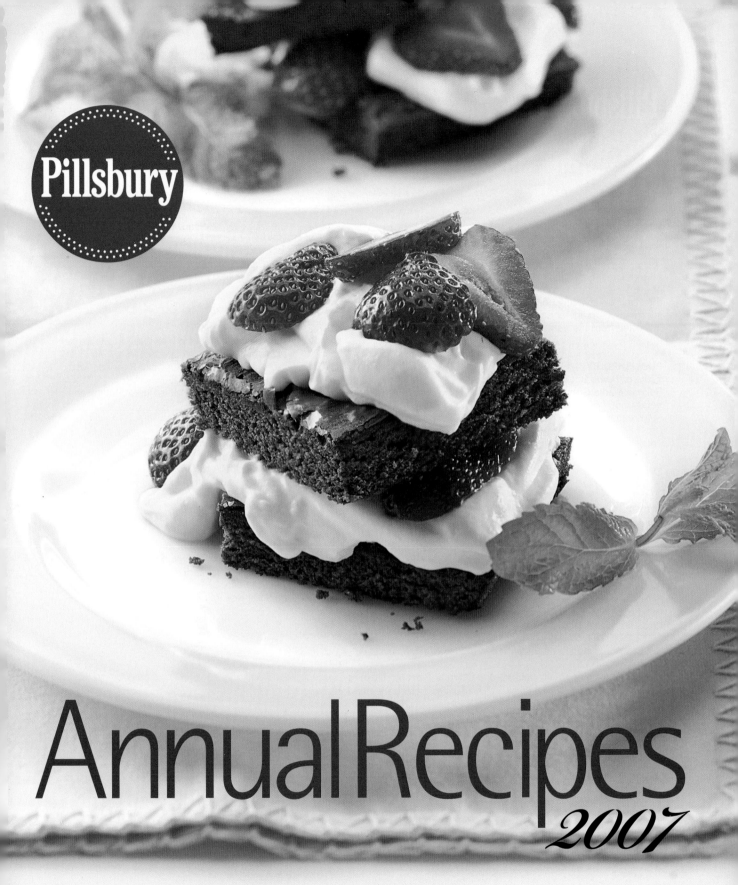

AnnualRecipes
2007

INCLUDING PILLSBURY BAKE-OFF CONTEST WINNERS

Pillsbury Annual Recipes 2007

Our recipes have been tested in the Pillsbury Kitchens and meet our standards of easy preparation, reliability and great taste.

For more great recipes, visit pillsbury.com

PUBLISHED BY
Taste of Home Books
Reiman Media Group, Inc.
5400 S. 60th St., Greendale WI 53129
www.reimanpub.com

This edition published by arrangement with Wiley Publishing, Inc.

Printed in U.S.A.

Taste of Home® is a registered trademark of Reiman Media Group, Inc.

Bake-Off® is a registered trademark of General Mills.

The trademarks referred to herein are trademarks of General Mills, Inc., or its affiliates, except as noted.

Hershey's, Kisses and Mounds trademarks and associated trade dress are registered trademarks of The Hershey Company.

SPLENDA is a registered trademark of McNeil Nutritionals, LLC.

All recipes were originally published in different form by Pillsbury Easy Meals℠ Magazine and Pillsbury® Magazines, both trademarks of General Mills, Inc.

International Standard Book Number (10):
0-89821-541-2
International Standard Book Number (13):
978-089821-541-0
International Standard Serial Number:
1930-7349

CREDITS
General Mills, Inc.
PUBLISHER, COOKBOOKS & MAGAZINES: Sheila Burke
MANAGER AND EDITOR, BOOK PUBLISHING: Lois Tlusty
RECIPE DEVELOPMENT AND TESTING: Pillsbury Test Kitchens
PHOTOGRAPHY: General Mills Photo Studios and Image Center

Reiman Media Group, Inc.
PRESIDENT: Barbara Newton
EDITOR IN CHIEF: Catherine Cassidy
CREATIVE DIRECTOR: Ardyth Cope
VICE PRESIDENT/BOOKS:
Heidi Reuter Lloyd
SENIOR BOOK EDITOR: Mark Hagen
EDITOR: Kathy Pohl
ART DIRECTOR: Gretchen Trautman
GRAPHIC ART ASSOCIATE: Nancy Novak
PROOFREADERS: Linne Bruskewitz, Jean Steiner
FOUNDER: Roy Reiman

FRONT COVER PHOTOGRAPHS:
Alfredo Chicken Pasta Toss, PG. 217; Crunchy Oven French Toast, PG. 143; Super Speedy Chili, PG. 122; Black Forest Cheesecake Dessert Cups, PG. 307; and Seafood Lasagna, PG. 152.

PAGE 5 PHOTOGRAPHS:
Lemony Fish and Tomatoes, PG. 231; Candy Bar Cheesecake, PG. 294; Cheesy Pasta-Vegetable Soup, PG. 122; and Ravioli Bolognese, PG. 189.

BACK COVER PHOTOGRAPHS:
Italian Marinated Pork Tenderloins, PG. 243; Key Lime Parfaits, PG. 323; Speedy Enchilada Bake, PG. 153; and Fruit-Topped Angel Food Cake Squares, PG. 314.

contents

"Our Very Best Recipes Are At Your Fingertips Inside This Annual Cookbook!"

introduction

A year ago, we launched a whole new line of Pillsbury cookbooks dedicated to bringing you the best of the best recipes year after year. Readers were thrilled with the first book in the series, *Pillsbury Annual Recipes 2006*, and asked for more. Hot off the presses, this brand-new annual is the second in the series, and we are convinced it is even better!

Pillsbury Annual Recipes 2007 contains 401 of the very best recipes from the popular cooking magazines over the past year, including a host of prize-winning recipes from the renowned Pillsbury Bake-Off Contests.

Good cooks have always relied on Pillsbury for quick-and-easy solutions to satisfy the what's-for-dinner dilemma, and this new annual helps you do just that—deliciously. It's never been easier to get dinner on the table fast for you and your family. In fact, many of these recipes can be ready in just 30 minutes or less! Each recipe comes with clear, step-by-step instructions...and every single recipe has been triple-tested by the Pillsbury Test Kitchens so you can be confident they will work in your kitchen, too. You'll find plenty of practical tips and timesaving hints, too. Plus, there's a gorgeous color photo for every recipe.

Planning complete meals is a breeze with all the choices offered here. From breakfast and brunch...to potlucks and picnics...to dinners and desserts, you'll find an amazing array of sensational choices for you and your family.

In this 2007 edition, we've added a Speedy Skillets chapter to help you satisfy your hungry bunch in a hurry! Many of these dishes can be prepared using just one pan, making cleanup a breeze—and most can be table-ready in 30 minutes or less.

If your gang prefers casseroles, turn to the Comforting Casseroles chapter. Try one of those scrumptious offerings ranging from Cheeseburger Lasagna to Chicken Dijon Shepherd's Pie to Nacho Casserole and much more!

And who doesn't like to play with their food? You'll find all kinds of clever and creative ways to present snacks and desserts in our new Fun with Food chapter. Whether you're looking for a way to liven up a birthday party, celebrate a holiday or put a little romance into a special occasion, this chapter has you covered.

Most of the recipes in this cookbook call for just a few simple ingredients you likely already have on hand or can easily find at your local grocery store. Best of all, many rely on brand-name products you've come to know and trust to give you fast, flavorful results without all the fuss of "from scratch" cooking.

HELPFUL ICONS

Time is precious these days, and time spent in the kitchen is certainly no exception. To help busy cooks out, we've highlighted the easy recipes in this book with an icon that looks like this so you can see them at a glance. These recipes call for 6 ingredients or less OR are ready to cook in 20 minutes or less OR are ready to eat in 30 minutes or less.

At the top of each recipe, we've also included "Prep" and "Ready in…" times. That way, you'll know exactly how long it takes to prepare each dish.

And because we know that today's family cooks are more health-conscious than ever, we've pinpointed the delicious but nutritious low-fat recipes in this book. Look for this symbol, which confirms that the recipe has 10 grams of fat or less (main dishes) or 3 grams of fat or less (all other recipes).

Plus, we've spotlighted the Pillsbury Bake-Off Contest Winners—the recipes judged to be the very best in the popular Pillsbury Bake-Off Contests over the years. These prize-winners from America's best home cooks are sure to win compliments from your family, just as they did

from the contest judges. Whether you're searching for a "company's coming" dish or a show-stopping dessert, look for the Bake-Off symbol as you page through this book.

HOW TO FIND A RECIPE

This cookbook is indexed in two helpful ways. Look up any major ingredient, and you'll find a list of the recipes in which it is included.

For instance, if you'd like to make a main dish with pork, turn to "pork" in the general index to find many tasty options.

The alphabetical index starts on page 344. Once you have found a few favorite recipes for your family, you can easily find them by title the next time you want to make them.

Or perhaps you just want to page through this book and look at all the eye-appealing photos until you find one that really whets your appetite for tonight's dinner.

Whichever recipe you choose, it's sure to become a new family favorite at your house. After all, that's why generations of good cooks have come to trust and rely on Pillsbury!

TROPICAL WAFFLE BAKE
PG. 18

Breakfast & Brunch

Greet the new day in a different way—
with delicious wake-up dishes!

SOUR CREAM-HAM ENCHILADAS
PG. 35

RISE 'N SHINE LATTICE PIZZA
PG. 26

SCRAMBLED EGGS BENEDICT
PG. 14

Spinach-Tomato Frittata

PREP TIME: 20 MINUTES (READY IN 35 MINUTES)
SERVINGS: 4

 EASY

6 eggs

⅓ cup grated Parmesan cheese

½ teaspoon garlic powder

½ teaspoon dried basil leaves

¼ teaspoon salt

¼ teaspoon pepper

⅛ teaspoon ground nutmeg

2 teaspoons olive oil

6 oz. fresh spinach, stems removed, torn into bite-size pieces (about 6 cups loosely packed)

5 to 6 cherry tomatoes, quartered

1) In small bowl with wire whisk or fork, beat eggs. Stir in cheese, garlic powder, basil, salt, pepper and nutmeg; set aside.

2) In 9- or 10-inch nonstick skillet with sloping sides (omelet or crepe pan), heat oil over medium heat. Add spinach; cover and cook 2 to 3 minutes, stirring once or twice and watching carefully to prevent burning, until spinach is slightly wilted (if necessary, add 2 tablespoons water if spinach becomes dry).

3) Reduce heat to low. Spread spinach evenly in skillet; top evenly with tomatoes. Pour egg mixture over top. Cover; cook 12 to 15 minutes or until bottom is lightly browned and top is set, lifting edges occasionally to allow uncooked egg mixture to flow to bottom of skillet. Cut into wedges.

HIGH ALTITUDE (3500-6500 FT.): No change.

Nutrition Information Per Serving:	
Calories: 190	From Fat: 120
Total Fat	13g
Saturated	4.5g
Cholesterol	325mg
Sodium	430mg
Total Carbohydrate	4g
Dietary Fiber	2g
Sugars	2g
Protein	14g

Vermont Maple Bread Pudding

BETH ROYALS | RICHMOND, VIRGINIA

PREP TIME: 25 MINUTES (READY IN 1 HOUR 35 MINUTES)
SERVINGS: 12

PUDDING

- 1 bag (12.4 oz.) Pillsbury® Oven Baked frozen crusty French dinner rolls
- 6 eggs
- 1/2 cup maple-flavored or real maple syrup
- 3/4 cup granulated sugar
- 1 1/2 teaspoons baking powder
- 1 pint (2 cups) half-and-half
- 1 cup milk
- 1/4 cup butter or margarine, melted
- 1/2 cup cream cheese creamy ready-to-spread frosting (from 16-oz. container)
- 1 container (6 oz.) Yoplait® Original 99% Fat Free French vanilla yogurt

GARNISHES, IF DESIRED

- Vanilla ice cream
- Fresh mint sprigs
- Powdered sugar

1) Heat oven to 350°F. Spray 13x9-inch pan with cooking spray. Let frozen rolls stand at room temperature 10 minutes. Cut each roll into 12 pieces; place in large bowl.

2) In another large bowl, slightly beat eggs. Reserve 1 tablespoon of the syrup in small microwavable bowl; add remaining syrup to eggs. Stir in sugar, baking powder, half-and-half, milk and melted butter until well blended. Pour mixture over roll pieces in bowl; stir to coat well. Pour mixture into pan, pressing bread into liquid with back of spoon. Let stand 5 minutes; press down bread again.

3) Bake 45 to 55 minutes or until top is golden brown and knife inserted in center comes out clean. Cool 20 minutes before serving.

4) To reserved tablespoon syrup, stir in frosting and yogurt. Microwave on High about 20 seconds or until melted. Stir; pour over warm bread pudding and spread to cover. Cut into 12 servings. Serve warm with ice cream; garnish with mint and sprinkle with powdered sugar.

HIGH ALTITUDE (3500-6500 FT.): Bake 50 to 60 minutes.

Nutrition Information Per Serving:	
Calories: 380	From Fat: 140
Total Fat	16g
Saturated	8g
Cholesterol	135mg
Sodium	360mg
Total Carbohydrate	50g
Dietary Fiber	0g
Sugars	30g
Protein	9g

Banana Pecan Pancake Bake

PAM IVBULS | OMAHA, NEBRASKA

PREP TIME: 20 MINUTES (READY IN 1 HOUR 25 MINUTES)
SERVINGS: 12

PANCAKES

- 2 boxes (16.4 oz. each) Pillsbury® frozen original pancakes (24 pancakes)
- 2 tablespoons butter or margarine, softened
- 3 eggs
- 1 cup half-and-half
- 1/4 cup maple-flavored syrup with butter
- 1/2 teaspoon ground cinnamon
- 2 containers (6 oz. each) Yoplait® Light Fat Free banana cream pie yogurt
- 4 medium bananas, cut diagonally into 1/4-inch-thick slices
- 1/2 cup chopped pecans

GARNISHES

- 3/4 cup extra-creamy whipped topping with real cream
- 12 diagonal slices bananas (1/4 inch thick)
- 3/4 cup maple-flavored syrup with butter
- 1/2 teaspoon ground cinnamon
- 2 tablespoons chopped pecans, if desired

   Additional ground cinnamon, if desired

1) Heat oven to 350°F. Remove frozen pancakes from boxes; unwrap and carefully separate. Set aside to partially thaw. With small pastry brush, coat bottom and sides of 15x10x1-inch pan with softened butter.

2) In 5-cup blender or large food processor, place eggs, half-and-half, 1/4 cup syrup, 1/2 teaspoon cinnamon and the yogurt; cover and blend on low speed 10 seconds until smooth. If necessary, scrape down sides of blender with rubber spatula and blend 5 to 10 seconds longer. Set aside.

3) Place 12 of the pancakes in 4 rows of 3 pancakes each, overlapping slightly if necessary, in pan. Pour 1 1/2 cups yogurt mixture evenly over pancakes (if necessary, use small spoon to coat surface of each pancake with yogurt mixture).

4) Place banana slices in single layer over pancakes. Place remaining 12 pancakes over banana-topped pancakes. Pour remaining yogurt mixture evenly over all pancakes. With large turkey baster, coat pancakes evenly with yogurt mixture from pan. Let stand 10 minutes to allow yogurt mixture to soak into pancakes. With baster, coat pancakes again with yogurt mixture from pan. Let stand 5 minutes longer. Sprinkle 1/2 cup pecans evenly over top.

5) Bake 30 to 40 minutes or until edges are set and light golden brown. Let stand 10 minutes before serving.

6) Cut into 12 servings; place on individual plates. Top each with 1 tablespoon whipped topping, 1 banana slice and 1 tablespoon syrup; sprinkle each with dash cinnamon and 1/2 teaspoon pecans. Sprinkle edge of each plate with additional cinnamon.

HIGH ALTITUDE (3500-6500 FT.): No change.

Nutrition Information Per Serving:		
Calories: 430	From Fat:	120
Total Fat		13g
Saturated		5g
Cholesterol		80mg
Sodium		520mg
Total Carbohydrate		70g
Dietary Fiber		2g
Sugars		29g
Protein		8g

Ranch Egg Salad Croissant Sandwiches

PREP TIME: 15 MINUTES (READY IN 15 MINUTES)
SERVINGS: 6

 EASY

9 hard-cooked eggs, peeled

¼ cup chopped green onions
(4 medium)

¼ teaspoon salt

¼ teaspoon coarse ground black pepper

½ cup ranch dressing

6 croissants, split

3 cups torn lettuce

Nutrition Information Per Serving:	
Calories: 470	From Fat: 300
Total Fat	33g
Saturated	13g
Cholesterol	385mg
Sodium	430mg
Total Carbohydrate	30g
Dietary Fiber	2g
Sugars	5g
Protein	15g

1) Cut each egg in half. Remove yolks; place in large bowl. Mash yolks with fork. Stir in onions, salt, pepper and ranch dressing. Chop egg whites; stir into yolk mixture.

2) To make each sandwich, top bottom half of 1 croissant with about ½ cup lettuce and ½ cup egg mixture. Cover with top half of croissant. Repeat for remaining sandwiches.

HIGH ALTITUDE (3500-6500 FT.): No change.

tip

To save time, purchase hard-cooked eggs from the deli section of the supermarket, or use leftover Easter eggs.

Strawberry Smoothies

| PREP TIME: | 5 MINUTES (READY IN 5 MINUTES) |
| SERVINGS: | 8 (1 CUP EACH) |

 EASY   LOW FAT

4 cups milk

1 package (10 oz.) frozen strawberries in syrup, partially thawed

2 cups vanilla or strawberry yogurt

1/2 cup strawberry-flavored syrup

Nutrition Information Per Serving:		
Calories: 210	From Fat:	30
Total Fat		3g
Saturated		2g
Cholesterol		15mg
Sodium		115mg
Total Carbohydrate		39g
Dietary Fiber		0g
Sugars		29g
Protein		7g

1) In blender container, combine 2 cups of the milk and the strawberries; blend until smooth and thick.

2) Add yogurt and syrup; blend at low speed until mixed. Pour into pitcher or container. Stir in remaining 2 cups milk; mix well. Garnish with fresh strawberries, if desired.

Blueberry Burrito Blintzes

KATHY ANNE SEPICH | GRESHAM, OREGON

| PREP TIME: | 30 MINUTES (READY IN 30 MINUTES) |
| SERVINGS: | 8 |

1 bag (10 oz.) Cascadian Farm® Organic frozen blueberries

1/2 cup small-curd 2% reduced-fat cottage cheese

2 tablespoons granulated sugar

1/2 teaspoon grated lemon peel

1/4 to 1/2 teaspoon ground nutmeg

1/4 to 1/2 teaspoon ground cinnamon

4 oz. reduced-fat cream cheese (Neufchâtel), softened

1 container (6 oz.) Yoplait® Light Fat Free blueberry patch yogurt

1 package (11.5 oz.) Old El Paso® flour tortillas for burritos, 8 inch (8 tortillas)

1 tablespoon butter or margarine

1/4 cup blueberry syrup

Powdered sugar, if desired

Lemon slices, if desired

Nutrition Information Per Serving:		
Calories: 300	From Fat:	80
Total Fat		9g
Saturated		4g
Cholesterol		15mg
Sodium		460mg
Total Carbohydrate		45g
Dietary Fiber		1g
Sugars		17g
Protein		8g

1) Thaw blueberries as directed on bag; drain, reserving liquid. In medium bowl, mix cottage cheese, sugar, lemon peel, nutmeg, cinnamon, cream cheese and yogurt until well blended. Gently stir in drained blueberries.

2) Place large sheet of waxed paper on work surface. For each blintz, place 1 flour tortilla on waxed paper. Spoon about 1/3 cup yogurt mixture in center. With pastry brush, moisten outer edge of tortilla with reserved blueberry liquid. Fold opposite sides of tortilla over filling, ends meeting in center; fold remaining 2 sides of tortilla over each other.

3) In 12-inch nonstick skillet, melt 1/2 tablespoon of the butter over medium heat. Cook 4 blintzes at a time, seam side down, about 2 minutes on each side until golden brown. Place blintzes, seam side down, on serving platter; drizzle with syrup. Sprinkle with powdered sugar; garnish with lemon slices.

HIGH ALTITUDE (3500-6500 FT.): Cook blintzes about 5 minutes on each side.

Asparagus Quiche

PREP TIME:	15 MINUTES (READY IN 1 HOUR 20 MINUTES)
SERVINGS:	6

 EASY

1 Pillsbury® refrigerated pie crust, softened as directed on box

1 can (10.5 oz.) Green Giant® cut spears asparagus, well drained

1 jar (2.5 oz.) Green Giant® sliced mushrooms, well drained

1 cup shredded Swiss cheese (4 oz.)

2 tablespoons all-purpose flour

3 eggs, slightly beaten

$1/2$ cup half-and-half

$1/2$ teaspoon salt

$1/8$ teaspoon pepper

$1/8$ teaspoon ground nutmeg

Nutrition Information Per Serving:

Calories:	310	From Fat:	180
Total Fat			20g
Saturated			9g
Cholesterol			135mg
Sodium			620mg
Total Carbohydrate			23g
Dietary Fiber			1g
Sugars			3g
Protein			11g

tip If fresh asparagus is in abundance, substitute $1/2$ pound for the canned asparagus. Remove the tough ends by breaking them off as far down as the stalks snap easily; cut the remaining into $1/2$-inch pieces.

1) Heat oven to 350°F. Place pie crust in 9-inch glass pie pan as directed on box for One-Crust Filled Pie. Place asparagus and mushrooms in crust.

2) In large bowl, toss cheese with flour. Stir in eggs, half-and-half, salt, pepper and nutmeg. Pour over asparagus and mushrooms.

3) Bake 55 to 60 minutes or until knife inserted in center comes out clean. Let stand 5 minutes before serving.

HIGH ALTITUDE (3500-6500 FT.): Cover crust edge with strips of foil after first 20 minutes of baking to prevent excessive browning.

Scrambled Eggs Benedict

PREP TIME:	10 MINUTES (READY IN 15 MINUTES)
SERVINGS:	4

 EASY

8 eggs

1/2 cup milk or water

1/8 teaspoon pepper

2 tablespoons butter

1 jar (7.5 oz.) hollandaise sauce

8 slices Canadian bacon (5 oz.)

4 English muffins, split, toasted

Paprika, if desired

Nutrition Information Per Serving:

Calories:	510	From Fat:	260
Total Fat			29g
Saturated			12g
Cholesterol			480mg
Sodium			1070mg
Total Carbohydrate			34g
Dietary Fiber			2g
Sugars			13g
Protein			27g

1) In medium bowl, beat eggs, milk and pepper with wire whisk or fork until well blended.

2) In 10-inch nonstick skillet, melt butter over medium heat. Pour egg mixture into skillet. As mixture begins to set on bottom and side, gently lift cooked portion with pancake turner so thin, uncooked portion can flow to bottom of skillet (avoid constant stirring). Cook 4 to 5 minutes or until eggs are thickened throughout but still moist and fluffy.

3) In 2-cup microwavable measuring cup, microwave hollandaise sauce on High 1 minute 30 seconds to 2 minutes or until hot; cover tightly to keep warm.

4) On large microwavable plate, place Canadian bacon slices in single layer. Microwave on High 45 to 60 seconds or until warm.

5) Place 2 toasted muffin halves on each plate. Top each muffin half with slice of Canadian bacon, about 1/3 cup eggs and 2 tablespoons hollandaise sauce; sprinkle with paprika.

HIGH ALTITUDE (3500-6500 FT.): No change.

Hollandaise sauce from a jar won't separate when it's heated so it's a nice alternative to the traditional sauce made from scratch that often has a tendency to separate.

Breakfast Quesadillas

JANE OZMENT | PURCELL, OKLAHOMA

Pillsbury Bake-Off

PREP TIME: 30 MINUTES (READY IN 35 MINUTES)
SERVINGS: 4 (2 QUESADILLAS EACH)

QUESADILLAS

- 1/3 lb. bulk pork sausage

- 6 eggs

- 2 tablespoons sour cream

- 2 tablespoons half-and-half

- 1 package (1.25 oz.) Old El Paso® taco seasoning mix

- 1 tablespoon butter or margarine

- 2 tablespoons finely chopped fresh chives

- 2 tablespoons finely chopped fresh cilantro

- 2 tablespoons chopped tomato

- 1 can (4.5 oz.) Old El Paso® chopped green chiles

- 1 package (11.5 oz.) Old El Paso® flour tortillas for burritos, 8 inch (8 tortillas)

- 1/2 cup shredded Cheddar cheese (2 oz.)

- 1/2 cup shredded Monterey Jack cheese (2 oz.)

TOPPINGS

- 2 to 4 tablespoons finely chopped fresh chives

- 2 to 4 tablespoons taco sauce

- 2 to 4 tablespoons sour cream

1) In 12-inch nonstick skillet, cook sausage over medium heat, stirring frequently, until browned and no longer pink. Remove sausage from skillet; drain on paper towels. Wipe skillet clean with paper towels; set aside. Meanwhile, in medium bowl, lightly beat eggs, 2 tablespoons sour cream, the half-and-half and taco seasoning mix with wire whisk until well blended.

2) In 10-inch nonstick skillet, melt butter over medium heat. Add egg mixture; cook 2 to 4 minutes, stirring frequently, until mixture is very moist. Stir in cooked sausage, 2 tablespoons chives, 2 tablespoons cilantro, the tomato and chiles. Cook 1 to 2 minutes longer or until egg mixture is set but still moist. Remove from heat.

3) Place tortillas on work surface. Top half of each tortilla with 2 to 3 tablespoons egg mixture; sprinkle each with 1 tablespoon of each of the cheeses. Fold untopped half of tortillas over egg mixture.

4) Heat same 12-inch skillet over medium heat. Place 2 quesadillas in skillet; cook 30 to 45 seconds on each side or until crisp and lightly browned. Remove from skillet; place on serving plate. Repeat with remaining quesadillas. With pizza cutter or sharp knife, cut each quesadilla into wedges. Top each serving (2 quesadillas) with about 1/2 tablespoon each of chives, taco sauce and sour cream.

HIGH ALTITUDE (3500-6500 FT.): No change.

Nutrition Information Per Serving:

Calories:	640	From Fat:	330
Total Fat			37g
Saturated			16g
Cholesterol			380mg
Sodium			2030mg
Total Carbohydrate			52g
Dietary Fiber			0g
Sugars			3g
Protein			27g

Broccoli, Potato and Bacon Quiche

TANYA NICOLE MARGALA | NEWPORT BEACH, CALIFORNIA

PREP TIME: 20 MINUTES (READY IN 1 HOUR)
SERVINGS: 8

1 bag (19 oz.) Green Giant® frozen roasted potatoes with broccoli & cheese sauce

1 Pillsbury® refrigerated pie crust (from 15-oz. box), softened as directed on box

4 eggs

2/3 cup whipping cream

7 slices bacon, cooked, crumbled (about 1/3 cup)

1 cup finely shredded Parmesan cheese (4 oz.)

1 cup finely shredded Cheddar cheese (4 oz.)

1/2 teaspoon dried basil leaves

1/2 teaspoon pepper

1/4 teaspoon parsley flakes

1/8 teaspoon salt, if desired

1 teaspoon finely chopped fresh chives

1) Heat oven to 350°F. Cook frozen potatoes with broccoli and cheese sauce in microwave as directed on bag.

2) Meanwhile, place pie crust in 9-inch glass pie plate as directed on box for One-Crust Filled Pie.

3) In large bowl, beat eggs and whipping cream with wire whisk until well blended. Stir in cooked potato mixture and remaining ingredients except chives. Pour filling into crust-lined plate; spread evenly. Sprinkle chives over filling.

4) Bake 30 to 40 minutes or until edge of filling is light golden brown and knife inserted in center comes out clean. Let stand 5 minutes before serving.

HIGH ALTITUDE (3500-6500 FT.): Heat oven to 375°F. Bake 33 to 43 minutes.

Nutrition Information Per Serving:		
Calories: 410	From Fat:	260
Total Fat		29g
Saturated		14g
Cholesterol		165mg
Sodium		880mg
Total Carbohydrate		21g
Dietary Fiber		1g
Sugars		3g
Protein		17g

Peanut Butter and Banana Waffle-Wiches

PREP TIME: 20 MINUTES (READY IN 20 MINUTES)
SERVINGS: 2

 EASY

- 4 Pillsbury® frozen buttermilk waffles
- 2 tablespoons creamy peanut butter
- 2 tablespoons strawberry or raspberry preserves
- 1 Nature Valley® oats 'n honey crunchy granola bar (1/2 pouch from 8.9-oz. box), coarsely crushed (about 1/4 cup)
- 1 small banana, thinly sliced

Nutrition Information Per Serving:	
Calories: 410	From Fat: 130
Total Fat	15g
Saturated	3.5g
Cholesterol	0mg
Sodium	610mg
Total Carbohydrate	63g
Dietary Fiber	3g
Sugars	23g
Protein	9g

tip

If you don't have the granola bar on hand, just use about 1/4 cup granola cereal instead.

1) Toast waffles as directed on box.

2) Spread 2 warm waffles with peanut butter and preserves. Sprinkle with crushed granola bar. Top with banana slices. Cover with remaining waffles, pressing down slightly. If desired, cut sandwiches in half diagonally to make triangles.

HIGH ALTITUDE (3500-6500 FT.): No change.

Tropical Waffle Bake

DIANE TOOMEY | ALLENTOWN, PENNSYLVANIA

Pillsbury Bake-Off

PREP TIME: 25 MINUTES (READY IN 1 HOUR 10 MINUTES)
SERVINGS: 6

5 Pillsbury® frozen buttermilk waffles (from 12-oz. bag), thawed

2 cans (8 oz. each) crushed pineapple in juice

1 1/2 cups finely chopped bananas (2 medium)

4 eggs

2/3 cup granulated sugar

5 tablespoons packed brown sugar

3 pouches (6 bars) Nature Valley® oats 'n honey crunchy granola bars (from 8.9-oz. box), crushed (heaping 1 cup)*

1/2 cup chopped macadamia nuts

3 tablespoons all-purpose flour

1/4 cup butter or margarine, softened

1 jar (10 oz.) strawberry spreadable fruit

Whipped cream, if desired

1) Heat oven to 350°F. Spray 8-inch square (2-quart) glass baking dish with cooking spray. Break waffles into 1- to 2-inch pieces; place in bottom of baking dish. Drain pineapple, reserving juice in small bowl; set pineapple aside. Gently stir bananas into juice to coat. With slotted spoon, place bananas evenly over waffles; discard any remaining juice.

2) In medium bowl, beat eggs, granulated sugar and 2 tablespoons of the brown sugar with wire whisk until blended. Stir in drained pineapple. Pour mixture over waffles and bananas in dish. In another medium bowl, mix crushed granola bars, nuts, flour, remaining 3 tablespoons brown sugar and the butter until crumbly; sprinkle over top.

3) Bake 30 to 35 minutes or until knife inserted in center comes out clean. Cool 10 minutes.

4) To serve, in small microwavable bowl, microwave spreadable fruit on High 1 minute. Stir; if necessary, continue to microwave on High in 15-second increments until melted and smooth. Cut into 6 servings. Top each serving with about 2 tablespoons warm fruit spread and 1 to 2 tablespoons whipped cream.

*NOTE: To easily crush granola bars, do not unwrap; use rolling pin to crush bars.

HIGH ALTITUDE (3500-6500 FT.): Heat oven to 375°F.

Nutrition Information Per Serving:	
Calories: 700	From Fat: 210
Total Fat	24g
Saturated	8g
Cholesterol	160mg
Sodium	410mg
Total Carbohydrate	111g
Dietary Fiber	7g
Sugars	80g
Protein	11g

Spinach Sausage Brunch Casserole

PREP TIME: 15 MINUTES (READY IN 50 MINUTES)
SERVINGS: 8

 EASY

- 1 lb. bulk Italian sausage

- 1 cup chopped onions

- 1 jar (7.25 oz.) mild roasted red bell peppers, drained, chopped

- 1 package (9 oz.) Green Giant® Harvest Fresh® frozen chopped spinach, thawed, well drained

- 1 cup all-purpose flour

- ¼ cup grated Parmesan cheese

- 1 tablespoon chopped fresh basil or 1 teaspoon dried basil leaves

- ½ teaspoon salt

- 2 cups milk

- 8 eggs

- 1 cup shredded Provolone cheese (4 oz.)

1) Heat oven to 425°F. Grease 13x9-inch pan. In 10-inch skillet, brown sausage and onions. Remove from skillet; drain on paper towels. Arrange sausage mixture in greased pan. Sprinkle chopped red peppers over sausage mixture; top with spinach.

2) In large bowl, combine flour, Parmesan cheese, basil and salt. In another large bowl, combine milk and eggs; beat until smooth. Add egg mixture to flour mixture; beat until well blended. Pour over spinach.*

3) Bake at 425°F. for 20 to 25 minutes or until knife inserted in center comes out clean. Sprinkle casserole with Provolone cheese. Bake at 425°F. for an additional 1 to 2 minutes or until cheese is melted.

4) Let stand 5 minutes. Cut into squares.

*NOTE: At this point, casserole can be covered and refrigerated up to 2 hours. Continue as directed.

Nutrition Information Per Serving:

Calories: 380	From Fat: 200
Total Fat	22g
Saturated	9g
Cholesterol	260mg
Sodium	810mg
Total Carbohydrate	21g
Dietary Fiber	2g
Sugars	7g
Protein	24g

Granola-Peanut Butter French Toast

KENDRA NORRIS | CROSSVILLE, TENNESSEE

PREP TIME: 20 MINUTES (READY IN 20 MINUTES)
SERVINGS: 6

2 cups Reese's® Puffs® cereal

4 eggs

¼ cup milk

1 teaspoon vanilla

12 tablespoons creamy peanut butter

12 slices white or wheat sandwich bread or slightly firm bread

4 Nature Valley® peanut butter crunchy granola bars (2 pouches from 8.9-oz. box), finely crushed (³/₄ cup)*

6 tablespoons marshmallow creme (from 7-oz. jar)

1) Place cereal in gallon-size resealable food-storage plastic bag. With flat side of meat mallet or rolling pin, crush cereal until very fine, making 1¹/₃ cups crumbs. Place on large plate; set aside.

2) In medium bowl, beat eggs, milk and vanilla with wire whisk until well blended. Spread 2 tablespoons peanut butter on each of 6 slices of bread. Sprinkle each with about 2 tablespoons crushed granola bars.

3) Spread 1 tablespoon marshmallow creme on remaining 6 slices of bread. Top peanut butter-spread bread with marshmallow-spread bread, marshmallow side down, making 6 sandwiches.

4) Spray griddle or 12-inch skillet with cooking spray; heat to 350°F. or over medium heat. Dip each side of each sandwich into egg mixture, then coat each side with cereal crumbs; place on hot griddle. Cook 2 to 4 minutes on each side or until golden brown. Serve warm; if desired, serve with maple- or chocolate-flavored syrup.

*NOTE: To easily crush granola bars, do not unwrap; use rolling pin to crush bars.

HIGH ALTITUDE (3500-6500 FT.): If using electric griddle or skillet, heat to 375°F.

Nutrition Information Per Serving:		
Calories: 530	From Fat: 230	
Total Fat		26g
Saturated		5g
Cholesterol		140mg
Sodium		690mg
Total Carbohydrate		57g
Dietary Fiber		4g
Sugars		20g
Protein		19g

Fruit-Topped Whole Grain Waffles

PREP TIME: 20 MINUTES (READY IN 20 MINUTES)
SERVINGS: 4 (8 SQUARE WAFFLES)

 EASY

TOPPING

1 cup frozen blueberries, thawed

1 cup fresh or frozen sliced
strawberries, thawed

1/4 cup maple-flavored syrup

WAFFLES

1/2 cup all-purpose flour

1/2 cup whole wheat flour

1/4 cup quick-cooking oats

2 teaspoons sugar

1 teaspoon baking powder

1/2 teaspoon baking soda

1 1/4 cups buttermilk

1/4 cup refrigerated or frozen fat-free
egg product, thawed, or 1 egg

2 tablespoons butter or margarine,
melted

1) Lightly spray waffle iron with cooking
spray; heat until hot. In medium bowl,
combine all topping ingredients; mix
well. Let stand while preparing waffles.

2) In large bowl, mix all-purpose flour,
whole wheat flour, oats, sugar, baking
powder and baking soda. Add buttermilk,
egg product and butter; beat well with
wire whisk.

3) For each waffle, spoon about 1/2 cup
batter into waffle iron, spreading batter
to edges. Bake about 3 minutes or until
waffle is golden brown. Serve
immediately with topping.

Nutrition Information Per Serving:

Calories:	360	From Fat:	80
Total Fat			8g
Saturated			5g
Cholesterol			20mg
Sodium			440mg
Total Carbohydrate			60g
Dietary Fiber			5g
Sugars			21g
Protein			10g

tip

Warm slices of ham
or Canadian bacon and
glasses of fresh juice
are perfect with these
hot toasty-crisp waffles.

Leek Quiche

PREP TIME: 25 MINUTES (READY IN 1 HOUR 15 MINUTES)
SERVINGS: 6

2 medium leeks

1 Pillsbury® refrigerated pie crust (from 15-oz. box), softened as directed on box

2 tablespoons butter or margarine

3 eggs

1 cup milk

1 cup shredded Swiss cheese (4 oz.)

1/2 teaspoon salt

1/4 teaspoon pepper

1/8 teaspoon ground nutmeg

Nutrition Information Per Serving:	
Calories: 340 From Fat: 200	
Total Fat	22g
Saturated	10g
Cholesterol	140mg
Sodium	470mg
Total Carbohydrate	24g
Dietary Fiber	0g
Sugars	4g
Protein	11g

1) Heat oven to 400°F. Wash leeks; remove any tough outer leaves. Trim roots from white bulb portion; cut leeks lengthwise and wash well. Cut crosswise into 1/2-inch-thick slices to make about 4 cups; set aside.

2) Place pie crust in 9-inch glass pie pan as directed on box for One-Crust Filled Pie. Partially bake crust 8 minutes or until very lightly browned.

3) Meanwhile, in 12-inch skillet, melt butter over medium heat. Add leeks; cook 7 to 9 minutes, stirring frequently, until tender but not brown. Remove from heat; set aside.

4) In small bowl, beat eggs with wire whisk. Stir in milk, cheese, salt, pepper and nutmeg until blended. Stir in cooked leeks. Pour mixture into partially baked crust.

5) Bake quiche 10 minutes. Cover crust edge with strips of foil to prevent excessive browning. Reduce oven temperature to 300°F.; bake 20 to 25 minutes longer or until knife inserted in center comes out clean. Cool 15 minutes before serving.

HIGH ALTITUDE (3500-6500 FT.): In Step 5, after covering crust edge with foil, reduce oven temperature to 350°F.; increase second bake time to 25 to 30 minutes.

Blueberry-Banana-Granola French Toast

CAROLYN ROBERTS | LOS ANGELES, CALIFORNIA

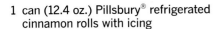

PREP TIME: 10 MINUTES (READY IN 1 HOUR 10 MINUTES)
SERVINGS: 8

1 can (12.4 oz.) Pillsbury® refrigerated cinnamon rolls with icing

8 Nature Valley® banana nut crunchy granola bars (4 pouches from 8.9-oz. box), crushed (1½ cups)*

4 eggs

¾ cup fat-free (skim) milk

1 can (14 oz.) fat-free sweetened condensed milk (not evaporated)

3 medium bananas, cut into 1-inch pieces

1 bag (10 oz.) Cascadian Farm® Organic frozen blueberries, thawed

1 aerosol can (7 oz.) fat-free whipped cream topping

1) Heat oven to 350°F. (325°F. for dark pan.) Spray 13x9-inch pan or 12x2-inch round cake pan with butter-flavor or regular cooking spray. Separate dough into 8 rolls; set icing aside. Cut each roll into quarters; arrange evenly in pan. Sprinkle ¾ cup of the crushed granola bars evenly over dough pieces.

2) In large food processor or 5-cup blender, place eggs, milk and condensed milk; cover and process 1 minute. Add bananas; cover and process 1 minute. Pour egg mixture over dough in pan. Sprinkle with remaining ¾ cup crushed granola bars.

3) Bake 35 to 45 minutes or until golden brown and set in center. Spoon and spread reserved icing over warm rolls. Cool 15 minutes before serving.

4) To serve, spoon baked French toast into shallow bowls or cut into 8 servings. Top each serving with 3 tablespoons blueberries; garnish with 2 tablespoons whipped cream topping.

*NOTE: To easily crush granola bars, do not unwrap; use rolling pin to crush bars.

HIGH ALTITUDE (3500-6500 FT.): Heat oven to 375°F. Add 2 tablespoons flour to ingredients in blender. Bake 30 to 40 minutes.

Nutrition Information Per Serving:

Calories:	500	From Fat:	100
Total Fat			11g
Saturated			3g
Cholesterol			110mg
Sodium			510mg
Total Carbohydrate			87g
Dietary Fiber			3g
Sugars			60g
Protein			13g

Breakfast Biscuit Cups with Green Chile Salsa

ERIN RENOUF MYLROIE | ST. GEORGE, UTAH

PREP TIME: 15 MINUTES (READY IN 50 MINUTES)
SERVINGS: 2

4 slices packaged precooked bacon (from 2.1-oz. package)

2 Pillsbury® Extra Large Easy Split® Oven Baked frozen biscuits (from 31.8-oz. bag), or 2 Pillsbury® Oven Baked frozen southern style biscuits (from 25-oz. bag)

1 can (4.5 oz.) Old El Paso® chopped green chiles

1/2 cup shredded sharp Cheddar cheese (2 oz.)

2 eggs

Salt and pepper, if desired

1 small tomato, finely chopped (1/2 cup)

1 tablespoon chopped fresh cilantro

1 tablespoon chopped red onion

1 tablespoon lime juice

Sliced cantaloupe, if desired

1) Heat oven to 375°F. Spray 2 (10-oz.) custard cups or soufflé dishes with cooking spray. If necessary, heat bacon in microwave on High 15 seconds or until warm and pliable. Line inner side of each custard cup (not bottom) with 2 bacon slices, overlapping as necessary.

2) Gently place frozen biscuit in each cup to fit inside bacon collar. Spoon 1 heaping tablespoon green chiles onto each biscuit; place remaining green chiles in small bowl and set aside. Sprinkle 2 tablespoons cheese over chiles on each biscuit. Carefully crack 1 egg over cheese on each. Sprinkle each with 2 tablespoons remaining cheese to cover; sprinkle with salt and pepper.

3) Place custard cups on cookie sheet; bake 25 to 35 minutes or until biscuits are baked and egg whites are set. Cool in cups 5 minutes. Meanwhile, add tomato, cilantro, onion and lime juice to green chiles in bowl; mix well. Season to taste with salt.

4) Carefully remove bacon-wrapped biscuits from custard cups; place on individual plates. Spoon green chile salsa over top and around sides. Serve with cantaloupe.

HIGH ALTITUDE (3500-6500 FT.): Heat oven to 400°F. In Step 2, do not sprinkle 2 tablespoons remaining cheese over each egg; sprinkle with salt and pepper. In Step 3, bake 30 minutes. Sprinkle remaining cheese over eggs; bake about 2 minutes longer or until cheese is melted.

Nutrition Information Per Serving:		
Calories: 580	From Fat: 310	
Total Fat		35g
Saturated		13g
Cholesterol		260mg
Sodium		1700mg
Total Carbohydrate		41g
Dietary Fiber		2g
Sugars		6g
Protein		26g

Spicy Sausage and Potato Squares

PREP TIME: 10 MINUTES (READY IN 1 HOUR 35 MINUTES)
SERVINGS: 6

 EASY

1 lb. bulk Italian sausage

4 cups frozen potatoes O'Brien with onions and peppers (from 28-oz. bag), thawed*

1 1/2 cups shredded Colby-Monterey Jack cheese (6 oz.)

1 box (9 oz.) Green Giant® frozen asparagus cuts, thawed**

4 eggs

3/4 cup milk

2 tablespoons shredded Parmesan cheese (1/2 oz.)

1) Heat oven to 350°F. Spray 8-inch square (2-quart) glass baking dish with cooking spray. In 8-inch skillet, cook sausage over medium heat 8 to 10 minutes, stirring occasionally, until no longer pink.

2) In baking dish, layer half of the thawed potatoes, half of the Colby-Monterey Jack cheese, the cooked sausage, thawed asparagus, remaining potatoes and cheese.

3) In medium bowl, beat eggs and milk until well blended. Pour evenly over potato mixture.

4) Cover tightly with foil; bake 1 hour. Uncover dish; sprinkle with Parmesan cheese. Bake uncovered 15 to 20 minutes longer or until knife inserted in center comes out clean. Let stand about 5 minutes before serving.

*NOTE: To quickly thaw the frozen potatoes, place in colander or strainer; rinse with warm water until thawed; drain well.

**NOTE: To quickly thaw the frozen asparagus, cut small slit in center of pouch. Microwave on High 2 to 3 minutes or until thawed; drain well.

HIGH ALTITUDE (3500-6500 FT.): No change.

Nutrition Information Per Serving:		
Calories: 480	From Fat:	250
Total Fat		28g
Saturated		12g
Cholesterol		215mg
Sodium		810mg
Total Carbohydrate		29g
Dietary Fiber		3g
Sugars		3g
Protein		28g

Rise 'n Shine Lattice Pizza

MARIA BALDWIN | MESA, ARIZONA

PREP TIME: 35 MINUTES (READY IN 1 HOUR 15 MINUTES)
SERVINGS: 8

1 box (9 oz.) Green Giant® frozen roasted potatoes with garlic & herbs

½ cup chives-and-onion cream cheese spread (from 8-oz. container)

1 teaspoon Italian seasoning

2 eggs

¾ to 1 cup basil pesto (6 to 8 oz.)

1 can (13.8 oz.) Pillsbury® refrigerated pizza crust

2 cups grated Asiago or Parmesan cheese (8 oz.)

1 package or jar (3 oz.) cooked real bacon bits

1 box (10.6 oz.) Pillsbury® refrigerated garlic with herbs breadsticks

Nutrition Information Per Serving:

Calories: 630	From Fat: 340
Total Fat	38g
Saturated	14g
Cholesterol	125mg
Sodium	1740mg
Total Carbohydrate	47g
Dietary Fiber	4g
Sugars	6g
Protein	24g

1) Heat oven to 350°F. Cut small slit in center of pouch of potatoes. Microwave on High 2 to 3 minutes or just until warm; set aside. In small bowl, beat cream cheese, Italian seasoning and eggs with electric mixer on medium speed until well blended; set aside.

2) Line large cookie sheet with cooking parchment paper. Place pesto in small strainer over bowl to drain off excess oil. Lightly brush oil from pesto onto parchment paper. Unroll pizza crust dough on paper-lined cookie sheet; starting at center, press out dough into 14-inch square.

3) Spread pesto over dough to within 1 inch of edges; sprinkle cheese over pesto. Roll up edges of dough to make 11-inch square. Spoon potatoes evenly over cheese. Pour egg mixture around potatoes. Sprinkle with bacon bits.

4) Separate breadstick dough into 10 strips; set garlic butter aside. Twist and stretch each strip of dough over potatoes in lattice pattern, tucking ends of strips under pizza dough. Remove cover from reserved garlic butter; microwave on High 10 seconds to soften. Brush garlic butter over edges and strips of dough.

5) Bake 30 to 40 minutes or until edges are browned and center is set, covering with foil during last 10 minutes of baking if necessary to prevent excessive browning. Immediately remove from cookie sheet. Cut into rectangles to serve.

HIGH ALTITUDE (3500-6500 FT.): Heat oven to 375°F.

Brunch Ham and Egg Muffins

PREP TIME: 45 MINUTES (READY IN 45 MINUTES)
SERVINGS: 4

8 large eggs

1 package (0.9-oz.) hollandaise sauce mix

1 cup milk

1/4 cup butter

1 teaspoon lemon juice

1/4 teaspoon dried dill weed

Dash pepper

8 oz. sliced cooked ham

4 English muffins, split, toasted

Nutrition Information Per Serving:		
Calories: 520	From Fat: 260	
Total Fat	29g	
Saturated	13g	
Cholesterol	490mg	
Sodium	1490mg	
Total Carbohydrate	32g	
Dietary Fiber	2g	
Sugars	11g	
Protein	31g	

1) Place eggs in single layer in large saucepan or Dutch oven; add enough cold water to cover eggs by 1 inch. Bring to a boil. Immediately remove from heat; cover and let stand 15 minutes. Drain; rinse with cold water. Place eggs in bowl of ice water; let stand 10 minutes. Peel eggs; cut into quarters. Set aside.

2) In medium saucepan, prepare sauce mix with milk and butter as directed on package. Stir in quartered hard-cooked eggs, lemon juice, dill and pepper. Cook and stir 2 to 3 minutes or until thoroughly heated.

3) Place ham on microwave-safe plate; cover loosely with microwave-safe plastic wrap. Microwave on Medium for 2 to 3 minutes or until thoroughly heated.

4) Place 2 muffin halves on each serving plate. Arrange ham slices on muffins. Spoon egg mixture over ham.

tip

If you have eight hard-cooked eggs on hand, you can save yourself some time by omitting the cooking directions in Step 1.

Pancake Banana Splits

PREP TIME: 25 MINUTES (READY IN 25 MINUTES)
SERVINGS: 6

 EASY LOW FAT

1 package (16.4-oz.) frozen microwave pancakes or buttermilk microwave pancakes (12 pancakes)

3 bananas

1 container (8 oz.) strawberry yogurt

1 container (8 oz.) vanilla yogurt

1 can (8 oz.) crushed pineapple in unsweetened juice, drained

$\frac{1}{2}$ cup fresh blueberries

2 tablespoons granola

Fresh strawberries

1) MICROWAVE DIRECTIONS: Remove plastic wrap from 2 stacks of pancakes; place on microwave-safe plate. Microwave on High for 2 minutes 15 seconds to 2 minutes 45 seconds or until pancakes are hot and no firm spots remain. DO NOT OVERHEAT. Repeat with remaining 2 stacks.

2) Cut each banana in half lengthwise and crosswise, making 4 pieces each.

3) To serve, place 2 pancakes on each serving plate. Top each with 2 banana pieces, $\frac{1}{6}$ each of strawberry yogurt, vanilla yogurt, pineapple and blueberries. Sprinkle each serving with granola. Garnish with strawberries.

Nutrition Information Per Serving:		
Calories: 340	From Fat:	40
Total Fat		4.5g
Saturated		1.5g
Cholesterol		10mg
Sodium		350mg
Total Carbohydrate		66g
Dietary Fiber		4g
Sugars		34g
Protein		9g

tip

Have all the topping ingredients ready before you microwave the pancakes to ensure that the pancakes will be hot when you serve them.

Great Day Granola

ANITA F. HUNTER | STILWELL, KANSAS

PREP TIME: 15 MINUTES (READY IN 2 HOURS 15 MINUTES)
SERVINGS: 32 (1/2 CUP EACH)

4 cups oats

3 cups Golden Grahams® cereal

3 cups Fiber One® cereal

1 cup chopped walnuts

1 cup sliced almonds

1 cup sunflower nuts

1 cup packed brown sugar

1/2 cup canola or vegetable oil

1/2 cup honey

1/2 cup water

1/2 teaspoon vanilla

1/2 teaspoon almond extract

1) Heat oven to 250°F. Spray 2 (15x10-inch) pans with sides with cooking spray. In very large bowl, mix oats, both cereals, the walnuts, almonds and sunflower nuts.

2) In 2-quart saucepan, cook brown sugar, oil, honey and water over medium-high heat 3 to 5 minutes, stirring constantly, until brown sugar is melted. Remove from heat. Stir in vanilla and almond extract. Pour over cereal mixture; stir until well coated. Spread mixture evenly in pans.

3) Bake 1 hour, rearranging pans once halfway through baking. Cool completely in pan, about 1 hour. Break into pieces. Store in tightly covered container. Serve as breakfast cereal, snack or as topping for ice cream, yogurt or fresh fruit.

HIGH ALTITUDE (3500-6500 FT.): No change.

Nutrition Information Per Serving:		
Calories: 220	From Fat:	90
Total Fat		10g
Saturated		1g
Cholesterol		0mg
Sodium		65mg
Total Carbohydrate		27g
Dietary Fiber		5g
Sugars		13g
Protein		4g

Savory Shrimp Crepes

PREP TIME: 45 MINUTES (READY IN 1 HOUR 10 MINUTES)
SERVINGS: 6 (2 CREPES EACH)

CREPES

3 eggs

²/₃ cup all-purpose flour

1 cup milk

FILLING

2 tablespoons butter

2 packages (8 oz. each) fresh whole mushrooms, thinly sliced

¼ cup butter

⅓ cup all-purpose flour

2 cups milk

2 tablespoons chopped fresh dill

¾ teaspoon salt

¼ teaspoon pepper

1 bag (12 oz.) frozen cooked deveined peeled small shrimp (about 90), thawed as directed on bag

1) Heat oven to 375°F. Spray 13x9-inch (3-quart) glass baking dish. In medium bowl, beat eggs and ²/₃ cup flour with electric mixer on medium speed until well blended. Slowly beat in 1 cup milk until smooth.

2) Heat 8-inch nonstick skillet over medium heat. Lift pan and pour about 3 tablespoons batter into center of skillet, then tilt skillet so batter evenly coats bottom. Cook 45 to 60 seconds or until top appears dry; turn crepe and cook 15 to 20 seconds longer. Remove from skillet; stack crepes on plate. Stir batter in bowl occasionally during cooking. Repeat with remaining batter, making about 11 more crepes.

3) In 10-inch skillet, melt 2 tablespoons butter over medium heat. Add mushrooms; cook 3 to 4 minutes, stirring occasionally, until mushrooms are lightly browned. Drain; set aside.

4) In 2-quart saucepan, melt ¼ cup butter over medium heat. Add ⅓ cup flour; cook, stirring constantly, until bubbly and smooth. Gradually stir in 2 cups milk, cooking and stirring until mixture boils. Boil and stir 1 minute. Reduce heat to low. Stir in dill, salt, pepper, thawed shrimp and 2 cups of the cooked mushrooms. Cook 2 to 3 minutes, stirring occasionally, until shrimp are thoroughly heated.

5) Place ⅓ cup shrimp mixture on each crepe; roll up and place in baking dish.

6) Cover tightly with foil; bake 20 minutes. Uncover; bake 5 minutes longer. Reheat remaining mushrooms over low heat 2 minutes. Serve crepes topped with mushrooms and if desired, garnished with fresh dill sprigs.

HIGH ALTITUDE (3500-6500 FT.): In Step 4, cook shrimp mixture 3 to 4 minutes. In Step 6, bake 25 minutes; uncover and bake 5 minutes longer.

Nutrition Information Per Serving:

Calories:	350	From Fat:	160
Total Fat			18g
Saturated			8g
Cholesterol			255mg
Sodium			590mg
Total Carbohydrate			25g
Dietary Fiber			2g
Sugars			7g
Protein			23g

Cheesy Rice and Broccoli in Egg Tortillas

LOANNE CHIU | FORT WORTH, TEXAS

Bake-Off®
Pillsbury

PREP TIME: 30 MINUTES (READY IN 30 MINUTES)
SERVINGS: 2

1 box (10 oz.) Green Giant® frozen cheesy rice & broccoli

1 cup shredded Mexican 4-cheese blend (4 oz.)

$^1/_2$ cup ranch-flavored sliced almonds

2 tablespoons finely chopped fresh cilantro

1 teaspoon chili powder

$^1/_2$ teaspoon dried Mexican oregano leaves

$^1/_4$ to $^3/_4$ teaspoon salt

3 eggs

4 tablespoons vegetable oil

4 Old El Paso® flour tortillas for soft tacos & fajitas, 6 inch (from 10.5-oz. package)

Fresh cilantro sprigs, if desired

Pickled jalapeño-flavored cucumbers, sliced, if desired

Chunky-style salsa, if desired

1) Cook rice and broccoli as directed on box. In medium bowl, mix rice and broccoli, the cheese, almonds, chopped cilantro, $^1/_2$ teaspoon of the chili powder, $^1/_4$ teaspoon of the oregano and $^1/_4$ teaspoon of the salt.

2) In pie plate or shallow bowl, beat eggs, remaining chili powder, oregano and remaining salt if desired with fork until well blended.

3) In 10-inch nonstick skillet, heat 1 tablespoon of the oil over medium heat. Dip 1 tortilla into egg mixture, letting egg mixture soak into tortilla; place in hot skillet. Cook until bottom of tortilla is browned, spooning 2 tablespoons egg mixture over tortilla (some egg mixture may run off).

4) Turn tortilla; place about $^1/_2$ cup rice mixture down center of tortilla. Fold sides of tortilla over rice mixture; press with pancake turner. Turn filled tortilla and press again. Cook 1 to 2 minutes longer or until tortilla is browned and filling is thoroughly heated. Place filled tortilla on plate; cover to keep warm. Repeat making 3 more filled tortillas. Cut each filled tortilla diagonally in half. Garnish with cilantro sprigs; serve with cucumbers and salsa or if desired, serve with green salad.

HIGH ALTITUDE (3500-6500 FT.): No change.

Nutrition Information Per Serving:	
Calories: 1070	From Fat: 680
Total Fat	76g
Saturated	20g
Cholesterol	375mg
Sodium	2320mg
Total Carbohydrate	60g
Dietary Fiber	5g
Sugars	7g
Protein	36g

Monte Cristos with Raspberry Yogurt Dip

COURTNEY BARRETT | LEWISVILLE, TEXAS

PREP TIME: 20 MINUTES (READY IN 20 MINUTES)
SERVINGS: 2

4 slices packaged precooked bacon (from 2.1-oz. package)

¼ cup seedless raspberry jam

1 container (6 oz.) Yoplait® Original 99% Fat Free red raspberry yogurt

1 tablespoon unsalted butter

4 Pillsbury® frozen homestyle waffles (from 12-oz. bag)

6 slices (³⁄₄ to 1 oz. each) Swiss cheese

4 slices (¹⁄₃ to ½ oz. each) cooked honey ham

4 slices (¹⁄₃ to ½ oz. each) cooked turkey

Powdered sugar

1) Heat bacon as directed on package; set aside. In small bowl, mix jam and yogurt; set aside.

2) In 12-inch skillet, melt butter over medium-low heat. Add 2 waffles; cook 3 to 4 minutes or until ridges are golden brown and tops begin to soften. Turn waffles; add remaining 2 waffles to skillet.

3) On each of first 2 toasted waffles, layer 1 Swiss cheese slice, 2 ham slices, 1 bacon slice, 1 Swiss cheese slice, 1 bacon slice, 2 turkey slices and 1 Swiss cheese slice (evenly arrange cheese so sandwich will hold together). Top each with remaining hot waffle, toasted side down. Cook about 2 minutes or until bottom waffles are browned.

4) Turn sandwiches; cover and cook about 4 minutes longer or until waffles are browned and cheese is melted. Cut sandwiches in half; lightly sprinkle with powdered sugar. Serve with raspberry sauce for dipping.

HIGH ALTITUDE (3500-6500 FT.): Cook over medium heat.

Nutrition Information Per Serving:	
Calories: 980	From Fat: 390
Total Fat	43g
Saturated	21g
Cholesterol	115mg
Sodium	2140mg
Total Carbohydrate	106g
Dietary Fiber	0g
Sugars	43g
Protein	41g

Make-Ahead Spring Brunch Bake

PREP TIME: 25 MINUTES (READY IN 9 HOURS 45 MINUTES)
SERVINGS: 12

- 2 tablespoons margarine or butter
- 2 medium leeks, quartered, sliced, using bulb and light green portions (about 2 cups)
- 8 oz. fresh asparagus spears, trimmed, broken into 1-inch pieces
- 5 cups frozen southern-style hash-brown potatoes (from 32-oz. package)
- 1/2 cup roasted red bell pepper strips (from 7.25-oz. jar)
- 1 teaspoon salt
- 1 teaspoon dried dill weed
- 8 eggs
- 1 pint (2 cups) half-and-half or milk
- 1 cup finely shredded fresh Parmesan cheese (4 oz.)

1) Spray 13x9-inch (3-quart) glass baking dish with cooking spray. Melt margarine in 12-inch skillet over medium-high heat. Add leeks and asparagus pieces; cook and stir 5 to 6 minutes or until crisp-tender.

2) Add potatoes, roasted pepper strips, salt and dill; mix lightly. Spoon evenly into sprayed baking dish.

3) Beat eggs in medium bowl. Add half-and-half; beat well. Add half of the cheese; mix well. Pour over vegetable mixture in baking dish. Sprinkle with remaining half of cheese. Cover with foil; refrigerate at least 8 hours or overnight.

4) Heat oven to 350°F. Bake, covered, 45 minutes. Uncover; bake an additional 20 to 25 minutes or until center is set. Let stand 10 minutes. Cut into squares. If desired, garnish with red bell pepper strips.

Nutrition Information Per Serving:

Calories:	250	From Fat:	110
Total Fat			13g
Saturated			6g
Cholesterol			165mg
Sodium			450mg
Total Carbohydrate			22g
Dietary Fiber			2g
Sugars			4g
Protein			11g

tip

The white bulb and light green portion of a leek are its most tender parts. The dark green leaves are usually tough and should be discarded. Sand and dirt hide between the layers of a leek, so rinse sliced leeks until they are free of any residue.

Dijon Ham and Asparagus Muffins

PREP TIME: 15 MINUTES (READY IN 15 MINUTES)
SERVINGS: 4

 EASY

½ lb. thin asparagus spears, trimmed, cut into 5-inch pieces

1 cup cubed (½ inch) cooked ham

¼ cup shredded Cheddar-American cheese blend (1 oz.)

2 tablespoons chopped green onions (2 medium)

¾ cup Alfredo pasta sauce

2 teaspoons Dijon mustard

2 English muffins, split, toasted

1) In microwavable pie plate, place asparagus spears; cover with microwavable plastic wrap and cut 1-inch slit in center of wrap. Microwave on High 2 to 3 minutes or until asparagus is crisp-tender; set aside.

2) Meanwhile, in 2-quart saucepan, mix remaining ingredients except muffins; cook over medium heat, stirring occasionally, until thoroughly heated.

3) Place 1 muffin half on each plate. Top each evenly with asparagus spears and ham mixture.

HIGH ALTITUDE (3500-6500 FT.): No change.

Nutrition Information Per Serving:		
Calories: 320	From Fat:	180
Total Fat		20g
Saturated		11g
Cholesterol		70mg
Sodium		960mg
Total Carbohydrate		18g
Dietary Fiber		1g
Sugars		5g
Protein		16g

tip

Cook the asparagus and make the ham mixture up to two days ahead, then cover and store in the refrigerator. Reheat the mixture before serving. Serve with fresh fruit if desired.

Sour Cream-Ham Enchiladas

PREP TIME: 15 MINUTES (READY IN 55 MINUTES)
SERVINGS: 6 (2 ENCHILADAS EACH)

 EASY

3 cups chopped cooked ham

1 container (8 oz.) sour cream
   (about 1 cup)

1 can (4.5 oz.) Old El Paso® chopped
   green chiles

3 cups shredded Cheddar cheese
   (12 oz.)

1 package (10.5 oz.) Old El Paso®
   flour tortillas for soft tacos & fajitas,
   6 inch (12 tortillas)

1 can (10 oz.) Old El Paso®
   enchilada sauce

Nutrition Information Per Serving:

Calories: 590	From Fat: 340
Total Fat	37g
Saturated	20g
Cholesterol	125mg
Sodium	2030mg
Total Carbohydrate	31g
Dietary Fiber	0g
Sugars	3g
Protein	33g

Try these enchiladas for brunch. Serve them with fresh orange slices and/or red grapes.

1) Heat oven to 350°F. Spray 13x9-inch (3-quart) glass baking dish with cooking spray. In large bowl, mix ham, sour cream, green chiles and 2^1/$_2$ cups of the cheese.

2) Spoon about ^{1}/$_3$ cup ham mixture evenly down center of each tortilla. Fold sides of tortilla over filling; place seam side down in baking dish. Pour enchilada sauce over filled tortillas.

3) Spray sheet of foil with cooking spray; cover dish tightly with foil, sprayed side down. Bake 30 to 35 minutes or until thoroughly heated. Uncover; sprinkle with remaining ^{1}/$_2$ cup cheese. Bake uncovered 5 minutes longer or until cheese is melted. If desired, serve with shredded lettuce and chopped tomatoes.

HIGH ALTITUDE (3500-6500 FT.): Bake 35 to 40 minutes.

Appetizers, Snacks & Beverages

Recipes for dipping, sipping and more
make party planning a breeze!

TOPPED MINI QUICHES
PG. 39

CHERRY FRUIT PUNCH
PG. 45

SPUNKY MONKEY SNACK MIX
PG. 47

HERB-CRAB SPREAD
PG. 59

Herbed Cheese Spread

PREP TIME: 15 MINUTES (READY IN 15 MINUTES)
SERVINGS: 12 (2 TABLESPOONS DIP AND 2 CRACKERS EACH)

 EASY

1 package (8 oz.) cream cheese, softened

¾ cup crumbled feta cheese (3 oz.)

2 tablespoons chopped fresh parsley

2 tablespoons cut (1-inch) fresh chives

1 tablespoon fresh thyme leaves

Dash coarse ground black pepper

1 small garlic clove

¼ cup finely chopped ripe olives

Crackers

1) In food processor bowl with metal blade, mix all ingredients except olives; process until well blended.

2) Stir in olives. Spoon into serving bowl. Serve with crackers.

HIGH ALTITUDE (3500-6500 FT.): No change.

Nutrition Information Per Serving:

Calories:	130	From Fat:	100
Total Fat			11g
Saturated			6g
Cholesterol			25mg
Sodium			230mg
Total Carbohydrate			6g
Dietary Fiber			0g
Sugars			1g
Protein			3g

 tip

Feta cheese is the classic Greek cheese made from sheep's or goat's milk. Cured and stored in brine, feta has a tangy, salty flavor that is great in this tasty dip.

Garnish the dip with a fresh sprig of thyme.

Topped Mini Quiches

PREP TIME: 25 MINUTES (READY IN 1 HOUR)
SERVINGS: 48 APPETIZERS

1 package (33.6 oz.) frozen Florentine or Lorraine mini quiches (48)

CREAMY PESTO TOPPER

2 tablespoons cream cheese spread (from 8-oz. container)

2 tablespoons basil pesto

1 tablespoon finely chopped red bell pepper or pimiento

RED AND GREEN TOPPER

3 tablespoons cream cheese spread (from 8-oz. container)

4 grape tomatoes, each cut into quarters

1 tablespoon chopped fresh parsley

DILL-SHRIMP TOPPER

2 tablespoons dill dip

16 ready-to-eat cooked tiny shrimp (from 8-oz. bag)

1) Bake quiches as directed on package. Meanwhile, prepare ingredients for toppers.

2) For Creamy Pesto Topper, mix cream cheese and pesto; spoon about $3/4$ teaspoon onto each of 16 quiches. Garnish each with bell pepper.

3) For Red and Green Topper, spoon about $1/2$ teaspoon cream cheese spread onto each of 16 quiches; place 1 tomato quarter in center of each. Garnish each with parsley.

4) For Dill-Shrimp Topper, spread about 1 teaspoon dill dip on each of 16 quiches; place shrimp with tail end facing upward in center of each. Sprinkle with dill, if desired.

HIGH ALTITUDE (3500-6500 FT.): No change.

Nutrition Information Per Serving:

Calories:	70	From Fat:	45
Total Fat			5g
Saturated			2g
Cholesterol			25mg
Sodium			115mg
Total Carbohydrate			5g
Dietary Fiber			0g
Sugars			0g
Protein			3g

tip If you don't want to make all three toppers, simply choose any topper and double or triple the ingredient amounts based on how many you plan to make.

Apricot Cooler

PREP TIME: 5 MINUTES (READY IN 5 MINUTES)
SERVINGS: 16 (1/2 CUP EACH)

 EASY LOW FAT

1 can (46 oz.) apricot nectar, chilled

3/4 cup frozen (thawed) lemonade concentrate (half 12-oz. can)

2 cups lemon-lime carbonated beverage, chilled

1) In 2½- to 3-quart nonmetal pitcher or punch bowl, mix apricot nectar and lemonade concentrate. If desired, refrigerate until serving time.

2) Just before serving, gently stir in carbonated beverage. Serve over ice.

HIGH ALTITUDE (3500-6500 FT.): No change.

To make cherry ice cubes, place 1 maraschino cherry in each section of an ice cube tray. Fill each section halfway with water. Freeze until firm, about 1 hour. Then, fill tray completely with water and freeze at least 1 hour or until serving.

Nutrition Information Per Serving:

Calories:	90	From Fat:	0
Total Fat			0g
Saturated			0g
Cholesterol			0mg
Sodium			5mg
Total Carbohydrate			21g
Dietary Fiber			0g
Sugars			20g
Protein			0g

Cocktail Sausages in Crimson Sauce

PREP TIME: 30 MINUTES (READY IN 30 MINUTES)
SERVINGS: 24 (ABOUT 3 SAUSAGES AND 1 TABLESPOON SAUCE EACH)

 EASY

1 can (16 oz.) whole berry cranberry sauce

1/3 cup seedless raspberry jam

1 teaspoon cornstarch

1/2 teaspoon red pepper sauce

2 packages (1 lb. each) cocktail-size smoked link sausages

2 tablespoons sliced green onions (2 medium)

Nutrition Information Per Serving:

Calories:	160	From Fat:	90
Total Fat			10g
Saturated			4g
Cholesterol			25mg
Sodium			360mg
Total Carbohydrate			12g
Dietary Fiber			0g
Sugars			10g
Protein			4g

1) In 3-quart saucepan, mix all ingredients except onions. Heat to boiling over medium-high heat, stirring frequently.

2) Reduce heat to low; cook uncovered 15 minutes, stirring occasionally, until sausages are hot. Spoon into serving dish; sprinkle with onions.

HIGH ALTITUDE (3500-6500 FT.): Add up to 1/4 cup water if sauce gets too thick.

Layered Reuben Spread

PREP TIME: 15 MINUTES (READY IN 40 MINUTES)
SERVINGS: 24 (2 TABLESPOONS SPREAD AND 3 CRACKERS EACH)

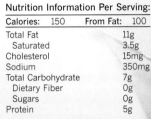 EASY

$^2/_3$ cup mayonnaise

$^1/_3$ cup Thousand Island dressing

1 can (8 oz.) sauerkraut, well drained

1 bag (8 oz.) shredded Swiss cheese
(2 cups)

1 package (6 oz.) thinly sliced
corned beef, chopped

2 tablespoons sliced green onions
(2 medium)

1 box (8 oz.) toasted wheat crackers
(about 72 crackers)

Nutrition Information Per Serving:	
Calories: 150	From Fat: 100
Total Fat	11g
Saturated	3.5g
Cholesterol	15mg
Sodium	350mg
Total Carbohydrate	7g
Dietary Fiber	0g
Sugars	0g
Protein	5g

1) Heat oven to 350°F. In small bowl, mix mayonnaise and dressing until well blended.

2) In ungreased 9-inch pie pan, layer sauerkraut, half of the cheese, the corned beef and mayonnaise mixture. To remaining half of cheese in bag, add onions; toss to mix. Sprinkle over top.

3) Bake 20 to 25 minutes or until bubbly around edge. Serve spread with crackers.

HIGH ALTITUDE (3500-6500 FT.): No change.

Fresh Fruit Salsa with Cinnamon Crisps

PREP TIME: 40 MINUTES (READY IN 1 HOUR)
SERVINGS: 16 (1/4 CUP SALSA AND 2 CRISPS EACH)

 LOW FAT

CINNAMON CRISPS

- 1 tablespoon sugar
- ½ teaspoon ground cinnamon
- 4 Old El Paso® flour tortillas for burritos, 8 inch (from 11.5-oz. package)
- 1 tablespoon water

SALSA

- 1 small orange
- 2 medium Granny Smith apples, peeled, cored and finely chopped (2 cups)
- ½ cup finely chopped fresh strawberries
- 1 medium peach, peeled, pitted and finely chopped (²/3 cup)
- 2 tablespoons packed brown sugar
- 2 tablespoons apple jelly

1) Heat oven to 400°F. Spray cookie sheet with cooking spray. In small bowl, mix sugar and cinnamon.

2) Lightly brush both sides of each tortilla with water. Lightly sprinkle about ½ teaspoon sugar-cinnamon mixture over each side of each tortilla. Cut each tortilla into 8 wedges; place on cookie sheet.

3) Bake 6 to 8 minutes or until light golden brown. Remove from cookie sheet; place on wire rack. Cool completely, about 10 minutes.

4) Meanwhile, grate peel from orange; squeeze orange to make about ¼ cup juice. In medium bowl, mix orange peel, orange juice and remaining salsa ingredients.

5) If desired, garnish salsa with strawberry fan. Serve salsa with cinnamon crisps.

HIGH ALTITUDE (3500-6500 FT.): No change.

Nutrition Information Per Serving:		
Calories: 70	From Fat:	10
Total Fat		1g
Saturated		0g
Cholesterol		0mg
Sodium		80mg
Total Carbohydrate		14g
Dietary Fiber		0g
Sugars		7g
Protein		0g

Blackberry-Almond Bruschetta

KAREN MACK | WEBSTER, NEW YORK

PREP TIME: 20 MINUTES (READY IN 1 HOUR)
SERVINGS: 24 APPETIZERS

1 can (11 oz.) Pillsbury® refrigerated crusty French loaf

Butter-flavor cooking spray

2 tablespoons granulated sugar

1 package (8 oz.) reduced-fat cream cheese (Neufchâtel), softened

1 to 2 teaspoons almond extract

¼ cup powdered sugar

1 bag (10 oz.) Cascadian Farm® frozen blackberries, thawed, well drained

⅓ cup sliced almonds, toasted, coarsely chopped*

3 tablespoons powdered sugar

1) Heat oven to 350°F. Bake French loaf as directed on can. Cool 5 minutes.

2) Cut ends off loaf; cut loaf crosswise into 24 slices, about ½ inch thick. Arrange slices on ungreased cookie sheet. Spray each slice with cooking spray until lightly coated; sprinkle with granulated sugar. Return to oven; bake 8 to 10 minutes longer or until lightly toasted.

3) Meanwhile, in small bowl, beat cream cheese, almond extract and ¼ cup powdered sugar with electric mixer on low speed until well combined.

4) Spread cheese mixture evenly onto toasted bread slices. Top each with 3 or 4 blackberries; sprinkle with almonds. With small strainer, sprinkle 3 tablespoons powdered sugar over bruschetta.

*NOTE: To toast almonds, spread on cookie sheet; bake at 350°F. 5 to 7 minutes or until golden brown, stirring occasionally. Coarsely chop.

HIGH ALTITUDE (3500-6500 FT.): No change.

Nutrition Information Per Appetizer:		
Calories: 90	From Fat: 30	
Total Fat		3.5g
Saturated		1.5g
Cholesterol		5mg
Sodium		115mg
Total Carbohydrate		11g
Dietary Fiber		0g
Sugars		5g
Protein		2g

Spinach Dip Crisps

STEPHANIE LAU-CHEN | MOUNTAIN VIEW, CALIFORNIA

Bake-Off

PREP TIME: 20 MINUTES (READY IN 35 MINUTES)
SERVINGS: 24 APPETIZERS

1 box (9 oz.) Green Giant® frozen spinach

24 wonton skins (about 3 1/4-inch squares; from 16-oz. package)

1 can (7 oz.) Old El Paso® chopped green chiles

1/3 cup reduced-fat mayonnaise or salad dressing

3/4 cup finely shredded Monterey Jack and Cheddar cheese blend

1) Heat oven to 350°F. Cook spinach as directed on box. Drain; set aside to cool.

2) Place 1 wonton skin in each of 24 ungreased regular-size muffin cups, gently pressing skin into bottom and up side of each cup (points of wonton skin will show above cup edge). Bake 7 to 10 minutes or until top 1/4 inch of wonton skins are golden brown.

3) Meanwhile, squeeze all excess water from spinach; place in large bowl. Stir in green chiles, mayonnaise and 1/4 cup of the cheese; mix well.

4) Spoon about 1 tablespoon spinach mixture into each wonton cup. Sprinkle each with 1 teaspoon remaining cheese. Bake 5 to 7 minutes longer or until cheese is melted and filling is hot. Remove from muffin cups; serve warm.

HIGH ALTITUDE (3500-6500 FT.): In step 4, bake 7 to 9 minutes.

Nutrition Information Per Appetizer:		
Calories: 50	From Fat:	20
Total Fat		2.5g
Saturated		1g
Cholesterol		5mg
Sodium		125mg
Total Carbohydrate		6g
Dietary Fiber		0g
Sugars		0g
Protein		2g

Cherry Fruit Punch

PREP TIME: 15 MINUTES (READY IN 15 MINUTES)
SERVINGS: 31 (1 CUP EACH)

 EASY   LOW FAT

1 box (4-serving size) cherry-flavored gelatin

1 cup boiling water

1 can (46 oz.) pineapple juice, chilled

1 quart (4 cups) apple cider, chilled

¼ cup lemon juice

1 bottle (33.8 oz.) ginger ale, chilled

Nutrition Information Per Serving:	
Calories: 70	From Fat: 0
Total Fat	0g
Saturated	0g
Cholesterol	0mg
Sodium	20mg
Total Carbohydrate	16g
Dietary Fiber	0g
Sugars	15g
Protein	0g

1) In 3-quart pitcher or bowl, mix gelatin and boiling water; stir until gelatin is dissolved. Stir in pineapple juice, apple cider and lemon juice. If desired, refrigerate until serving time.

2) Just before serving, pour mixture into punch bowl. Gently stir in ginger ale.

HIGH ALTITUDE (3500-6500 FT.): No change.

Fire-It-Up Snack Mix

PREP TIME: 10 MINUTES (READY IN 1 HOUR 10 MINUTES)
SERVINGS: 40 (1/4 CUP EACH)

 EASY

2 cups corn chips

2 cups small pretzel twists

2 cups oyster crackers

2 cups honey-roasted peanuts

2 cups pumpkin seeds

¼ cup butter or margarine, melted

¼ cup packed brown sugar

1 teaspoon chili powder

2 teaspoons Worcestershire sauce

1 teaspoon hot pepper sauce

Nutrition Information Per Serving:	
Calories: 110	From Fat: 60
Total Fat	6g
Saturated	1.5g
Cholesterol	0mg
Sodium	125mg
Total Carbohydrate	9g
Dietary Fiber	1g
Sugars	3g
Protein	3g

Tailor this snack mix to your taste by using your favorite crackers, chips and nuts.

1) Heat oven to 300°F. In large bowl, mix corn chips, pretzel twists, oyster crackers, peanuts and pumpkin seeds.

2) In small bowl, mix remaining ingredients. Pour butter mixture over corn chip mixture; toss to coat. Spread in 2 ungreased 15x10x1-inch pans.

3) Bake 25 to 30 minutes or until peanuts are golden brown, stirring every 10 minutes. Cool completely, about 30 minutes. (Mixture crisps as it cools.)

HIGH ALTITUDE (3500-6500 FT.): No change.

Pepper Jack-Artichoke Dip

PREP TIME:	15 MINUTES (READY IN 30 MINUTES)	EASY
SERVINGS:	32 (2 TABLESPOONS AND 2 MELBA TOAST ROUNDS EACH)	

2 cans (14 oz. each) quartered
artichoke hearts, drained, chopped

1 cup mayonnaise

10 oz. pepper Jack cheese, shredded
(2 1/2 cups)

1/4 cup Progresso® Italian-style
bread crumbs

Red bell pepper, chopped, if desired

Chopped parsley

8 oz. melba toast rounds (about 64)

Nutrition Information Per Serving:

Calories:	120	From Fat:	70
Total Fat			8g
Saturated			2g
Cholesterol			10mg
Sodium			220mg
Total Carbohydrate			9g
Dietary Fiber			1g
Sugars			0g
Protein			4g

This is an easy
recipe to cut in
half if your group
is smaller. Bake in
an 8-inch square
baking dish.

1) Heat oven to 400°F. In medium bowl, mix artichokes, mayonnaise and
2 cups of the cheese. Spread mixture in ungreased 13x9-inch (3-quart)
glass baking dish.

2) In small bowl, mix remaining 1/2 cup cheese and the bread crumbs;
sprinkle over artichoke mixture.

3) Bake 10 to 12 minutes or until thoroughly heated. Garnish with red bell
pepper and parsley. Serve dip with melba toast rounds.

HIGH ALTITUDE (ABOVE 3500-6500 FT.): No change.

Spunky Monkey Snack Mix

PREP TIME: 5 MINUTES (READY IN 5 MINUTES)
SERVINGS: 14 (1/2 CUP EACH)

 EASY

3 cups Golden Grahams® cereal

1 bag (7 oz.) malted milk balls (2 cups)

1 cup dried banana chips

1 cup honey-roasted peanuts

1) In covered container or large resealable food-storage plastic bag, gently toss all ingredients. Tightly cover container or seal bag.

HIGH ALTITUDE (3500-6500 FT.): No change.

Nutrition Information Per Serving:		
Calories: 190	From Fat:	80
Total Fat		8g
Saturated		3.5g
Cholesterol		0mg
Sodium		150mg
Total Carbohydrate		27g
Dietary Fiber		2g
Sugars		16g
Protein		4g

Veggie Ranch Scoops

PREP TIME: 35 MINUTES (READY IN 35 MINUTES)
SERVINGS: 10 (3 CHIPS EACH)

 EASY

1/3 cup ranch dressing

3 cups scoop-style tortilla chips (about 30 chips)

1 small carrot, shredded (about 1/3 cup)

2 tablespoons finely chopped red bell pepper

1 cup very small (1/2 inch) broccoli florets (about 30)

1) Spoon scant 1/2 teaspoon dressing in center of each chip. Top each with pinch of carrot, bell pepper and 1 broccoli floret. Place on serving plate or tray; serve immediately.

HIGH ALTITUDE (3500-6500 FT.): No change.

Nutrition Information Per Serving:		
Calories: 80	From Fat:	50
Total Fat		6g
Saturated		1g
Cholesterol		0mg
Sodium		105mg
Total Carbohydrate		6g
Dietary Fiber		0g
Sugars		0g
Protein		0g

 Take the stress out of last-minute party preparations by placing the chips on your serving tray and measuring out the other ingredients so they are ready to go. When it's time to serve, it will only take minutes to have these appetizers on the table.

Fresh Mango Salsa

KIM ROULEAU | MOUNT PROSPECT, ILLINOIS

PREP TIME: 25 MINUTES (READY IN 25 MINUTES)
SERVINGS: 18 (1/4 CUP EACH)

1 bag (10 oz.) Cascadian Farm®
Organic frozen sliced peaches
(1 1/2 cups), thawed

2 cups finely chopped peeled fresh
mango (about 2) or 1 jar (24 oz.)
mango slices, drained, chopped

1 jar (16 oz.) Old El Paso® Wild for
Mild® Thick 'n Chunky salsa (2 cups)

1/4 cup chopped fresh cilantro

2 tablespoons fresh lime juice (about
2 medium)

1 small clove garlic, finely chopped

1) If desired, coarsely chop peaches. In
medium bowl, gently mix all ingredients.
Serve with chips for dipping or as sauce
for chicken, fish or meat.

HIGH ALTITUDE (3500-6500 FT.): No change.

Nutrition Information Per Serving:

Calories: 30	From Fat: 0
Total Fat	0g
Saturated	0g
Cholesterol	0mg
Sodium	190mg
Total Carbohydrate	7g
Dietary Fiber	0g
Sugars	4g
Protein	0g

If you can't find
Cascadian Farm®
Organic frozen
sliced peaches
at your grocery
store, look for
another brand
instead.

Elegant Cheese and Fruit Platter

PREP TIME: 15 MINUTES (READY IN 45 MINUTES)
SERVINGS: 24

 EASY

- 1 block (8 oz.) white Cheddar cheese
- 1 wedge (8 oz.) blue cheese (such as Stilton or Gorgonzola)
- 1 round (8 oz.) Brie cheese
- 1 large crisp red eating apple, sliced
- 1 medium pear, sliced
- 1 pint (2 cups) strawberries, halved
- 3/4 lb. seedless green grapes, cut into small clusters
- 3/4 lb. seedless red grapes, cut into small clusters
- 1 package (7 oz.) dried apricots
- 1/4 cup dried cherries or sweetened dried cranberries
- Fresh rosemary sprigs, if desired

1) On large serving platter, arrange cheeses in center. Cover; let stand at room temperature about 30 minutes.

2) Arrange fresh fruit in groups around cheese. Sprinkle dried apricots and cherries over cheese and fruit. Tuck rosemary sprigs among fruit.

3) To serve, provide cheese planes for harder cheeses and cheese spreaders for soft cheeses. If desired, serve cheese and fruit with crackers.

HIGH ALTITUDE (3500-6500 FT.): No change.

Nutrition Information Per Serving:		
Calories: 170	From Fat:	80
Total Fat		9g
Saturated		5g
Cholesterol		25mg
Sodium		250mg
Total Carbohydrate		16g
Dietary Fiber		2g
Sugars		12g
Protein		7g

Trail Mix-Peanut Butter Bark

PREP TIME: 25 MINUTES (READY IN 55 MINUTES)
SERVINGS: 12 (2 PIECES EACH)

 EASY

2 cups small pretzel twists (from 15-oz. bag)

1 cup Cheerios® cereal

2/3 cup sweetened dried cranberries

1/2 cup cashew halves

10 oz. vanilla-flavored candy coating (almond bark), cut into small pieces

1/3 cup creamy peanut butter

1) Cut 24x12-inch sheet of waxed paper. In large bowl, mix pretzels, cereal, cranberries and cashews.

2) In small microwavable bowl, microwave candy coating and peanut butter on High 1 minute. Stir well; microwave 15 to 30 seconds longer or until melted and mixture can be stirred smooth.

3) Gradually pour melted candy coating mixture over pretzel mixture, stirring to coat all pieces. Quickly spread mixture onto waxed paper into 12x8-inch rectangle, about 1/2 inch thick. Let stand 30 minutes or until set. Break into 2x2-inch pieces.

HIGH ALTITUDE (3500-6500 FT.): No change.

Nutrition Information Per Serving:

Calories:	270	From Fat:	130
Total Fat			14g
Saturated			6g
Cholesterol			0mg
Sodium			190mg
Total Carbohydrate			30g
Dietary Fiber			1g
Sugars			21g
Protein			5g

Store the bark in a sealed container in the refrigerator for up to one week. The refrigerator prevents the pretzels and cereal from getting soggy.

Coconut Shrimp with Gingered Cocktail Sauce

PREP TIME: 15 MINUTES (READY IN 30 MINUTES)
SERVINGS: 16 (2 SHRIMP AND 1 TABLESPOON SAUCE EACH)

 EASY   LOW FAT

SHRIMP

1 cup shredded coconut

½ cup Progresso® plain bread crumbs

¼ teaspoon salt

Dash ground red pepper (cayenne)

1½ lb. uncooked medium shrimp, peeled, deveined

¼ cup honey

SAUCE

1 jar (12 oz.) cocktail sauce

¼ teaspoon ground ginger

1) Heat oven to 425°F. Line large cookie sheet with foil; lightly spray foil with cooking spray. In food processor, place coconut, bread crumbs, salt and ground red pepper; process 10 seconds to mix slightly. Place in pie pan or shallow dish.

2) Pat shrimp dry with paper towels; place in medium bowl. In 1-quart saucepan, heat honey over low heat just until melted. Pour over shrimp; toss to coat. Roll shrimp in coconut mixture to coat; place in single layer on cookie sheet.

3) Bake 9 to 12 minutes or until shrimp turn pink and coconut begins to brown.

4) In small serving bowl, mix sauce ingredients. Arrange shrimp on serving platter; serve with sauce.

HIGH ALTITUDE (3500-6500 FT.): No change.

Nutrition Information Per Serving:		
Calories: 110	From Fat:	25
Total Fat		2.5g
Saturated		2g
Cholesterol		40mg
Sodium		380mg
Total Carbohydrate		15g
Dietary Fiber		0g
Sugars		12g
Protein		5g

To devein peeled shrimp, run a sharp knife down the back of the shrimp and lift the sandy-colored vein from the shrimp. Rinse to remove any excess vein.

Cereal-Almond Brittle

ENNY WILLIAMS | HONOLULU, HAWAII

PREP TIME: 15 MINUTES (READY IN 1 HOUR 10 MINUTES)
SERVINGS: 14 (1/2 CUP EACH)

2 cups Cheerios® cereal

2 cups Cinnamon Toast Crunch® cereal

2 cups oats

1 cup sliced almonds

½ cup butter or margarine

¼ cup packed brown sugar

⅓ cup real maple or maple-flavored syrup

1) Heat oven to 300°F. Line 1 large (17x14-inch) cookie sheet or 2 (15x10x1-inch) pans with foil; spray foil with cooking spray. In large bowl, mix both cereals, the oats and almonds; set aside.

2) In 1-quart saucepan, heat butter, brown sugar and syrup over medium heat, stirring frequently, until butter is melted and mixture boils. Pour over cereal mixture; stir until well coated. Spread mixture evenly on cookie sheet with rubber spatula until about ½ inch thick.

3) Bake 35 to 40 minutes or until almonds are golden brown. Cool completely, about 15 minutes. Break into pieces with fingers. Store in tightly covered container.

HIGH ALTITUDE (3500-6500 FT.): No change.

Nutrition Information Per Serving:		
Calories: 220	From Fat:	100
Total Fat		12g
Saturated		4.5g
Cholesterol		15mg
Sodium		120mg
Total Carbohydrate		26g
Dietary Fiber		3g
Sugars		11g
Protein		4g

Smoky Bean Dip

PREP TIME: 35 MINUTES (READY IN 35 MINUTES)
SERVINGS: 8

2 dried chipotle chiles

2 cans (15.5 or 15 oz. each) pinto beans, drained, rinsed

1/8 teaspoon liquid smoke, if desired

1 large garlic clove, minced

2 tablespoons chopped fresh cilantro

1/2 each of green, yellow and red bell pepper

2 Italian plum tomatoes, chopped

1 cup shredded Mexican cheese blend (4 oz.)

8 oz. tortilla chips

Nutrition Information Per Serving:	
Calories: 340	From Fat: 110
Total Fat	12g
Saturated	3.5g
Cholesterol	15mg
Sodium	270mg
Total Carbohydrate	45g
Dietary Fiber	9g
Sugars	3g
Protein	14g

1) Heat oven to 375°F. Place chiles in small bowl; cover with boiling water. Let stand 10 minutes or until soft. Drain chiles, reserving 3 tablespoons of soaking water. Remove and discard seeds from chiles; coarsely chop chiles.

2) In food processor bowl with metal blade or blender container, place beans, chiles, reserved water, liquid smoke and garlic; process on high speed until well combined. Stir in cilantro. Place mixture in ungreased shallow 9-inch glass pie pan. Cover with foil.

3) Bake 15 to 20 minutes or until mixture is thoroughly heated. Meanwhile, cut bell peppers with cactus, coyote and moon-shaped cookie cutters; set aside.

4) Uncover dip; sprinkle with tomatoes and cheese. Bake 2 to 3 minutes longer or until cheese is melted. Garnish top of dip with bell pepper cutouts. Serve with tortilla chips.

HIGH ALTITUDE (3500-6500 FT.): No change.

If you use canned chipotle chiles in this dip, it is not necessary to soak them as directed in the recipe. Add the canned chiles directly to the beans in the food processor, along with 3 tablespoons of the adobo sauce from the can in place of the soaking liquid.

Apple Snack Stacks

PREP TIME: 15 MINUTES (READY IN 45 MINUTES)
SERVINGS: 4

🄴 EASY

2 medium apples

4 tablespoons peanut butter, process cheese dip or sauce, or cream cheese

Nutrition Information Per Serving:	
Calories: 150	From Fat: 80
Total Fat	8g
Saturated	1.5g
Cholesterol	0mg
Sodium	75mg
Total Carbohydrate	14g
Dietary Fiber	2g
Sugars	8g
Protein	4g

1) Wash apples; remove core, leaving apples whole. Fill center of each apple with about 2 tablespoons peanut butter, packing gently. Wrap each tightly in plastic wrap. Refrigerate until filling is set, about 30 minutes.

2) Cut each apple crosswise into 1/2-inch-thick slices. Divide slices into 4 portions; wrap each portion tightly in plastic wrap. Refrigerate until serving time.

HIGH ALTITUDE (3500-6500 FT.): No change.

Southwestern Shrimp Cocktail

PREP TIME:	10 MINUTES (READY IN 40 MINUTES)	
SERVINGS:	20 (2 SHRIMP AND 1 TEASPOON SAUCE EACH)	EASY

SHRIMP

  2 lb. cooked deveined peeled large shrimp (total 41 to 50 shrimp), patted dry

SASSY COCKTAIL SAUCE

  ¼ cup Old El Paso® Thick 'n Chunky salsa

  ¼ cup cocktail sauce

TANGY LIME SAUCE

  ½ cup mayonnaise

  ¼ cup chopped fresh cilantro or parsley

  1 to 2 tablespoons lime juice

  1½ teaspoons Old El Paso® taco seasoning mix (from 1.25-oz. package)

1) Arrange shrimp in wreath pattern.

2) In separate small serving bowls, mix ingredients for both sauces. Serve shrimp with sauces.

HIGH ALTITUDE (3500-6500 FT.): No change.

Nutrition Information Per Serving:		
Calories: 90	From Fat:	45
Total Fat		5g
Saturated		1g
Cholesterol		90mg
Sodium		220mg
Total Carbohydrate		2g
Dietary Fiber		0g
Sugars		1g
Protein		10g

We've used shrimp with the tail shells, but you can also use shrimp without the tails on if you prefer.

Golden Glow Punch

PREP TIME: 10 MINUTES (READY IN 10 MINUTES)
SERVINGS: 25 (1/2 CUP EACH)

 EASY   LOW FAT

1 can (6 oz.) frozen lemonade concentrate, thawed

1 can (6 oz.) frozen orange juice concentrate, thawed

1 can (6 oz.) frozen tangerine juice concentrate, thawed

2 cups cold water

2 bottles (33 oz. each) ginger ale, chilled

Ice cubes or ice mold

Nutrition Information Per Serving:		
Calories: 70	From Fat:	0
Total Fat		0g
Saturated		0g
Cholesterol		0mg
Sodium		10mg
Total Carbohydrate		17g
Dietary Fiber		0g
Sugars		16g
Protein		0g

1) In large nonmetal pitcher or punch bowl, combine juice concentrates and water; mix well.

2) Just before serving, add ginger ale and ice; stir to blend. Garnish as desired.

Sugar-and-Spice Snack Mix

PREP TIME:	15 MINUTES (READY IN 1 HOUR 35 MINUTES)	
SERVINGS:	9 (1 CUP EACH)	**e** EASY

6 cups popped popcorn

3 cups Bugles® original flavor snacks
(from 14.5-oz. bag)

2 cups holiday-shaped pretzels

1 cup honey-roasted peanuts

½ cup sweetened dried cranberries

5 tablespoons butter or margarine,
melted

2 tablespoons sugar

2 tablespoons apple cider or
apple juice

2 teaspoons apple pie spice

1) Heat oven to 275°F. In large bowl, mix
popcorn, snacks, pretzels, peanuts and
cranberries.

2) In small bowl, mix butter, sugar, apple
cider and apple pie spice. Drizzle over
snack mixture, stirring until evenly
coated. Spread in ungreased shallow
roasting pan.

3) Bake 45 to 50 minutes, stirring every
15 minutes, until light brown and crisp.
Cool 30 minutes. Store in tightly covered
container.

HIGH ALTITUDE (3500-6500 FT.): No change.

Nutrition Information Per Serving:

Calories:	330	From Fat:	180
Total Fat			20g
Saturated			7g
Cholesterol			15mg
Sodium			420mg
Total Carbohydrate			29g
Dietary Fiber			3g
Sugars			11g
Protein			6g

Bread and Veggie Dippers with Garlic Dip

PREP TIME:	25 MINUTES (READY IN 25 MINUTES)	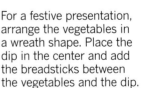 EASY
SERVINGS:	10	

1 box (10.6 oz.) Pillsbury® refrigerated garlic breadsticks and herbs

1 cup sour cream

½ cup mayonnaise

2 tablespoons finely chopped fresh parsley

About 4 cups assorted vegetables (baby-cut carrots, grape or cherry tomatoes, small broccoli and cauliflower florets, bell pepper strips, green onions and/or radishes)

Nutrition Information Per Serving:

Calories:	230	From Fat:	150
Total Fat		16g	
Saturated		4.5g	
Cholesterol		20mg	
Sodium		360mg	
Total Carbohydrate		16g	
Dietary Fiber		2g	
Sugars		4g	
Protein		3g	

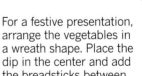

For a festive presentation, arrange the vegetables in a wreath shape. Place the dip in the center and add the breadsticks between the vegetables and the dip.

1) Heat oven to 375°F. Remove dough from can; reserve garlic seasoning for dip. Separate dough into 10 breadsticks. Cut each in half crosswise to make 20 strips; place 1 inch apart on ungreased large cookie sheet. Bake 13 to 18 minutes or until golden brown.

2) Meanwhile, in medium bowl, mix garlic seasoning from box, the sour cream, mayonnaise and parsley until well blended. Spoon into serving bowl.

3) On large platter, arrange vegetables, dip and breadsticks.

HIGH ALTITUDE (3500-6500 FT.): No change.

Southwestern Layered Dip

PREP TIME: 15 MINUTES (READY IN 15 MINUTES)
SERVINGS: 18 (3 TABLESPOONS DIP AND 3/4 OUNCE CHIPS EACH)

e EASY

1 can (16 oz.) Old El Paso® vegetarian refried beans

4 tablespoons chopped fresh cilantro

1 can (11 oz.) Green Giant® Mexicorn® whole kernel corn with red and green peppers, drained

1 container (8 oz.) sour cream (about 1 cup)

1 package (1.25 oz.) Old El Paso® 40%-less-sodium taco seasoning mix

½ cup shredded taco-seasoned cheese (2 oz.)

15 oz. tortilla chips

1) In bottom of 9-inch deep-dish pie pan, spread refried beans. Sprinkle 3 tablespoons of the cilantro over beans. Spoon corn evenly over cilantro.

2) In small bowl, mix sour cream and taco seasoning mix; spread over corn. Sprinkle with cheese and remaining 1 tablespoon cilantro. Serve with tortilla chips.

HIGH ALTITUDE (3500-6500 FT.): No change.

Nutrition Information Per Serving:		
Calories: 200	From Fat: 90	
Total Fat		10g
Saturated		3g
Cholesterol		10mg
Sodium		450mg
Total Carbohydrate		24g
Dietary Fiber		2g
Sugars		2g
Protein		4g

For more spicy heat, chop one fresh jalapeño chile and sprinkle over the refried beans.

Cinnamon-Fruit Snack Mix

REBECCA NURSE | WATERFORD, PENNSYLVANIA

PREP TIME: 20 MINUTES (READY IN 1 HOUR 50 MINUTES)
SERVINGS: 32 (1/2 CUP EACH)

2 cups Cinnamon Toast Crunch® cereal

1 cup Fiber One® cereal

1½ cups Mounds® coconut flakes

1 cup pecan halves

1 cup blanched whole almonds

½ cup sunflower nuts

½ cup wheat germ

½ cup ground flax seed

1 teaspoon salt

1 teaspoon ground cinnamon

1 cup chopped dried apricots

1 cup banana chips

1 cup sweetened dried cranberries

½ cup dried cherries

½ cup golden raisins

¼ cup vegetable oil

1 can (14 oz.) fat-free sweetened condensed milk (not evaporated)

Nutrition Information Per Serving:		
Calories: 220	From Fat: 100	
Total Fat		11g
Saturated		3g
Cholesterol		0mg
Sodium		125mg
Total Carbohydrate		27g
Dietary Fiber		4g
Sugars		19g
Protein		4g

1) Heat oven to 300°F. Spray 15x10x1-inch pan with cooking spray. In large bowl, place both cereals, coconut, pecans, almonds, sunflower nuts, wheat germ, flax seed, salt and cinnamon; mix well. In small bowl, mix oil and condensed milk. Pour over cereal mixture; toss until well coated. Spread evenly in pan.

2) Bake 50 to 60 minutes, stirring every 15 minutes to break up any large clumps, until light golden brown. Cool 30 minutes (mixture will crisp as it cools).

3) In large bowl, mix cereal mixture, apricots, banana chips, cranberries, cherries and raisins. Store in tightly covered container.

HIGH ALTITUDE (3500-6500 FT.): No change.

Herb-Crab Spread

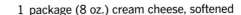

PREP TIME: 15 MINUTES (READY IN 45 MINUTES)
SERVINGS: 24 (1 TABLESPOON SPREAD AND 2 CRACKERS EACH)   EASY

1 package (8 oz.) cream cheese, softened

1 can (6 oz.) lump crabmeat, drained

½ teaspoon minced garlic

¼ teaspoon red pepper sauce

3 tablespoons chopped fresh basil

2 tablespoons chopped fresh oregano

1 sprig fresh basil

48 crackers or sliced bell peppers

Nutrition Information Per Serving:		
Calories: 80	From Fat: 50	
Total Fat		6g
Saturated		2.5g
Cholesterol		15mg
Sodium		120mg
Total Carbohydrate		5g
Dietary Fiber		0g
Sugars		0g
Protein		3g

1) In medium bowl with spoon, mix cream cheese, crabmeat, garlic, pepper sauce, chopped basil and oregano until well blended. Spoon into serving bowl. Cover; refrigerate at least 30 minutes to blend flavors. Garnish with oregano or basil sprig.

2) Serve crab spread with crackers or sliced bell peppers.

HIGH ALTITUDE (3500-6500 FT.): No change.

Cinco de Mayo Glazed Chicken Wings

LINDA DRUMM | VICTOR, IDAHO

PREP TIME: 50 MINUTES (READY IN 50 MINUTES)
SERVINGS: 5 (4 CHICKEN WINGS EACH)

1 tablespoon canola or vegetable oil

2¹/₂ lb. chicken wings, cut apart at joints, wing tips discarded

2 medium green onions, thinly sliced including tops (about 2 tablespoons)

1 teaspoon crushed red pepper flakes

2 cans (12 oz. each) lemon-lime carbonated beverage

1 can (4.5 oz.) Old El Paso® chopped green chiles, drained

1 package (1.25 oz.) Old El Paso® taco seasoning mix

10 lettuce leaves, if desired

1) In 12-inch nonstick skillet, heat oil over medium-high heat. Add chicken wings and onions; sprinkle with pepper flakes. Cook uncovered 5 to 8 minutes, stirring occasionally, until browned; drain.

2) Stir in carbonated beverage, green chiles and taco seasoning mix. Increase heat to high; cook uncovered 15 minutes, stirring occasionally. Reduce heat to medium-high; cook 5 to 10 minutes, stirring frequently, until chicken wings are completely glazed, small amount of glaze remains in skillet and juice of chicken is clear when thickest part is cut to bone (180°F.).

3) To serve, line serving plate with lettuce; arrange chicken wings over lettuce. Serve immediately.

HIGH ALTITUDE (3500-6500 FT.): In Step 1, cook 8 to 11 minutes.

Nutrition Information Per Serving:		
Calories: 350	From Fat:	170
Total Fat		19g
Saturated		5g
Cholesterol		70mg
Sodium		850mg
Total Carbohydrate		20g
Dietary Fiber		0g
Sugars		14g
Protein		23g

Ranch Roll-Up Snacks

PREP TIME: 15 MINUTES (READY IN 2 HOURS 15 MINUTES)
SERVINGS: 40 APPETIZERS

 EASY   LOW FAT

1 package (3 oz.) cream cheese, softened

1 container (8 oz.) ranch sour cream dip

½ cup finely chopped broccoli

½ cup shredded carrot

¼ cup finely chopped red onion

4 slices precooked bacon, chopped

5 Old El Paso® flour tortillas for burritos, 8 inch (from 11.5-oz. package)

Nutrition Information Per Serving:		
Calories: 40	From Fat:	25
Total Fat		2.5g
Saturated		1g
Cholesterol		0mg
Sodium		100mg
Total Carbohydrate		3g
Dietary Fiber		0g
Sugars		0g
Protein		1g

For a fun change of flavor, feel free to use French onion dip and flavored flour tortillas instead.

1) In small bowl with electric mixer, beat cream cheese on medium speed until smooth. Beat in dip until well blended. Stir in broccoli, carrot, onion and bacon.

2) Spread mixture evenly onto each tortilla to edges. Roll up each; wrap tightly in plastic wrap. Refrigerate at least 2 hours or up to 8 hours before serving.

3) To serve, cut each roll into 8 pieces.

HIGH ALTITUDE (3500-6500 FT.): No change.

Perfect Deviled Eggs

PREP TIME: 25 MINUTES (READY IN 50 MINUTES)
SERVINGS: 12

 EASY

6 eggs

3 tablespoons ranch dressing

½ teaspoon prepared yellow mustard

¼ cup finely chopped celery

⅛ teaspoon salt

Paprika

Nutrition Information Per Serving:		
Calories: 60	From Fat:	40
Total Fat		4.5g
Saturated		1g
Cholesterol		105mg
Sodium		90mg
Total Carbohydrate		0g
Dietary Fiber		0g
Sugars		0g
Protein		3g

1) In 2-quart saucepan, place eggs in single layer; add enough water to cover eggs by 1 inch. Heat to boiling. Immediately remove from heat; cover and let stand 15 minutes.

2) Drain water from eggs; rinse eggs with cold water. Place eggs in bowl of ice water; let stand 10 minutes.

3) Peel eggs; cut in half lengthwise. Carefully remove yolks; place in small bowl. Mash yolks with fork until smooth. Stir in remaining ingredients except paprika until well blended.

4) Spoon yolk mixture into egg white halves. Sprinkle with paprika.

HIGH ALTITUDE (3500-6500 FT.): When cooking eggs, after heating water with eggs to boiling, boil gently 5 minutes. Remove from heat; cover and let stand 15 minutes. Continue as directed above.

To save time, purchase hard-cooked eggs in the refrigerated section of the grocery store.

Cranberry-Turkey Quesadillas

PREP TIME: 10 MINUTES (READY IN 20 MINUTES)
SERVINGS: 16

 EASY

1 package (11.5 oz.) Old El Paso® flour tortillas for burritos (8 tortillas)

3 cups shredded pepper Jack cheese (12 oz.)

6 oz. smoked cooked turkey, chopped (1 cup)

½ cup sweetened dried cranberries

2 tablespoons butter or margarine, melted

1 tablespoon chopped fresh parsley

Nutrition Information Per Serving:		
Calories: 170	From Fat:	80
Total Fat		9g
Saturated		4.5g
Cholesterol		30mg
Sodium		450mg
Total Carbohydrate		14g
Dietary Fiber		0g
Sugars		4g
Protein		8g

1) Heat oven to 400°F. On ungreased large cookie sheet, place 4 of the tortillas. Sprinkle ½ cup of the cheese over each tortilla. Top each evenly with turkey and cranberries. Sprinkle ¼ cup remaining cheese over each. Top with remaining tortillas.

2) In small bowl, mix melted butter and parsley. Brush butter mixture over tops of filled tortillas.

3) Bake 6 to 8 minutes or until cheese is melted and edges begin to turn light golden brown. Cut into wedges; serve warm.

HIGH ALTITUDE (3500-6500 FT.): No change.

Vegetable Tree with Nacho Cheese Dip

PREP TIME: 20 MINUTES (READY IN 20 MINUTES)
SERVINGS: 12 (2 VEGETABLE PIECES AND 2 TABLESPOONS DIP EACH)

 EASY

1 loaf (16 oz.) mild Mexican prepared cheese product with jalapeño peppers, cubed

1½ cups ready-to-eat baby-cut carrots

1½ cups celery sticks

1 cup fresh broccoli or cauliflower florets

1 large red, green and/or yellow bell pepper, cut into strips

1 small jicama (about 1 lb.), cut into sticks

Nutrition Information Per Serving:		
Calories: 150	From Fat:	80
Total Fat		8g
Saturated		5g
Cholesterol		30mg
Sodium		590mg
Total Carbohydrate		11g
Dietary Fiber		3g
Sugars		6g
Protein		7g

1) In medium microwavable bowl, microwave cheese product cubes on High 3 to 4 minutes, stirring once halfway through cooking, until melted. Pour into serving bowl.

2) To serve, arrange vegetables on serving platter; serve with warm cheese dip.

HIGH ALTITUDE (3500-6500 FT.): No change.

VEGETABLE MEDLEY
WITH CREAMY
PARMESAN SAUCE
PG. 89

Salads & Sides

Toss together one of these sensational salads or side dishes to round out any meal.

CONFETTI SPAGHETTI SALAD
PG. 68

TORTILLA TACO SALAD
PG. 90

SPINACH, STRAWBERRY AND
GRAPEFRUIT TOSS
PG. 77

Grilled Caesar Steak and Potato Salad

PREP TIME: 45 MINUTES (READY IN 45 MINUTES)
SERVINGS: 8 (1-1/2 CUPS EACH)

 EASY

2 lb. boneless beef sirloin steak
(1 inch thick)

2 tablespoons refrigerated Caesar
dressing

$3/4$ teaspoon salt

$1/4$ teaspoon pepper

2 packages (1 lb. 4 oz. each)
refrigerated new potato wedges

Cooking spray

$2/3$ cup shredded Parmesan cheese
($2^2/3$ oz.)

$2/3$ cup refrigerated Caesar dressing

Chopped romaine lettuce, if desired

$1/2$ cup sliced green onions
(8 medium)

1) Heat gas or charcoal grill. Brush steak with 2 tablespoons dressing; sprinkle with $1/4$ teaspoon of the salt and the pepper.

2) Cut 4 (18x12-inch) sheets of heavy-duty foil. Generously spray half of one side of each foil sheet with cooking spray. Place $1/4$ of potatoes evenly in center of each sprayed portion of foil. Generously spray potatoes with cooking spray; sprinkle with remaining $1/2$ teaspoon salt. Fold unsprayed half of foil loosely over potatoes so edges meet; seal edges with tight $1/2$-inch folds and fold again.

3) When grill is heated, place packets on gas grill over medium-high heat or on charcoal grill over medium-high coals; cover grill. Cook packets 10 minutes, turning over several times. Place steak on grill with packets; cook 10 to 15 minutes longer, turning steak over once and turning packets several times, until steak is desired doneness and potatoes are tender.

4) In large bowl, toss cooked potatoes, cheese and $2/3$ cup dressing. Cut steak across grain into thin slices. Place lettuce onto serving plates. Divide potato mixture evenly over lettuce; top each with steak slices and sprinkle with onions.

HIGH ALTITUDE (3500-6500 FT.): Cook packets and steak on gas grill over medium-low heat or on charcoal grill over medium-low coals. Continue as directed above.

Nutrition Information Per Serving:		
Calories: 400	From Fat:	190
Total Fat		21g
Saturated		5g
Cholesterol		65mg
Sodium		1020mg
Total Carbohydrate		27g
Dietary Fiber		4g
Sugars		2g
Protein		29g

Buffalo Chicken Layered Salad

PREP TIME: 40 MINUTES (READY IN 40 MINUTES)
SERVINGS: 8 (1 CUP EACH)

2 teaspoons red pepper sauce

2 cups chopped deli rotisserie chicken
(from 2- to 2¹/₂-lb. chicken)

1 bag (10 oz.) torn romaine lettuce

¹/₄ cup chopped red onion

1 cup thinly sliced celery
(2¹/₂ medium stalks)

1¹/₂ cups halved cherry tomatoes

1 bottle (8 oz.) ranch dressing (1 cup)

¹/₂ cup chopped packaged precooked
bacon (about 8 slices)

Nutrition Information Per Serving:		
Calories: 250	From Fat:	170
Total Fat		19g
Saturated		3.5g
Cholesterol		45mg
Sodium		510mg
Total Carbohydrate		5g
Dietary Fiber		2g
Sugars		2g
Protein		13g

1) In medium bowl, sprinkle red pepper sauce over chicken; stir to mix well.

2) In 13x9-inch (3-quart) glass baking dish, layer lettuce, onion, celery, 1 cup of the tomatoes and the chicken.

3) Pour dressing evenly over salad. Sprinkle with bacon and remaining ¹/₂ cup tomatoes.

HIGH ALTITUDE (3500-6500 FT.): No change.

Tuna Twist Pasta Salad

PREP TIME: 25 MINUTES (READY IN 25 MINUTES)
SERVINGS: 4 (1-1/2 CUPS EACH)

⊖ EASY

3 cups uncooked rotini (spiral) pasta
(3 oz.)

1 cup Green Giant® frozen sweet peas
(from 1-lb. bag)

¹/₄ cup chopped celery

1 can (6 oz.) albacore tuna in water,
drained, flaked

³/₄ cup Parmesan peppercorn dressing

Leaf lettuce

Nutrition Information Per Serving:		
Calories: 340	From Fat:	180
Total Fat		20g
Saturated		3g
Cholesterol		20mg
Sodium		710mg
Total Carbohydrate		24g
Dietary Fiber		2g
Sugars		5g
Protein		17g

1) Cook pasta as directed on package, adding frozen peas during last 4 minutes of cooking time. Drain; rinse with cold water to cool. Drain well.

2) In large bowl, gently toss cooled cooked pasta and peas, celery and tuna. Pour dressing over salad; toss to coat well. Spoon salad onto lettuce-lined plates.

HIGH ALTITUDE (3500-6500 FT.): No change.

Confetti Spaghetti Salad

PREP TIME: 25 MINUTES (READY IN 1 HOUR 25 MINUTES)
SERVINGS: 8 (3/4 CUP EACH)

 EASY

1 package (7 oz.) spaghetti, broken into thirds

2 cups Green Giant® frozen mixed vegetables (from 1-lb. bag)

¼ cup coarsely chopped red onion

1 medium tomato, chopped

½ cup Italian dressing

Nutrition Information Per Serving:		
Calories: 190	From Fat:	60
Total Fat		7g
Saturated		0.5g
Cholesterol		0mg
Sodium		250mg
Total Carbohydrate		28g
Dietary Fiber		4g
Sugars		4g
Protein		5g

1) Cook spaghetti as directed on package, adding frozen mixed vegetables during last 5 to 7 minutes of cooking time; cook until mixed vegetables are tender. Drain; rinse with cold water to cool. Drain well.

2) In medium bowl, gently toss cooled cooked spaghetti and vegetables, and remaining ingredients to coat. Cover; refrigerate at least 1 hour to blend flavors before serving.

HIGH ALTITUDE (3500-6500 FT.): No change.

Italian-Dressed Vegetable Salad

PREP TIME: 20 MINUTES (READY IN 1 HOUR 20 MINUTES)
SERVINGS: 8 (2/3 CUP EACH)

 EASY

2 cups Green Giant Select® frozen broccoli florets (from 14-oz. bag)

2 cups Green Giant® frozen cauliflower florets (from 1-lb. bag)

1 cup cherry tomatoes, halved

1 cup sliced fresh carrots

¾ cup Italian dressing

Nutrition Information Per Serving:		
Calories: 120	From Fat:	80
Total Fat		9g
Saturated		0.5g
Cholesterol		0mg
Sodium		210mg
Total Carbohydrate		7g
Dietary Fiber		2g
Sugars		4g
Protein		2g

1) In 3-quart saucepan, heat 8 cups water to boiling. Add broccoli and cauliflower; return to boiling. Boil 2 minutes. Drain; rinse with cold water to cool. Drain well. Separate broccoli and cauliflower.

2) In large glass bowl, layer cauliflower, tomatoes and carrots. Pour dressing evenly over salad. Top with broccoli. Cover; refrigerate at least 1 hour to blend flavors before serving.

HIGH ALTITUDE (3500-6500 FT.): No change.

Smoky Potato Packets

PREP TIME: 55 MINUTES (READY IN 55 MINUTES)
SERVINGS: 4

 EASY

1 bag (28 oz.) frozen potatoes O'Brien with onions and peppers

1 package (16 oz.) miniature smoked Polish sausages

3/4 cup ranch dressing

1 cup shredded Cheddar and American cheese blend (4 oz.)

2 tablespoons chopped chives or green onions

Nutrition Information Per Serving:		
Calories: 860	From Fat:	570
Total Fat		64g
Saturated		21g
Cholesterol		110mg
Sodium		1750mg
Total Carbohydrate		52g
Dietary Fiber		5g
Sugars		7g
Protein		24g

1) Heat gas or charcoal grill. Cut 4 (18x12-inch) sheets of heavy-duty (or nonstick) foil. If using heavy-duty foil, spray foil with cooking spray.

2) In large bowl, gently mix potatoes, sausages and dressing. Spoon mixture evenly onto foil sheets. Wrap each packet securely using double-fold seals, allowing room for heat expansion.

3) When grill is heated, place foil packets on gas grill over medium heat or on charcoal grill over medium coals; cover grill. Cook 30 to 35 minutes, rotating and turning packets over several times, until potatoes are tender.

4) Remove packets from grill; open carefully to allow steam to escape. Sprinkle each with cheese and chives. Close packets; let stand until cheese is melted.

HIGH ALTITUDE (3500-6500 FT.): Cook foil packets on covered grill over medium-low heat. Continue as directed above.

Creamy Dill-Cucumber Salad

PREP TIME: 20 MINUTES (READY IN 50 MINUTES)
SERVINGS: 8 (1/2 CUP EACH)

e EASY   **f** LOW FAT

2 medium cucumbers, halved lengthwise and cut into 1/2-inch-thick slices

8 cherry tomatoes, halved

1/4 cup chopped red onion

1/2 cup sour cream

1 tablespoon chopped fresh dill weed

1 1/2 teaspoons vinegar

1/2 teaspoon sugar

1/4 teaspoon salt

Nutrition Information Per Serving:		
Calories: 40	From Fat:	25
Total Fat		3g
Saturated		2g
Cholesterol		10mg
Sodium		80mg
Total Carbohydrate		4g
Dietary Fiber		0g
Sugars		2g
Protein		0g

1) In medium bowl, mix cucumbers, tomatoes and onion.

2) In small bowl, mix remaining ingredients; stir into cucumber mixture. Cover; refrigerate at least 30 minutes or until serving time.

HIGH ALTITUDE (3500-6500 FT.): No change.

Cheese, Peas and Shells Salad

PREP TIME: 25 MINUTES (READY IN 55 MINUTES)
SERVINGS: 5 (3/4 CUP EACH)

SALAD

1 cup uncooked small pasta shells (4 oz.)

1 cup Green Giant® frozen sweet peas (from 1-lb. bag)

1 cup sliced celery (1 3/4 stalks)

1/2 cup thinly sliced radishes (4 medium)

4 oz. sharp Cheddar cheese, cubed (1 cup)

DRESSING

1/3 cup reduced-fat mayonnaise

2 tablespoons milk

2 tablespoons sweet honey mustard

1/2 teaspoon salt

1/4 teaspoon pepper

1) Cook pasta as directed on package, adding peas during last 3 minutes of cooking time. Drain; rinse with cold water to cool. Drain well.

2) Meanwhile, in medium bowl, mix remaining salad ingredients. In small bowl, mix dressing ingredients until well blended.

3) Gently stir cooked pasta and peas into salad. Add dressing; toss gently to coat. Cover; refrigerate 30 minutes to blend flavors before serving.

HIGH ALTITUDE (3500-6500 FT.): No change.

Nutrition Information Per Serving:		
Calories: 260	From Fat:	120
Total Fat		14g
Saturated		6g
Cholesterol		30mg
Sodium		690mg
Total Carbohydrate		25g
Dietary Fiber		3g
Sugars		4g
Protein		11g

Mexicorn®-Topped Tomatoes

ROXANNE CHAN | ALBANY, CALIFORNIA

PREP TIME: 20 MINUTES (READY IN 20 MINUTES)
SERVINGS: 6

1 can (11 oz.) Green Giant® Mexicorn® whole kernel corn with red and green peppers, drained

1 can (4.5 oz.) Old El Paso® chopped green chiles, drained

1/2 cup finely chopped fresh or refrigerated mango

2 tablespoons finely chopped green onions (2 medium)

2 tablespoons sliced ripe olives

1 tablespoon finely chopped fresh cilantro

1 tablespoon chopped chipotle chile in adobo sauce (from 7-oz. can)

1 tablespoon lime juice (1/2 medium)

1 teaspoon olive oil

4 large firm ripe tomatoes, cut crosswise into 1/4-inch-thick slices

Pumpkin seeds*

1) In medium bowl, mix all ingredients except tomatoes and pumpkin seeds.

2) On serving platter, arrange tomatoes, overlapping slices. Spoon corn mixture down center of tomatoes. Sprinkle with pumpkin seeds.

*NOTE: Roasted hulled pumpkin seeds (pepitas) can be used as garnish.

High Altitude (3500-6500 FT.): No change.

Nutrition Information Per Serving:

Calories:	110	From Fat:	25
Total Fat			2.5g
Saturated			0g
Cholesterol			0mg
Sodium			300mg
Total Carbohydrate			18g
Dietary Fiber			3g
Sugars			8g
Protein			3g

Asian Fresh Slaw

| PREP TIME: | 10 MINUTES (READY IN 10 MINUTES) |
| SERVINGS: | 10 (1/2 CUP EACH) |

 EASY

1 bag (16 oz.) coleslaw mix
(shredded cabbage and carrots)

1/2 cup sweet-spicy French dressing

1/4 cup chopped red bell pepper
(1/4 medium)

1/4 cup loosely packed fresh cilantro
leaves, coarsely chopped

1/4 cup coarsely chopped salted
dry-roasted peanuts

Nutrition Information Per Serving:		
Calories: 80	From Fat:	50
Total Fat		6g
Saturated		1g
Cholesterol		0mg
Sodium		190mg
Total Carbohydrate		7g
Dietary Fiber		2g
Sugars		4g
Protein		2g

1) In 2-quart bowl, mix coleslaw mix and dressing. Top with bell pepper, cilantro and peanuts.

2) Just before serving, toss salad.

HIGH ALTITUDE (3500-6500 FT.): No change.

Fresh and Light Turkey and Bow-Tie Salad

| PREP TIME: | 35 MINUTES (READY IN 35 MINUTES) |
| SERVINGS: | 8 (1-1/2 CUPS EACH) |

5 cups uncooked bow-tie (farfalle)
pasta (12 oz.)

1 lb. fresh asparagus spears, trimmed,
cut into 1-inch pieces

4 cups diced cooked turkey

1 medium red bell pepper, chopped
(1 cup)

1/4 cup chopped or shredded fresh basil

3/4 cup reduced-fat salad dressing or
mayonnaise

2 containers (6 oz. each) Yoplait®
Original lemon burst yogurt

1/2 teaspoon onion salt

1/2 teaspoon grated lemon peel,
if desired

Red leaf lettuce, if desired

Nutrition Information Per Serving:		
Calories: 390	From Fat:	100
Total Fat		11g
Saturated		2.5g
Cholesterol		70mg
Sodium		470mg
Total Carbohydrate		48g
Dietary Fiber		3g
Sugars		11g
Protein		28g

1) Cook pasta in salted water as directed on package, adding asparagus during last 2 to 3 minutes of cooking. Drain; rinse with cold water to cool. Drain well.

2) Meanwhile, in very large (5-quart) bowl, mix turkey, bell pepper and basil. In small bowl, mix salad dressing, yogurt, onion salt and lemon peel.

3) Stir cooled cooked pasta with asparagus into turkey mixture. Pour dressing over salad; toss gently to mix. Refrigerate at least 1 hour to blend flavors and chill salad.

4) In shallow serving bowl or on platter, arrange lettuce. Spoon salad onto lettuce. If desired, garnish with additional basil.

HIGH ALTITUDE (3500-6500 FT.): No change.

Baked Taco Salad

SUSAN BAZAN | SEQUIM, WASHINGTON

PREP TIME: 45 MINUTES (READY IN 1 HOUR 15 MINUTES)
SERVINGS: 10 (3 CUPS EACH)

3 tablespoons olive oil

6 boneless skinless chicken breasts
(1½ lb.), cut into bite-size pieces

1 medium onion, chopped (½ cup)

5 medium cloves garlic, finely chopped
(2½ teaspoons)

12 corn tortillas (6 inch), torn or cut
into small pieces (2½ cups)

1 cup sour cream

1 can (19 oz.) Progresso® Vegetable
Classics hearty tomato soup

1 can (15.25 oz.) Green Giant®
whole kernel corn, drained

1 can (15 oz.) Progresso® black beans,
drained, rinsed

1 can (4.5 oz.) Old El Paso® chopped
green chiles

1 package (1.25 oz.) Old El Paso®
taco seasoning mix

½ to 1 teaspoon salt

1 teaspoon ground cumin

¼ teaspoon pepper

2 cups shredded Colby-Monterey
Jack cheese blend (8 oz.)

1 can (2¼ oz.) sliced ripe olives,
drained

1 to 2 heads romaine lettuce,
shredded (about 16 cups)

4 tomatoes, chopped (3 cups)

8 medium green onions,
chopped (½ cup)

Mango-peach salsa, if desired

1) Heat oven to 350°F. Spray 13x9-inch
(3-quart) glass baking dish with cooking
spray. In 12-inch skillet, heat oil over
medium-high heat. Add chicken, onion
and garlic; cook about 8 minutes,
stirring frequently, until chicken is no
longer pink in center. Remove skillet
from heat.

2) Stir in tortillas, sour cream, soup, corn,
beans, green chiles, taco seasoning mix, salt, cumin and pepper. Pour into
baking dish. Sprinkle with cheese and olives.

3) Cover tightly with foil; bake 30 minutes. Uncover; bake 15 minutes longer
or until cheese is melted and mixture is bubbly.

4) In 6-quart bowl, mix lettuce, tomatoes and green onions. Divide lettuce
mixture evenly among individual plates. Top each with baked taco mixture
and mango-peach salsa.

HIGH ALTITUDE (3500-6500 FT.): In Step 2, do not add cheese and olives. In Step 3, after uncovering
baking dish, sprinkle with cheese and olives; bake 15 minutes longer.

Nutrition Information Per Serving:		
Calories: 490	From Fat:	180
Total Fat		20g
Saturated		9g
Cholesterol		80mg
Sodium		1230mg
Total Carbohydrate		48g
Dietary Fiber		9g
Sugars		10g
Protein		30g

Sunny Broccoli-Pasta Salad

PREP TIME: 30 MINUTES (READY IN 1 HOUR)
SERVINGS: 8 (3/4 CUP EACH)

DRESSING
- ½ cup reduced-fat mayonnaise or salad dressing
- ⅓ cup milk
- 1 tablespoon cider vinegar
- 2 teaspoons sugar
- ½ teaspoon salt

SALAD
- 1½ cups uncooked radiatore (nuggets) pasta (5 oz.)
- 8 slices bacon
- 2 cups small fresh broccoli florets
- 1 cup small fresh cauliflower florets
- ¼ cup chopped red onion
- ¼ cup golden raisins
- 3 tablespoons sunflower nuts

1) In small bowl, mix dressing ingredients until well blended. Refrigerate while cooking pasta.

2) Cook pasta as directed on package. Drain; rinse with cold water to cool. Drain well.

3) Meanwhile, cook bacon until crisp. Drain on paper towels; crumble bacon.

4) In large bowl, gently mix cooled cooked pasta, bacon and remaining salad ingredients. Pour dressing over salad; toss gently to coat. Cover; refrigerate at least 30 minutes or until serving time.

HIGH ALTITUDE (3500-6500 FT.): No change.

Nutrition Information Per Serving:		
Calories: 210	From Fat: 100	
Total Fat		11g
Saturated		2.5g
Cholesterol		15mg
Sodium		460mg
Total Carbohydrate		23g
Dietary Fiber		3g
Sugars		6g
Protein		7g

Peach-Pecan Cornbread Dressing

PREP TIME: 15 MINUTES (READY IN 40 MINUTES)
SERVINGS: 6 (3/4 CUP EACH)

 EASY

1¼ cups water

1 cup chicken broth

1 package (8 oz.) cornbread stuffing mix

1 cup chopped celery (2 stalks)

½ cup cut-up dried peaches

¼ cup chopped pecans

Nutrition Information Per Serving:

Calories:	230	From Fat:	50
Total Fat			5g
Saturated			0g
Cholesterol			0mg
Sodium			610mg
Total Carbohydrate			39g
Dietary Fiber			4g
Sugars			8g
Protein			5g

1) Heat oven to 375°F. Spray 2-quart casserole with cooking spray. In 3-quart saucepan, heat water and broth to boiling. Stir in remaining ingredients. Spoon into casserole; cover.

2) Bake 20 to 25 minutes or until thoroughly heated.

HIGH ALTITUDE (3500-6500 FT.): No change.

This tasty side dish is the perfect accompaniment to roast chicken. You can vary the flavor by substituting ½ cup cut-up dried apricots for the peaches.

Pea Pod and Chicken Salad Oriental

PREP TIME: 30 MINUTES (READY IN 3 HOURS 30 MINUTES)
SERVINGS: 6 (1-1/3 CUPS EACH)

SALAD

1½ cups uncooked rotini pasta (3½ oz.)

¾ lb. fresh snow pea pods (3 cups), trimmed, cut in half crosswise

3 cups cubed cooked chicken or turkey

¾ cup sliced green onions (12 medium)

1 can (8 oz.) sliced water chestnuts, drained

Lettuce leaves, if desired

⅓ cup slivered almonds, toasted

DRESSING

¾ cup mayonnaise or salad dressing

2 teaspoons soy sauce

¼ teaspoon pepper

⅛ teaspoon ground ginger

1) Cook pasta as directed on package, adding pea pods during last 1 to 2 minutes of cooking. Drain; rinse with cold water to cool. Drain well.

2) Meanwhile, in large bowl, mix chicken, onions and water chestnuts. In small bowl, mix dressing ingredients until well blended.

3) Gently stir cooled cooked pasta and pea pods into chicken mixture. Pour dressing over salad; stir gently to coat. Cover; refrigerate at least 3 hours or until serving time.

4) To serve, line serving bowl with lettuce leaves. Spoon salad over lettuce. Sprinkle with almonds.

HIGH ALTITUDE (3500-6500 FT.): No change.

Nutrition Information Per Serving:		
Calories: 500	From Fat:	270
Total Fat		30g
Saturated		5g
Cholesterol		75mg
Sodium		440mg
Total Carbohydrate		34g
Dietary Fiber		5g
Sugars		4g
Protein		27g

Spinach, Strawberry and Grapefruit Toss

PREP TIME: 25 MINUTES (READY IN 25 MINUTES)
SERVINGS: 12

ALMONDS AND DRESSING

$1/3$ cup oil

$1/2$ cup sliced almonds

3 tablespoons honey

Dash cinnamon

$1/2$ teaspoon grated lime peel

3 tablespoons lime juice

1 teaspoon Dijon mustard

$1/4$ teaspoon salt

SALAD

1 package (10 oz.) spinach leaves, torn (10 cups)

1 pint (2 cups) fresh strawberries, sliced

1 grapefruit, peeled, sectioned

1) Line cookie sheet with foil. Spray foil with cooking spray. Heat 2 teaspoons of the oil in small skillet over medium heat until hot. Add almonds; cook and stir until lightly browned. Add 1 tablespoon of the honey and the cinnamon; cook and stir an additional 1 to 2 minutes or until almonds are glazed and golden brown. Place on foil-lined cookie sheet. Set aside to cool.

2) In jar with tight-fitting lid, combine remaining oil and honey, the lime peel, lime juice, mustard and salt; shake until well blended.

3) In large serving bowl, combine spinach, strawberries and grapefruit.

4) Just before serving, drizzle dressing over salad; toss lightly to coat. Sprinkle with glazed almonds.

Nutrition Information Per Serving:

Calories:	130	From Fat:	80
Total Fat			9g
Saturated			1g
Cholesterol			0mg
Sodium			80mg
Total Carbohydrate			11g
Dietary Fiber			2g
Sugars			7g
Protein			2g

tip To section a grapefruit, use a sharp serrated knife to remove its peel and outer membrane. Then, cut along 1 side of each section next to the dividing membrane, using the knife to help release the fruit from the membrane on the other side of the section.

Fresh Tomato-Onion Salad

PREP TIME: 20 MINUTES (READY IN 20 MINUTES)
SERVINGS: 8

 EASY

SALAD

- 2 medium red tomatoes, cut into bite-size wedges
- 2 medium yellow tomatoes, cut into bite-size wedges
- 1/2 small onion, sliced
- 2 tablespoons coarsely chopped fresh basil
- 1 tablespoon chopped fresh Italian parsley

DRESSING

- 1 1/2 teaspoons red wine vinegar
- 1/8 teaspoon salt
- 1/8 teaspoon coarse ground black pepper
- 1/4 teaspoon Dijon mustard
- 2 tablespoons olive or vegetable oil

1) In large bowl, toss salad ingredients to mix.

2) In small bowl, mix dressing ingredients except oil. Slowly add oil, beating with wire whisk until well blended. Pour dressing over salad; toss to coat.

HIGH ALTITUDE (3500-6500 FT.): No change.

Nutrition Information Per Serving:

Calories: 45	From Fat: 35
Total Fat	3.5g
Saturated	0.5g
Cholesterol	0mg
Sodium	45mg
Total Carbohydrate	3g
Dietary Fiber	0g
Sugars	1g
Protein	0g

If yellow tomatoes aren't available, use all red tomatoes.

Two teaspoons dried basil and one teaspoon dried parsley can be used instead of fresh herbs.

Almond-Parmesan Asparagus

PREP TIME: 20 MINUTES (READY IN 20 MINUTES)
SERVINGS: 8

 EASY

2 tablespoons sliced almonds

2 teaspoons butter or margarine

2 teaspoons all-purpose flour

1/2 cup half-and-half

1/8 teaspoon salt

Dash pepper

Dash ground nutmeg, if desired

2 lb. fresh asparagus spears, trimmed

1/2 cup chopped yellow bell pepper
(1/2 medium)

1/4 cup shredded Parmesan cheese
(1 oz.)

1) In 8-inch skillet, cook almonds over medium-low heat 4 to 6 minutes, stirring frequently, until fragrant and lightly browned. Remove from skillet; set aside.

2) In same skillet, melt butter over medium-low heat. With wire whisk, stir in flour until blended. Stir in half-and-half, salt, pepper and nutmeg. Cook, stirring constantly, until mixture boils. Cook 2 to 3 minutes longer, stirring constantly, until thickened. Remove from heat; cover to keep warm.

3) In 4-quart saucepan or Dutch oven, place asparagus; add 1/2 cup water. Heat to boiling over medium heat. Cook uncovered 3 to 5 minutes or until asparagus is crisp-tender, adding bell pepper during last minute of cooking; drain.

4) On large serving platter, arrange asparagus and bell pepper. Spoon sauce over top; sprinkle with cheese and almonds.

HIGH ALTITUDE (3500-6500 FT.): No change.

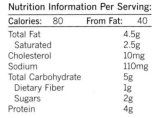

Nutrition Information Per Serving:		
Calories: 80	From Fat:	40
Total Fat		4.5g
Saturated		2.5g
Cholesterol		10mg
Sodium		110mg
Total Carbohydrate		5g
Dietary Fiber		1g
Sugars		2g
Protein		4g

Cherry-Cranberry Sauce

PREP TIME: 20 MINUTES (READY IN 2 HOURS 20 MINUTES)
SERVINGS: 8 (1/4 CUP EACH)

 EASY   LOW FAT

1 bag (12 oz.) fresh cranberries

1/3 cup dried sweet red cherries

1 cup sugar

1 cup water

2 tablespoons orange marmalade

Nutrition Information Per Serving:	
Calories: 150	From Fat: 0
Total Fat	0g
Saturated	0g
Cholesterol	0mg
Sodium	0mg
Total Carbohydrate	38g
Dietary Fiber	2g
Sugars	33g
Protein	0g

1) In 3-quart saucepan, mix cranberries, cherries, sugar and water. Heat to boiling. Reduce heat to low; simmer uncovered 10 to 12 minutes, stirring occasionally, until cranberries have popped open.

2) Stir in marmalade. Cool 1 hour. Spoon into serving dish; cover and refrigerate at least 1 hour before serving.

HIGH ALTITUDE (3500-6500 FT.): No change.

Apple Slaw

PREP TIME: 15 MINUTES (READY IN 15 MINUTES)
SERVINGS: 10

 EASY   LOW FAT

SALAD

4 cups coleslaw mix (from 16-oz. bag)

1/4 cup sliced green onions (4 medium)

2 medium Granny Smith apples, cubed

DRESSING

3 tablespoons sugar

1/4 teaspoon salt

1/4 teaspoon apple pie spice

3 tablespoons cider vinegar

2 tablespoons vegetable oil

Nutrition Information Per Serving:	
Calories: 70	From Fat: 25
Total Fat	3g
Saturated	0g
Cholesterol	0mg
Sodium	65mg
Total Carbohydrate	10g
Dietary Fiber	1g
Sugars	8g
Protein	0g

tip

The apple pie spice in the dressing can be replaced with cinnamon.

1) In large bowl, toss salad ingredients to mix.

2) In small bowl, mix dressing ingredients until well blended. Pour dressing over salad; toss gently to coat. Serve immediately, or refrigerate until serving time.

HIGH ALTITUDE (3500-6500 FT.): No change.

Orange-Honey-Sweet Potato Salad

PREP TIME: 35 MINUTES (READY IN 1 HOUR 35 MINUTES)
SERVINGS: 6 (2/3 CUP EACH)

 EASY   LOW FAT

1½ lb. dark-orange sweet potatoes, peeled, cut into ½-inch pieces (4 cups)

½ cup sliced celery (1 stalk)

⅓ cup sweetened dried cranberries

1 tablespoon honey

1 teaspoon grated orange peel

1 container (6 oz.) Yoplait® Original 99% Fat Free orange crème yogurt

1) In 2-quart saucepan, place potatoes; add enough water to cover potatoes. Heat to boiling over medium-high heat. Reduce heat to low; simmer 9 to 11 minutes or until potatoes are fork-tender. Drain; cool 15 minutes.

2) Meanwhile, in large bowl, mix remaining ingredients.

3) Gently stir cooled potatoes into celery mixture until well coated. Refrigerate at least 1 hour before serving.

HIGH ALTITUDE (3500-6500 FT.): No change.

Nutrition Information Per Serving:

Calories:	160	From Fat:	0
Total Fat			0.5g
Saturated			0g
Cholesterol			0mg
Sodium			35mg
Total Carbohydrate			36g
Dietary Fiber			3g
Sugars			26g
Protein			3g

Shrimp and Rice Salad

NINA HUTCHISON | WINDSOR, CALIFORNIA

PREP TIME: 25 MINUTES (READY IN 3 HOURS 45 MINUTES)
SERVINGS: 6 (1-2/3 CUPS EACH)

1½ cups water

1 box (6.4 oz.) chicken fried rice skillet-meal mix for chicken

½ cup frozen sweet peas (from 1-lb. bag)

1 bag (12 oz.) frozen cooked cocktail shrimp (60 to 80 count/lb.), thawed

¾ cup chopped fresh cilantro

¾ cup sliced pimiento-stuffed green olives

½ cup chopped red onion

2 medium tomatoes, chopped (1½ cups)

1 large Anaheim chile, finely chopped (3 tablespoons)

5 tablespoons balsamic vinegar

2 tablespoons vegetable oil

1 can (15 oz.) Progresso® black beans, drained, rinsed

1 can (11 oz.) Green Giant® Niblets® white shoepeg corn, drained

1) In 10-inch skillet, heat water, uncooked rice and seasoning mix to boiling over high heat, stirring occasionally. Reduce heat to low; cover and simmer 7 minutes.

2) Stir in frozen peas. Cover; cook 3 to 5 minutes longer or until water is completely absorbed. Pour rice mixture into large bowl. Cool about 15 minutes.

3) Stir in all remaining ingredients. Cover; refrigerate 3 to 4 hours before serving.

HIGH ALTITUDE (3500-6500 FT.): Make rice following High Altitude directions on skillet-meal box.

Nutrition Information Per Serving:

Calories:	400	From Fat:	80
Total Fat		9g	
Saturated		1.5g	
Cholesterol		110mg	
Sodium		1190mg	
Total Carbohydrate		57g	
Dietary Fiber		7g	
Sugars		7g	
Protein		23g	

Jiggle Bell Salad

PREP TIME: 10 MINUTES (READY IN 5 HOURS 5 MINUTES)
SERVINGS: 8

e EASY   **f** LOW FAT

1¹/₂ cups cranberry-apple juice drink

2 boxes (4-serving size each) wild strawberry flavored gelatin

2 cups sparkling water, chilled

1 can (15 oz.) mandarin orange segments, drained

Lettuce leaves

Nutrition Information Per Serving:		
Calories: 130	From Fat:	0
Total Fat		0g
Saturated		0g
Cholesterol		0mg
Sodium		100mg
Total Carbohydrate		30g
Dietary Fiber		0g
Sugars		28g
Protein		2g

1) Oil 7-cup mold with vegetable oil. In 2-quart saucepan, heat cranberry-apple juice drink to boiling. Remove from heat. Stir in gelatin until dissolved. Refrigerate 15 minutes.

2) Stir in sparkling water. Refrigerate 40 minutes longer.

3) Fold orange segments into gelatin; spoon into mold. Refrigerate until firm, about 4 hours.

4) To serve, line serving platter with lettuce. Unmold gelatin onto lined platter. Cut into wedges to serve.

HIGH ALTITUDE (3500-6500 FT.): No change.

Apple-Squash

PREP TIME: 20 MINUTES (READY IN 20 MINUTES)
SERVINGS: 6 (1/2 CUP EACH)

e EASY   **f** LOW FAT

1 small butternut or buttercup squash (about 1 lb.)

¹/₂ cup apple cider or water

2 small apples, peeled, cubed

2 tablespoons sugar

¹/₂ teaspoon ground cinnamon

¹/₄ teaspoon ground nutmeg

1 tablespoon butter or margarine, if desired

Nutrition Information Per Serving:		
Calories: 70	From Fat:	0
Total Fat		0g
Saturated		0g
Cholesterol		0mg
Sodium		0mg
Total Carbohydrate		17g
Dietary Fiber		2g
Sugars		12g
Protein		0g

1) With vegetable peeler, peel squash. Remove seeds; cut squash into ¹/₂-inch cubes. In 1¹/₂-quart microwavable casserole, place squash and cider. Cover; microwave on High 5 to 7 minutes, stirring once halfway through cooking, until squash is tender.

2) Stir in remaining ingredients. Cover; microwave on High 2 to 3 minutes longer, stirring once halfway through cooking, until squash and apples are very tender. Serve immediately. If desired, mash before serving.

HIGH ALTITUDE (3500-6500 FT.): No change.

You Won't Know It's Not Potato Salad

LORI HOLTSCLAW | ROCHESTER HILLS, MICHIGAN

PREP TIME: 40 MINUTES (READY IN 2 HOURS 5 MINUTES)
SERVINGS: 16 (1/2 CUP EACH)

4 eggs

2 bags (1 lb. each) Green Giant® frozen cauliflower florets

1 bag (10 oz.) Cascadian Farm® Organic frozen peas & carrots

1³/₄ cups reduced-fat mayonnaise or salad dressing

1 teaspoon granulated sugar

1 teaspoon salt

¹/₄ teaspoon pepper

¹/₄ teaspoon paprika

1 tablespoon cider vinegar

1 teaspoon yellow mustard

1 cup chopped celery (2¹/₂ stalks)

²/₃ cup chopped onion (about 1 medium)

1) In 2-quart saucepan, place eggs in single layer; add enough cold water to cover eggs by 1 inch. Cover; heat to boiling. Remove from heat; let stand covered 15 minutes. Drain eggs. Immediately run cold water over eggs until completely cooled. Peel and chop eggs.

2) Meanwhile, in large (4-quart) microwavable bowl, place frozen cauliflower and frozen peas and carrots; cover with microwavable waxed paper. Microwave on High 20 to 25 minutes, stirring once halfway through microwaving. Drain vegetables in colander; rinse with cold water to cool. Place colander over same large bowl; refrigerate at least 30 minutes or until cooled.

3) In small bowl, mix mayonnaise, sugar, salt, pepper, ¹/₈ teaspoon of the paprika, the vinegar and mustard; set aside.

4) Remove vegetables from refrigerator; discard any liquid in bowl. Pat drained vegetables dry with paper towels; chop any large cauliflower pieces into ³/₄-inch chunks to resemble chopped potatoes. Place cauliflower, peas and carrots in same bowl. Add celery, onion and chopped eggs.

5) Pour mayonnaise mixture over salad; stir until vegetables and eggs are well coated. Sprinkle remaining ¹/₈ teaspoon paprika over salad. If desired, cover and refrigerate at least 1 hour or until well chilled before serving.

HIGH ALTITUDE (3500-6500 FT.): In Step 1, after heating water with eggs to boiling, boil gently 5 minutes. Remove from heat; cover and let stand 15 minutes.

Nutrition Information Per Serving:		
Calories: 130	From Fat:	90
Total Fat		10g
Saturated		2g
Cholesterol		60mg
Sodium		370mg
Total Carbohydrate		7g
Dietary Fiber		2g
Sugars		3g
Protein		3g

Tropical Fruit Salad with Poppy Seed Dressing

PREP TIME: 20 MINUTES (READY IN 20 MINUTES)
SERVINGS: 6

 EASY   LOW FAT

DRESSING
- ½ cup plain yogurt
- 2 tablespoons apricot preserves or orange marmalade
- ¼ teaspoon poppy seed

SALAD
- 1 small pineapple, peeled, cored and cut into wedges
- 1 mango or papaya, peeled, seeded and sliced (about 1½ cups)
- 1 medium banana, sliced (about ¾ cup)
- 2 kiwifruit, peeled, sliced (about ⅔ cup)
- ½ cup seedless red grapes
- 2 tablespoons coconut, toasted if desired*

1) In small bowl, mix dressing ingredients.

2) On serving platter, arrange fruit in decorative pattern; sprinkle with coconut. Drizzle dressing over salad.

*NOTE: To toast coconut, spread on cookie sheet; bake at 350°F. 7 to 8 minutes, stirring occasionally, until light golden brown. Or spread in thin layer in microwavable pie plate; microwave on Low 4 minutes 30 seconds to 8 minutes, tossing with fork after each minute, until light golden brown.

High Altitude (3500-6500 FT.): No change.

Nutrition Information Per Serving:			
Calories:	160	From Fat:	15
Total Fat			1.5g
Saturated			1g
Cholesterol			0mg
Sodium			25mg
Total Carbohydrate			33g
Dietary Fiber			3g
Sugars			23g
Protein			2g

Wondering how to cut fresh pineapple? With long sharp knife, cut off top and bottom of pineapple; cut pineapple into quarters lengthwise. Remove core from each quarter. Using knife, cut pineapple away from rind. Cut pineapple into wedges.

Southwestern Shrimp Taco Salad

| PREP TIME: | 15 MINUTES (READY IN 15 MINUTES) | EASY |
| SERVINGS: | 4 (2 CUPS EACH) | |

½ cup southwestern sour cream dip
(from 15.5-oz. container)

½ cup Old El Paso® Thick 'n Chunky
salsa

1 bag (10 oz.) romaine and leaf lettuce

12 oz. cooked deveined shelled medium
shrimp, tail shells removed

1 cup shredded Mexican cheese
blend (4 oz.)

Nutrition Information Per Serving:	
Calories: 270	From Fat: 130
Total Fat	15g
Saturated	9g
Cholesterol	200mg
Sodium	850mg
Total Carbohydrate	8g
Dietary Fiber	1g
Sugars	5g
Protein	26g

1) In large bowl, mix sour cream dip and salsa. Add lettuce, shrimp
and ½ cup of the cheese; toss to coat well.

2) Divide salad evenly onto serving plates. Sprinkle with remaining
½ cup cheese.

HIGH ALTITUDE (3500-6500 FT.): No change.

Cheesy Tortellini Salad

| PREP TIME: | 15 MINUTES (READY IN 1 HOUR 15 MINUTES) | EASY |
| SERVINGS: | 8 (3/4 CUP EACH) | |

1 package (9 oz.) refrigerated three-
cheese-filled tortellini

2 cups Green Giant Select® frozen
broccoli florets (from 14-oz. bag)

½ cup Italian vinaigrette dressing

2 tablespoons chopped fresh or
1 teaspoon dried basil leaves

1½ cups grape tomatoes or halved
cherry tomatoes

1 cup thin red onion wedges, halved

½ cup finely shredded Cheddar
cheese (2 oz.)

Nutrition Information Per Serving:	
Calories: 210	From Fat: 100
Total Fat	11g
Saturated	3g
Cholesterol	20mg
Sodium	290mg
Total Carbohydrate	21g
Dietary Fiber	2g
Sugars	4g
Protein	7g

1) Cook tortellini and broccoli as directed on packages. Drain; rinse with cold
water to cool. Drain well; place in large serving bowl.

2) Meanwhile, in small bowl, mix dressing and basil.

3) Gently stir tomatoes, onion and cheese into tortellini mixture. Pour dressing
over salad; stir to coat evenly. Cover; refrigerate at least 1 hour to blend
flavors before serving.

HIGH ALTITUDE (3500-6500 FT.): No change.

Mexican Macaroni Salad

CHERYL AMATO | SOUTH AMBOY, NEW JERSEY

Pillsbury
Bake-Off

PREP TIME: 30 MINUTES (READY IN 1 HOUR 30 MINUTES)
SERVINGS: 8 (1-1/4 CUPS EACH)

6 cups uncooked rotini pasta (1 lb.)

1 to 2 tablespoons grated lime peel (from 2 medium limes)

3 to 4 tablespoons lime juice (from 2 medium limes)

1 cup ranch dressing

1 package (1.25 oz.) Old El Paso® taco seasoning mix

1 large avocado, pitted, peeled and finely chopped

1 pint (2 cups) cherry or grape tomatoes, cut in half

1 cup shredded Cheddar cheese (4 oz.)

2 tablespoons finely chopped fresh cilantro

2 medium green onions, sliced (including tops)

1 can (19 oz.) Progresso® red kidney beans, drained, rinsed

1 can (6 oz.) pitted large ripe olives, drained, cut in half

1 can (4.5 oz.) Old El Paso® chopped green chiles, drained

1) Cook and drain pasta as directed on package. Rinse with cold water to cool; drain well.

2) Meanwhile, grate peel from limes; place in small bowl. Squeeze juice from limes; add to peel in bowl. Stir in dressing and taco seasoning mix. Stir avocado into dressing mixture.

3) In large serving bowl, toss pasta with all remaining ingredients. Pour dressing mixture over salad; toss gently to mix. Cover; refrigerate at least 1 hour before serving to blend flavors.

HIGH ALTITUDE (3500-6500 FT.): No change.

Nutrition Information Per Serving:

Calories:	560	From Fat:	250
Total Fat			27g
Saturated			7g
Cholesterol			75mg
Sodium			1210mg
Total Carbohydrate			61g
Dietary Fiber			8g
Sugars			4g
Protein			17g

Fresh Greens with Green Chile Vinaigrette

PREP TIME:	10 MINUTES (READY IN 10 MINUTES)
SERVINGS:	8

 EASY

VINAIGRETTE

- 1 can (4.5 oz.) Old El Paso® chopped green chiles
- 1/3 cup extra-virgin olive oil
- 2 tablespoons balsamic vinegar
- 2 tablespoons orange juice
- 1/2 teaspoon salt

SALAD

- 8 cups torn washed seasonal salad greens (such as spinach and other lettuce of choice)
- 1 cup cherry tomatoes, halved

Nutrition Information Per Serving:			
Calories:	100	From Fat:	80
Total Fat		9g	
Saturated		1g	
Cholesterol		0mg	
Sodium		220mg	
Total Carbohydrate		4g	
Dietary Fiber		1g	
Sugars		2g	
Protein		1g	

1) In blender container, place chiles, oil, vinegar, orange juice and salt; blend until smooth.

2) Place salad greens in serving bowl. Add vinaigrette; toss gently. Scatter cherry tomato halves over top.

HIGH ALTITUDE (3500-6500 FT.): No change.

Red and Green Tossed Salad

PREP TIME:	10 MINUTES (READY IN 10 MINUTES)
SERVINGS:	6 (1-1/2 CUPS EACH)

 EASY

- 1 bag (10 oz.) torn mixed salad greens (about 7 cups)
- 1 large apple, cubed (1 1/2 cups)
- 1/2 cup walnuts
- 1/3 cup sweetened dried cranberries
- 1/3 cup raspberry vinaigrette dressing

Nutrition Information Per Serving:			
Calories:	160	From Fat:	100
Total Fat		11g	
Saturated		1.5g	
Cholesterol		0mg	
Sodium		40mg	
Total Carbohydrate		14g	
Dietary Fiber		3g	
Sugars		10g	
Protein		2g	

1) In large bowl, gently mix all ingredients except dressing.

2) Just before serving, toss with dressing.

HIGH ALTITUDE (3500-6500 FT.): No change.

Vegetable Medley with Creamy Parmesan Sauce

PREP TIME: 10 MINUTES (READY IN 10 MINUTES)
SERVINGS: 6 (1/2 CUP VEGETABLES AND ABOUT 2 TABLESPOONS SAUCE EACH)

 EASY

1 bag (1 lb.) Green Giant Select® frozen broccoli, carrots and cauliflower

2 oz. 1/3-less-fat cream cheese (Neufchâtel)

1/4 cup grated Parmesan cheese

1/3 cup milk

Nutrition Information Per Serving:		
Calories: 70	From Fat:	35
Total Fat	4g	
Saturated	2.5g	
Cholesterol	10mg	
Sodium	135mg	
Total Carbohydrate	5g	
Dietary Fiber	2g	
Sugars	2g	
Protein	5g	

1) Cook vegetables as directed on bag; drain and keep warm.

2) Meanwhile, in 1-quart saucepan, heat cream cheese, Parmesan cheese and milk over medium heat, stirring constantly, until cream cheese is melted and mixture is smooth and hot.

3) Serve sauce with vegetables; sprinkle with chopped basil, if desired.

HIGH ALTITUDE (3500-6500 FT.): No change.

For a little more flavor, add some fresh basil—just chop and add to the cooked sauce before serving.

Tortilla Taco Salad

PREP TIME: 20 MINUTES (READY IN 20 MINUTES)
SERVINGS: 6

 EASY

6 Old El Paso® flour tortillas for burritos, 8 inch (from 11.5-oz. package)

1 container (18 oz.) refrigerated taco sauce with seasoned ground beef

1 can (15 oz.) Progresso® pinto beans, drained

2 tablespoons sweet-spicy French dressing

1½ cups shredded lettuce

¾ cup chopped tomato (1 medium)

¾ cup shredded Mexican or taco-seasoned cheese blend (3 oz.)

Old El Paso® taco sauce, if desired

1) Heat oven to 400°F. To make tortilla bowls, cut 6 (25x12-inch) sheets of foil. Slightly crush each sheet to make 4-inch ball; flatten balls slightly with palm of hand.

2) On ungreased large cookie sheet, place tortillas in single layer; cover completely with another sheet of foil. Heat in oven 1 minute or just until warm. Remove tortillas from cookie sheet; place foil balls on same sheet. Top each ball with 1 warm tortilla, shaping tortilla gently to fit around ball.

3) Bake 6 to 8 minutes or until tortillas are crisp and lightly browned. Remove tortilla bowls from foil balls; place on wire rack. Cool 2 minutes.

4) Meanwhile, in medium microwavable bowl, mix taco sauce with ground beef, pinto beans and dressing. Cover with microwavable plastic wrap, folding back one edge ¼ inch to vent steam. Microwave on High 4 to 6 minutes or until hot.

5) Place tortilla bowls on plates. Spoon about ½ cup hot beef mixture into each tortilla bowl. Top each with ¼ cup lettuce, 2 tablespoons tomato and 2 tablespoons cheese. Serve with taco sauce.

HIGH ALTITUDE (3500-6500 FT.): No change.

Nutrition Information Per Serving:		
Calories: 420	From Fat:	150
Total Fat		17g
Saturated		6g
Cholesterol		35mg
Sodium		1170mg
Total Carbohydrate		47g
Dietary Fiber		6g
Sugars		5g
Protein		21g

Nutty Chicken Dinner Salad

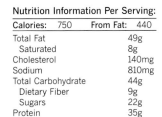

HOLLY YOUNG | BOUNTIFUL, UTAH

PREP TIME: 40 MINUTES (READY IN 40 MINUTES)
SERVINGS: 4

1 bag (10 oz.) Cascadian Farm® Organic frozen raspberries

1/2 cup oil and vinegar dressing

1/4 cup chopped pecans

1 tablespoon packed brown sugar

2 tablespoons mayonnaise or salad dressing

2 tablespoons maple-flavored syrup or real maple syrup

4 Nature Valley® cinnamon crunchy granola bars (2 pouches from 8.9-oz. box), finely crushed (3/4 cup)*

1 egg

1 lb. uncooked chicken breast tenders (not breaded)

1/2 teaspoon salt

1/8 teaspoon pepper

3 tablespoons vegetable oil

1 bag (10 oz.) or 2 bags (5 oz. each) mixed baby salad greens

1/2 cup thinly sliced red onion

2 slices (3/4 to 1 oz. each) Swiss cheese, cut into thin julienne strips

1/4 cup pecan halves, toasted ** or glazed

1) Spread frozen raspberries on paper towel; let stand to thaw while making dressing and salad. In small bowl, mix dressing, chopped pecans, brown sugar, mayonnaise and syrup with wire whisk until well blended. Refrigerate until serving time.

2) Place finely crushed granola bars on paper plate or in pie plate. In shallow bowl or another pie plate, beat egg with fork. Sprinkle chicken with salt and pepper.

3) In 12-inch nonstick skillet, heat oil over medium heat. Add chicken to beaten egg; stir to coat. Dip each chicken strip lightly into crushed granola bars; add to skillet. Cook 6 to 8 minutes, turning once, until chicken is no longer pink in center and browned on all sides. Remove from skillet; drain on paper towels.

4) In large serving bowl, mix salad greens, onion, cheese and thawed raspberries. Toss, adding only enough dressing to evenly coat ingredients. Arrange greens mixture on individual plates. Place chicken evenly over greens. Arrange pecan halves on top. Drizzle with remaining dressing.

*NOTE: To crush granola bars, unwrap and place in small resealable food-storage plastic bag; use rolling pin to finely crush bars.

**NOTE: To toast pecans, bake uncovered in ungreased shallow pan in 350°F. oven about 10 minutes, stirring occasionally, until golden brown.

HIGH ALTITUDE (3500-6500 FT.): In Step 3, cook over medium-high heat.

Nutrition Information Per Serving:		
Calories: 750	From Fat:	440
Total Fat		49g
Saturated		8g
Cholesterol		140mg
Sodium		810mg
Total Carbohydrate		44g
Dietary Fiber		9g
Sugars		22g
Protein		35g

Spinach Waldorf Salad with Cinnamon-Apple Dressing

PREP TIME: 20 MINUTES (READY IN 20 MINUTES)
SERVINGS: 8 (1 CUP EACH)

🥚 EASY　　🍃 LOW FAT

1/2 cup mayonnaise

2 tablespoons frozen apple juice concentrate, thawed

1/4 teaspoon ground cinnamon

2 large red eating apples, cubed (about 4 cups)

1/2 cup seedless red grapes, halved

1/2 cup chopped celery (1 medium stalk)

1/2 cup chopped walnuts

4 cups torn fresh spinach leaves

Nutrition Information Per Serving:	
Calories: 210	From Fat: 140
Total Fat	16g
Saturated	2g
Cholesterol	10mg
Sodium	100mg
Total Carbohydrate	15g
Dietary Fiber	3g
Sugars	10g
Protein	2g

1) In large bowl, mix mayonnaise, juice concentrate and cinnamon until well blended.

2) Stir in apples, grapes, celery and walnuts to coat.

3) Before serving, place spinach in large salad bowl. Spoon apple mixture over spinach; toss to mix and coat.

HIGH ALTITUDE (3500-6500 FT.): No change.

Basil Scalloped Corn

PREP TIME: 10 MINUTES (READY IN 1 HOUR 5 MINUTES)
SERVINGS: 10 (1/2 CUP EACH)

🥚 EASY　　🍃 LOW FAT

1 tablespoon butter or margarine

1/2 cup chopped onion (1 medium)

2 cans (11 oz. each) Green Giant® Mexicorn® whole kernel corn with red and green peppers, undrained

2 tablespoons all-purpose flour

1 can (14.75 oz.) Green Giant® cream style corn

1 teaspoon dried basil leaves

1/2 teaspoon seasoned salt

2 eggs, beaten

Nutrition Information Per Serving:	
Calories: 130	From Fat: 30
Total Fat	3g
Saturated	1g
Cholesterol	45mg
Sodium	380mg
Total Carbohydrate	21g
Dietary Fiber	2g
Sugars	5g
Protein	4g

1) Heat oven to 350°F. Spray 1½-quart casserole or soufflé dish with cooking spray. In 10-inch nonstick skillet, melt butter over medium-high heat. Add onion; cook 2 to 4 minutes, stirring occasionally, until crisp-tender.

2) Stir in remaining ingredients until well blended. Pour into casserole.

3) Bake uncovered 45 to 55 minutes or until set and knife inserted 1 inch from edge comes out clean.

HIGH ALTITUDE (3500-6500 FT.): Heat oven to 375°F. Increase flour to 1/4 cup and bake time to 55 to 65 minutes.

Warm Chicken Taco Salad

DIANNA WARA | WASHINGTON, ILLINOIS

PREP TIME: 30 MINUTES (READY IN 30 MINUTES)
SERVINGS: 8 (1-1/2 CUPS EACH)

SAUCE

- 1 cup fresh parsley
- 1/2 cup fresh cilantro leaves
- 3/4 cup part skim ricotta cheese
- 1 tablespoon green pepper sauce
- 1 container (6 oz.) Yoplait® Light Fat Free Key lime pie yogurt

SALAD

- 1 1/2 lb. ground chicken
- 1/3 cup warm water
- 1 package (1.25 oz.) Old El Paso® 40% less-sodium taco seasoning mix
- 1 can (11 oz.) Green Giant® Mexicorn® whole kernel corn with red and green peppers, drained
- 1 bag (16 oz.) lettuce salad mix (iceberg lettuce, cabbage and carrots)
- 2 large tomatoes, coarsely chopped (2 cups)
- 1 cup shredded Cheddar-Monterey Jack cheese (4 oz.)
- 1 cup coarsely crushed blue corn tortilla chips (1 1/2 oz.)
- 1 large tomato, if desired for garnish

1) In food processor, process parsley and cilantro with on-and-off motions until finely chopped. Add ricotta cheese, pepper sauce and yogurt; process until well blended. Pour into quart-size resealable food-storage plastic bag. Seal bag; refrigerate sauce until needed.

2) In 10-inch nonstick skillet, cook ground chicken over medium-high heat, stirring frequently, until no longer pink; drain if necessary. Stir in water, taco seasoning mix and corn. Cook 2 to 3 minutes, stirring occasionally, until thoroughly heated and slightly thickened.

3) In 3- to 4-quart glass bowl, layer salad mix, chopped tomatoes, cheese, chicken mixture and tortilla chips. Cut hole in one bottom corner of bag of sauce; pipe sauce in coil over salad. For garnish, cut skin of large tomato to form a rose; place in center of salad.

HIGH ALTITUDE (3500-6500 FT.): No change.

Nutrition Information Per Serving:			
Calories:	310	From Fat:	110
Total Fat		12g	
Saturated		5g	
Cholesterol		70mg	
Sodium		610mg	
Total Carbohydrate		23g	
Dietary Fiber		3g	
Sugars		8g	
Protein		26g	

Baked Tomatoes with Zucchini

PREP TIME:	20 MINUTES (READY IN 1 HOUR)
SERVINGS:	6

e EASY

6 medium tomatoes

2 medium zucchini, unpeeled, cut into ¼-inch slices

4 cloves garlic, minced

1 teaspoon parsley flakes

¼ teaspoon salt

¼ teaspoon pepper

3 tablespoons olive oil

Nutrition Information Per Serving:

Calories:	110	From Fat:	70
Total Fat			7g
Saturated			1g
Cholesterol			0mg
Sodium			110mg
Total Carbohydrate			8g
Dietary Fiber			3g
Sugars			3g
Protein			2g

Using serrated knife, cut tomatoes into quarters, cutting to about ½ inch from bottom. Cut wedges in half again, not all the way through.

1) Heat oven to 400°F. Place tomatoes stem side down on cutting board. Cut each tomato into 8 wedges, cutting to about ½ inch from bottom (not all the way through). Place tomatoes, cut side up, in ungreased 12x8-inch (2-quart) glass baking dish. Insert 2 zucchini slices between each slice in each tomato.

2) In small bowl, mix remaining ingredients; drizzle over tomatoes.

3) Bake uncovered 30 to 40 minutes or until tomatoes are slightly soft. Serve tomatoes with slotted spoon.

HIGH ALTITUDE (3500-6500 FT.): No change.

Chicken Fiesta Salad

HEIDI VAWDREY | RIVERTON, UTAH

Pillsbury Bake-Off

PREP TIME: 1 HOUR (READY IN 1 HOUR)
SERVINGS: 4 (3 CUPS EACH)

TORTILLA STRIPS

Vegetable oil for frying

4 corn tortillas

SALAD

16 leaves red or green leaf lettuce (about 1 head)

1 large yellow or orange bell pepper, cut into thin bite-size strips

1 large mango, peeled, seeded and cut into chunks

1 large avocado, pitted, peeled and cut into thin slices

2 large plum (Roma) tomatoes, finely chopped

1 can (15 oz.) Progresso® black beans

1 cup shredded pepper Jack cheese (4 oz.)

CHICKEN

4 boneless skinless chicken breasts, cut into ¼-inch-wide strips

1 package (1.25 oz.) Old El Paso® 40% less-sodium taco seasoning mix

1 teaspoon ground chipotle chili powder

2 tablespoons water

DRESSING

⅓ cup vegetable oil

⅓ cup lime juice

2 tablespoons honey

⅓ cup loosely packed cilantro leaves and stems

2 teaspoons Dijon mustard

Dash salt

1) In 8-inch skillet, heat ½ inch oil for frying over medium heat. With pizza cutter, cut corn tortillas into ¼-inch-wide strips. Fry strips in batches in hot oil 1 to 2 minutes or until golden and crisp. With tongs, place fried tortilla strips on paper towels to drain.

2) On individual plates, evenly layer lettuce, bell pepper, mango, avocado, tomatoes, beans and cheese.

3) Lightly spray 10-inch skillet with cooking spray. Add chicken strips; sprinkle with taco seasoning mix, chipotle chili powder and water. Cook uncovered over medium heat 5 to 6 minutes, stirring occasionally, until chicken is no longer pink in center. Set aside.

4) In food processor or blender, process all dressing ingredients until well blended and cilantro is finely chopped. Arrange chicken evenly over salads. Drizzle about 3 tablespoons dressing over each salad. Top each evenly with tortilla strips.

HIGH ALTITUDE (3500-6500 FT.): In Steps 1 and 3, cook over medium-high heat.

Nutrition Information Per Serving:		
Calories: 880	From Fat: 420	
Total Fat		47g
Saturated		11g
Cholesterol		100mg
Sodium		1330mg
Total Carbohydrate		71g
Dietary Fiber		13g
Sugars		23g
Protein		45g

TURKEY JOE CALZONES
PG. 118

Soups & Sandwiches

Ladle up steaming bowls and layer simple sandwiches for a quick-to-fix lunch.

SPANISH CHICKEN AND RICE SOUP
PG. 100

GRILLED STUFFED PIZZA BURGERS
PG. 112

GRILLED TOMATO-CHEESE
SANDWICHES
PG. 121

Grands!® Tuna and Green Chile Melt

CYNTHIA GEDLING | LITTLE ROCK, ARKANSAS

PREP TIME: 25 MINUTES (READY IN 25 MINUTES)
SERVINGS: 8 OPEN-FACE SANDWICHES

1 can (16.3 oz.) Pillsbury® Grands!® Homestyle refrigerated reduced-fat buttermilk biscuits

1 egg yolk

1/4 teaspoon water

1 tablespoon sesame seed

1/3 cup reduced-fat mayonnaise or salad dressing

2 tablespoons finely chopped fresh cilantro

1/8 teaspoon salt

1/8 teaspoon pepper

1/8 teaspoon Cajun seasoning

1 can (4.5 oz.) Old El Paso® chopped green chiles

2 cans (6 oz. each) albacore tuna in water, drained

2 cups shredded reduced-fat Cheddar cheese (8 oz.)

Chopped tomato, if desired

Shredded lettuce, if desired

1) Heat oven to 350°F. Spray large cookie sheet with cooking spray. Separate dough into 8 biscuits; place 2½ inches apart on cookie sheet. With bottom of flat 2-inch-diameter glass or with fingers, press biscuits into 3½-inch rounds with ¼-inch rim around outer edge.

2) In small bowl, beat egg yolk and water with fork until well blended. Brush over tops and sides of biscuits. Sprinkle each with sesame seed. Bake 13 to 17 minutes or until golden brown.

3) Meanwhile, in medium bowl, mix mayonnaise, cilantro, salt, pepper, Cajun seasoning and green chiles. Stir in tuna; set aside.

4) Set oven control to broil. Spoon about ¼ cup tuna mixture into indentation in each biscuit; sprinkle each with ¼ cup cheese. Broil 4 to 6 inches from heat 1 to 2 minutes or until cheese is melted. Carefully remove biscuits from cookie sheet. Garnish with tomato and lettuce.

HIGH ALTITUDE (3500-6500 FT.): No change.

Nutrition Information Per Sandwich:	
Calories: 310	From Fat: 110
Total Fat	13g
Saturated	4g
Cholesterol	45mg
Sodium	1150mg
Total Carbohydrate	27g
Dietary Fiber	0g
Sugars	5g
Protein	21g

Easy Chunky Tomato Soup

PREP TIME: 25 MINUTES (READY IN 25 MINUTES)
SERVINGS: 4 (1-3/4 CUPS EACH)

 EASY

2 tablespoons vegetable oil

1 medium onion, chopped ($1/2$ cup)

2 tablespoons all-purpose flour

$1/2$ cup milk

1 jar (26 to 28 oz.) tomato pasta sauce

1 can (14.5 oz.) diced tomatoes with basil, garlic and oregano, undrained

1 can (14 oz.) chicken broth

$3/4$ cup finely shredded Cheddar-American cheese blend (3 oz.)

1) In 4-quart saucepan, heat oil over medium heat. Add onion; cook and stir until softened. Add flour; cook and stir until moistened. Gradually add milk, cooking and stirring about 2 minutes or until smooth and bubbly.

2) Stir in pasta sauce, tomatoes and broth. Cover; cook over medium heat about 15 minutes, stirring frequently, just until mixture boils. Top each serving with 3 tablespoons cheese.

HIGH ALTITUDE (3500-6500 FT.): No change.

Nutrition Information Per Serving:

Calories:	430	From Fat:	190
Total Fat			22g
Saturated			7g
Cholesterol			25mg
Sodium			1630mg
Total Carbohydrate			46g
Dietary Fiber			4g
Sugars			19g
Protein			12g

tip

Serve the soup with grilled cheese sandwiches or Pillsbury® refrigerated breadsticks sprinkled with Parmesan cheese before baking.

Easy Pizza Burgers

PREP TIME: 20 MINUTES (READY IN 20 MINUTES)
SERVINGS: 8 SANDWICHES

  EASY LOW FAT

½ lb. extra-lean (at least 90%) ground beef

¼ cup finely chopped onion (½ medium)

1 can (6 oz.) tomato paste

¾ teaspoon Italian seasoning

1 can (4 oz.) Green Giant® mushroom pieces and stems, drained, if desired

4 English muffins, split

1 cup shredded mozzarella cheese (4 oz.)

Nutrition Information Per Serving:	
Calories: 170	From Fat: 50
Total Fat	6g
Saturated	3g
Cholesterol	25mg
Sodium	390mg
Total Carbohydrate	18g
Dietary Fiber	2g
Sugars	5g
Protein	12g

1) In 10-inch nonstick skillet, cook ground beef and onion over medium-high heat, stirring frequently, until beef is thoroughly cooked; drain. Stir in tomato paste, Italian seasoning and mushrooms. Cover and refrigerate; use within 3 days.

2) To prepare each sandwich, spread about ¼ cup beef mixture on English muffin half. Sprinkle 2 tablespoons cheese over top. Place on microwavable napkin or paper towel (to absorb moisture).

3) Microwave 1 sandwich uncovered on High 1 to 2 minutes or until beef mixture is hot and cheese is melted.

HIGH ALTITUDE (3500-6500 FT.): No change.

Spanish Chicken and Rice Soup

PREP TIME: 15 MINUTES (READY IN 20 MINUTES)
SERVINGS: 5 (1-1/3 CUPS EACH)

 EASY LOW FAT

2 cans (19 oz. each) Progresso® Traditional chicken vegetable soup

1 can (14½ oz.) diced tomatoes with jalapeño chiles, undrained

1 pouch (8.8 oz.) precooked Spanish-style rice mix

1 cup Green Giant® frozen corn (from 1-lb. bag)

Nutrition Information Per Serving:	
Calories: 220	From Fat: 30
Total Fat	3g
Saturated	0g
Cholesterol	10mg
Sodium	1340mg
Total Carbohydrate	38g
Dietary Fiber	5g
Sugars	7g
Protein	10g

1) In 3-quart saucepan, mix soup, tomatoes, rice from mix and corn. Heat to boiling over medium-high heat, stirring occasionally.

2) Reduce heat to low; cook uncovered 5 minutes.

HIGH ALTITUDE (3500-6500 FT.): No change.

Black Bean-Chorizo Soup in Tortilla Bowls

SITA LEPCZYK WILLIAMS | BLACKSBURG, VIRGINIA

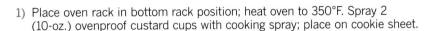

PREP TIME: 25 MINUTES (READY IN 25 MINUTES)
SERVINGS: 2

2 flour tortillas (8 to 10 inch)

5 oz. smoked chorizo sausage links, coarsely chopped

1 large clove garlic, finely chopped

1/3 cup dry sherry or chicken broth

1/2 teaspoon chili powder

1 can (19 oz.) Progresso® Vegetable Classics hearty black bean soup

1 can (4.5 oz.) Old El Paso® chopped green chiles

1/3 cup shredded Mexican 4-cheese blend (1 1/3 oz.)

2 tablespoons sour cream

2 tablespoons chopped fresh cilantro

1) Place oven rack in bottom rack position; heat oven to 350°F. Spray 2 (10-oz.) ovenproof custard cups with cooking spray; place on cookie sheet.

2) Place tortillas on microwavable plate; cover with microwavable plastic wrap. Microwave on High 45 to 60 seconds, turning after 30 seconds, until very soft. Center tortillas over cups, press into cups so top edges are even. Press tortilla folds against side of each cup to make bowl as large as possible.

3) Bake on bottom oven rack 8 to 10 minutes or until tortillas are stiff enough to hold their shape. Remove tortilla bowls from cups; place on cookie sheet. Return to middle oven rack in oven; bake 5 to 7 minutes longer or until browned and stiff. Remove tortilla bowls from cookie sheet; place on wire rack.

4) Meanwhile, heat 10-inch regular or cast iron skillet over high heat. Add sausage; cook and stir about 30 seconds or until browned. Add garlic; cook and stir 30 to 60 seconds longer. Remove skillet from heat; stir in sherry. Return skillet to high heat; cook and stir 2 to 3 minutes or until liquid has almost evaporated. Stir in chili powder, soup and green chiles. Reduce heat to medium-low; cook, stirring occasionally, until thoroughly heated.

5) Place tortilla bowls on individual plates. Divide soup evenly among bowls. Top each with cheese, sour cream and cilantro. Serve immediately.

HIGH ALTITUDE (3500-6500 FT.): No change.

Nutrition Information Per Serving:

Calories:	740	From Fat:	360
Total Fat			40g
Saturated			16g
Cholesterol			85mg
Sodium			2250mg
Total Carbohydrate			62g
Dietary Fiber			10g
Sugars			5g
Protein			34g

Chicken Marsala Sandwiches

KELLY MADEY | QUAKERTOWN, PENNSYLVANIA

Bake-Off

PREP TIME: 30 MINUTES (READY IN 30 MINUTES)
SERVINGS: 4

¼ cup olive oil

3 cloves garlic, finely chopped

¼ cup all-purpose flour

Salt and pepper, if desired

1 lb. chicken breast cut for scaloppine by butcher (or 1 lb. boneless skinless chicken breasts pounded to ⅛-inch thickness)

1 can (6 oz.) Green Giant® B in B® sliced mushrooms, drained

½ cup Marsala (sweet) wine or apple juice

1 can (18.5 oz.) Progresso® Vegetable Classics French onion soup

4 kaiser rolls

4 oz. fontina cheese, sliced, shaved or grated*

1 tablespoon parsley flakes, if desired

Nutrition Information Per Serving:

Calories:	580	From Fat:	260
Total Fat			29g
Saturated			9g
Cholesterol			105mg
Sodium			1200mg
Total Carbohydrate			41g
Dietary Fiber			2g
Sugars			4g
Protein			39g

1) In small microwavable bowl, mix oil and garlic. Microwave on High 1 minute; set aside. Place flour on plate; stir in salt and pepper. Coat chicken with flour, shaking off excess.

2) In 12-inch nonstick skillet (1½ inches deep), place 1 tablespoon of the heated oil without garlic pieces. Heat oil over medium-high heat 1 to 2 minutes or until hot but not smoking. Add chicken, cutting large pieces in half, if necessary, so all chicken fits in skillet; cook 4 to 6 minutes, turning once, until no longer pink in center and golden brown. Remove chicken from skillet; place on plate and cover to keep warm.

3) In same skillet, cook mushrooms over medium-high heat 1 minute, stirring occasionally, until thoroughly heated. Stir in wine and soup with heatproof rubber spatula or wooden spoon to scrape up brown bits from bottom of skillet. Cook 5 to 7 minutes, stirring occasionally, until thoroughly heated.

4) Meanwhile, set oven control to broil. Split rolls; place cut side up on large cookie sheet. Broil 6 to 8 inches from heat 1 to 2 minutes or until toasted and golden brown. Brush cut sides with remaining oil mixture with garlic pieces; top evenly with fontina cheese. Broil 30 to 60 seconds or until cheese is melted.

5) Return chicken to skillet. Reduce heat to medium-low; simmer uncovered 2 to 3 minutes, turning chicken occasionally, until chicken is coated with sauce. Divide chicken evenly among rolls. With slotted spoon, divide mushrooms and onions over chicken. Pour wine sauce into 4 (4-oz.) ramekins or dipping bowls. Sprinkle parsley on individual plates; place sandwiches and ramekins of sauce for dipping on plates.

*NOTE: If sliced or grated fontina cheese is unavailable, purchase wedge and shave with vegetable peeler into slices.

HIGH ALTITUDE (3500-6500 FT.): No change.

Squash and Mushroom Soup

PREP TIME: 45 MINUTES (READY IN 50 MINUTES)
SERVINGS: 6 (1-1/3 CUPS EACH)

 LOW FAT

1 butternut squash (3 lb.)

1 tablespoon butter or margarine

1 medium onion, chopped (1/2 cup)

1 package (8 oz.) sliced fresh
mushrooms (3 cups)

3 cloves garlic, minced

1 teaspoon salt

1/2 teaspoon ground ginger

1/4 teaspoon ground cumin

1/4 teaspoon black pepper

     Dash ground red pepper (cayenne)

2 cans (14 oz. each) chicken broth

1 cup half-and-half

1) Cut squash in half lengthwise; remove seeds. Cover each squash half with microwavable plastic wrap; place on microwavable plate. Microwave on High 8 to 16 minutes or until fork-tender. Cool 10 to 15 minutes before handling.

2) Meanwhile, in 4-quart Dutch oven, melt butter over medium heat. Add onion and mushrooms; cook about 10 minutes, stirring occasionally, until tender. Stir in garlic, salt, ginger, cumin, black pepper and ground red pepper. Add broth; heat to boiling over high heat. Reduce heat to low; simmer uncovered 5 minutes to blend flavors.

3) Scoop flesh from cooled squash into blender or food processor. Add half-and-half; blend until smooth. Stir squash mixture into mushroom mixture in Dutch oven. Simmer uncovered 10 minutes longer, stirring occasionally, until thoroughly heated.

HIGH ALTITUDE (3500-6500 FT.): No change.

Nutrition Information Per Serving:		
Calories: 190	From Fat:	70
Total Fat		8g
Saturated		4g
Cholesterol		20mg
Sodium		1030mg
Total Carbohydrate		23g
Dietary Fiber		3g
Sugars		9g
Protein		7g

Tomato-Crab Bisque

ROBIN SPIRES | TAMPA, FLORIDA

PREP TIME: 15 MINUTES (READY IN 15 MINUTES)
SERVINGS: 2 (2 CUPS EACH)

e EASY

1 can (19 oz.) Progresso® Vegetable Classics tomato basil soup

1 can (7 oz.) Old El Paso® chopped green chiles

1 cup whipping cream

½ cup drained refrigerated pasteurized crabmeat (about 3 oz.), flaked

1 tablespoon chopped fresh Italian (flat-leaf) parsley

Nutrition Information Per Serving:

Calories: 570	From Fat: 370
Total Fat	41g
Saturated	24g
Cholesterol	165mg
Sodium	1550mg
Total Carbohydrate	40g
Dietary Fiber	1g
Sugars	21g
Protein	12g

1) In 2-quart saucepan, heat soup and green chiles over medium heat to boiling. Reduce heat to low; beat in whipping cream with wire whisk until blended. Cook just until thoroughly heated (do not boil).

2) Meanwhile, in small microwavable bowl, microwave crabmeat on High 30 to 45 seconds or until thoroughly heated.

3) Ladle soup into individual soup bowls. Top each serving with ¼ cup crabmeat and parsley.

HIGH ALTITUDE (3500-6500 FT.): No change.

Beefy Bean and Corn Chili

PREP TIME: 25 MINUTES (READY IN 25 MINUTES)
SERVINGS: 5 (1-1/2 CUPS EACH)

e EASY

1 lb. lean (at least 80%) ground beef

2 cans (15 oz. each) spicy chili beans, undrained

1 can (14.5 oz.) diced tomatoes, undrained

1 can (11 oz.) Green Giant® Niblets® whole kernel corn, undrained

1 can (4.5 oz.) Old El Paso® chopped green chiles

Nutrition Information Per Serving:

Calories: 380	From Fat: 110
Total Fat	12g
Saturated	4g
Cholesterol	55mg
Sodium	1030mg
Total Carbohydrate	42g
Dietary Fiber	9g
Sugars	5g
Protein	26g

1) In 3-quart saucepan, cook ground beef over medium-high heat, stirring frequently, until thoroughly cooked; drain well.

2) Stir in remaining ingredients. Reduce heat to medium; cook 10 to 15 minutes, stirring occasionally, until thoroughly heated and flavors are blended.

HIGH ALTITUDE (3500-6500 FT.): No change.

Ground Beef Reuben Melts

PREP TIME: 25 MINUTES (READY IN 25 MINUTES)
SERVINGS: 6

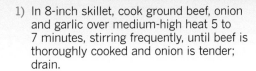 EASY

1 lb. lean (at least 80%) ground beef

1/4 cup chopped onion (1/2 medium)

2 cloves garlic, minced

1 cup undrained sauerkraut (from 14-oz. can)

6 slices dark rye bread, toasted

1/2 cup Thousand Island dressing

6 thin slices (1/2 oz. each) Swiss cheese

1) In 8-inch skillet, cook ground beef, onion and garlic over medium-high heat 5 to 7 minutes, stirring frequently, until beef is thoroughly cooked and onion is tender; drain.

2) Meanwhile, set oven control to broil. In 1-quart saucepan, heat sauerkraut; drain. Arrange toasted slices of bread on broiler pan.

3) Stir salad dressing into beef mixture. Spoon beef mixture evenly onto bread slices. Top each with sauerkraut and Swiss cheese.

4) Broil sandwiches 4 to 6 inches from heat 3 to 4 minutes or until cheese is melted and bubbly.

HIGH ALTITUDE (3500-6500 FT.): No change.

Nutrition Information Per Serving:	
Calories: 330	From Fat: 180
Total Fat	20g
Saturated	7g
Cholesterol	65mg
Sodium	720mg
Total Carbohydrate	17g
Dietary Fiber	2g
Sugars	3g
Protein	20g

 tip

For a quick New York deli-style meal, serve these sandwiches with Kosher dill pickles and deli potato salad.

Chicken-Ramen Soup

PREP TIME: 30 MINUTES (READY IN 45 MINUTES)
SERVINGS: 6 (1 CUP EACH)

 LOW FAT

1 tablespoon olive oil

1 cup ready-to-eat baby-cut carrots, sliced into 1/4-inch slices

1 cup sliced (1/4 inch) celery (2 medium stalks)

1 medium onion, chopped (1/2 cup)

2 cloves garlic, minced

2 cups cut-up deli rotisserie chicken (from 2- to 2 1/2-lb. chicken)

6 cups water

1 package (3 oz.) chicken-flavor ramen noodle soup mix

1/4 teaspoon salt

1/4 teaspoon pepper

1) In 5-quart Dutch oven, heat oil over medium heat. Add carrots, celery, onion and garlic; cook 3 to 4 minutes, stirring frequently, until tender.

2) Stir in chicken, water, contents of seasoning packet from soup mix, salt and pepper. Heat to boiling over high heat. Reduce heat to medium; simmer uncovered 10 to 15 minutes.

3) Stir in noodles from soup mix; simmer uncovered 3 minutes longer or until noodles are tender.

HIGH ALTITUDE (3500-6500 FT.): No change.

Nutrition Information Per Serving:

Calories: 170	From Fat: 70
Total Fat	8g
Saturated	2g
Cholesterol	40mg
Sodium	340mg
Total Carbohydrate	11g
Dietary Fiber	2g
Sugars	2g
Protein	15g

Cheesy Chili Dogs

PREP TIME:	15 MINUTES (READY IN 15 MINUTES)
SERVINGS:	8

e EASY

1 package (1 lb.) cocktail-size smoked link sausages, each cut into 3 pieces

1 can (15 oz.) or box (14.3 oz.) chili without beans

$1/3$ cup chopped celery

$1/2$ cup cheese dip (from 15-oz. jar)

2 tablespoons buffalo wing sauce (from 12-oz. jar)

8 bratwurst buns, split

1 medium tomato, chopped ($3/4$ cup)

Nutrition Information Per Serving:		
Calories: 380	From Fat: 200	
Total Fat		22g
Saturated		8g
Cholesterol		45mg
Sodium		1120mg
Total Carbohydrate		30g
Dietary Fiber		2g
Sugars		5g
Protein		15g

1) In large bowl, mix all ingredients except buns and tomato. Cover; refrigerate up to 3 days.

2) To make 1 chili dog, in small microwavable bowl, microwave about $1/2$ cup sausage mixture, loosely covered, on High about 1 minute, stirring once halfway through heating, until hot. Spoon sausage mixture into bun; sprinkle with heaping tablespoon tomato.

HIGH ALTITUDE (3500-6500 FT.): No change.

Ranch-Style Chicken Tacos

PREP TIME:	25 MINUTES (READY IN 25 MINUTES)
SERVINGS:	5 (2 TACOS EACH)

e EASY

1 box (4.7 oz.) Old El Paso® Stand 'N Stuff™ taco shells (10 shells)

2 cups cut-up deli rotisserie chicken (from 2- to $2^1/2$-lb. chicken)

1 bottle (8 oz.) ranch dressing

$1^1/2$ cups shredded lettuce

1 cup chopped tomato (1 large)

1 cup shredded Cheddar cheese (4 oz.)

$1/4$ cup chopped green onions (4 medium)

1 can ($2^1/4$ oz.) sliced ripe olives, if desired

Nutrition Information Per Serving:		
Calories: 560	From Fat: 370	
Total Fat		41g
Saturated		11g
Cholesterol		85mg
Sodium		670mg
Total Carbohydrate		23g
Dietary Fiber		3g
Sugars		3g
Protein		24g

1) Heat oven to 325°F. Heat taco shells as directed on box.

2) Meanwhile, if chicken is cold, place in medium microwavable bowl; microwave on High 1 to 2 minutes or until hot. Stir in $1/2$ cup of the dressing to coat.

3) Spoon warm chicken mixture into warm taco shells. Top with lettuce, tomato, cheese, onions and olives. Drizzle or serve with remaining dressing.

HIGH ALTITUDE (3500-6500 FT.): No change.

Creamy Ham and Potato Soup

PREP TIME: 15 MINUTES (READY IN 35 MINUTES)
SERVINGS: 4 (1-1/2 CUPS EACH)

⊜ EASY

1 large carrot, chopped (about $1/2$ cup)

1 medium stalk celery, chopped (about $1/2$ cup)

2 cups milk

2 cups water

1 tablespoon butter or margarine

1 box (4.8 oz.) sour cream 'n chives potato mix

1 package (8 oz.) diced cooked ham (about $1^1/2$ cups)

$1/2$ teaspoon dried dill weed

1) In 3-quart saucepan, mix all ingredients. Heat to boiling over medium-high heat, stirring frequently.

2) Reduce heat to low; cover and cook 20 minutes or until potatoes are tender.

HIGH ALTITUDE (3500-6500 FT.): No change.

Nutrition Information Per Serving:

Calories:	320	From Fat:	110
Total Fat			12g
Saturated			5g
Cholesterol			55mg
Sodium			1770mg
Total Carbohydrate			33g
Dietary Fiber			2g
Sugars			8g
Protein			20g

Ham and Mozzarella Sandwich Wedges

PREP TIME: 15 MINUTES (READY IN 15 MINUTES)
SERVINGS: 6

⊜ EASY

1 round loaf (12 to 16 oz.) focaccia bread (9 inch)

$1/3$ cup sandwich spread or mayonnaise

$1/2$ lb. thinly sliced cooked ham

$1/2$ cup very thinly sliced red onion, if desired

6 slices ($3/4$ oz. each) mozzarella cheese

2 or 3 leaves leaf lettuce

Nutrition Information Per Serving:

Calories:	310	From Fat:	120
Total Fat			14g
Saturated			4g
Cholesterol			30mg
Sodium			1160mg
Total Carbohydrate			31g
Dietary Fiber			1g
Sugars			3g
Protein			17g

1) Cut bread in half horizontally to make 2 layers. Spread cut sides with sandwich spread.

2) On bottom half of bread, layer ham, onion, cheese and lettuce. Cover with top half of bread. Cut into 6 wedges. Serve immediately, or wrap each sandwich in plastic wrap and refrigerate up to 24 hours.

HIGH ALTITUDE (3500-6500 FT.): No change.

Warm Grilled Veggie Sandwiches

PREP TIME: 1 HOUR (READY IN 1 HOUR)
SERVINGS: 4

 LOW FAT

1 medium zucchini, cut in half crosswise, cut lengthwise into $1/4$-inch-thick strips

$1/4$ medium red bell pepper, seeded, cut into $1/2$-inch-wide strips

$1/2$ red onion, cut into $3/4$-inch-thick slices

1 tablespoon olive oil

1 tablespoon chopped fresh oregano

1 clove garlic, minced

$1/2$ loaf French bread (about 11 inch)

$1/4$ cup ranch dressing

3 thin slices ($1/2$ oz. each) Swiss cheese (from deli)

1) Heat gas or charcoal grill. In 8-inch (2-quart) glass baking dish, mix zucchini, bell pepper and onion. Drizzle with oil; toss to coat. With tongs, place vegetables in grill basket (grill "wok").

2) When grill is heated, place grill basket on gas grill over medium heat or on charcoal grill over medium coals; cover grill. Cook 15 to 20 minutes, stirring occasionally, until vegetables are crisp-tender. Remove grill basket from grill; place vegetables in 8-inch dish. Stir in oregano and garlic.

3) Cut 18x18-inch sheet of heavy-duty foil; lightly spray foil with cooking spray. Cut loaf of bread in half lengthwise. Spread cut sides of bread with dressing.

4) Top bottom half with grilled vegetable mixture. Place cheese slices diagonally over vegetables, overlapping slightly. Cover with top half of bread. Place on foil; wrap securely using double-fold seals, allowing room for heat expansion.

5) Reduce gas grill to low heat or adjust coals for low heat. Place wrapped loaf on grill; cover grill. Cook 7 to 10 minutes or until warm. Carefully unwrap loaf to allow steam to escape. Cut loaf into 4 sandwiches.

HIGH ALTITUDE (3500-6500 FT.): No change.

Nutrition Information Per Serving:		
Calories: 230	From Fat: 80	
Total Fat		9g
Saturated		2.5g
Cholesterol		5mg
Sodium		400mg
Total Carbohydrate		30g
Dietary Fiber		2g
Sugars		1g
Protein		7g

Flaky Ham and Turkey Sandwich Slices

PREP TIME: 15 MINUTES (READY IN 40 MINUTES)
SERVINGS: 8 (2 SLICES EACH)

 EASY

1 box (15 oz.) Pillsbury® refrigerated pie crusts, softened as directed on box

2 teaspoons yellow mustard

1/2 lb. sliced cooked turkey

1 cup shredded Cheddar cheese (4 oz.)

2 small plum (Roma) tomatoes, thinly sliced

1/2 lb. sliced cooked ham

Nutrition Information Per Serving:		
Calories: 400	From Fat:	210
Total Fat		23g
Saturated		9g
Cholesterol		65mg
Sodium		770mg
Total Carbohydrate		27g
Dietary Fiber		0g
Sugars		2g
Protein		20g

1) Heat oven to 425°F. Remove pie crusts from pouches; place crusts flat on work surface. Brush each crust with 1 teaspoon mustard to within 1/2 inch of edge.

2) Layer turkey, cheese, tomato slices and ham in 4 1/2-inch-wide strip down center of each crust to within 1 inch of top and bottom of edges. Fold top and bottom edges up onto filling. Bring both sides up over filling, meeting in center; press crust edges together forming 1/2-inch-high seam to seal (flute edge if desired). Place on ungreased cookie sheet. Cut 3 or 4 slits in top crust of each to allow steam to escape.

3) Bake 20 to 25 minutes or until golden brown. Cool 5 minutes. Cut each roll into 8 slices; serve warm.

HIGH ALTITUDE (3500-6500 FT.): Bake 17 to 22 minutes.

Chili Burgers

PREP TIME: 25 MINUTES (READY IN 25 MINUTES)
SERVINGS: 4 SANDWICHES

 EASY

1 lb. lean (at least 80%) ground beef

1 teaspoon chili powder

1/8 teaspoon ground red pepper (cayenne), if desired

4 slices onion

Cooking spray or vegetable oil

4 burger buns, split

4 slices (1 oz. each) hot pepper Monterey Jack cheese

Nutrition Information Per Serving:		
Calories: 440	From Fat:	220
Total Fat		25g
Saturated		11g
Cholesterol		95mg
Sodium		440mg
Total Carbohydrate		23g
Dietary Fiber		2g
Sugars		4g
Protein		31g

1) Heat gas or charcoal grill. In medium bowl, mix ground beef, chili powder and ground red pepper. Shape mixture into 4 (4-inch) patties, 1/2 inch thick. Spray both sides of onion slices with cooking spray or brush with oil.

2) When grill is heated, place patties and onion slices on gas grill over medium heat or on charcoal grill over medium coals; cover grill. Cook 11 to 13 minutes, turning patties and onion slices once, until thermometer inserted in center of patties reads 160°F. During last 2 minutes of cooking, place buns, cut sides down, on grill and cheese on patties; cook 1 to 2 minutes or until buns are golden brown and cheese is melted.

3) Place patties on bottom halves of buns. Top with onion slices. Cover with top halves of buns.

HIGH ALTITUDE (3500-6500 FT.): Cook patties on covered grill over medium-low heat. Continue as directed above.

Barbecue Chicken Wraps

PREP TIME:	20 MINUTES (READY IN 20 MINUTES)	EASY
SERVINGS:	4	

2 cups Lloyd's® refrigerated original barbeque sauce with shredded chicken (from 18-oz. container)

4 slices precooked bacon, cut into pieces

4 flour tortillas (10 to 12 inch)

1 cup shredded Cheddar cheese (4 oz.)

1 cup creamy coleslaw (from deli)

Nutrition Information Per Serving:

Calories:	650	From Fat:	290
Total Fat			32g
Saturated			11g
Cholesterol			75mg
Sodium			1560mg
Total Carbohydrate			64g
Dietary Fiber			3g
Sugars			22g
Protein			28g

Use ¼ cup bacon bits or crumbled bacon in place of the four slices precooked if it is more convenient.

1) In 1-quart saucepan, cook barbeque sauce with chicken and bacon over medium heat 5 to 10 minutes, stirring occasionally, until thoroughly heated.

2) Meanwhile, heat tortillas as directed on package.

3) Spoon ½ cup chicken mixture down center of each warm tortilla. Top each with cheese. Spoon coleslaw down sides of each. Fold up bottom of each tortilla; fold in sides. If desired, enclose bottom of wraps in foil or waxed paper.

HIGH ALTITUDE (3500-6500 FT.): No change.

Grilled Stuffed Pizza Burgers

PREP TIME: 35 MINUTES (READY IN 35 MINUTES)
SERVINGS: 6

2 lb. lean (at least 80%) ground beef

½ teaspoon salt

¼ cup chopped pepperoni (about 1 oz.)

2 tablespoons sliced ripe olives

½ cup pizza sauce

6 slices (³/4 oz. each) mozzarella cheese, cut in half diagonally

6 burger buns, split, toasted

6 leaves lettuce

1) Heat gas or charcoal grill. In large bowl, mix ground beef and salt. Shape mixture into 12 thin patties, each about 4 inches in diameter.

2) In small bowl, mix pepperoni, olives and ⅓ cup of the pizza sauce. Spoon rounded tablespoon pepperoni mixture onto center of 6 patties; spread slightly. Top with remaining patties; press edges together firmly to seal.

3) Place patties on grill; cover grill. Cook with medium heat 8 to 12 minutes, turning once, until thermometer inserted in center of patties reads 160°F (avoid inserting in filling). During last 1 to 2 minutes of cooking time, top each patty with cheese and rounded teaspoon of remaining pizza sauce, and place buns, cut side down, on grill; cook until cheese is melted and buns are lightly toasted.

4) To serve, place lettuce and patties in bottom halves of buns. Cover with top halves of buns.

HIGH ALTITUDE (3500-6500 FT.): No change.

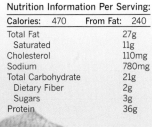

Nutrition Information Per Serving:		
Calories: 470	From Fat: 240	
Total Fat	27g	
Saturated	11g	
Cholesterol	110mg	
Sodium	780mg	
Total Carbohydrate	21g	
Dietary Fiber	2g	
Sugars	3g	
Protein	36g	

Chicken-Bacon-Ranch Wraps

PREP TIME: 15 MINUTES (READY IN 15 MINUTES)
SERVINGS: 8

e EASY

- 3 cups coarsely shredded deli rotisserie chicken (from 2 to 2$\frac{1}{2}$-lb. chicken)
- 1 cup shredded Monterey Jack cheese (4 oz.)
- 8 slices cooked bacon, chopped (about $\frac{1}{2}$ cup)
- $\frac{1}{4}$ cup chopped green onions (4 medium)
- 1 cup ranch dressing
- 1 package (11.5 oz.) Old El Paso® flour tortillas for burritos, 8 inch (8 tortillas)
- 4 cups shredded romaine lettuce

1) In large bowl, gently mix all ingredients except tortillas and lettuce. Cover; refrigerate up to 3 days.

2) To make 1 wrap, in small microwavable bowl, microwave generous $\frac{1}{3}$ cup chicken mixture, loosely covered, on High 30 to 45 seconds or until hot. Spread chicken mixture on tortilla and top with $\frac{1}{2}$ cup shredded lettuce; roll up.

HIGH ALTITUDE (3500-6500 FT.): No change.

Nutrition Information Per Serving:

Calories: 470	From Fat:	280
Total Fat		31g
Saturated		8g
Cholesterol		75mg
Sodium		880mg
Total Carbohydrate		24g
Dietary Fiber		0g
Sugars		2g
Protein		24g

Smothered Beef Sandwiches

PREP TIME: 10 MINUTES (READY IN 30 MINUTES)
SERVINGS: 6 SANDWICHES

 EASY

- 1 package (10 oz.) frozen garlic bread
- 1 container (18 oz.) refrigerated original barbeque sauce with shredded beef
- 1 cup finely shredded Cheddar-American cheese blend (4 oz.)

Nutrition Information Per Serving:

Calories: 370	From Fat:	140
Total Fat		16g
Saturated		6g
Cholesterol		40mg
Sodium		970mg
Total Carbohydrate		37g
Dietary Fiber		1g
Sugars		14g
Protein		19g

1) Heat oven to 375°F. On ungreased cookie sheet, place bread halves, garlic side up. Top each half of bread evenly with barbeque sauce with shredded beef. Sprinkle each with $\frac{1}{2}$ cup cheese.

2) Bake 18 to 20 minutes or until beef mixture is thoroughly heated and cheese is melted.

3) To serve, cut each half of bread into 3 pieces.

HIGH ALTITUDE (3500-6500 FT.): No change.

Toasted Mexi-Meatball Hoagies

JENNY FLAKE | GILBERT, ARIZONA

PREP TIME: 45 MINUTES (READY IN 1 HOUR 15 MINUTES)
SERVINGS: 4 (1/2 SANDWICH EACH)

ROLLS

2 cans (11 oz. each) Pillsbury® refrigerated crusty French loaf

MEATBALLS

2 tablespoons extra-virgin olive oil

1 package (1.25 oz.) Old El Paso® taco seasoning mix

1 egg, slightly beaten

1 lb. lean (at least 80%) ground beef

½ cup Progresso® garlic herb bread crumbs

½ cup chopped fresh cilantro

½ cup finely chopped onion (1 medium)

½ teaspoon finely chopped garlic

¼ teaspoon freshly ground black pepper

2 tablespoons chunky-style salsa

1 teaspoon red pepper sauce

SAUCE

1¼ cups ranch dressing

¼ cup chopped fresh cilantro

¼ cup chunky-style salsa

1 tablespoon fresh lime juice

Reserved 1 teaspoon Old El Paso® taco seasoning mix

TOPPINGS

2 cups shredded iceberg lettuce

1 cup shredded Cheddar cheese (4 oz.)

1 cup diced tomatoes (2 small)

¼ cup chopped fresh cilantro

Nutrition Information Per Serving:		
Calories: 1240	From Fat: 660	
Total Fat		74g
Saturated		20g
Cholesterol		175mg
Sodium		3000mg
Total Carbohydrate		98g
Dietary Fiber		5g
Sugars		14g
Protein		45g

1) Heat oven to 350°F. Grease large cookie sheet with cooking spray or shortening. Remove dough from both cans; place seam side down and 3 inches apart on cookie sheet. Cut 4 or 5 diagonal slashes (½-inch deep) with sharp knife on top of each loaf. Bake 26 to 30 minutes or until deep golden brown. Cool slightly while preparing meatballs, about 25 minutes.

2) Spread oil in bottom of 13x9-inch (3-quart) glass baking dish. Reserve 1 teaspoon of the taco seasoning mix for sauce; place remaining seasoning mix in large bowl. Add remaining meatball ingredients; mix well. Shape mixture into 1-inch balls; place in baking dish. Bake uncovered 25 to 30 minutes, turning meatballs once halfway through baking, until meat thermometer inserted in center of meatballs reads 160°F.

3) Meanwhile, in food processor, place all sauce ingredients; process until smooth. Set aside.

4) Set oven control to broil. Cut each loaf in half horizontally, cutting to but not completely through one long side; place cut side up on cookie sheet. Broil 5 to 6 inches from heat 1 to 2 minutes or just until lightly toasted.

5) Spread ¼ cup sauce on each toasted cut side. Spoon hot meatballs evenly onto bottom halves of loaf. Top evenly with toppings. Drizzle with remaining sauce. If desired, close sandwiches. Cut each sandwich in half. Serve immediately.

HIGH ALTITUDE (3500-6500 FT.): No change.

Cheesy Pork Quesadillas

PREP TIME: 15 MINUTES (READY IN 15 MINUTES)
SERVINGS: 4

e EASY

1 container (18 oz.) Lloyd's®
   refrigerated original barbeque sauce
   with shredded pork

4 Old El Paso® flour tortillas for
   burritos, 8 inch (from 11.5-oz.
   package)

$1/4$ cup sour cream

$3/4$ cup Old El Paso® Thick 'n Chunky
   salsa

4 slices (1 oz. each) Monterey Jack
   cheese, cut in half

1) In 2-quart saucepan, mix barbeque
   sauce with pork. Cook over medium-high
   heat, stirring occasionally, until
   thoroughly heated.

2) Meanwhile, spread half of each tortilla
   with sour cream.

3) Top sour cream side of each tortilla with
   $1/4$ of pork mixture, 1 tablespoon salsa
   and 2 half-slices cheese. Fold tortilla over
   onto filling.

4) Spray 12-inch skillet with cooking spray;
   heat over medium-high heat. Add
   2 quesadillas at a time to skillet; cook
   about 3 minutes, turning once, until
   filling is heated and tortillas are golden
   brown. Repeat with remaining
   2 quesadillas. Cut into wedges;
   serve with remaining salsa.

HIGH ALTITUDE (3500-6500 FT.): No change.

Nutrition Information Per Serving:

Calories:	480	From Fat:	180
Total Fat			20g
Saturated			9g
Cholesterol			70mg
Sodium			1680mg
Total Carbohydrate			51g
Dietary Fiber			0g
Sugars			23g
Protein			24g

Bagel Shop Chicken Salad Sandwiches

PREP TIME: 30 MINUTES (READY IN 30 MINUTES)
SERVINGS: 4

ⓔ EASY

- 2 cups chopped cooked chicken
- ½ cup chopped precooked bacon (about 6 or 7 slices)
- ¼ cup finely chopped celery
- 2 tablespoons finely chopped green onions (2 medium)
- ½ teaspoon dried basil leaves
- ¼ teaspoon garlic powder
- ¼ cup mayonnaise or salad dressing
- 4 bagels (whole-grain, pumpernickel or sesame seed), split

  Thin cucumber slices or lettuce leaves, if desired

1) In medium bowl, mix chicken, bacon, celery, onions, basil, garlic powder and mayonnaise.

2) Spread chicken mixture on bottom halves of bagels. Top with cucumber slices. Cover with top halves of bagels. Serve immediately, or wrap each sandwich in plastic wrap and refrigerate up to 24 hours.

HIGH ALTITUDE (3500-6500 FT.): No change.

Nutrition Information Per Serving:		
Calories: 440	From Fat: 200	
Total Fat		22g
Saturated		5g
Cholesterol		90mg
Sodium		590mg
Total Carbohydrate		31g
Dietary Fiber		2g
Sugars		2g
Protein		29g

Tropical Barbeque Pork Sandwiches

PREP TIME: 15 MINUTES (READY IN 15 MINUTES)
SERVINGS: 6

e EASY

6 sesame seed-topped sandwich buns, split

3 cups Lloyd's® refrigerated original barbeque sauce with shredded pork (from two 18-oz. containers), heated as directed on container

6 slices drained canned pineapple

6 thin rings green bell pepper

6 slices (1 oz. each) Monterey Jack cheese

Nutrition Information Per Serving:	
Calories: 420	From Fat: 130
Total Fat	15g
Saturated	7g
Cholesterol	55mg
Sodium	1150mg
Total Carbohydrate	49g
Dietary Fiber	1g
Sugars	24g
Protein	23g

1) Set oven control to broil. On ungreased cookie sheet, place bun halves, cut side up. Broil 2 to 3 minutes or until golden brown.

2) Divide warm barbeque sauce with pork evenly onto bottom halves of buns. Top each with pineapple, bell pepper and cheese.

3) Broil 2 to 3 minutes or until cheese is melted and begins to turn golden. Remove from cookie sheet; cover with top halves of buns.

HIGH ALTITUDE (3500-6500 FT.): No change.

Sassy Southwestern Burgers

PREP TIME: 20 MINUTES (READY IN 20 MINUTES)
SERVINGS: 4

e EASY

1 lb. lean (at least 80%) ground beef

2 tablespoons Old El Paso® 40% less-sodium taco seasoning mix (from 1.25-oz. package)

6 tablespoons Old El Paso® Thick 'n Chunky salsa

4 slices (³/4 oz. each) pepper Jack cheese

4 burger buns, split

Nutrition Information Per Serving:	
Calories: 390	From Fat: 180
Total Fat	21g
Saturated	9g
Cholesterol	90mg
Sodium	990mg
Total Carbohydrate	24g
Dietary Fiber	1g
Sugars	4g
Protein	27g

1) Heat gas or charcoal grill. In medium bowl, mix ground beef, taco seasoning mix and 2 tablespoons of the salsa. Shape mixture into 4 patties, ¹/2 inch thick.

2) Place patties on grill; cover grill. Cook with medium heat 11 to 13 minutes, turning once, until thermometer inserted in center of patties reads 160°F. During last 2 minutes of cooking time, place buns, cut sides down, on grill; cook 1 to 2 minutes or until lightly toasted. During last minute of cooking time, place cheese on patties; cook until melted.

3) To serve, place patties on bottom halves of buns. Top each with 1 tablespoon remaining salsa and top halves of buns.

HIGH ALTITUDE (3500-6500 FT.): No change.

Turkey Joe Calzones

PREP TIME: 35 MINUTES (READY IN 55 MINUTES)
SERVINGS: 6 CALZONES

 EASY   LOW FAT

1 lb. lean ground turkey

1 package (1.31 oz.) sloppy joe seasoning mix

1 can (8 oz.) tomato sauce

1 can (13.8 oz.) Pillsbury® refrigerated pizza crust

¼ cup chopped dill pickles

1 egg, beaten

Nutrition Information Per Serving:	
Calories: 330	From Fat: 90
Total Fat	10g
Saturated	2.5g
Cholesterol	60mg
Sodium	1240mg
Total Carbohydrate	38g
Dietary Fiber	2g
Sugars	6g
Protein	21g

1) Heat oven to 400°F. Grease large cookie sheet with shortening or spray with cooking spray. In 12-inch skillet, cook ground turkey over medium heat, stirring frequently, until turkey is no longer pink; drain. Stir in seasoning mix and tomato sauce. Cook 2 minutes, stirring frequently, until sauce is thickened. Remove from heat; cool 10 minutes.

2) Meanwhile, unroll dough; cut in half lengthwise and into thirds crosswise to make 6 pieces. Press each piece into 5½-inch round. Place dough rounds on cookie sheet. Sprinkle about 2 teaspoons pickles over each round.

3) Spoon about ½ cup turkey mixture onto center of each. Fold each dough round in half over filling; press edges with fork to seal. Lightly brush tops with beaten egg.

4) Bake 14 to 18 minutes or until golden brown.

HIGH ALTITUDE (3500-6500 FT.): No change.

Cook the turkey mixture the night before, then cover and refrigerate it until you're ready to make the calzones. Heat the mixture in the microwave just until it's warm before assembling the calzones.

Honey Barbecue Meatball Sandwiches

PREP TIME: 15 MINUTES (READY IN 15 MINUTES)
SERVINGS: 6

 EASY

1 package (16 oz.) frozen cooked meatballs, thawed

¼ cup chopped red bell pepper

¼ cup chopped green bell pepper

¼ cup chopped onion (½ medium)

1 cup barbecue sauce

2 tablespoons lemon juice

1 tablespoon honey

6 hero sandwich rolls or hoagie buns (6 to 7 inch)

1 cup shredded Cheddar cheese (4 oz.)

1) In large bowl, mix all ingredients except rolls and cheese. Cover; refrigerate up to 3 days.

2) To make 1 sandwich, in small microwavable bowl, microwave ⅔ cup meatball mixture, loosely covered, on High about 1 minute or until hot. Fill roll with meatball mixture; sprinkle with about 2 tablespoons cheese.

HIGH ALTITUDE (3500-6500 FT.): No change.

Nutrition Information Per Serving:	
Calories: 530	From Fat: 170
Total Fat	19g
Saturated	8g
Cholesterol	100mg
Sodium	1410mg
Total Carbohydrate	65g
Dietary Fiber	3g
Sugars	22g
Protein	27g

Granola-Chicken Salad Sandwiches

JEREMY HODGES | PELHAM, ALABAMA

PREP TIME: 15 MINUTES (READY IN 25 MINUTES)
SERVINGS: 6 SANDWICHES

1 can (10.1 oz.) Pillsbury® Big & Flaky refrigerated crescent dinner rolls

2 cups plain chicken salad for sandwiches (from deli)

1/4 cup seedless green grapes, cut into quarters

1/4 cup chopped fresh pineapple or drained canned pineapple tidbits

1/4 cup chopped red apple

1/4 cup drained canned mandarin orange segments

1 tablespoon packed brown sugar

4 Nature Valley® roasted almond crunchy granola bars (2 pouches from 8.9-oz. box), crushed (3/4 cup)*

1/2 cup salad dressing or mayonnaise

1) Heat oven to 350°F. Bake crescent rolls as directed on can. Remove from cookie sheet; cool on wire rack 5 minutes.

2) Meanwhile, in medium bowl, mix all remaining ingredients; refrigerate until needed.

3) Cut rolls horizontally in half. Fill with chicken salad mixture.

*NOTE: To easily crush granola bars, do not unwrap; use rolling pin to crush bars.

HIGH ALTITUDE (3500-6500 FT.): No change.

Nutrition Information Per Sandwich:

Calories:	490	From Fat:	270
Total Fat			30g
Saturated			6g
Cholesterol			40mg
Sodium			700mg
Total Carbohydrate			42g
Dietary Fiber			2g
Sugars			18g
Protein			13g

Mexican Egg Salad Wraps

CAROLE RESNICK | CLEVELAND, OHIO

Bake-Off

PREP TIME: 25 MINUTES (READY IN 25 MINUTES)
SERVINGS: 8 WRAPS

12 hard-cooked eggs, peeled, coarsely
chopped

1/2 cup mayonnaise or salad dressing

1/4 cup finely chopped celery

1/4 to 1/2 teaspoon salt

1 can (4.5 oz.) Old El Paso® chopped
green chiles

2 medium avocados, pitted, peeled and
coarsely chopped (2 cups)

2 teaspoons fresh lime juice

1 tablespoon finely chopped onion

1 package (11.5 oz.) Old El Paso® flour
tortillas for burritos, 8 inch (8 tortillas)

1/3 cup small fresh cilantro leaves,
stems removed

Fresh cilantro sprigs

Fresh medium strawberries

1) In large bowl, mix chopped eggs,
mayonnaise, celery, salt and chiles. Place
avocado in medium bowl; sprinkle with
lime juice. Add onion; mash with spoon.

2) Spread 1/4 cup avocado mixture on each
tortilla to within 1/2 inch of edge. Spread
each with about 1/3 cup egg salad
mixture. Sprinkle cilantro leaves over
each. Fold in sides of each tortilla; roll up.
Arrange wraps on large serving platter;
garnish with cilantro sprigs and strawberries.

HIGH ALTITUDE (3500-6500 FT.): No change.

Nutrition Information Per Wrap:		
Calories: 430	From Fat:	260
Total Fat		29g
Saturated		6g
Cholesterol		325mg
Sodium		620mg
Total Carbohydrate		28g
Dietary Fiber		3g
Sugars		2g
Protein		14g

French Dip Burgers

PREP TIME: 25 MINUTES (READY IN 25 MINUTES)
SERVINGS: 4 SANDWICHES

 EASY

- 1 cup water
- 1 package (1 oz.) dry onion soup mix
- 2 tablespoons water
- 1 lb. lean (at least 80%) ground beef
- 8 diagonal slices French bread (1/2 inch thick)

1) Heat gas or charcoal grill. To make hot broth in 1-quart saucepan, mix 1 cup water and 2 tablespoons of the soup mix. Heat to boiling. Reduce heat to low; cover and simmer while making and grilling patties.

2) In medium bowl, mix 2 tablespoons water and the remaining soup mix until well blended. Stir in ground beef. Shape mixture into 4 oval-shaped patties, 1/2 inch thick.

3) Place patties on grill; cover grill. Cook with medium heat 11 to 13 minutes, turning once, until thermometer inserted in center of patties reads 160°F. During last 2 minutes of cooking time, place bread slices on grill; cook 1 to 2 minutes, turning once, until lightly toasted.

4) To serve, place each patty between 2 slices French bread. Serve with hot broth for dipping.

HIGH ALTITUDE (3500-6500 FT.): No change.

Nutrition Information Per Serving:

Calories:	260	From Fat:	120
Total Fat			13g
Saturated			5g
Cholesterol			70mg
Sodium			780mg
Total Carbohydrate			14g
Dietary Fiber			0g
Sugars			2g
Protein			22g

Grilled Tomato-Cheese Sandwiches

PREP TIME: 15 MINUTES (READY IN 15 MINUTES)
SERVINGS: 2

 EASY

- 4 teaspoons butter or margarine, softened
- 4 slices bread
- 4 slices (1 oz. each) Colby-Monterey Jack cheese
- 4 slices tomato (1/4- to 1/2-inch-thick)

Nutrition Information Per Serving:

Calories:	430	From Fat:	250
Total Fat			27g
Saturated			15g
Cholesterol			75mg
Sodium			650mg
Total Carbohydrate			24g
Dietary Fiber			1g
Sugars			2g
Protein			18g

1) Spread butter on one side of each slice of bread. On 2 bread slices, butter side down, layer 1 slice of cheese, 2 tomato slices and another slice of cheese. Top with remaining bread slices, butter side up.

2) Heat 12-inch skillet over medium heat. Add sandwiches; cook 2 to 3 minutes or until bottom is golden brown. Turn; cover skillet and cook 2 to 3 minutes longer or until golden brown and cheese is melted.

HIGH ALTITUDE (3500-6500 FT.): No change.

Super Speedy Chili

PREP TIME: 15 MINUTES (READY IN 15 MINUTES)
SERVINGS: 4 (1-1/3 CUPS EACH)

 EASY   LOW FAT

½ lb. lean (at least 80%) ground beef

2 cans (14.5 oz. each) stewed tomatoes, undrained, cut up

1 can (15 oz.) spicy chili beans, undrained

3 teaspoons chili powder

Shredded Cheddar cheese, if desired

Nutrition Information Per Serving:

Calories:	270	From Fat:	70
Total Fat			8g
Saturated			2.5g
Cholesterol			35mg
Sodium			1020mg
Total Carbohydrate			33g
Dietary Fiber			7g
Sugars			11g
Protein			17g

1) In 3-quart saucepan or 10-inch skillet, cook ground beef over medium-high heat, stirring frequently, until thoroughly cooked; drain.

2) Stir in remaining ingredients. Heat to boiling. Reduce heat to medium-low; simmer uncovered 5 minutes, stirring occasionally. Top individual servings with cheese.

HIGH ALTITUDE (3500-6500 FT.): No change.

Cheesy Pasta-Vegetable Soup

PREP TIME: 20 MINUTES (READY IN 30 MINUTES)
SERVINGS: 4 (1-1/2 CUPS EACH)

 EASY   LOW FAT

2 cans (14 oz. each) chicken broth

1 cup Green Giant® frozen cut green beans (from 1-lb. bag)

1 bag (24 oz.) Green Giant® Pasta Accents® frozen pasta, broccoli, sugar snap peas & garlic sauce

½ cup cheese dip or process cheese sauce (from 8-oz. jar)

Nutrition Information Per Serving:

Calories:	310	From Fat:	130
Total Fat			14g
Saturated			6g
Cholesterol			25mg
Sodium			1630mg
Total Carbohydrate			33g
Dietary Fiber			4g
Sugars			7g
Protein			13g

1) In 3-quart saucepan, heat broth over high heat to boiling. Stir in green beans and pasta with vegetables and garlic sauce. Return to boiling.

2) Reduce heat to medium; simmer uncovered 6 to 8 minutes, stirring occasionally, until vegetables are crisp-tender.

3) Remove from heat. Stir in cheese dip until melted.

HIGH ALTITUDE (3500-6500 FT.): No change.

Garlic Pepper-Blue Cheese Burgers

PREP TIME: 25 MINUTES (READY IN 25 MINUTES)
SERVINGS: 4

 EASY

1 lb. lean (at least 80%) ground beef

½ cup crumbled blue cheese (2 oz.)

1 teaspoon garlic-pepper blend

½ teaspoon salt

4 onion buns, split

4 slices tomato

Nutrition Information Per Serving:	
Calories: 350	From Fat: 170
Total Fat	19g
Saturated	8g
Cholesterol	80mg
Sodium	730mg
Total Carbohydrate	20g
Dietary Fiber	1g
Sugars	3g
Protein	26g

1) Heat gas or charcoal grill. In medium bowl, mix ground beef, blue cheese, garlic-pepper blend and salt. Shape mixture into 4 (4-inch) patties, about ½ inch thick.

2) Place patties on grill; cover grill. Cook with medium heat 11 to 13 minutes, turning once, until thermometer inserted in center of patties reads 160°F. If desired, during last 1 to 2 minutes of cooking, toast buns, cut sides down, on grill.

3) Place patties on bottom halves of buns. Top each with tomato slice. If desired, top with additional blue cheese. Cover with top halves of buns.

HIGH ALTITUDE (3500-6500 FT.): No change.

Offer blue cheese-lovers more flavor: Crumble extra blue cheese over the burgers or mix blue cheese with mayonnaise to spread on the buns.

Yummy Hero Sandwiches

PREP TIME:	15 MINUTES (READY IN 45 MINUTES)
SERVINGS:	8

 EASY

1 tablespoon butter or margarine

1 medium onion, halved, thinly sliced

1 medium bell pepper (any color), thinly sliced

2 cans (13.8 oz. each) Pillsbury® refrigerated pizza crust

2 tablespoons creamy Dijon mustard-mayonnaise spread

1/2 lb. thinly sliced cooked chicken

40 thin slices pepperoni, 1 1/2-inch diameter (about 3 oz.)

8 oz. thinly sliced Cheddar cheese or mozzarella

1 egg

1 teaspoon sesame seed

1) Heat oven to 400°F. Grease 13x9-inch pan with shortening or spray with cooking spray. In 10-inch skillet, melt butter over medium-high heat. Add onion and bell pepper; cook 3 to 5 minutes, stirring occasionally, until tender.

2) Unroll 1 can of the dough; place in pan. Starting at center, press out dough just to edge of pan (do not go up sides). Spread mustard-mayonnaise over dough. Top evenly with chicken, pepperoni, onion mixture and cheese.

3) Unroll remaining can of dough over cheese, stretching to edges. In small bowl, beat egg; brush over top. Sprinkle with sesame seed.

4) Bake 23 to 28 minutes or until golden brown and thoroughly heated. Let stand 10 minutes. Cut into 8 pieces to serve.

HIGH ALTITUDE (3500-6500 FT.): Bake 28 to 33 minutes.

Nutrition Information Per Serving:		
Calories: 470	From Fat:	160
Total Fat		18g
Saturated		8g
Cholesterol		80mg
Sodium		1170mg
Total Carbohydrate		51g
Dietary Fiber		2g
Sugars		8g
Protein		26g

Toasted Turkey and Roasted Pepper Sandwiches

PREP TIME: 25 MINUTES (READY IN 25 MINUTES)
SERVINGS: 4 SANDWICHES

 EASY

3 tablespoons mayonnaise

1 tablespoon Dijon mustard

8 thin slices sourdough bread

1/2 lb. sliced cooked turkey breast
(from deli)

4 thin slices Cheddar cheese

1 jar (7 or 7.25 oz.) roasted red bell
peppers, drained, sliced

Nutrition Information Per Serving:		
Calories: 420	From Fat:	190
Total Fat		21g
Saturated		8g
Cholesterol		60mg
Sodium		1330mg
Total Carbohydrate		33g
Dietary Fiber		2g
Sugars		5g
Protein		23g

1) In small bowl, mix mayonnaise and mustard. Spread 1 tablespoon mayonnaise mixture on each of 4 slices of bread. Top each evenly with turkey, cheese and roasted peppers. Cover with remaining slices of bread.

2) Spray 12-inch skillet with cooking spray; place 2 sandwiches in skillet. Cover and cook over medium-low heat 2 minutes on each side or until bread is golden brown and cheese is melted. Repeat with remaining 2 sandwiches.

HIGH ALTITUDE (3500-6500 FT.): No change.

Vegetable-Beef-Barley Soup

PREP TIME: 35 MINUTES (READY IN 35 MINUTES)
SERVINGS: 4 (1-1/2 CUPS EACH)

 EASY   LOW FAT

1/2 lb. extra-lean (at least 90%)
ground beef

1 can (14.5 oz.) stewed tomatoes,
undrained, cut up

1 can (14 oz.) beef broth

1 can (8 oz.) no-salt-added tomato
sauce

1 cup Green Giant® frozen mixed
vegetables (from 1-lb. bag)

1/3 cup uncooked quick-cooking barley

Nutrition Information Per Serving:		
Calories: 230	From Fat:	45
Total Fat		5g
Saturated		2g
Cholesterol		35mg
Sodium		760mg
Total Carbohydrate		30g
Dietary Fiber		6g
Sugars		9g
Protein		16g

1) In 3-quart saucepan, cook ground beef over medium-high heat, stirring frequently, until thoroughly cooked; drain.

2) Stir in remaining ingredients. Heat to boiling. Reduce heat to medium; cover and cook 10 to 15 minutes, stirring occasionally, until vegetables and barley are tender.

HIGH ALTITUDE (3500-6500 FT.): Add up to 1/2 cup water if soup becomes too thick.

Philly Cheese Steak Onion Soup

ANNE JOHNSON | VINCENT, OHIO

PREP TIME: 10 MINUTES (READY IN 35 MINUTES)
SERVINGS: 2 (1-3/4 CUPS EACH)

1 can (11 oz.) Pillsbury® refrigerated crusty French loaf

1/2 teaspoon butter or margarine

1 boneless beef rib-eye steak (1/2 lb.), trimmed of fat, cut into bite-size strips

1/4 teaspoon salt

Dash pepper

1 can (18.5 oz.) Progresso® Vegetable Classics French onion soup

1 can (4 oz.) Green Giant® mushroom pieces and stems, drained

1/2 cup shredded provolone cheese (2 oz.)

3 tablespoons chopped green bell pepper

1) Heat oven to 350°F. Bake French loaf as directed on can. Meanwhile, in 2-quart saucepan, melt butter over medium heat. Add beef strips; sprinkle with salt and pepper. Cook and stir until browned. Stir in soup; heat to boiling. Reduce heat to medium-low; simmer uncovered 20 minutes.

2) Stir mushrooms into soup; cook until thoroughly heated. Cut 2 (1-inch-thick) diagonal slices from warm loaf; reserve remaining loaf to serve with soup.

3) Set oven control to broil. Ladle soup into 2 (15-oz.) ovenproof bowls. Sprinkle 2 tablespoons of the cheese onto each serving. Top each with bread slice. Sprinkle bell pepper and remaining cheese evenly over each.

4) Place bowls on cookie sheet; broil 4 to 6 inches from heat 1 to 2 minutes or until cheese is bubbly and bread is toasted. Serve soup with remaining slices of loaf.

HIGH ALTITUDE (3500-6500 FT.): No change.

Nutrition Information Per Serving:		
Calories: 730	From Fat:	210
Total Fat		23g
Saturated		10g
Cholesterol		75mg
Sodium		2720mg
Total Carbohydrate		83g
Dietary Fiber		4g
Sugars		13g
Protein		48g

Toasted Beef and Mozzarella Sandwiches

PREP TIME: 20 MINUTES (READY IN 20 MINUTES)
SERVINGS: 4

 EASY

8 slices (about 5x4 inch each) sourdough or Vienna bread

¼ cup refrigerated French onion dip

½ lb. sliced cooked roast beef (from deli)

1 medium tomato, very thinly sliced

4 slices (¾ oz. each) mozzarella cheese

Nutrition Information Per Serving:	
Calories: 480	From Fat: 190
Total Fat	21g
Saturated	9g
Cholesterol	70mg
Sodium	740mg
Total Carbohydrate	45g
Dietary Fiber	3g
Sugars	2g
Protein	29g

1) Heat closed contact grill for 5 minutes.
Spread 4 slices of the bread with dip. Top with beef, tomato and cheese. Cover with remaining bread slices.

2) When grill is heated, place sandwiches on bottom grill surface (2 at a time if necessary). Close grill; cook 3 to 4 minutes or until bread is toasted and cheese is melted.

HIGH ALTITUDE (3500-6500 FT.): No change.

Mini Tuna-Cheese Buns

PREP TIME: 20 MINUTES (READY IN 20 MINUTES)
SERVINGS: 8

 EASY

1 can (6 oz.) solid white tuna in water, drained, flaked

1 cup finely shredded Cheddar cheese (4 oz.)

¼ cup finely chopped celery

2 tablespoons finely chopped red onion

3 tablespoons mayonnaise or salad dressing

1 tablespoon Dijon mustard

8 miniature sandwich buns (about 3 inch), split

8 small leaves lettuce

Nutrition Information Per Serving:	
Calories: 240	From Fat: 110
Total Fat	12g
Saturated	4.5g
Cholesterol	25mg
Sodium	450mg
Total Carbohydrate	23g
Dietary Fiber	1g
Sugars	3g
Protein	12g

1) In medium bowl, mix tuna, cheese, celery, onion, mayonnaise and mustard.

2) Spread tuna mixture on bottom halves of buns. Top with lettuce. Cover with top halves of buns. Serve immediately, or wrap each sandwich in plastic wrap and refrigerate up to 24 hours.

HIGH ALTITUDE (3500-6500 FT.): No change.

ALMOND SCONES
PG. 133

Breads & Pastries

Yum! Baked goods loaded with homemade taste, without all the work.

ORANGE-CARAMEL PECAN BISCUITS
PG. 138

CRUNCHY OVEN FRENCH TOAST
PG. 143

PIZZA BISCUIT WREATH
PG. 137

Pesto-Cheese Bread

PREP TIME: 20 MINUTES (READY IN 20 MINUTES)
SERVINGS: 12 (1 PIECE EACH)

 EASY

1 loaf Italian bread (10 to 12 inch)

⅓ cup refrigerated basil pesto (from 7-oz. container)

¾ cup shredded mozzarella cheese (3 oz.)

Nutrition Information Per Serving:		
Calories: 110	From Fat:	50
Total Fat		6g
Saturated		2g
Cholesterol		0mg
Sodium		220mg
Total Carbohydrate		11g
Dietary Fiber		0g
Sugars		0g
Protein		4g

1) Heat gas or charcoal grill. Cut 18x18-inch sheet of heavy-duty foil. Cut loaf of bread in half lengthwise. Spread each half with pesto. Sprinkle with cheese.

2) Place bread, cheese sides together, on foil; wrap securely using double fold seals, allowing room for heat expansion.

3) When grill is heated, place wrapped bread on gas grill over medium heat or on charcoal grill over medium coals; cover grill. Cook 10 to 12 minutes, rotating and turning over occasionally, until bread is warm and cheese is melted.

4) Carefully unwrap bread to allow steam to escape. Separate loaf into 2 halves; cut each into 6 pieces. Serve immediately.

HIGH ALTITUDE (3500-6500 FT.): Cook wrapped bread on covered grill over medium-low heat. Continue as directed above.

Cheesy Surprise Cornbread Biscuits

PREP TIME: 25 MINUTES (READY IN 40 MINUTES)
SERVINGS: 10 BISCUITS

 EASY

1 can (12 oz.) Pillsbury® Golden Layers® refrigerated buttermilk biscuits

2 sticks (1 oz. each) mozzarella string cheese, each cut crosswise into 5 pieces

3 tablespoons butter or margarine, melted

¼ cup cornmeal

2 teaspoons sugar

Nutrition Information Per Serving:		
Calories: 180	From Fat:	100
Total Fat		11g
Saturated		4g
Cholesterol		10mg
Sodium		400mg
Total Carbohydrate		18g
Dietary Fiber		0g
Sugars		4g
Protein		4g

1) Heat oven to 375°F. Spray 10 regular-size muffin cups with cooking spray. Separate dough into 10 biscuits; separate each into 2 layers. Place 1 piece of cheese on bottom layer of each biscuit; place top layer over cheese and press edges together to seal.

2) Place melted butter in shallow bowl. In another shallow bowl, mix cornmeal and sugar. Dip each filled biscuit into butter; coat lightly with cornmeal mixture. Place each in muffin cup.

3) Bake 10 to 14 minutes or until light golden brown. If necessary, run knife around edge of each muffin cup; remove biscuits from cups. Serve warm.

HIGH ALTITUDE (3500-6500 FT.): In Step 3, bake 14 to 18 minutes; continue as directed above.

Gooey Caramel Apple Pull-Aparts

LISA MCDANIEL | HIGHLAND, ILLINOIS

PREP TIME: 10 MINUTES (READY IN 1 HOUR 20 MINUTES)
SERVINGS: 12

4 Nature Valley® pecan crunch crunchy granola bars (2 pouches from 8.9-oz. box), crushed (³/4 cup)*

¹/4 cup chopped pecans

1 teaspoon ground cinnamon

1 cup whipping cream

¹/2 cup packed light brown sugar

2 cans (17.5 oz. each) Pillsbury® Grands!® refrigerated cinnamon rolls with icing

1 medium Granny Smith apple, peeled, coarsely chopped (about 1¹/4 cups)

1) Heat oven to 350°F. Spray 12-cup fluted tube cake pan with cooking spray. In small bowl, mix crushed granola bars, pecans and ¹/2 teaspoon of the cinnamon. Sprinkle mixture evenly in bottom of pan.

2) In large bowl, mix whipping cream, brown sugar and remaining ¹/2 teaspoon cinnamon. Separate both cans of dough into 10 rolls; set icing aside. Cut each roll into quarters. Stir roll pieces and apples into whipping cream mixture to coat. Spoon mixture into pan; spread evenly.

3) Bake 50 to 60 minutes or until deep golden brown. Immediately place heatproof serving plate or platter upside down over pan; turn plate and pan over (do not remove pan). Cool 5 minutes. Remove pan; scrape any remaining topping in pan onto coffee cake. Cool 5 minutes longer. Drizzle reserved icing over top. Serve warm.

*NOTE: To easily crush granola bars, do not unwrap; use rolling pin to crush bars.

HIGH ALTITUDE (3500-6500 FT.): Heat oven to 375°F. Bake 40 to 50 minutes.

Nutrition Information Per Serving:

Calories:	420	From Fat:	160
Total Fat			18g
Saturated			7g
Cholesterol			20mg
Sodium			600mg
Total Carbohydrate			60g
Dietary Fiber			2g
Sugars			32g
Protein			6g

White Chocolate-Iced Blueberry Loaf

PREP TIME: 10 MINUTES (READY IN 3 HOURS 10 MINUTES)
SERVINGS: 12 SLICES

 EASY

LOAF

2½ cups all-purpose flour

1 cup granulated sugar

3 teaspoons baking powder

½ teaspoon salt

¼ teaspoon ground allspice, if desired

1 cup buttermilk*

¼ cup butter or margarine, melted

2 eggs

1½ cups fresh or frozen (do not thaw) blueberries

½ cup chopped pecans

ICING

¼ cup white vanilla baking chips

3 tablespoons powdered sugar

1 to 2 tablespoons milk

1) Heat oven to 350°F. Grease bottom only of 9x5-inch loaf pan. In large bowl, mix flour, sugar, baking powder, salt and allspice with spoon. Beat in buttermilk, butter and eggs until blended. Stir in blueberries and pecans. Spread batter in pan.

2) Bake 1 hour 15 minutes to 1 hour 20 minutes or until toothpick inserted in center comes out clean. Cool in pan on wire rack 10 minutes.

3) Run knife around edges of pan to loosen loaf. Remove loaf from pan; place on wire rack. Cool completely, about 1 hour 30 minutes.

4) In small microwavable bowl, microwave vanilla baking chips on High 30 seconds. Stir until melted; if necessary, microwave in additional 10-second increments until melted. Beat in powdered sugar and enough milk until smooth and desired drizzling consistency. Drizzle icing over loaf. Let stand until icing is set before storing.

*NOTE: To substitute for buttermilk, use 1 tablespoon vinegar or lemon juice plus milk to make 1 cup.

HIGH ALTITUDE (3500-6500 FT.): Decrease baking powder to 1-1/2 teaspoons.

Nutrition Information Per Serving:		
Calories: 290	From Fat:	90
Total Fat		9g
Saturated		3g
Cholesterol		45mg
Sodium		280mg
Total Carbohydrate		45g
Dietary Fiber		2g
Sugars		23g
Protein		5g

tip

This delicious loaf makes a great gift. Place toothpicks into the top surface of the loaf to protect the icing from sticking. Then wrap the loaf in colored cellophane and tie with a pretty bow.

Almond Scones

PREP TIME: 20 MINUTES (READY IN 50 MINUTES)
SERVINGS: 12

 EASY

2 cups all-purpose flour

¼ cup sugar

2 teaspoons baking powder

¼ teaspoon salt

6 tablespoons butter

⅓ cup almond paste, cut into small
  pieces

½ cup milk

¼ teaspoon almond extract

1 egg, beaten

  Sliced almonds, if desired

  Coarse sugar, if desired

1) Heat oven to 400°F. Lightly spray cookie sheet with cooking spray. In large bowl, combine flour, sugar, baking powder and salt; mix well. With pastry blender or fork, cut in butter until mixture resembles coarse crumbs. Stir in almond paste, separating pieces to coat each with flour mixture.

2) In small bowl, combine milk, almond extract and egg; blend well. Add to flour mixture. Stir just until dry ingredients are moistened.

3) On floured surface, gently knead dough about 6 times. Divide dough in half; shape each into ball. Pat each ball into 5-inch round with center higher than edges. Brush with milk; sprinkle with almonds and sugar. Cut each round into 6 wedges. Place wedges 1 inch apart on sprayed cookie sheet.

4) Bake at 400°F. for 13 to 15 minutes or until light golden brown. Cool 10 minutes before serving.

HIGH ALTITUDE (3500-6500 FT.): Increase flour to 2-1/3 cups. Bake as directed above.

Nutrition Information Per Serving:

Calories:	190	From Fat:	70
Total Fat			8g
Saturated			4g
Cholesterol			35mg
Sodium			180mg
Total Carbohydrate			24g
Dietary Fiber			1g
Sugars			8g
Protein			4g

Easy Cherry-Almond Coffee Cake

PREP TIME: 10 MINUTES (READY IN 50 MINUTES)
SERVINGS: 6

 EASY

1 can (12.4 oz.) Pillsbury® refrigerated cinnamon rolls with icing

1 cup cherry pie filling (from 21-oz. can)

1 tablespoon slivered almonds

1) Heat oven to 375°F. Spray 9-inch round cake pan with cooking spray. Separate dough into 8 rolls. Cut each into 4 pieces; place rounded side down in pan. Spoon pie filling over dough. Sprinkle with almonds.

2) Bake 25 to 35 minutes or until deep golden brown. Cool in pan 3 minutes. Place wire rack upside down over pan; turn rack and pan over. Remove pan. Place heatproof plate upside down over coffee cake; turn over.

3) Remove cover from icing; microwave on High 3 to 7 seconds. Stir icing; drizzle desired amount over warm coffee cake. Cut into wedges; serve warm.

HIGH ALTITUDE (3500-6500 FT.): No change.

Nutrition Information Per Serving:

Calories:	250	From Fat:	70
Total Fat			8g
Saturated			2g
Cholesterol			0mg
Sodium			450mg
Total Carbohydrate			43g
Dietary Fiber			2g
Sugars			24g
Protein			3g

Fruit and Nut Pastries

ARLENE SWIATEK GILLEN | HOLLAND, NEW YORK

PREP TIME: 25 MINUTES (READY IN 1 HOUR)
SERVINGS: 7 PASTRIES

PASTRIES

- ½ cup Progresso® plain bread crumbs
- 2 to 2½ tablespoons golden raisins
- 2 tablespoons packed light brown sugar
- 2 tablespoons Mounds® coconut flakes
- 2 tablespoons finely chopped walnuts
- 1 egg white
- ½ teaspoon vanilla
- 5 tablespoons apricot fruit spread
- 1 tablespoon powdered sugar
- 1 can (10.1 oz.) Pillsbury® Big & Flaky refrigerated crescent dinner rolls

GLAZE

- ½ cup powdered sugar
- ⅛ teaspoon vanilla
- 1½ to 1¾ teaspoons water

Nutrition Information Per Pastry:

Calories:	310	From Fat:	100
Total Fat			11g
Saturated			2.5g
Cholesterol			0mg
Sodium			390mg
Total Carbohydrate			48g
Dietary Fiber			2g
Sugars			26g
Protein			5g

1) Heat oven to 350°F. Line large cookie sheet with foil; lightly spray foil with cooking spray. In medium bowl, mix bread crumbs, raisins, brown sugar, coconut and walnuts.

2) In small bowl, beat egg white and ½ teaspoon vanilla with wire whisk about 30 seconds or until frothy. Stir into brown sugar mixture until well blended. In another small bowl, place fruit spread; stir with fork to break up any large pieces of fruit.

3) Cut 16x12-inch sheet of waxed paper; place on work surface. With fine strainer, sift 1 tablespoon powdered sugar onto paper. Unroll dough onto sugared paper; press into 14x7-inch rectangle, firmly pressing perforations to seal. Spread fruit spread over dough to edges. With pizza cutter, cut dough in half crosswise to make 2 (7-inch) squares.

4) Top 1 dough square with brown sugar mixture, spreading evenly over fruit spread to edges of dough. With waxed paper, lift remaining dough square and turn upside down over brown sugar mixture; lightly press. Remove paper. With pizza cutter, cut filled dough into 7 (1-inch-wide) strips. Carefully twist each strip 3 times; shape into loose knot, tucking ends under (dough will be sticky). Place 3 inches apart on cookie sheet.

5) Bake 17 to 25 minutes or until golden brown. Remove pastries from cookie sheet; place on wire racks. Cool 15 minutes.

6) In small bowl, blend ½ cup powdered sugar, ⅛ teaspoon vanilla and enough water for desired drizzling consistency. Drizzle glaze over cooled pastries. If desired, place small bowl of softened butter in center of serving platter; arrange pastries on platter around bowl.

*NOTE: To reheat 1 pastry, place in microwave on paper towel; microwave on High 15 to 20 seconds or until warm.

HIGH ALTITUDE (3500-6500 FT.): Bake 18 to 21 minutes.

Overnight Lemon Country Coffee Cake

PREP TIME: 15 MINUTES (READY IN 9 HOURS 10 MINUTES)
SERVINGS: 15

 EASY

COFFEE CAKE

- ½ cup margarine or butter, softened
- 1 cup granulated sugar
- 2 eggs
- 2 containers (6 oz. each) Yoplait® original lemon burst yogurt
- 2 teaspoons grated lemon peel
- 2⅓ cups all-purpose flour
- 1½ teaspoons baking powder
- ½ teaspoon salt
- ¼ teaspoon baking soda

TOPPING

- ¾ cup firmly packed brown sugar
- ¾ cup chopped pecans
- ½ teaspoon nutmeg

1) Spray bottom only of 13x9-inch pan with cooking spray. In large bowl, combine margarine and granulated sugar; beat until light and fluffy. Add eggs 1 at a time, beating well after each addition. Add yogurt and lemon peel; beat well.

2) Add flour, baking powder, salt and baking soda; beat at low speed until smooth. Spread batter in sprayed pan. Cover; refrigerate 8 hours or overnight.

3) In small resealable plastic bag, combine brown sugar, pecans and nutmeg; mix well. Refrigerate.

4) When ready to bake, let coffee cake stand at room temperature while heating oven to 350°F. Uncover coffee cake; sprinkle with topping.

5) Bake at 350°F. for 30 to 40 minutes or until toothpick inserted in center comes out clean. Cool 15 minutes. Serve warm.

HIGH ALTITUDE (3500-6500 FT.): Increase flour to 2-1/2 cups. Bake as directed above.

Nutrition Information Per Serving:

Calories:	290	From Fat:	100
Total Fat			11g
Saturated			2g
Cholesterol			30mg
Sodium			250mg
Total Carbohydrate			43g
Dietary Fiber			1g
Sugars			27g
Protein			5g

Ham and Swiss Sandwich Roll

PREP TIME: 10 MINUTES (READY IN 30 MINUTES)
SERVINGS: 6

 EASY

1 can (13.8 oz.) Pillsbury® refrigerated pizza crust

2 tablespoons honey-mustard

6 oz. thinly sliced or shaved cooked ham

6 slices ($^3/_4$ oz. each) Swiss cheese

1 egg, beaten

1 teaspoon sesame seed

Nutrition Information Per Serving:		
Calories: 320	From Fat: 100	
Total Fat		12g
Saturated		5g
Cholesterol		70mg
Sodium		990mg
Total Carbohydrate		35g
Dietary Fiber		1g
Sugars		7g
Protein		19g

tip

Ham with Swiss cheese is a great combination, but you can use any of your favorite cheeses in this hearty, hot sandwich roll. Try Colby-Monterey Jack, Cheddar or mozzarella.

1) Heat oven to 400°F. Spray cookie sheet with cooking spray or grease with shortening. Unroll dough onto cookie sheet. Starting at center, press out dough into 14x8-inch rectangle.

2) Spread honey-mustard over dough to within 1 inch of edges. Layer ham and cheese over mustard.

3) Fold long sides of dough over filling to center of rectangle; pinch to seal. Pinch short sides to seal and tuck under. Brush with egg; sprinkle with sesame seed.

4) Bake 16 to 18 minutes or until crust is golden brown. Cut into 6 pieces; serve warm.

HIGH ALTITUDE (3500-6500 FT.): Bake 18 to 20 minutes.

Pizza Biscuit Wreath

PREP TIME:	20 MINUTES (READY IN 40 MINUTES)
SERVINGS:	10 (2 BISCUITS EACH)

 EASY

2 cans (12 oz. each) Pillsbury® Golden Layers® refrigerated buttermilk biscuits

60 small slices (1½ inch) pepperoni (3½ oz.)

5 sticks (¾ oz. each) Colby-Monterey Jack cheese, each cut crosswise into 4 pieces

1 egg, beaten

2 tablespoons shredded Parmesan cheese

½ teaspoon Italian seasoning

1 can (8 oz.) pizza sauce

Nutrition Information Per Serving:

Calories:	350	From Fat:	190
Total Fat			21g
Saturated			7g
Cholesterol			40mg
Sodium			1090mg
Total Carbohydrate			30g
Dietary Fiber			1g
Sugars			8g
Protein			10g

1) Heat oven to 375°F. Spray large cookie sheet with cooking spray. Separate 1 can of dough into 10 biscuits; keep second can refrigerated. Press each biscuit into 3-inch round.

2) Place 3 pepperoni slices and 1 piece of cheese on each dough round. Wrap dough around filling, pinching edges to seal and form ball. Repeat with remaining can of dough, pepperoni and cheese.

3) Leaving a 4-inch hole in center, arrange 8 balls, seam side down and sides almost touching, into ring on cookie sheet. Arrange remaining 12 balls, sides almost touching, around outer edge of first ring. Brush rings with beaten egg. Sprinkle with Parmesan cheese and Italian seasoning.

4) Bake 18 to 20 minutes or until golden brown. Meanwhile, in small microwavable bowl, microwave pizza sauce, loosely covered, on High 45 to 60 seconds or until warm.

5) Carefully slide wreath from cookie sheet onto serving platter. Place bowl of pizza sauce in center of wreath. Garnish with fresh oregano, if desired. Serve warm.

HIGH ALTITUDE (3500-6500 FT.): Heat oven to 350°F. Bake 25 to 27 minutes.

Orange-Caramel Pecan Biscuits

PREP TIME: 10 MINUTES (READY IN 40 MINUTES)
SERVINGS: 6

 EASY

1 tablespoon butter, softened

½ cup butterscotch caramel ice cream topping

⅓ cup chopped pecans

2 teaspoons grated orange peel

6 Pillsbury® Home Baked Classics™ frozen buttermilk biscuits (from 25 oz. package)

Nutrition Information Per Serving:		
Calories: 320	From Fat:	140
Total Fat		15g
Saturated		4g
Cholesterol		5mg
Sodium		690mg
Total Carbohydrate		41g
Dietary Fiber		0g
Sugars		17g
Protein		5g

1) Heat oven to 375°F. With 1 tablespoon butter, generously butter bottom and sides of 9-inch round cake pan. Spread ice cream topping in buttered pan. Sprinkle with pecans and orange peel. Place frozen biscuits over pecans and orange peel.

2) Bake at 375°F. for 25 to 28 minutes or until golden brown and biscuits are no longer doughy. Immediately invert on serving platter; spread any topping remaining in pan over biscuits. Serve warm.

HIGH ALTITUDE (3500-6500 FT.): Bake at 400°F. for 25 to 28 minutes.

Crescent Hot Cross Buns

PREP TIME: 15 MINUTES (READY IN 40 MINUTES)
SERVINGS: 8

 EASY

BUNS

1 can (8 oz.) Pillsbury® refrigerated crescent dinner rolls

⅓ cup raisins

¼ teaspoon grated lemon peel, if desired

ICING

¼ cup powdered sugar

1 to 2 teaspoons milk

Nutrition Information Per Serving:		
Calories: 140	From Fat:	50
Total Fat		6g
Saturated		2g
Cholesterol		0mg
Sodium		220mg
Total Carbohydrate		20g
Dietary Fiber		0g
Sugars		9g
Protein		2g

1) Heat oven to 375°F. Unroll dough and separate into 8 triangles.

2) In small bowl, mix raisins and lemon peel; spoon about 1 teaspoon raisin mixture onto short side of each triangle. Gently wrap corners of dough over filling and roll to opposite point; pinch to seal. Place point side down on ungreased cookie sheet.

3) Bake 12 to 14 minutes or until golden brown. Remove from cookie sheet; place on wire rack. Cool 10 minutes.

4) In small bowl, mix powdered sugar and enough milk until smooth and drizzling consistency. With spoon, drizzle icing in cross shape on top of each bun.

HIGH ALTITUDE (3500-6500 FT.): No change.

Add a little extra color and a twist of flavor by substituting diced dried fruit and raisin mixture for the raisins.

Turkey Caesar Focaccia Wedges

PREP TIME: 10 MINUTES (READY IN 10 MINUTES)
SERVINGS: 6

 EASY

1 package (12 oz.) cheese or garlic focaccia bread (8 to 10 inch)

3 cups torn romaine lettuce

9 oz. cooked turkey, cut into bite-size strips (2 cups)

1/3 cup creamy Caesar dressing

1/4 cup grated Parmesan cheese

1/4 teaspoon coarse ground black pepper

Nutrition Information Per Serving:	
Calories: 320	From Fat: 140
Total Fat	15g
Saturated	4g
Cholesterol	45mg
Sodium	440mg
Total Carbohydrate	22g
Dietary Fiber	0g
Sugars	2g
Protein	22g

1) Cut focaccia bread in half horizontally; set aside. In large bowl, mix remaining ingredients.

2) Spoon turkey mixture evenly onto bottom half of bread. Cover with top half of bread. Cut into 6 wedges to serve.

HIGH ALTITUDE (3500-6500 FT.): No change.

Look for the garlic focaccia bread in the deli or bakery. Plain focaccia bread or a loaf of soft French bread can also be used for this sandwich.

Garlic, Chive and Cheese Bread

PREP TIME: 20 MINUTES (READY IN 20 MINUTES)
SERVINGS: 16

 EASY

1 container (8 oz.) garden vegetable cream cheese spread

2 tablespoons chopped fresh chives

1 small garlic clove, minced

1 loaf (16 oz.) French bread, split lengthwise

1) Heat gas or charcoal grill. In small bowl, mix cream cheese spread, chives and garlic.

2) When grill is heated, place bread halves, cut side down, on gas grill over medium heat or on charcoal grill over medium coals. Cook 1 to 2 minutes or until light golden brown.

3) Turn bread halves; spread cream cheese mixture on toasted sides of bread. Cook cheese side up 3 to 4 minutes longer or until thoroughly heated.

HIGH ALTITUDE (3500-6500 FT.): Cook over medium-low heat.

Nutrition Information Per Serving:

Calories:	120	From Fat:	45
Total Fat			5g
Saturated			3g
Cholesterol			15mg
Sodium			260mg
Total Carbohydrate			15g
Dietary Fiber			0g
Sugars			0g
Protein			4g

Raspberry-Nut Dreams

KATHY SWEETON | LONG BEACH, CALIFORNIA

PREP TIME: 25 MINUTES (READY IN 55 MINUTES)
SERVINGS: 16 SWEET ROLLS

½ cup salted roasted macadamia nuts

⅓ cup packed brown sugar

2 packages (3 oz. each) cream cheese, softened

1 cup Cascadian Farm® Organic frozen raspberries (from 10-oz. bag), thawed as directed on bag, drained and liquid reserved

1 can (16.3 oz.) Pillsbury® Grands!® Flaky Layers refrigerated buttermilk biscuits

⅓ cup Mounds® coconut flakes

1) Heat oven to 350°F. Lightly spray 16 regular-size muffin cups with cooking spray. In food processor, process macadamia nuts with on-and-off motions until coarsely chopped. Add brown sugar; process until combined. Place in small bowl; set aside.

2) In same food processor, process cream cheese, 2 tablespoons nut mixture and 1 to 2 tablespoons reserved raspberry liquid until smooth.

3) Separate dough into 8 biscuits; separate each into 2 layers, making a total of 16 rounds. Lightly press each round in bottom and up side of muffin cup. Spoon about ½ tablespoon cream cheese mixture into each dough-lined cup. Top each evenly with raspberries, 1 tablespoon remaining nut mixture and 1 teaspoon coconut.

4) Bake 14 to 22 minutes or until coconut is lightly browned. Cool in pan 5 minutes before serving.

HIGH ALTITUDE (3500-6500 FT.): No change.

Nutrition Information Per Sweet Roll:		
Calories: 190	From Fat: 100	
Total Fat	11g	
Saturated	4g	
Cholesterol	10mg	
Sodium	320mg	
Total Carbohydrate	19g	
Dietary Fiber	2g	
Sugars	8g	
Protein	3g	

Granola Streusel Cranberry Muffin Mix

PREP TIME: 10 MINUTES (READY IN 30 MINUTES)
SERVINGS: 12 MUFFINS

 EASY

MUFFIN MIX

- 2 cups all-purpose flour
- ³/4 cup sweetened dried cranberries
- ¹/2 cup sugar
- ¹/2 cup nonfat dry milk
- 3 teaspoons baking powder
- ¹/2 teaspoon pumpkin pie spice
- ¹/2 teaspoon salt

STREUSEL MIX

- 2 Nature Valley® oats 'n honey crunchy granola bars (1 pouch from 8.9-oz. box), finely crushed (about ¹/3 cup)
- 2 tablespoons sugar

TO MAKE MUFFINS:

- ³/4 cup water
- ¹/3 cup vegetable oil
- 1 egg, slightly beaten
- 2 tablespoons butter or margarine, melted

1) In large bowl, mix Muffin Mix ingredients. Spoon into jar with lid or resealable food-storage plastic bag; cover jar or seal bag. In another jar or bag, mix Streusel Mix ingredients; cover or seal.

2) To make muffins, heat oven to 375°F. Line 12 regular-size muffin cups with paper baking cups or spray bottoms only of muffin cups with cooking spray. In large bowl, mix Muffin Mix, water, oil and egg with spoon just until dry ingredients are moistened. Spoon batter evenly into muffin cups.

3) In small bowl, mix Streusel Mix with melted butter. Sprinkle mixture evenly over batter in cups; press in lightly.

4) Bake 14 to 18 minutes or until toothpick inserted in center comes out clean. Remove from muffin cups; serve warm.

HIGH ALTITUDE (3500-6500 FT.): No change.

Nutrition Information Per Serving:		
Calories: 250	From Fat:	80
Total Fat		9g
Saturated		2g
Cholesterol		25mg
Sodium		270mg
Total Carbohydrate		37g
Dietary Fiber		1g
Sugars		19g
Protein		4g

Be sure to attach the recipe when giving this mix as a gift. When baking these muffins, check for doneness at the minimum baking time. They're light in color when they're done.

Crunchy Oven French Toast

PREP TIME: 20 MINUTES (READY IN 2 HOURS 40 MINUTES)
SERVINGS: 4 (2 SLICES EACH)

 EASY

3 eggs

1 cup half-and-half

2 tablespoons sugar

1 teaspoon vanilla

¼ teaspoon salt

3 cups corn flakes cereal, crushed to 1 cup

8 (³/4-inch-thick) diagonally cut slices French bread

Strawberry syrup

Fresh strawberries, raspberries and/or blueberries

1) Grease 15x10x1-inch baking pan. In shallow bowl, combine eggs, half-and-half, sugar, vanilla and salt; beat well. Place crushed cereal in another shallow bowl. Dip each bread slice in egg mixture, making sure all egg mixture is absorbed. Coat each slice with crumbs. Place in greased pan; cover. Freeze 1 to 2 hours or until firm.

2) Heat oven to 425°F. Bake bread slices 15 to 20 minutes or until golden brown, turning once. Serve with syrup and strawberries. If desired, garnish with whipped topping.

Nutrition Information Per Serving:

Calories:	390	From Fat:	120
Total Fat			13g
Saturated			6g
Cholesterol			180mg
Sodium			690mg
Total Carbohydrate			55g
Dietary Fiber			2g
Sugars			11g
Protein			13g

Crescent Bear Claws

MAUREEN MCBRIDE | SAN JOSE, CALIFORNIA

Pillsbury Bake-Off

PREP TIME: 20 MINUTES (READY IN 45 MINUTES)
SERVINGS: 6 BEAR CLAWS

FILLING

1 egg

2 tablespoons milk

1 cup Progresso® plain bread crumbs

2 tablespoons granulated sugar

2 tablespoons butter, melted

1/4 cup water

2 teaspoons almond extract

GLAZE

1/2 cup granulated sugar

1/4 cup water

1 tablespoon light corn syrup

ROLLS

1 can (8 oz.) Pillsbury® refrigerated crescent dinner rolls

1/3 to 1/2 cup sliced almonds

ICING

1 cup powdered sugar

2 tablespoons water

1) Heat oven to 375°F. Line cookie sheet with cooking parchment paper. In medium bowl, beat egg lightly with wire whisk. Place half of egg (about 1½ tablespoons) in custard cup; beat in milk until blended and set aside. To remaining egg in bowl, stir in remaining filling ingredients until well blended.

2) Meanwhile, in 1-quart heavy saucepan, mix glaze ingredients. Heat to boiling. Remove from heat; cool while making rolls.

3) On lightly floured work surface, unroll dough; press into 12x8-inch rectangle, firmly pressing perforations to seal. Spoon filling into 12x2-inch strip lengthwise down center 1/3 of dough. Fold 1/3 of dough over filling. Fold filling-topped section over last 1/3 of dough so seam is on bottom of folded dough. With hand, gently flatten 1-inch-wide strip of dough along one long side of folded dough. Cut folded dough crosswise into 6 (2-inch) pastries. Along flattened edge of each pastry, cut 1-inch-long cuts about 1/2 inch apart.

4) Lightly brush egg-milk mixture over each pastry. Place almonds on plate; invert each pastry onto almonds and press gently so almonds stick to dough. Place almond side up on cookie sheet, spreading each cut slightly to form claw shape. Sprinkle remaining almonds over top of pastries.

5) Bake 15 to 18 minutes or until golden brown. Remove to wire rack; cool 5 minutes. Drizzle cooled glaze over each pastry. In another small bowl, mix icing ingredients until smooth (if icing is too thick, add 1/2 teaspoon water at a time until drizzling consistency). Drizzle icing over cooled pastries.

HIGH ALTITUDE (3500-6500 FT.): Bake 14 to 17 minutes.

Nutrition Information Per Bear Claw:

Calories: 470	From Fat: 150
Total Fat	16g
Saturated	6g
Cholesterol	45mg
Sodium	480mg
Total Carbohydrate	72g
Dietary Fiber	2g
Sugars	45g
Protein	8g

Two-Cheese and Ham French Loaf

PREP TIME: 10 MINUTES (READY IN 45 MINUTES)
SERVINGS: 6

 EASY

1 loaf (1 lb.) French bread

¼ cup honey mustard

8 slices (³/₄ to 1 oz. each) Swiss cheese

8 slices (³/₄ to 1 oz. each) Cheddar cheese

¼ lb. thinly sliced cooked ham

³/₄ cup strawberry or raspberry preserves

If 18-inch-wide foil is not available, use a double-fold seal to secure two 12-inch-wide sheets of foil together.

1) Heat oven to 375°F. Cut 30x18-inch sheet of heavy-duty foil. Cut French bread in half horizontally. Spread cut sides of bread halves with honey mustard. Place bottom half of bread on foil.

2) Layer Swiss and Cheddar cheeses, and ham evenly on bottom half of bread. Cover with top half of bread. Wrap tightly in foil using double-fold seals.

3) Bake 30 to 35 minutes or until cheeses are melted and loaf is thoroughly heated.

4) Carefully unwrap loaf to allow steam to escape. Cut loaf into 6 pieces; serve with preserves for dipping.

HIGH ALTITUDE (3500-6500 FT.): No change.

Nutrition Information Per Serving:

Calories:	560	From Fat:	190
Total Fat			21g
Saturated			12g
Cholesterol			65mg
Sodium			950mg
Total Carbohydrate			68g
Dietary Fiber			2g
Sugars			22g
Protein			26g

Easy Stromboli

PREP TIME: 15 MINUTES (READY IN 35 MINUTES)
SERVINGS: 4

 EASY

½ lb. lean (at least 80%) ground beef

1 can (13.8 oz.) Pillsbury® refrigerated pizza crust

⅓ cup pizza sauce

1 cup shredded mozzarella cheese (4 oz.)

¼ cup chopped green and/or red bell pepper, if desired

¼ teaspoon Italian seasoning

1) Heat oven to 400°F. Spray large cookie sheet with cooking spray. In 8-inch skillet, cook ground beef over medium-high heat, stirring frequently, until thoroughly cooked; drain. Set aside.

2) Unroll dough; place on cookie sheet. Starting at center, press out dough into 15x11-inch rectangle.

3) Spread pizza sauce over dough to within 2 inches of long sides and ½ inch of short sides. Spoon and spread cooked ground beef lengthwise down center, forming 3-inch-wide strip and to within ½ inch of short sides. Top with cheese, bell pepper and Italian seasoning. Fold long sides of dough up over filling; press edges and ends to seal.

4) Bake uncovered 15 to 20 minutes or until crust is golden brown. Cut stromboli into slices to serve.

HIGH ALTITUDE (3500-6500 FT.): In Step 4, bake uncovered 14 to 17 minutes.

Nutrition Information Per Serving:		
Calories: 430	From Fat: 140	
Total Fat		15g
Saturated		7g
Cholesterol		50mg
Sodium		970mg
Total Carbohydrate		49g
Dietary Fiber		2g
Sugars		7g
Protein		25g

Granola Sweet Rolls on a Stick

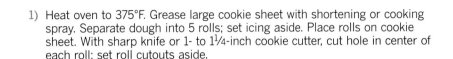

ROBIN ROSS | ST. PETERSBURG, FLORIDA

PREP TIME: 15 MINUTES (READY IN 40 MINUTES)
SERVINGS: 5

1 can (7.3 oz.) Pillsbury® refrigerated cinnamon rolls with icing (5 rolls)

1 container (6 oz.) Yoplait® Original 99% Fat Free French vanilla yogurt

4 Nature Valley® cinnamon crunchy granola bars (2 pouches from 8.9-oz. box), finely crushed (3/4 cup)*

1 large banana

5 round wooden sticks with one pointed end (10 inch)

Nutrition Information Per Serving:

Calories: 280	From Fat: 70
Total Fat	8g
Saturated	2g
Cholesterol	0mg
Sodium	430mg
Total Carbohydrate	46g
Dietary Fiber	2g
Sugars	24g
Protein	6g

1) Heat oven to 375°F. Grease large cookie sheet with shortening or cooking spray. Separate dough into 5 rolls; set icing aside. Place rolls on cookie sheet. With sharp knife or 1- to 1¼-inch cookie cutter, cut hole in center of each roll; set roll cutouts aside.

2) Place yogurt in shallow bowl. Place crushed granola bars in another shallow bowl. Peel banana; cut off small slice from each end and cut remaining banana into 5 equal pieces. Place banana pieces in yogurt; stir with spoon until coated. Roll banana pieces in crushed granola bars to coat well. Place 1 coated banana piece in hole in each roll, making hole larger if necessary. Set remaining yogurt aside.

3) Thread stick through side of each roll, through banana and out other side of roll. Slide roll down stick about ⅓ of length. Thread 1 reserved roll cutout onto stick.

4) Bake 12 to 17 minutes or until golden brown and dough around center of roll is no longer doughy. Cool 5 minutes. Meanwhile, stir reserved icing into remaining yogurt for sauce. If desired, cut off sharp ends from sticks with kitchen scissors. Loosen rolls and remove from cookie sheet. Serve with yogurt sauce for dipping.

*NOTE: To easily crush granola bars, do not unwrap; use rolling pin to crush bars.

HIGH ALTITUDE (3500-6500 FT.): No change.

Raspberry Cream Cheese Coffee Cake

PREP TIME: 25 MINUTES (READY IN 1 HOUR 35 MINUTES)
SERVINGS: 16

2¼ cups all-purpose flour

¾ cup sugar

¾ cup margarine or butter

½ teaspoon baking powder

½ teaspoon baking soda

¼ teaspoon salt

¾ cup sour cream

1 teaspoon almond extract

1 egg

1 package (8 oz.) cream cheese, softened

¼ cup sugar

1 egg

½ cup raspberry preserves

½ cup sliced almonds

1) Heat oven to 350°F. Grease and flour bottom and sides of 9 or 10-inch springform pan. In large bowl, combine flour and ¾ cup sugar; mix well. With pastry blender or fork, cut in margarine until mixture resembles coarse crumbs. Reserve 1 cup of crumb mixture.

2) To remaining crumb mixture, add baking powder, baking soda, salt, sour cream, almond extract and 1 egg; blend well. Spread batter over bottom and 2 inches up sides (about ¼ inch thick) of greased and floured pan.

3) In small bowl, combine cream cheese, ¼ cup sugar and 1 egg; blend well. Pour into batter-lined pan. Carefully spoon preserves evenly over cream cheese mixture. In another small bowl, combine reserved crumb mixture and sliced almonds. Sprinkle over preserves.

4) Bake at 350°F. for 45 to 55 minutes or until cream cheese filling is set and crust is deep golden brown. Cool 15 minutes; remove sides of pan. Serve warm or cool. Store in refrigerator.

HIGH ALTITUDE (3500-6500 FT.): No change.

Nutrition Information Per Serving:	
Calories: 320	From Fat: 160
Total Fat	18g
Saturated	7g
Cholesterol	50mg
Sodium	250mg
Total Carbohydrate	34g
Dietary Fiber	0g
Sugars	18g
Protein	5g

Banana Crème Pastries

JAIMIE CALTABELLATTA | MIDLAND PARK , NEW JERSEY

Pillsbury Bake-Off

PREP TIME: 15 MINUTES (READY IN 35 MINUTES)
SERVINGS: 2

1 can (4 oz.) Pillsbury® refrigerated crescent dinner rolls (4 rolls)

2 tablespoons finely chopped walnuts

1 tablespoon granulated sugar

1 teaspoon milk

1 container (6 oz.) Yoplait® Original 99% Fat Free banana crème yogurt

1 snack-size container (3.5 oz.) banana pudding

1 medium banana, sliced

Whipped cream topping (from aerosol can), if desired

Powdered sugar, if desired

1) Heat oven to 375°F. Spray cookie sheet with cooking spray. Unroll dough; separate into 4 triangles. On cookie sheet, make 2 kite shapes by placing longest sides of 2 dough triangles together; press edges to seal.

2) In small bowl, mix walnuts and granulated sugar. Lightly brush dough with milk; sprinkle each evenly with walnut mixture.

3) Bake 8 to 12 minutes or until bottoms are golden brown. Meanwhile, in another small bowl, mix yogurt and pudding until well blended. Stir in banana.

4) Remove pastries from oven. Immediately turn pastries over with pancake turner; gently fold each in half along sealed seam, walnut mixture side out. Remove from cookie sheet; place on wire rack. Cool completely, about 15 minutes.

5) To serve, place pastries on individual dessert plates; fill each with about ³/₄ cup yogurt mixture. Garnish each with dollop of whipped cream topping; sprinkle with powdered sugar.

HIGH ALTITUDE (3500-6500 FT.): No change.

Nutrition Information Per Serving:	
Calories: 500	From Fat: 180
Total Fat	20g
Saturated	5g
Cholesterol	5mg
Sodium	560mg
Total Carbohydrate	70g
Dietary Fiber	3g
Sugars	40g
Protein	11g

Comforting Casseroles

Hearty and homey, all-in-one
casserole dishes are oh-so-satisfying.

BARBEQUE PORK-CHEESY POTATO
BAKE
PG. 167

HOME-STYLE TURKEY AND
BISCUIT CASSEROLE
PG. 162

GREEK SHRIMP AND PASTA BAKE
PG. 163

PIZZA LASAGNA
PG. 158

Seafood Lasagna

PREP TIME: 35 MINUTES (READY IN 1 HOUR 55 MINUTES)
SERVINGS: 12

 LOW FAT

9 uncooked lasagna noodles

1 cup chicken broth

3 tablespoons cornstarch

3 cups milk

3 teaspoons dried dill weed

1 package (12 oz.) frozen cooked deveined shelled small shrimp, thawed, drained

1 box (9 oz.) Green Giant® frozen spinach, thawed, squeezed to drain

2 cups shredded Swiss cheese (8 oz.)

2 packages (8 oz. each) salad-style imitation crabmeat, chopped

1/2 cup shredded Parmesan cheese (2 oz.)

1) Cook and drain lasagna noodles as directed on package.

2) Meanwhile, heat oven to 350°F. In 2-quart saucepan, mix broth and cornstarch until smooth. Stir in milk and dill weed. Heat to boiling over medium-high heat, stirring constantly. Reduce heat to medium; cook 2 to 3 minutes, stirring constantly, until sauce is bubbly and slightly thickened.

3) In ungreased 13x9-inch (3-quart) glass baking dish, spread 1/2 cup of the sauce. Top with 3 cooked noodles. In medium bowl, mix shrimp, spinach and 1 cup of the sauce; spoon half of shrimp mixture over noodles, spreading evenly. Sprinkle with 2/3 cup of the Swiss cheese.

4) In another medium bowl, mix crabmeat and 1 cup of the sauce; spoon crabmeat mixture over cheese, spreading evenly. Top with 3 noodles. Spoon remaining shrimp mixture over noodles, spreading evenly. Sprinkle with 2/3 cup of the Swiss cheese. Top with remaining noodles and any remaining sauce.

5) Cover tightly with foil; bake 50 to 60 minutes or until hot and bubbly. Uncover; sprinkle with remaining 2/3 cup Swiss cheese and the Parmesan cheese. Bake 5 to 7 minutes longer or until cheese is melted. Let stand 10 minutes before serving. Garnish with dill weed, if desired.

HIGH ALTITUDE (3500-6500 FT.): No change.

Nutrition Information Per Serving:		
Calories: 260	From Fat:	80
Total Fat		9g
Saturated		5g
Cholesterol		90mg
Sodium		700mg
Total Carbohydrate		21g
Dietary Fiber		1g
Sugars		4g
Protein		24g

Nacho Casserole

PREP TIME: 20 MINUTES (READY IN 1 HOUR)
SERVINGS: 6 (1-1/4 CUPS EACH)

 EASY

1 lb. lean (at least 80%) ground beef

1 tablespoon Old El Paso® taco seasoning mix (from 1.25-oz. package)

$1/3$ cup sweet-spicy French dressing

1 can ($10^3/_4$ oz.) condensed fiesta nacho cheese soup

1 can (14.5 oz.) Mexican-style diced tomatoes, undrained

1 can (15 oz.) Progresso® pinto beans, drained, rinsed

$1 1/2$ cups shredded Cheddar cheese (6 oz.)

4 cups nacho-flavored tortilla chips (about 4 oz.), coarsely crushed (2 cups)

1 cup shredded lettuce

1 can ($2^1/_4$ oz.) sliced ripe olives, drained, if desired

Nutrition Information Per Serving:

Calories:	550	From Fat:	270
Total Fat			31g
Saturated			12g
Cholesterol			80mg
Sodium			1170mg
Total Carbohydrate			40g
Dietary Fiber			8g
Sugars			8g
Protein			29g

1) Heat oven to 375°F. In 10-inch skillet, cook ground beef over medium-high heat, stirring frequently, until thoroughly cooked; drain. Stir in taco seasoning mix, dressing and soup. Spoon evenly into ungreased 8-inch square (2-quart) glass baking dish.

2) Spread tomatoes and beans on top of beef mixture. Sprinkle cheese evenly over top. Cut 12x9-inch sheet of foil; spray with cooking spray. Cover dish with foil, sprayed side down.

3) Bake 30 minutes. Uncover dish; bake 8 to 10 minutes longer or until edges are bubbly. Top with chips, lettuce and olives before serving.

HIGH ALTITUDE (3500-6500 FT.): In Step 3, bake covered 40 minutes. Uncover dish; continue as directed above.

Speedy Enchilada Bake

PREP TIME: 15 MINUTES (READY IN 55 MINUTES)
SERVINGS: 6 (1 CUP EACH)

 EASY

1 cup chopped Italian plum tomatoes (3 medium)

1 can (11 oz.) Green Giant® Mexicorn® whole kernel corn with red and green peppers

1 can (10 oz.) Old El Paso® enchilada sauce

1 container (18 oz.) refrigerated taco sauce with seasoned ground beef

4 cups small round corn tortilla chips (5 oz.)

2 cups shredded Cheddar cheese (8 oz.)

$1/4$ cup sliced green onions (4 medium)

1) Heat oven to 375°F. Spray 8-inch square (2-quart) glass baking dish with cooking spray. In medium bowl, mix tomatoes, corn and enchilada sauce.

2) In baking dish, layer half of the taco sauce with ground beef, $1^1/2$ cups of the chips, $1/2$ cup of the cheese and half of corn mixture. Top with remaining taco sauce with ground beef, $1^1/2$ cups chips, $1/2$ cup cheese and remaining corn mixture.

3) Sprinkle with remaining 1 cup cheese and the onions. Arrange remaining 1 cup chips upright around edge of dish, overlapping as necessary.

4) Bake uncovered 35 to 40 minutes or until bubbly and thoroughly heated.

HIGH ALTITUDE (3500-6500 FT.): Heat oven to 400°F.; continue as directed above.

Nutrition Information Per Serving:

Calories:	460	From Fat:	240
Total Fat			26g
Saturated			11g
Cholesterol			60mg
Sodium			1200mg
Total Carbohydrate			35g
Dietary Fiber			3g
Sugars			6g
Protein			22g

Doubly Cheesy Ham Divan Bake

PREP TIME: 25 MINUTES (READY IN 55 MINUTES)
SERVINGS: 6 (1-1/4 CUPS EACH)

3 cups uncooked medium egg
noodles (6 oz.)

2 boxes (10 oz. each) Green Giant®
frozen broccoli & cheese flavored sauce

2 cups cubed cooked ham

1 cup finely shredded Cheddar-
American cheese blend (4 oz.)

1 cup milk

¼ teaspoon pepper

1 jar (2.5 oz.) Green Giant® sliced
mushrooms, drained

¾ cup coarsely crushed bite-size
cheese crackers

Nutrition Information Per Serving:

Calories:	340	From Fat:	150
Total Fat			16g
Saturated			7g
Cholesterol			75mg
Sodium			1670mg
Total Carbohydrate			26g
Dietary Fiber			3g
Sugars			6g
Protein			22g

1) In 4-quart saucepan or Dutch oven, cook noodles as directed on package. Drain; return to Dutch oven.

2) Meanwhile, heat oven to 350°F. Spray 8-inch square (2-quart) glass baking dish with cooking spray. Cut small slit in top of each pouch of vegetables; place both on microwavable plate. Microwave on High 4 to 5 minutes or until broccoli is crisp-tender.

3) Into cooked noodles in Dutch oven, gently stir broccoli with cheese sauce, ham, cheese, milk, pepper and mushrooms. Spoon into baking dish.

4) Bake uncovered 20 to 30 minutes or until thoroughly heated. Sprinkle crushed crackers over top before serving.

HIGH ALTITUDE (3500-6500 FT.): Heat oven to 375°F. In Step 4, cover baking dish with sprayed foil, sprayed side down; bake covered 20 minutes. Uncover dish; bake 5 to 10 minutes longer or until thoroughly heated. Continue as directed above.

Baked Chicken Nugget Spaghetti

PREP TIME: 15 MINUTES (READY IN 35 MINUTES)
SERVINGS: 4 (1-3/4 CUPS EACH)

 EASY

8 oz. uncooked spaghetti, broken in half

1 jar (26 to 28 oz. tomato pasta sauce

1 box (11 oz.) frozen breaded chicken breast nuggets

1½ cups shredded mozzarella cheese (6 oz.)

Nutrition Information Per Serving:

Calories:	770	From Fat:	250
Total Fat			28g
Saturated			10g
Cholesterol			60mg
Sodium			1780mg
Total Carbohydrate			95g
Dietary Fiber			6g
Sugars			14g
Protein			33g

1) In 3-quart saucepan, cook spaghetti as directed on package. Drain; return to saucepan.

2) Meanwhile, heat oven to 400°F. Spray 13x9-inch (3-quart) glass baking dish with cooking spray.

3) Stir pasta sauce into cooked spaghetti. Pour into baking dish, spreading evenly to cover bottom of dish. Arrange frozen chicken nuggets in single layer over spaghetti mixture.

4) Bake uncovered 8 minutes. Remove from oven. Turn chicken nuggets over; sprinkle cheese over top.

5) Return to oven; bake 6 to 8 minutes longer or until chicken is thoroughly heated and cheese is melted.

HIGH ALTITUDE (3500-6500 FT.): In Step 4, bake uncovered 10 minutes. In Step 5, bake 10-12 minutes longer.

Pineapple-Black Bean Enchiladas

MARY IOVINELLI BUESCHER | BLOOMINGTON, MINNESOTA

PREP TIME: 30 MINUTES (READY IN 1 HOUR 10 MINUTES)
SERVINGS: 8

2 teaspoons vegetable oil

1 large yellow onion, chopped (about 1 cup)

1 medium red bell pepper, chopped (about 1 cup)

1 can (20 oz.) pineapple tidbits in juice, drained, 1/3 cup juice reserved

1 can (15 oz.) Progresso® black beans, drained, rinsed

1 can (4.5 oz.) Old El Paso® chopped green chiles

1 teaspoon salt

1/2 cup chopped fresh cilantro

3 cups shredded reduced-fat Cheddar cheese (12 oz.)

1 can (10 oz.) Old El Paso® mild enchilada sauce

8 whole wheat flour tortillas (8 or 9 inch)

1/2 cup reduced-fat sour cream

8 teaspoons chopped fresh cilantro

1) Heat oven to 350°F. Spray 13x9-inch (3-quart) glass baking dish with cooking spray. In 12-inch nonstick skillet, heat oil over medium heat. Add onion and bell pepper; cook 4 to 5 minutes or until softened. Stir in pineapple, beans, green chiles and salt. Cook and stir until thoroughly heated. Remove skillet from heat. Stir in 1/2 cup cilantro and 2 cups of the cheese.

2) Spoon and spread 1 tablespoon enchilada sauce onto each tortilla. Spoon about 3/4 cup vegetable mixture over sauce on each. Roll up tortillas; place seam side down in baking dish.

3) In small bowl, mix reserved 1/3 cup pineapple juice and remaining enchilada sauce; pour over entire surface of enchiladas in dish. Sprinkle with remaining 1 cup cheese. Spray sheet of foil large enough to cover baking dish with cooking spray; place sprayed side down over baking dish and seal tightly.

4) Bake 35 to 40 minutes, removing foil during last 5 to 10 minutes of baking, until cheese is melted and sauce is bubbly. Top each baked enchilada with 1 tablespoon sour cream and and 1 teaspoon cilantro.

HIGH ALTITUDE (3500-6500 FT.): Bake 40 to 45 minutes, removing foil during last 5 to 10 minutes of baking.

Nutrition Information Per Serving:		
Calories: 330	From Fat:	70
Total Fat		7g
Saturated		3g
Cholesterol		15mg
Sodium		1110mg
Total Carbohydrate		48g
Dietary Fiber		7g
Sugars		17g
Protein		19g

Lasagna Roll-Ups

PREP TIME: 30 MINUTES (READY IN 1 HOUR 20 MINUTES)
SERVINGS: 8

8 uncooked lasagna noodles

1/2 lb. lean ground turkey

2 cloves garlic, minced

1 jar (26 oz.) tomato pasta sauce

2 teaspoons Italian seasoning

1/2 teaspoon fennel seed, if desired

1 cup part-skim ricotta or cottage cheese

1/2 cup shredded carrot (1 small)

1 box (9 oz.) Green Giant® frozen spinach, thawed, drained and squeezed dry

2 egg whites or 1 egg

1 cup shredded mozzarella cheese (4 oz.)

1) Heat oven to 350°F. Cook lasagna noodles as directed on package. Drain; rinse with hot water.

2) Meanwhile, in 10-inch skillet, cook ground turkey and garlic over medium-high heat, stirring frequently, until turkey is no longer pink; drain, if necessary. Stir in pasta sauce, Italian seasoning and fennel. Reduce heat to low; simmer uncovered about 15 minutes, stirring occasionally.

3) In small bowl, mix ricotta cheese, carrot, spinach and egg whites. Spread each cooked lasagna noodle with generous 1/4 cup spinach filling to within 1 inch of one short end. Roll up firmly toward unfilled end.

4) Reserve 1 1/2 cups sauce. In ungreased 12x8-inch (2-quart) glass baking dish, pour remaining sauce. Arrange roll-ups, seam side down, in sauce. Pour reserved sauce over roll-ups.

5) Cover tightly with foil; bake 30 to 40 minutes or until hot and bubbly. Sprinkle with mozzarella cheese; bake uncovered 3 to 5 minutes longer or until cheese is melted. Let stand 5 minutes before serving.

HIGH ALTITUDE (3500-6500 FT.): Heat oven to 375°F.

Nutrition Information Per Serving:		
Calories:	320	From Fat: 90
Total Fat		11g
Saturated		4.5g
Cholesterol		35mg
Sodium		700mg
Total Carbohydrate		37g
Dietary Fiber		3g
Sugars		8g
Protein		19g

Chicken Dijon Shepherd's Pie

PREP TIME: 20 MINUTES (READY IN 50 MINUTES)
SERVINGS: 5 (1-1/3 CUPS EACH)

 EASY

FILLING

- 1 lb. boneless skinless chicken breasts, cut into $1/2$-inch pieces
- 1 cup coarsely chopped onions (2 medium)
- 2 cups Green Giant® frozen mixed vegetables (from 1-lb. bag)
- 1 jar (12 oz.) chicken gravy
- $1/2$ cup milk
- 1 tablespoon Dijon mustard
- $1/4$ teaspoon dried thyme leaves

TOPPING

- 1 $1/4$ cups water
- $3/4$ cup milk
- $1/4$ cup sour cream
- $1/2$ teaspoon garlic salt
- 2 cups plain mashed potato mix (dry)
- Paprika

1) Heat oven to 350°F. In 12-inch nonstick skillet, cook chicken and onions, stirring occasionally, until chicken is browned and no longer pink in center.

2) Stir in remaining filling ingredients. Spoon into ungreased 8-inch square (2-quart) glass baking dish.

3) In 2-quart saucepan, heat water to boiling. Remove from heat. Stir in remaining topping ingredients except paprika. Spoon topping over chicken mixture; sprinkle with paprika.

4) Bake uncovered 25 to 30 minutes or until bubbly.

HIGH ALTITUDE (3500-6500 FT.): Thaw and drain frozen vegetables before using; continue as directed above.

Nutrition Information Per Serving:

Calories:	350	From Fat:	100
Total Fat			11g
Saturated			4g
Cholesterol			70mg
Sodium			690mg
Total Carbohydrate			35g
Dietary Fiber			5g
Sugars			9g
Protein			28g

This traditional English casserole is topped with mashed potatoes. Serve chocolate-dipped shortbread cookies for dessert.

Garlic-Herb Cheesy Potatoes

PREP TIME: 15 MINUTES (READY IN 1 HOUR 10 MINUTES)
SERVINGS: 18 (1/2 CUP EACH)

 EASY

$\frac{1}{2}$ cup butter or margarine, melted

2 cups herb-seasoned croutons, coarsely crushed

1 bag (32 oz.) frozen southern-style diced hash brown potatoes, thawed

2 cups shredded Cheddar cheese (8 oz.)

1 cup chive-and-onion sour cream potato topper

$\frac{1}{4}$ cup chopped onion ($\frac{1}{2}$ onion)

$\frac{1}{4}$ teaspoon pepper

1 can ($10\frac{3}{4}$ oz.) condensed cream of mushroom soup

1 container (5.2 to 6.5 oz.) garlic-and-herb spreadable cheese

1) Heat oven to 350°F. Spray 13x9-inch (3-quart) glass baking dish with cooking spray. In small bowl, mix $\frac{1}{4}$ cup of the melted butter and the crushed croutons; set aside.

2) In large bowl, mix remaining $\frac{1}{4}$ cup melted butter and all remaining ingredients. Spoon into baking dish, spreading evenly.

3) Bake 40 minutes or until browned and bubbly around edges. Sprinkle crouton mixture over potato mixture; bake 10 to 15 minutes longer or until topping is browned.

HIGH ALTITUDE (3500-6500 FT.): In Step 3, cover baking dish with foil; bake 40 minutes. Remove foil and add crouton mixture; bake 15 to 20 minutes longer.

Nutrition Information Per Serving:

Calories:	250	From Fat:	150
Total Fat			16g
Saturated			9g
Cholesterol			40mg
Sodium			370mg
Total Carbohydrate			20g
Dietary Fiber			2g
Sugars			2g
Protein			6g

Pizza Lasagna

PREP TIME: 45 MINUTES (READY IN 1 HOUR 30 MINUTES)
SERVINGS: 8

9 uncooked lasagna noodles

1 can (15 oz.) pizza sauce

1 can (14.5 oz.) diced tomatoes with green pepper and onion, undrained

1 container (15 oz.) ricotta cheese

1 teaspoon Italian seasoning

2 cups shredded mozzarella cheese (8 oz.)

2 packages ($3\frac{1}{2}$ oz. each) pepperoni slices

1 jar (4.5 oz.) Green Giant® sliced mushrooms, drained

1 can ($2\frac{1}{4}$ oz.) sliced ripe olives, drained

$\frac{1}{2}$ cup chopped green bell pepper ($\frac{1}{2}$ medium)

2 tablespoons grated Parmesan cheese

1) Cook lasagna noodles as directed on package; drain.

2) Meanwhile, heat oven to 350°F. Spray 12x8-inch (2-quart) glass baking dish with cooking spray. In 2-quart saucepan, mix pizza sauce and tomatoes. Cook over medium heat, stirring frequently, until thoroughly heated. In medium bowl, mix ricotta cheese and Italian seasoning.

3) Spread $\frac{1}{4}$ cup pizza sauce mixture in bottom of baking dish. Arrange 3 cooked noodles over sauce. Spoon and spread half of ricotta mixture over noodles. Top with $\frac{1}{2}$ cup of the mozzarella cheese, 1 cup sauce mixture, $\frac{1}{3}$ each of the pepperoni slices, mushrooms, olives and bell pepper. Repeat layers once.

4) Top with remaining noodles, sauce mixture, mozzarella cheese, pepperoni slices, mushrooms, olives and bell pepper. Sprinkle Parmesan cheese over top.

5) Bake uncovered 30 to 35 minutes or until bubbly. Let stand 15 minutes before serving.

HIGH ALTITUDE (3500-6500 FT.): Heat oven to 375°F. In Step 5, cover baking dish with sprayed foil, sprayed side down. Bake 45 minutes. Uncover dish; bake 5 to 10 minutes longer or until bubbly. Continue as directed above.

Nutrition Information Per Serving:

Calories:	430	From Fat:	200
Total Fat			23g
Saturated			11g
Cholesterol			55mg
Sodium			1340mg
Total Carbohydrate			32g
Dietary Fiber			3g
Sugars			8g
Protein			24g

Zucchini 'n Hamburger Casserole

PREP TIME: 25 MINUTES (READY IN 1 HOUR 20 MINUTES)
SERVINGS: 6 (1-1/2 CUPS EACH)

1 lb. lean (at least 80%) ground beef

1 medium onion, chopped (1/2 cup)

1/2 teaspoon salt

1/8 teaspoon pepper

3/4 cup uncooked medium-grain white rice

1 cup water

1 medium zucchini, cut into 1/4-inch-thick slices (2 cups)

1 large tomato, chopped (1 cup)

1 can (19 oz.) Progresso® Vegetable Classics tomato basil soup

2 cups shredded mozzarella cheese (8 oz.)

1) Heat oven to 375°F. Spray 13x9-inch (3-quart) glass baking dish with cooking spray. In 10-inch skillet, cook ground beef and onion over medium-high heat, stirring frequently, until beef is thoroughly cooked; drain. Sprinkle with salt and pepper.

2) Place rice and water in baking dish; stir to mix. Layer cooked ground beef, zucchini and tomato over rice. Pour soup over top. Cut 16x12-inch sheet of foil; spray with cooking spray. Cover dish with foil, sprayed side down.

3) Bake 40 minutes. Uncover dish; sprinkle cheese over top. Bake uncovered 10 to 15 minutes longer or until edges are bubbly and cheese is lightly browned.

HIGH ALTITUDE (3500-6500 FT.): In Step 3, bake covered 45 minutes. Uncover dish; continue as directed above.

Nutrition Information Per Serving:		
Calories: 410	From Fat:	160
Total Fat		17g
Saturated		8g
Cholesterol		65mg
Sodium		830mg
Total Carbohydrate		36g
Dietary Fiber		2g
Sugars		7g
Protein		27g

Mile-High Mexican Torta

PREP TIME: 25 MINUTES (READY IN 50 MINUTES)
SERVINGS: 6

1   lb. lean (at least 80%) ground beef

1   can (14.5 oz.) diced tomatoes with sweet onions, drained

1   can (15 oz.) spicy chili beans, undrained

4   tablespoons chopped fresh cilantro

1/2 cup sour cream

1   tablespoon Old El Paso® taco seasoning mix (from 1.25-oz. package)

3   Old El Paso® flour tortillas for burritos, 8 inch (from 11.5-oz. package)

2   cups finely shredded taco-flavored cheese blend (8 oz.)

1) Heat oven to 375°F. Spray 9-inch glass pie pan with cooking spray. In 12-inch nonstick skillet, cook ground beef over medium-high heat, stirring occasionally, until thoroughly cooked; drain. Stir in tomatoes, chili beans and 2 tablespoons of the cilantro.

2) Meanwhile, in small bowl, mix sour cream and taco seasoning mix.

3) Place 1 flour tortilla in bottom of pie pan. Spread about 2$\frac{1}{2}$ tablespoons sour cream mixture over tortilla. Top with $\frac{1}{3}$ of ground beef mixture and $\frac{1}{2}$ cup of the cheese. Repeat layers 2 more times. Sprinkle with remaining cheese.

4) Bake uncovered 20 to 25 minutes or until thoroughly heated and cheese is melted. Sprinkle with remaining 2 tablespoons cilantro before serving; cut into wedges.

HIGH ALTITUDE (3500-6500 FT.): Use deep-dish 9-inch glass pie pan. In Step 4, bake uncovered 30 to 35 minutes; continue as directed above.

Nutrition Information Per Serving:		
Calories: 490	From Fat: 250	
Total Fat		28g
Saturated		14g
Cholesterol		100mg
Sodium		1100mg
Total Carbohydrate		31g
Dietary Fiber		4g
Sugars		5g
Protein		30g

Speedy Ravioli Bake

PREP TIME: 20 MINUTES (READY IN 30 MINUTES)
SERVINGS: 6 (1 CUP EACH)

 EASY

2 packages (9 oz. each) refrigerated cheese-filled ravioli

1 jar (25 to 26 oz.) chunky tomato pasta sauce

1 teaspoon dried basil leaves

2 cups shredded mozzarella cheese (8 oz.)

Nutrition Information Per Serving:	
Calories: 400	From Fat: 170
Total Fat	19g
Saturated	9g
Cholesterol	105mg
Sodium	1480mg
Total Carbohydrate	37g
Dietary Fiber	2g
Sugars	10g
Protein	21g

1) Heat oven to 400°F. In 3-quart saucepan or 4-quart Dutch oven, cook ravioli as directed on package; drain and set aside.

2) In same saucepan, mix pasta sauce and basil. Cook over medium heat 5 minutes, stirring occasionally, until thoroughly heated. Stir in cooked ravioli. Pour into ungreased 13x9-inch (3-quart) glass baking dish. Sprinkle cheese over top.

3) Bake uncovered 10 minutes or until sauce is bubbly and cheese is melted.

HIGH ALTITUDE (3500-6500 FT.): No change.

Make-Ahead Pizza Casserole

PREP TIME: 20 MINUTES (READY IN 9 HOURS 40 MINUTES)
SERVINGS: 6 (1-1/3 CUPS EACH)

 EASY

1 lb. mild Italian pork sausage

2 cups water

1 can (15 oz.) pizza sauce

1 can (14.5 oz.) diced tomatoes with sweet onion, undrained

4 cups uncooked rotini pasta (10 oz.)

1 can (2 1/4 oz.) sliced ripe olives, drained

1 1/2 cups shredded mozzarella or pizza cheese blend (6 oz.)

Nutrition Information Per Serving:	
Calories: 500	From Fat: 200
Total Fat	22g
Saturated	9g
Cholesterol	60mg
Sodium	1250mg
Total Carbohydrate	50g
Dietary Fiber	5g
Sugars	8g
Protein	26g

1) In 10-inch skillet, cook sausage over medium-high heat 8 to 10 minutes, stirring frequently, until no longer pink; drain.

2) In ungreased 13x9-inch (3-quart) glass baking dish, mix water, pizza sauce and tomatoes. Stir in cooked sausage, uncooked pasta and olives (pasta should be completely covered with sauce). Cover tightly with foil; refrigerate at least 8 hours or overnight.

3) When ready to bake, heat oven to 350°F. Stir casserole; cover with foil and bake 1 hour to 1 hour 15 minutes or until bubbly.

4) Uncover baking dish; stir mixture. Sprinkle with cheese; bake uncovered 5 minutes longer or until cheese is melted.

HIGH ALTITUDE (3500-6500 FT.): No change.

Home-Style Turkey and Biscuit Casserole

PREP TIME: 15 MINUTES (READY IN 50 MINUTES)
SERVINGS: 4

 EASY

1 can (10³/₄ oz.) condensed cream of celery soup

¹/₂ cup milk

2 cups Green Giant® frozen mixed vegetables (from 1-lb. bag)

2 cups cubed cooked turkey

1 cup chive-and-onion sour cream

¹/₄ teaspoon poultry seasoning

4 Pillsbury® Oven Baked frozen buttermilk biscuits (from 25-oz. bag)

Nutrition Information Per Serving:	
Calories: 560	From Fat: 270
Total Fat	30g
Saturated	12g
Cholesterol	105mg
Sodium	1240mg
Total Carbohydrate	42g
Dietary Fiber	5g
Sugars	11g
Protein	30g

1) Heat oven to 375°F. Spray 8-inch square (2-quart) glass baking dish with cooking spray. In 2-quart saucepan, mix soup, milk and vegetables. Heat to boiling over medium heat, stirring occasionally to prevent sticking.

2) Stir in turkey, sour cream and poultry seasoning. Cook and stir just until thoroughly heated. Spoon into baking dish. Arrange frozen biscuits over hot mixture.

3) Bake uncovered 30 to 35 minutes or until biscuits are golden brown.

HIGH ALTITUDE (3500-6500 FT.): Increase milk to 3/4 cup.

Cheesy Spinach Manicotti

PREP TIME: 30 MINUTES (READY IN 1 HOUR 45 MINUTES)
SERVINGS: 7 (2 SHELLS EACH)

1 tablespoon olive oil

³/₄ cup chopped onion (1 large)

1 clove garlic, minced

1 bag (1 lb.) Green Giant® frozen cut leaf spinach

¹/₄ to ¹/₂ teaspoon salt

1 cup ricotta cheese

1 cup finely shredded mild Cheddar cheese (4 oz.)

1 jar (26 oz.) tomato pasta sauce

1 can (14.5 oz.) diced tomatoes with basil, garlic and oregano, undrained

1 package (8 oz.) manicotti pasta (14 manicotti)

1¹/₂ cups shredded mozzarella cheese (6 oz.)

1) Heat oven to 350°F. Spray 13x9-inch (3-quart) glass baking dish with cooking spray. In 10-inch nonstick skillet, heat oil over medium-high heat. Add onion and garlic; cook 2 to 3 minutes, stirring occasionally, until tender.

2) Stir in frozen spinach; sprinkle with salt to taste. Cover; cook 5 to 6 minutes, stirring occasionally, until spinach is thawed and liquid has evaporated. Remove from heat. Stir in ricotta and Cheddar cheeses.

3) In large bowl, mix pasta sauce and tomatoes; spread about 1¹/₂ cups in bottom of baking dish. With table knife, push about ¹/₄ cup spinach mixture into each uncooked manicotti pasta, pushing filling in from both ends. Place filled pasta diagonally over sauce in dish. Pour remaining sauce mixture over top.

4) Cover tightly with foil; bake 55 to 65 minutes or until pasta around outer edge is fork-tender. Uncover dish; sprinkle with mozzarella cheese. Bake uncovered 5 to 10 minutes longer or until cheese is melted and casserole is bubbly.

HIGH ALTITUDE (3500-6500 FT.): Heat oven to 375°F.

Nutrition Information Per Serving:	
Calories: 480	From Fat: 170
Total Fat	19g
Saturated Fat	9g
Cholesterol	40mg
Sodium	1000mg
Total Carbohydrate	54g
Dietary Fiber	6g
Sugars	11g
Protein	22g

Greek Shrimp and Pasta Bake

PREP TIME: 30 MINUTES (READY IN 50 MINUTES)
SERVINGS: 6 (1-1/2 CUPS EACH)

2 1/2 cups uncooked penne pasta (8 oz.)

3/4 lb. uncooked medium shrimp, peeled, deveined and tail shells removed

3 cups fresh spinach, stems removed, torn into pieces

1 cup grape tomatoes, cut in half

1 teaspoon salt

1 teaspoon dried oregano leaves

2 tablespoons olive oil

1 package (4 oz.) crumbled feta cheese (about 1 cup)

1 can (2 1/4 oz.) sliced ripe olives, drained

1) In 4-quart saucepan or Dutch oven, cook pasta as directed on package, adding shrimp during last 2 to 3 minutes of cooking. Cook until pasta is tender and shrimp turn pink. Drain; return to saucepan.

2) Meanwhile, heat oven to 350°F. Spray 13x9-inch (3-quart) glass baking dish with cooking spray.

3) Stir remaining ingredients into cooked pasta and shrimp. Pour into baking dish; spread evenly.

4) Bake uncovered 15 to 20 minutes or until thoroughly heated.

HIGH ALTITUDE (3500-6500 FT.): In Step 4, bake uncovered 20 to 25 minutes.

Nutrition Information Per Serving:

Calories:	280	From Fat:	100
Total Fat			11g
Saturated			4g
Cholesterol			70mg
Sodium			910mg
Total Carbohydrate			33g
Dietary Fiber			3g
Sugars			2g
Protein			14g

Cheeseburger Lasagna

PREP TIME: 15 MINUTES (READY IN 1 HOUR 45 MINUTES)
SERVINGS: 8

 EASY

1 lb. lean (at least 80%) ground beef

2 cans (15 oz. each) tomato sauce

1 cup ketchup

1/2 cup water

2 tablespoons dry onion soup mix (half 1-oz. package)

2 eggs

2 cups cottage cheese

1/2 cup grated Parmesan cheese

8 uncooked lasagna noodles

1 cup shredded Cheddar cheese (4 oz.)

1 cup shredded Colby-Monterey Jack cheese blend (4 oz.)

1) Heat oven to 375°F. In 3-quart saucepan, cook ground beef over medium-high heat, stirring frequently, until thoroughly cooked; remove from heat and drain. Stir in tomato sauce, ketchup, water and soup mix.

2) In medium bowl, beat eggs well. Stir in cottage cheese and Parmesan cheese.

3) Spoon 1 1/2 cups of meat sauce in bottom of ungreased 13x9-inch (3-quart) glass baking dish. Top with 4 uncooked lasagna noodles (noodles may not reach ends of dish). Top with half of cottage cheese mixture and half of remaining meat sauce.

4) Repeat layers with remaining lasagna noodles, cottage cheese mixture and meat sauce. Sprinkle shredded cheese over top. Cut 16x12-inch sheet of regular or nonstick foil; if using regular foil, spray with cooking spray. Cover dish loosely with foil, sprayed side down.

5) Bake 1 hour or until lasagna is bubbly and noodles can be easily pierced with tip of sharp knife. Uncover dish; bake 10 to 15 minutes longer or until cheese on top is melted. Let stand 15 minutes before serving.

HIGH ALTITUDE (3500-6500 FT.): In Step 5, bake covered 1 hour 10 minutes. Uncover dish; continue as directed above.

Nutrition Information Per Serving:		
Calories: 450	From Fat:	180
Total Fat		20g
Saturated		11g
Cholesterol		125mg
Sodium		1710mg
Total Carbohydrate		35g
Dietary Fiber		3g
Sugars		15g
Protein		33g

Biscuits and Sloppy Joe Casserole

PREP TIME:	20 MINUTES (READY IN 50 MINUTES)	EASY
SERVINGS:	5	

1 lb. lean (at least 80%) ground beef

¼ cup chopped onion (½ medium)

¼ cup chopped celery (½ stalk)

1 can (10¾ oz.) condensed chicken gumbo soup

1 can (10¾ oz.) condensed tomato soup

2 tablespoons Dijon mustard

1 tablespoon Worcestershire sauce

1 can (12 oz.) Pillsbury® Golden Layers® refrigerated buttermilk biscuits

Nutrition Information Per Serving:		
Calories: 490	From Fat:	220
Total Fat		24g
Saturated		7g
Cholesterol		60mg
Sodium		1750mg
Total Carbohydrate		45g
Dietary Fiber		2g
Sugars		11g
Protein		23g

1) Heat oven to 375°F. In 10-inch skillet, cook ground beef, onion and celery over medium-high heat, stirring frequently, until beef is thoroughly cooked; drain.

2) Stir in remaining ingredients except biscuits. Cook 2 to 3 minutes, stirring occasionally, until thoroughly heated. Spoon mixture into ungreased 8-inch square (2-quart) glass baking dish.

3) Separate dough into 10 biscuits; cut each in half crosswise. Arrange biscuit pieces, cut side down, on hot beef mixture.

4) Bake uncovered 20 to 28 minutes or until biscuits are deep golden brown.

HIGH ALTITUDE (3500-6500 FT.): No change.

Green Bean and Turkey Casserole

PREP TIME:	20 MINUTES (READY IN 35 MINUTES)	EASY
SERVINGS:	6 (1-1/4 CUPS EACH)	

2 cups cubed cooked turkey or chicken

2 cups Green Giant® frozen cut green beans, (from 1-lb. bag)

1 can (10¾ oz.) condensed cream of mushroom soup

1 cup milk

1¾ cups water

3 tablespoons butter or margarine

½ teaspoon salt

2 cups plain mashed potato mix (dry)

1 cup shredded Cheddar cheese (4 oz.)

½ can (2.8 oz.) french fried onions (½ cup)

Nutrition Information Per Serving:		
Calories: 370	From Fat:	190
Total Fat		22g
Saturated		10g
Cholesterol		80mg
Sodium		920mg
Total Carbohydrate		23g
Dietary Fiber		2g
Sugars		4g
Protein		22g

1) Heat oven to 375°F. In 2-quart saucepan, mix turkey, green beans, soup and ⅓ cup of the milk. Cook over medium heat 6 to 8 minutes, stirring occasionally, until mixture is hot.

2) Make mashed potatoes in microwave as directed on box using water, remaining ⅔ cup milk, butter, salt and mashed potato mix.

3) Remove turkey mixture from heat. Stir in cheese until melted. Pour into ungreased 2-quart casserole. Top with mashed potatoes.

4) Bake uncovered 10 minutes. Sprinkle with onions; bake 3 to 5 minutes longer or until mixture is bubbly and onions are warm.

HIGH ALTITUDE (3500-6500 FT.): Increase water to 2 cups and first bake time to 20 minutes.

Meatball Sandwich Casserole

PREP TIME: 25 MINUTES (READY IN 1 HOUR 5 MINUTES)
SERVINGS: 6

 EASY

18 to 24 slices (¼ inch thick) baguette French bread

¼ cup olive or vegetable oil

1 package (1 lb.) frozen cooked Italian-style or regular meatballs (32), thawed

1 bag (1 lb.) frozen bell pepper and onion stir-fry, thawed, drained

1 ½ cups tomato pasta sauce

1 cup shredded mozzarella cheese (4 oz.)

1) Heat oven to 350°F. Brush 1 side of each bread slice with oil. In ungreased 9½-inch deep-dish pie plate, line bottom and side with bread, oil side up and slightly overlapping slices.

2) Bake 5 to 10 minutes or until edges are light golden brown.

3) Meanwhile, in large bowl, gently mix meatballs, bell pepper and onion stir-fry, and pasta sauce to coat.

4) Spoon meatball mixture into crust; bake uncovered 25 to 30 minutes or until thoroughly heated in center. Sprinkle with cheese; bake 5 to 10 minutes longer or until cheese is melted.

HIGH ALTITUDE (3500-6500 FT.): In Step 4, bake 35 to 40 minutes. Sprinkle with cheese; bake 5 to 10 minutes longer.

Nutrition Information Per Serving:

Calories: 550	From Fat: 240
Total Fat	27g
Saturated	8g
Cholesterol	90mg
Sodium	1130mg
Total Carbohydrate	50g
Dietary Fiber	4g
Sugars	9g
Protein	26g

Mashed Potato Casserole

PREP TIME: 20 MINUTES (READY IN 45 MINUTES)
SERVINGS: 14 (1/2 CUP EACH)

 EASY

3 cups water

¼ cup butter or margarine

1 cup milk

3 cups plain mashed potato mix (dry)

1 container (8 oz.) sour cream

1 cup shredded Cheddar cheese (4 oz.)

⅓ cup cooked real bacon pieces (from 3-oz. jar)

1 can (2.8 oz.) french-fried onions (about 1 cup)

Nutrition Information Per Serving:

Calories: 190	From Fat: 120
Total Fat	13g
Saturated	6g
Cholesterol	30mg
Sodium	230mg
Total Carbohydrate	12g
Dietary Fiber	0g
Sugars	2g
Protein	5g

1) Heat oven to 350°F. In 3-quart saucepan, heat water and butter to boiling. Boil 1 minute, stirring constantly. Add milk; remove from heat.

2) Stir in mashed potato mix with fork until potatoes are desired consistency. Stir in sour cream and cheese. Spoon into ungreased 13x9-inch (3-quart) glass baking dish. Sprinkle bacon and onions over top.

3) Bake 20 to 25 minutes or until hot.

HIGH ALTITUDE (3500-6500 FT.): Heat oven to 375°F.

Barbeque Pork-Cheesy Potato Bake

PREP TIME: 15 MINUTES (READY IN 1 HOUR 20 MINUTES)
SERVINGS: 4 (1-1/4 CUPS EACH)

 EASY

- 1 package (1 lb. 4 oz.) refrigerated sliced potatoes
- 1 container (18 oz.) Lloyd's® refrigerated original barbeque sauce with shredded pork
- 1/3 cup water
- 8 oz. pasteurized prepared cheese product, cut into cubes (1 1/2 cups)
- 1/2 cup sliced green onions (8 medium)
- 1/2 cup chive-and-onion sour cream potato topper (from 12-oz. container), if desired

1) Heat oven to 350°F. Spray 13x9-inch (3-quart) glass baking dish with cooking spray. Arrange potatoes evenly in dish.

2) In large bowl, mix barbeque sauce with pork and water; pour mixture evenly over potatoes. Cover tightly with foil.

3) Bake 40 to 50 minutes or until potatoes are tender and mixture is hot and bubbly.

4) Uncover dish; sprinkle cheese and onions over top. Bake uncovered 10 to 15 minutes longer or until cheese is melted. Top individual servings with potato topper.

HIGH ALTITUDE (3500-6500 FT.): Increase water to 3/4 cup. Bake at 375°F. 45 to 55 minutes. Continue as directed above.

Nutrition Information Per Serving:	
Calories: 540	From Fat: 200
Total Fat	22g
Saturated	12g
Cholesterol	90mg
Sodium	2270mg
Total Carbohydrate	61g
Dietary Fiber	3g
Sugars	28g
Protein	27g

Speedy Skillet Suppers

Most of these fast-to-fix stovetop suppers
can be on the table in 30 minutes!

MEATBALLS AND RICE SKILLET DINNER
PG. 172

PINEAPPLE SHRIMP STIR-FRY
PG. 175

PORK AND ASPARAGUS SCALOPPINE
PG. 191

PROVENÇAL CHICKEN AND TOMATOES
PG. 178

Quick Italian Chicken and Rice

PREP TIME: 15 MINUTES (READY IN 20 MINUTES)
SERVINGS: 3

 EASY  LOW FAT

2 teaspoons vegetable oil

1 package (12 to 14 oz.) chicken breast tenders (not breaded)

1/2 teaspoon Italian seasoning

1 can (14.5 oz.) Italian-style stewed tomatoes, undrained

3/4 cup water

1 1/2 cups uncooked instant white rice

1) In 10-inch nonstick skillet, heat oil over medium-high heat. Sprinkle chicken tenders on all sides with Italian seasoning; add to skillet. Cook 5 to 6 minutes, stirring constantly, until chicken is browned and no longer pink in center.

2) Stir in tomatoes and water. Heat to boiling. Stir in rice. Cover; remove from heat. Let stand 5 minutes or until liquid is absorbed.

HIGH ALTITUDE (3500-6500 FT.): Increase water to 1-1/4 cups. In Step 2, let stand 10 minutes or until liquid is absorbed.

Nutrition Information Per Serving:

Calories:	410	From Fat:	70
Total Fat			7g
Saturated			1.5g
Cholesterol			70mg
Sodium			440mg
Total Carbohydrate			57g
Dietary Fiber			2g
Sugars			7g
Protein			30g

Turkey Stroganoff

PREP TIME: 20 MINUTES (READY IN 20 MINUTES)
SERVINGS: 4 (1-1/2 CUPS EACH)

 EASY

1 lb. lean ground turkey

1/2 teaspoon pepper

3 1/2 cups water

1 package (1.5 oz.) beef stroganoff sauce mix

3 cups uncooked medium egg noodles (6 oz.)

1/2 cup sour cream

Chopped parsley, if desired

Nutrition Information Per Serving:		
Calories: 400	From Fat: 130	
Total Fat		15g
Saturated		6g
Cholesterol		135mg
Sodium		630mg
Total Carbohydrate		35g
Dietary Fiber		2g
Sugars		1g
Protein		32g

After stirring in the sour cream, don't let the mixture boil or the sauce will have a curdled appearance.

1) In 10-inch skillet, crumble ground turkey; sprinkle with pepper. Cook over medium-high heat 5 to 6 minutes, stirring frequently, until turkey is no longer pink.

2) Stir in water, sauce mix and noodles; heat to boiling. Stir; reduce heat to medium-low. Cover; cook 6 to 8 minutes, stirring occasionally, until noodles are tender.

3) Stir in sour cream. Cook and stir just until thoroughly heated. Sprinkle with chopped parsley.

HIGH ALTITUDE (3500-6500 FT.): No change.

Skillet Pizza Potatoes

PREP TIME: 35 MINUTES (READY IN 35 MINUTES)
SERVINGS: 5 (1-1/2 CUPS EACH)

 EASY

1 lb. bulk Italian pork sausage

1/2 cup pepperoni slices (about 3 oz.)

1 jar (14 oz.) pizza sauce

1/2 cup water

1 bag (28 oz.) frozen potatoes O'Brien
with onions and peppers

1 cup shredded Italian cheese blend
(4 oz.)

Nutrition Information Per Serving:	
Calories: 610	From Fat: 300
Total Fat	34g
Saturated	13g
Cholesterol	80mg
Sodium	1550mg
Total Carbohydrate	52g
Dietary Fiber	6g
Sugars	5g
Protein	27g

1) In Dutch oven or 12-inch nonstick skillet, cook sausage over medium-high heat, stirring frequently, until no longer pink. Stir in pepperoni; cook 2 minutes. Drain.

2) Stir in pizza sauce and water. Add potatoes; stir to mix. Reduce heat to medium; cover and cook 10 to 15 minutes, stirring occasionally, until potatoes are tender.

3) Sprinkle cheese over top. Remove from heat; cover and let stand 5 minutes or until cheese is melted.

HIGH ALTITUDE (3500-6500 FT.): If potato mixture looks too dry, add up to 1/4 cup additional water.

If you can't find shredded Italian cheese blend, use shredded mozzarella cheese instead.

Meatballs and Rice Skillet Dinner

PREP TIME: 10 MINUTES (READY IN 35 MINUTES)
SERVINGS: 3 (1-1/2 CUPS EACH)

 EASY

1 tablespoon butter or margarine

1 package (6.8 oz.) beef-flavored rice and vermicelli mix

2 1/3 cups water

16 frozen cooked meatballs (8 oz.)

2 cups Green Giant® frozen broccoli cuts (from 1-lb. bag), thawed

1/2 cup red bell pepper strips

Nutrition Information Per Serving:	
Calories: 520	From Fat: 140
Total Fat	16g
Saturated	6g
Cholesterol	90mg
Sodium	1320mg
Total Carbohydrate	69g
Dietary Fiber	5g
Sugars	5g
Protein	27g

1) In 10-inch skillet, melt butter over medium heat. Stir in rice and vermicelli from mix; cook and stir until lightly browned. Add water, contents of seasoning packet from mix and meatballs; heat to boiling. Stir; reduce heat to medium-low. Cover; cook 15 minutes.

2) Gently stir in broccoli and bell pepper. Increase heat to medium; cover and cook 7 to 9 minutes or until broccoli is crisp-tender and rice is tender. Before serving, stir to fluff rice.

HIGH ALTITUDE (3500-6500 FT.): Increase water to 2-2/3 cups.

Sweet-and-Sour Ham Steak

PREP TIME: 15 MINUTES (READY IN 15 MINUTES)
SERVINGS: 4

 EASY   LOW FAT

¼ cup sweet-and-sour sauce

2 tablespoons frozen orange juice concentrate, thawed

1 slice (about 1 lb.) center-cut smoked ham

1 tablespoon chopped fresh chives, if desired

1) In small bowl, mix sweet-and-sour sauce and juice concentrate; set aside.

2) In 10- to 12-inch nonstick skillet, cook ham slice over medium heat 6 minutes, turning once.

3) Spoon sauce mixture over ham. Cook 4 to 6 minutes longer, turning ham once or twice, until thoroughly heated. Sprinkle with chives.

HIGH ALTITUDE (3500-6500 FT.): No change.

Nutrition Information Per Serving:

Calories:	180	From Fat:	70
Total Fat			8g
Saturated			2.5g
Cholesterol			50mg
Sodium			1290mg
Total Carbohydrate			7g
Dietary Fiber			0g
Sugars			6g
Protein			19g

Cheesy Tomato-Chicken Skillet

PREP TIME: 20 MINUTES (READY IN 25 MINUTES)
SERVINGS: 4 (1-1/4 CUPS EACH)

 EASY

2 cups uncooked pasta nuggets or radiatore (7 oz.)

³/4 lb. chicken breast strips for stir-fry

1 can (10³/4 oz.) condensed cream of chicken soup

1½ cups chopped plum (Roma) tomatoes (4 to 5 medium)

½ cup milk

2 tablespoons chopped fresh basil

1 cup shredded mozzarella cheese (4 oz.)

1) Cook pasta as directed on package. Drain; cover to keep warm.

2) Meanwhile, heat 10-inch nonstick skillet over medium-high heat. Add chicken; cook 4 to 6 minutes, stirring frequently, until chicken is no longer pink in center. Reduce heat to medium; stir in soup, tomatoes, milk and basil.

3) Stir in cooked pasta. Cook about 8 minutes, stirring occasionally, until bubbly and thoroughly heated. Sprinkle with cheese. Remove from heat. Cover; let stand until cheese is melted, 2 to 3 minutes.

HIGH ALTITUDE (3500-6500 FT.): No change.

Nutrition Information Per Serving:

Calories:	510	From Fat:	140
Total Fat		15g	
Saturated		6g	
Cholesterol		75mg	
Sodium		990mg	
Total Carbohydrate		58g	
Dietary Fiber		4g	
Sugars		4g	
Protein		37g	

Italian plum tomatoes, also called Roma tomatoes, are small, oval tomatoes that retain their shape when cooked.

Pineapple Shrimp Stir-Fry

PREP TIME: 25 MINUTES (READY IN 25 MINUTES)
SERVINGS: 4 (1 CUP EACH)

 EASY   LOW FAT

1 lb. uncooked deveined shelled medium shrimp, thawed if frozen, tail shells removed

½ teaspoon salt

¼ teaspoon pepper

1 cup matchstick-cut carrots

1 medium red bell pepper, cut into 1-inch pieces

1 can (8 oz.) pineapple chunks, drained

⅔ cup sweet-and-sour sauce

1) Heat nonstick wok or 12-inch nonstick skillet over medium-high heat. Add shrimp; sprinkle with salt and pepper. Cook and stir 1 minute. Add carrots and bell pepper; cook and stir 2 to 3 minutes or until shrimp turn pink and opaque, and vegetables are crisp-tender.

2) Add pineapple chunks and sweet-and-sour sauce; cook and stir 2 to 3 minutes longer or until pineapple is thoroughly heated. If desired, serve over hot cooked rice.

HIGH ALTITUDE (3500-6500 FT.): No change.

Nutrition Information Per Serving:

Calories:	180	From Fat:	20
Total Fat			2g
Saturated			0g
Cholesterol			160mg
Sodium			650mg
Total Carbohydrate			25g
Dietary Fiber			3g
Sugars			20g
Protein			18g

tip
Matchstick-cut carrots can be found already cut in the produce department of the supermarket.

Sweet-and-Sour Pork and Vegetables

PREP TIME:	20 MINUTES (READY IN 20 MINUTES)	EASY
SERVINGS:	4 (1-1/2 CUPS EACH)	

³/4 lb. boneless pork loin chops, cut into thin bite-size strips

1¹/4 cups water

1 bag (1 lb. 5 oz.) Green Giant® Create a Meal!® frozen sweet & sour stir-fry meal starter

1 package (3 or 3.5 oz.) pork or chicken-flavor ramen noodle soup mix

Nutrition Information Per Serving:

Calories:	350	From Fat:	100
Total Fat			11g
Saturated			3.5g
Cholesterol			50mg
Sodium			780mg
Total Carbohydrate			43g
Dietary Fiber			3g
Sugars			22g
Protein			22g

1) Heat 12-inch nonstick skillet over medium-high heat. Add pork strips; cook and stir 3 to 5 minutes or until pork is no longer pink in center.

2) Add water, frozen vegetables with pineapple and frozen sauce from meal starter packet. Increase heat to high; heat to boiling.

3) Break noodles into small pieces; add to skillet. Stir in contents of seasoning packet from soup mix. Reduce heat to low; cover and simmer 5 to 7 minutes, stirring occasionally, until vegetables are crisp-tender and noodles are tender.

HIGH ALTITUDE (3500-6500 FT.): If mixture is too thick, add up to 1/4 cup additional water.

Ham, Broccoli and Rice Skillet Dinner

PREP TIME:	25 MINUTES (READY IN 35 MINUTES)	EASY	LOW FAT
SERVINGS:	4 (1 CUP EACH)		

2 teaspoons butter or margarine

¹/2 cup chopped onion (1 medium)

1 package (4.3 oz.) long grain and wild rice mix

1²/3 cups water

2 cups Green Giant Select® frozen broccoli florets (from 14-oz. bag)

1¹/2 cups cubed cooked ham

Nutrition Information Per Serving:

Calories:	240	From Fat:	70
Total Fat			7g
Saturated			3g
Cholesterol			35mg
Sodium			1130mg
Total Carbohydrate			28g
Dietary Fiber			2g
Sugars			2g
Protein			17g

1) In 10-inch nonstick skillet, melt butter over medium heat. Add onion and rice from mix; cook and stir 1 to 2 minutes or until onion begins to cook. Stir in water and contents of seasoning packet from mix; heat to boiling. Reduce heat to medium-low; cover and cook 10 minutes.

2) Stir in broccoli and ham; return to boiling. Reduce heat to medium-low; cover and cook 10 to 15 minutes, stirring occasionally, until broccoli is crisp-tender and rice is tender.

HIGH ALTITUDE (3500-6500 FT.): Increase water to 1-3/4 cups. After stirring in water and contents of seasoning packet from mix, heat to boiling. Reduce heat to medium-low; cover and cook 15 minutes. Continue as directed above.

Skillet Canadian Bacon and Potatoes

PREP TIME: 15 MINUTES (READY IN 30 MINUTES)
SERVINGS: 4 (1-1/2 CUPS EACH)

e EASY

3$\frac{1}{2}$ cups water

2 teaspoons butter or margarine

1 box (7.7 oz.) creamy scalloped potato mix with bread crumb topping

1$\frac{1}{4}$ cups fat-free (skim) milk

$\frac{1}{2}$ lb. Canadian bacon slices, cut into strips

1 box (9 oz.) Green Giant® frozen sugar snap peas, thawed, drained

1) In 10-inch deep-sided nonstick skillet, heat water and butter to boiling over medium-high heat. Stir in potato slices from mix; return to boiling. Boil 15 minutes.

2) Do not drain potatoes. Stir in contents of sauce packet from mix, the milk, bacon and sugar snap peas. Return to boiling. Reduce heat to medium; cook 4 to 5 minutes longer, stirring occasionally, until sauce is slightly thickened.

3) Sprinkle with contents of topping packet from mix. If desired, season to taste with pepper.

HIGH ALTITUDE (3500-6500 FT.): Increase water to 3-3/4 cups. Boil potato slices 17 minutes; continue as directed above.

Nutrition Information Per Serving:

Calories: 320	From Fat: 100
Total Fat	11g
Saturated	4.5g
Cholesterol	40mg
Sodium	1550mg
Total Carbohydrate	37g
Dietary Fiber	3g
Sugars	10g
Protein	20g

tip

Applesauce is a nice side for this skillet recipe. Serve some easy-to-bake brownies for a no-fuss dessert.

Provençal Chicken and Tomatoes

PREP TIME:	15 MINUTES (READY IN 35 MINUTES)
SERVINGS:	4

 EASY

4 slices bacon, cut into 1-inch pieces

1 cup frozen small whole onions (from 1-lb. bag)

1 lb. boneless skinless chicken thighs

1 can (15.8 oz.) Great Northern beans, drained, rinsed

1 can (14.5 oz.) diced tomatoes with basil, garlic and oregano, undrained

¼ cup water

¼ teaspoon pepper

1) Heat 12-inch skillet over medium heat. Add bacon; cook about 5 minutes or until bacon begins to brown. Add onions; cook 3 to 5 minutes, stirring occasionally, until onions begin to turn light golden.

2) Add chicken thighs; cook 5 to 6 minutes or until chicken is lightly browned on both sides.

3) Stir in remaining ingredients, scraping up any brown bits from bottom of skillet; heat to boiling. Reduce heat to low; cover and cook 10 minutes.

4) Uncover; cook 5 to 10 minutes longer or until chicken is no longer pink in center and sauce is slightly thickened.

HIGH ALTITUDE (3500-6500 FT.): No change.

Nutrition Information Per Serving:		
Calories: 390	From Fat:	120
Total Fat		14g
Saturated		4.5g
Cholesterol		75mg
Sodium		350mg
Total Carbohydrate		35g
Dietary Fiber		9g
Sugars		4g
Protein		39g

Mom's Skillet Goulash

PREP TIME: 30 MINUTES (READY IN 30 MINUTES)
SERVINGS: 6

 EASY   LOW FAT

2²/₃ cups uncooked rotini pasta (8 oz.)

1 lb. lean (at least 80%) ground beef

1¹/₂ cups chopped celery (about 3 stalks)

1 cup chopped onions (2 medium)

2 cans (14.5 oz. each) diced tomatoes, undrained

1 can (10³/₄ oz.) condensed tomato soup

1 teaspoon dried basil leaves

¹/₂ teaspoon salt

¹/₄ teaspoon pepper

Nutrition Information Per Serving:		
Calories: 350	From Fat:	90
Total Fat		10g
Saturated		3.5g
Cholesterol		45mg
Sodium		910mg
Total Carbohydrate		46g
Dietary Fiber		5g
Sugars		8g
Protein		21g

For extra-quick prep, use 1 cup frozen chopped onions. Look for 12-ounce packages near the frozen potatoes and other vegetables.

1) Cook pasta as directed on package; drain.

2) Meanwhile, in 12-inch nonstick skillet or Dutch oven, cook ground beef, celery and onions over medium-high heat 5 to 7 minutes, stirring frequently, until beef is thoroughly cooked; drain.

3) Stir in cooked pasta and remaining ingredients. Heat to boiling. Reduce heat to low; simmer uncovered 10 minutes, stirring occasionally.

HIGH ALTITUDE (3500-6500 FT.): In Step 3, add 1/2 cup water to skillet with other ingredients. Heat to boiling; continue as directed above.

Creamy Ham and Tortellini

| PREP TIME: | 30 MINUTES (READY IN 30 MINUTES) |
| SERVINGS: | 4 (1-1/2 CUPS EACH) |

 EASY

1 package (9 oz.) refrigerated cheese-filled tortellini

1 tablespoon olive oil

1 medium onion, chopped ($\frac{1}{2}$ cup)

2 cups cubed ($\frac{1}{2}$ inch) cooked ham

2 cups Green Giant® frozen chopped broccoli (from 1-lb. bag)

1 cup whipping cream

$\frac{1}{4}$ cup shredded Parmesan cheese (1 oz.)

Nutrition Information Per Serving:	
Calories: 590	From Fat: 310
Total Fat	35g
Saturated	18g
Cholesterol	135mg
Sodium	1380mg
Total Carbohydrate	39g
Dietary Fiber	4g
Sugars	6g
Protein	30g

1) Cook and drain tortellini as directed on package.

2) Meanwhile, in 12-inch skillet, heat oil over medium heat. Add onion; cook 4 to 5 minutes, stirring frequently, until lightly browned.

3) Stir in ham and broccoli. Cook 5 minutes, stirring occasionally.

4) Stir in cream and cheese. Heat just to boiling over high heat. Stir in tortellini. Reduce heat to medium; simmer uncovered 4 to 5 minutes or until thoroughly heated.

HIGH ALTITUDE (3500-6500 FT.): Increase whipping cream to 1-1/4 cups. In Step 4, simmer uncovered 6 to 7 minutes.

Garlic-Basil Chicken

| PREP TIME: | 20 MINUTES (READY IN 35 MINUTES) |
| SERVINGS: | 2 |

 EASY

3 cloves garlic, minced

1 tablespoon dried basil leaves

$\frac{1}{2}$ teaspoon pepper

$\frac{1}{4}$ teaspoon salt

1 tablespoon lemon juice

2 tablespoons olive oil

2 bone-in chicken breasts (1$\frac{1}{4}$ lb.)

Nutrition Information Per Serving:	
Calories: 400	From Fat: 220
Total Fat	25g
Saturated	5g
Cholesterol	115mg
Sodium	390mg
Total Carbohydrate	3g
Dietary Fiber	0g
Sugars	0g
Protein	42g

1) In shallow dish or pie pan, mix garlic, basil, pepper, salt, lemon juice and 1 tablespoon of the oil. Coat chicken with garlic-basil mixture.

2) In 10-inch skillet, heat remaining tablespoon oil over medium heat. Add chicken; cook 5 minutes on each side or until browned.

3) Reduce heat to medium-low; cover and cook 10 to 15 minutes or until juice of chicken is clear when thickest part is cut to bone (170°F.).

HIGH ALTITUDE (3500-6500 FT.): In Step 3, cover and cook 20 to 30 minutes.

Peanut-Chicken Stir-Fry

PREP TIME: 10 MINUTES (READY IN 10 MINUTES)
SERVINGS: 4

EASY

- 1 tablespoon vegetable oil
- 1 package (14 to 16 oz.) chicken breast strips for stir-fry
- 2¾ cups water
- 1 package (1 oz.) stir-fry seasoning mix
- ⅓ cup creamy peanut butter
- 1 can (14 oz.) fancy mixed Chinese vegetables, drained
- 2 cups frozen bell pepper and onion stir-fry (from 1-lb. bag), thawed, patted dry with paper towels
- 2 cups instant white rice
- ¼ cup chopped peanuts

Nutrition Information Per Serving:	
Calories: 610 From Fat: 200	
Total Fat	23g
Saturated	4.5g
Cholesterol	60mg
Sodium	1050mg
Total Carbohydrate	67g
Dietary Fiber	5g
Sugars	6g
Protein	37g

If chicken breast strips are unavailable in the fresh poultry counter, cut boneless skinless chicken breasts crosswise into strips instead.

1) In 12-inch nonstick skillet, heat oil over medium-high heat. Add chicken; cook and stir 5 to 6 minutes or until no longer pink in center.

2) Reduce heat to medium. Stir in ¾ cup of the water, stir-fry seasoning mix and peanut butter until smooth. Stir in vegetables and bell pepper and onion stir-fry; cook and stir until thoroughly heated.

3) Meanwhile, cook rice in remaining 2 cups water as directed on package.

4) Serve chicken mixture over rice; sprinkle with peanuts.

HIGH ALTITUDE (3500-6500 FT.): Increase water to 3 cups. Use 1 cup in Step 2; use 2 cups when cooking rice.

Home-Style Hamburger Hash

PREP TIME: 30 MINUTES (READY IN 30 MINUTES)
SERVINGS: 4

 EASY

1 lb. lean (at least 80%) ground beef

4 cups frozen potatoes O'Brien with onions and peppers (from 24-oz. bag)

1 can (11 oz.) Green Giant® Mexicorn® whole kernel corn with red and green peppers, undrained

3/4 cup water

1 teaspoon beef bouillon granules

1 tablespoon chopped fresh parsley, if desired

Nutrition Information Per Serving:	
Calories: 410 From Fat: 120	
Total Fat	13g
Saturated	5g
Cholesterol	70mg
Sodium	760mg
Total Carbohydrate	50g
Dietary Fiber	5g
Sugars	3g
Protein	25g

tip

Enjoy this hash with ripe pear slices and a glass of cold milk.

1) In 10-inch nonstick skillet, cook ground beef over medium-high heat 5 to 7 minutes, stirring frequently, until thoroughly cooked; drain.

2) Stir in remaining ingredients except parsley. Reduce heat to medium; cover and cook 20 minutes, stirring occasionally, until potatoes are tender. If desired, season to taste with salt and pepper. Sprinkle with parsley.

HIGH ALTITUDE (3500-6500 FT.): No change.

Tuna Noodle Skillet

PREP TIME: 20 MINUTES (READY IN 20 MINUTES)
SERVINGS: 4 (1-1/2 CUPS EACH)

 EASY

3$\frac{1}{2}$ cups mini lasagna (mafalda) noodles (8 oz.)

1 cup chopped celery (1$\frac{1}{2}$ to 2 stalks)

2 tablespoons water

$\frac{1}{2}$ cup reduced-fat sour cream

$\frac{1}{2}$ cup reduced-fat ranch dressing

1 can (12 oz.) tuna in water, drained, flaked

1 jar (2 oz.) chopped pimientos, drained

Nutrition Information Per Serving:		
Calories: 410	From Fat:	100
Total Fat		11g
Saturated		3g
Cholesterol		40mg
Sodium		810mg
Total Carbohydrate		52g
Dietary Fiber		4g
Sugars		4g
Protein		29g

1) Cook and drain noodles as directed on package.

2) Meanwhile, in 12-inch nonstick skillet, place celery and water. Cover; cook over medium heat 3 to 4 minutes or until celery is crisp-tender.

3) Gently stir in cooked noodles and remaining ingredients. Cook about 5 minutes, stirring frequently, until thoroughly heated.

HIGH ALTITUDE (3500-6500 FT.): No change.

Meatball Lo Mein

PREP TIME: 20 MINUTES (READY IN 20 MINUTES)
SERVINGS: 3

 EASY

18 frozen cooked original flavor meatballs (about 9 oz.)

1 bag (1 lb. 5 oz.) Green Giant® Create A Meal!® frozen lo mein stir-fry meal starter

1 small red or green bell pepper, cut into 1-inch pieces

$\frac{1}{3}$ cup water

Nutrition Information Per Serving:		
Calories: 380	From Fat:	120
Total Fat		13g
Saturated		4.5g
Cholesterol		90mg
Sodium		1290mg
Total Carbohydrate		42g
Dietary Fiber		4g
Sugars		12g
Protein		23g

1) Heat meatballs in microwave as directed on package.

2) In 10-inch nonstick skillet, mix frozen sauce, noodles and vegetables from meal starter, the bell pepper and water. Cover; cook over medium-high heat 8 to 10 minutes, stirring frequently, until vegetables are crisp-tender. Stir in hot meatballs.

HIGH ALTITUDE (3500-6500 FT.): Increase water to 1/2 cup.

Cheesy Chicken and Vegetables

PREP TIME: 25 MINUTES (READY IN 25 MINUTES)
SERVINGS: 4 (1-1/2 CUPS EACH)

 EASY

1 tablespoon vegetable oil

1 lb. chicken breast tenders

1/4 teaspoon pepper

1 package (24 oz.) Green Giant® frozen broccoli, carrots, cauliflower and cheese flavored sauce

2 teaspoons dried basil leaves

1/4 cup grated Parmesan cheese

Nutrition Information Per Serving:	
Calories: 280	From Fat: 100
Total Fat	11g
Saturated	3.5g
Cholesterol	80mg
Sodium	780mg
Total Carbohydrate	12g
Dietary Fiber	4g
Sugars	7g
Protein	31g

1) In 12-inch nonstick skillet or Dutch oven, heat oil over medium-high heat. Add chicken; sprinkle with pepper. Cook 4 to 5 minutes, stirring occasionally, until brown.

2) Stir in frozen vegetables with cheese sauce. Reduce heat to medium-low; cook 10 minutes, stirring frequently, until chicken is no longer pink in center, cheese sauce has melted and vegetables are tender.

3) Stir in basil and Parmesan cheese. Cook 2 to 3 minutes longer, stirring occasionally, until thoroughly heated.

HIGH ALTITUDE (3500-6500 FT.): After adding frozen vegetables with cheese sauce, heat to boiling. Reduce heat and continue as directed above.

tip

If you like, serve with buttered pasta and sprinkle with additional Parmesan cheese.

Bow Ties with Bacon and Tomatoes

PREP TIME: 30 MINUTES (READY IN 30 MINUTES)
SERVINGS: 3 (1-1/3 CUPS EACH)

EASY

4 slices bacon, cut into 1-inch pieces

1 medium onion, finely chopped (1/2 cup)

1 can (14.5 oz.) diced tomatoes with roasted garlic and onion, undrained

1 can (14 oz.) chicken broth

3 cups uncooked bow-tie (farfalle) pasta (7 oz.)

1/8 teaspoon pepper

Nutrition Information Per Serving:	
Calories: 580	From Fat: 260
Total Fat	28g
Saturated	11g
Cholesterol	30mg
Sodium	1330mg
Total Carbohydrate	66g
Dietary Fiber	4g
Sugars	10g
Protein	16g

1) In 12-inch skillet, cook bacon over medium-high heat 8 to 10 minutes, stirring frequently, until bacon is brown. Reduce heat to medium. Add onion; cook 2 to 3 minutes, stirring frequently, until onion is tender.

2) Stir in tomatoes, broth, uncooked pasta and pepper. Heat to boiling over high heat. Reduce heat to medium; cook uncovered 10 to 12 minutes, stirring occasionally, until pasta is tender and mixture is desired consistency.

HIGH ALTITUDE (3500-6500 FT.): Increase cook time in Step 2 to 12 to 14 minutes.

Sweet-and-Sour Chicken Nuggets

PREP TIME: 20 MINUTES (READY IN 20 MINUTES)
SERVINGS: 4

 EASY

2 tablespoons vegetable oil

20 frozen breaded chicken breast nuggets (about 12 oz.)

1 bag (1 lb. 5 oz.) Green Giant® Create a Meal!® frozen sweet & sour stir-fry meal starter

1 package (3 oz.) chicken-flavor ramen noodle soup mix

1 cup water

1) In 12-inch nonstick skillet, heat oil over medium heat. Add chicken nuggets; cook 4 to 5 minutes, stirring and turning occasionally, until thoroughly heated. Remove chicken from skillet; place on plate and cover to keep warm.

2) Wipe skillet clean with paper towel. In skillet, mix frozen sauce, vegetables and pineapple from meal starter. Cover; cook over medium heat 5 minutes, stirring occasionally.

3) Crumble ramen noodles. Stir noodles, contents of seasoning packet from soup mix and water into vegetable mixture. Cover; cook 4 to 5 minutes, stirring occasionally and separating noodles, until vegetables and noodles are tender. Serve topped with chicken nuggets.

HIGH ALTITUDE (3500-6500 FT.): No change.

Nutrition Information Per Serving:	
Calories: 510	From Fat: 230
Total Fat	26g
Saturated	6g
Cholesterol	35mg
Sodium	1040mg
Total Carbohydrate	55g
Dietary Fiber	4g
Sugars	24g
Protein	16g

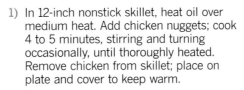

At the grocery store you will find package sizes for chicken nuggets that range from 11 to 16 ounces. Any size can be used for this recipe.

Turkey Stroganoff Skillet Supper

PREP TIME: 25 MINUTES (READY IN 35 MINUTES)
SERVINGS: 4 (1-1/3 CUPS EACH)

1 can (14 oz.) chicken broth

1 jar (12 oz.) turkey gravy

2½ cups uncooked wide egg noodles (4 oz.)

1 cup sliced fresh carrots (2 medium)

1 cup Green Giant® frozen sweet peas (from 1-lb. bag)

½ cup sour cream

⅛ teaspoon ground nutmeg

⅛ teaspoon pepper

2 cups cubed cooked turkey

Nutrition Information Per Serving:		
Calories: 400	From Fat: 160	
Total Fat	17g	
Saturated	6g	
Cholesterol	105mg	
Sodium	1020mg	
Total Carbohydrate	32g	
Dietary Fiber	3g	
Sugars	5g	
Protein	29g	

Start off your meal with a tossed salad of mixed greens and your favorite dressing.

1) In 10-inch skillet, mix broth and gravy until well blended. Heat to boiling. Stir in noodles, carrots, peas, sour cream, nutmeg and pepper. Return to boiling. Reduce heat to low; cover and simmer 10 minutes.

2) Stir in turkey. Cook about 4 minutes, stirring occasionally, until noodles and vegetables are tender.

HIGH ALTITUDE (3500-6500 FT.): No change.

Chicken and Vegetable Gravy over Biscuits

PREP TIME: 25 MINUTES (READY IN 25 MINUTES)
SERVINGS: 4

 EASY

- 1 tablespoon vegetable oil
- 1 lb. boneless skinless chicken thighs, cut into quarters
- 1 jar (12 oz.) chicken gravy
- 1 tablespoon Worcestershire sauce
- 1/2 teaspoon onion salt
- 2 cups Green Giant® frozen mixed vegetables (from 1-lb. bag)
- 4 Pillsbury® Microwave frozen buttermilk biscuits (from 1-lb. bag)

Nutrition Information Per Serving:		
Calories: 530	From Fat: 250	
Total Fat	27g	
Saturated	7g	
Cholesterol	70mg	
Sodium	1440mg	
Total Carbohydrate	41g	
Dietary Fiber	4g	
Sugars	7g	
Protein	32g	

tip

If you prefer, this yummy and creamy chicken can be served over mashed potatoes.

1) In 10-inch nonstick skillet, heat oil over medium-high heat. Add chicken; cook 5 minutes, stirring occasionally, until browned on all sides. Reduce heat to low; cover and cook 5 minutes or until juice of chicken is clear when center of thickest part is cut (180°F.).

2) Stir in remaining ingredients except biscuits. Cover; cook over high heat until mixture boils. Reduce heat; cover and cook 5 to 7 minutes, stirring occasionally, until vegetables are tender.

3) Meanwhile, microwave biscuits as directed on bag. Serve chicken mixture over split warm biscuits.

HIGH ALTITUDE (3500-6500 FT.): No change.

Stove-Top Chicken Enchilada Lasagna

LAURA WARE | FORT WORTH, TEXAS

PREP TIME: 15 MINUTES (READY IN 45 MINUTES)
SERVINGS: 2

1 tablespoon butter or vegetable oil

1/3 cup finely chopped onion (1 small)

1 can (10 oz.) Old El Paso® red enchilada sauce

1 to 3 teaspoons ground cumin

1 can (12.5 oz.) chunk chicken breast in water, drained

4 Old El Paso® flour tortillas for burritos, 8 inch (from 11.5-oz. package)

1 cup shredded pepper Jack cheese (4 oz.)

1 cup shredded Cheddar cheese (4 oz.)

1/3 cup sliced jalapeño chiles (from jar)

1 can (7 oz.) Old El Paso® chopped green chiles

Sour cream

1) In 2-quart saucepan, melt butter over medium heat. Add onion; cook 3 to 5 minutes, stirring frequently, until tender. Reserve 1/4 cup enchilada sauce; add remaining sauce to onion. Stir in cumin and chicken. Reduce heat to medium-low; simmer uncovered 5 minutes.

2) Lightly grease 10-inch skillet with butter or cooking spray; heat over low heat. Place 1 tortilla in skillet; top evenly with pepper Jack cheese and second tortilla. Spread chicken mixture over second tortilla; top with third tortilla. Sprinkle evenly with Cheddar cheese; top with jalapeño chiles and green chiles. Place fourth tortilla over chiles; spread reserved 1/4 cup enchilada sauce over top.

3) Cover skillet; cook over low heat 18 to 20 minutes or until thoroughly heated. Remove from heat; let stand 10 minutes before serving. Cut into 4 wedges; serve topped with sour cream and if desired, several additional jalapeño chile slices.

HIGH ALTITUDE (3500-6500 FT.): In Step 3, cook over medium-low heat 21 to 23 minutes.

Nutrition Information Per Serving:

Calories:	970	From Fat:	510
Total Fat			57g
Saturated			30g
Cholesterol			205mg
Sodium			3040mg
Total Carbohydrate			59g
Dietary Fiber			1g
Sugars			7g
Protein			56g

Ravioli Bolognese

PREP TIME: 40 MINUTES (READY IN 40 MINUTES)
SERVINGS: 4 (1-3/4 CUPS EACH)

 EASY

- 1 lb. lean (at least 80%) ground beef
- 1 cup frozen small whole onions (from 1-lb. bag)
- 1 jar (26 oz.) sun-dried tomato pasta sauce
- 1 jar (4.5 oz.) Green Giant® whole mushrooms, drained
- 1 package (9 oz.) refrigerated cheese-filled ravioli
- 1 cup water

1) In 12-inch skillet, cook ground beef and onions over medium heat 8 to 10 minutes, stirring frequently, until beef is thoroughly cooked; drain.

2) Add remaining ingredients; heat to boiling. Reduce heat to low; cover and simmer 20 to 25 minutes, stirring occasionally, until sauce is thoroughly heated and ravioli are tender.

HIGH ALTITUDE (3500-6500 FT.): Increase water to 1-1/2 cups.

Nutrition Information Per Serving:

Calories:	520	From Fat:	220
Total Fat			25g
Saturated			8g
Cholesterol			135mg
Sodium			1620mg
Total Carbohydrate			49g
Dietary Fiber			4g
Sugars			16g
Protein			30g

tip To make this dish even more special, add $1/2$ cup chopped pitted kalamata olives and sprinkle each serving with shredded Parmesan or mozzarella cheese.

Crunchy Asian Chicken and Vegetables

PREP TIME: 20 MINUTES (READY IN 20 MINUTES)
SERVINGS: 4

⊜ EASY   ⓕ LOW FAT

2 cups uncooked instant white rice

2 cups water

2 tablespoons vegetable oil

14 to 16 oz. uncooked chicken breast tenders (not breaded)

$\frac{1}{2}$ cup thinly sliced onion

$\frac{1}{2}$ cup teriyaki baste and glaze (from 12-oz. bottle)

$\frac{1}{2}$ cup water

1 cup julienne cut ($2x\frac{1}{8}x\frac{1}{8}$ inch) carrots

1 cup Green Giant Select® frozen sugar snap peas (from 1-lb. bag), thawed

1 can (11 oz.) mandarin orange segments, drained

1) In 2-quart saucepan, cook rice in 2 cups water as directed on package, omitting salt.

2) In 12-inch nonstick skillet, heat oil over medium heat. Add chicken and onion; cook 6 to 8 minutes, turning chicken and stirring onion occasionally, until onion is tender and chicken is no longer pink.

3) Stir in teriyaki baste and glaze, $\frac{1}{2}$ cup water, the carrots and sugar snap peas. Heat to boiling; boil 1 minute. Reduce heat; cover and simmer 4 to 6 minutes longer, stirring occasionally, until vegetables are crisp-tender. Gently stir in orange segments. Serve chicken mixture over rice.

HIGH ALTITUDE (3500-6500 FT.): No change.

Nutrition Information Per Serving:

Calories:	490	From Fat:	70
Total Fat		8g	
Saturated		1g	
Cholesterol		50mg	
Sodium		960mg	
Total Carbohydrate		73g	
Dietary Fiber		3g	
Sugars		20g	
Protein		31g	

tip

If desired, substitute chicken breast strips for stir-fry, for the chicken breast tenders, or you can cut boneless chicken breasts into $\frac{1}{2}$-inch-thick strips instead.

Pork and Asparagus Scaloppine

PREP TIME: 30 MINUTES (READY IN 30 MINUTES)
SERVINGS: 4

e EASY

- ⅓ cup lemon-herb dressing
- ⅓ cup all-purpose flour
- 1 lb. boneless thin-cut pork loin chops (about 6), cut in half
- ½ cup chicken broth
- 2 tablespoons lemon-herb dressing
- ¾ lb. fresh asparagus spears, trimmed, cut into 1-inch pieces (1¾ cups)

Nutrition Information Per Serving:	
Calories: 310	From Fat: 130
Total Fat	14g
Saturated	4g
Cholesterol	70mg
Sodium	370mg
Total Carbohydrate	19g
Dietary Fiber	1g
Sugars	9g
Protein	27g

tip

Serve with buttered egg noodles or fettuccine and purchased Caesar salad.

1) Heat 12-inch nonstick skillet over medium-high heat. In separate shallow bowls, place ⅓ cup dressing and flour. Dip pork pieces into dressing; coat with flour. Add pork to skillet; cook 1 to 2 minutes on each side or until brown. Meanwhile, in small bowl, mix broth and 2 tablespoons dressing.

2) Reduce heat to medium; add broth mixture to skillet, moving pork with wooden spoon to scrape up any brown bits. Add asparagus; cover and cook 2 to 3 minutes or until asparagus is crisp-tender and pork is no longer pink in center.

HIGH ALTITUDE (3500-6500 FT.): No change.

CORNISH HENS WITH APPLE-RAISIN STUFFING
PG. 216

Main Dishes

Menu choices your family will love...from pizza and pork chops to pot roast and meat loaf.

POLKA DOT MEAT LOAF
PG. 209

CHICKEN SALAD CRESCENT CANNOLI
PG. 224

LEMONY FISH AND TOMATOES
PG. 231

Barbeque Pork and Veggie Pizza

PREP TIME: 10 MINUTES (READY IN 35 MINUTES)
SERVINGS: 4

 EASY

1 can (13.8 oz.) Pillsbury® refrigerated pizza crust

1 container (18 oz.) Lloyd's® refrigerated original barbeque sauce with shredded pork

1½ cups shredded Monterey Jack cheese (6 oz.)

½ medium red onion, cut in thin wedges

1 medium green bell pepper, cut into thin bite-size strips

Nutrition Information Per Serving:

Calories:	610	From Fat:	180
Total Fat			21g
Saturated			10g
Cholesterol			70mg
Sodium			1800mg
Total Carbohydrate			75g
Dietary Fiber			2g
Sugars			28g
Protein			32g

1) Heat oven to 425°F. Spray 12-inch pizza pan with cooking spray. Unroll dough on pan; starting at center, press out dough to edge of pan to form crust. Bake 7 to 9 minutes or until light golden brown.

2) Remove partially baked crust from oven. Top with barbeque sauce with pork, cheese, onion and bell pepper.

3) Return to oven; bake 10 to 12 minutes longer or until crust is golden brown and cheese is melted.

HIGH ALTITUDE (3500-6500 FT.): No change.

tip

Serve with fruit slices such as apples, oranges or pears for an easy supper.

Crispy Oven-Fried Chicken

PREP TIME: 25 MINUTES (READY IN 1 HOUR 10 MINUTES)
SERVINGS: 4

 LOW FAT

2 cups Total® Corn Flakes cereal,
crushed to 1 cup

2 egg whites

1 teaspoon paprika

½ teaspoon salt

½ teaspoon garlic powder

½ teaspoon dried oregano leaves

¼ teaspoon ground red pepper
(cayenne)

3 to 3½ lb. cut-up broiler-fryer
chicken, skin removed

Nutrition Information Per Serving:	
Calories: 300	From Fat: 90
Total Fat	10g
Saturated	3g
Cholesterol	120mg
Sodium	510mg
Total Carbohydrate	11g
Dietary Fiber	0g
Sugars	1g
Protein	41g

tip

For easy cleanup, coat the chicken with the corn flake mixture by shaking the egg white-dipped pieces in a large resealable food storage plastic bag.

1) Heat oven to 400°F. Spray rack in broiler pan with cooking spray.

2) In shallow bowl, place crushed cereal. In another shallow bowl, beat remaining ingredients except chicken with fork until well blended. Dip chicken pieces into egg white mixture; coat with cereal. Place on rack in broiler pan.

3) Bake about 45 minutes or until thermometer inserted in center of breast reads 170°F. and in center of thighs, legs and wings reads 180°F.

HIGH ALTITUDE (3500-6500 FT.): No change.

Italian Meatballs and Fettuccine

PREP TIME: 25 MINUTES (READY IN 25 MINUTES)
SERVINGS: 4 (1-1/2 CUPS EACH)

 EASY

1 package (9 oz.) refrigerated
    fettuccine

8 oz. frozen Italian meatballs (about 8)

1½ cups coarsely chopped plum (Roma)
    tomatoes (4 to 5 medium)

½ cup Italian dressing

½ teaspoon dried basil leaves

¼ cup shredded Parmesan cheese
    (1 oz.), if desired

Nutrition Information Per Serving:		
Calories: 450	From Fat: 190	
Total Fat	22g	
Saturated	4g	
Cholesterol	65mg	
Sodium	730mg	
Total Carbohydrate	46g	
Dietary Fiber	3g	
Sugars	6g	
Protein	20g	

You'll find a variety
of sizes and flavors
of meatballs in the
freezer case at the
grocery store. If the
meatballs are small,
you may need a few
extra to equal the
8 ounces of meatballs
needed for this recipe.

1) Cook fettuccine as directed on package. Drain; return to saucepan. If
    necessary, cover to keep warm.

2) Meanwhile, in small microwavable bowl, microwave meatballs, uncovered,
    on High 3 to 6 minutes, stirring once, until thoroughly heated.

3) Gently stir meatballs, tomatoes, dressing and basil into cooked fettuccine.
    Cook over low heat 2 to 3 minutes, stirring occasionally, just until
    thoroughly heated. Sprinkle with cheese.

HIGH ALTITUDE (3500-6500 FT.): No change.

Sweet-and-Sour Pork Chops

PREP TIME:	25 MINUTES (READY IN 25 MINUTES)
SERVINGS:	4

 EASY

½ cup sweet-and-sour sauce

2 tablespoons chili sauce

¼ teaspoon ground ginger

4 boneless pork loin chops
(about ¾ inch thick)

½ teaspoon garlic powder

½ teaspoon paprika

Nutrition Information Per Serving:

Calories:	270	From Fat:	100
Total Fat			11g
Saturated			4g
Cholesterol			85mg
Sodium			280mg
Total Carbohydrate			10g
Dietary Fiber			0g
Sugars			7g
Protein			31g

1) Heat gas or charcoal grill. In 1-quart saucepan, mix sweet-and-sour sauce, chili sauce and ginger. Sprinkle pork chops with garlic powder and paprika.

2) When grill is heated, place pork chops on gas grill over medium heat or on charcoal grill over medium coals; cover grill. Cook 8 to 10 minutes, turning once or twice and brushing with sauce mixture during last 5 minutes of cooking, until pork chops are no longer pink and meat thermometer inserted in center of pork reads 160°F.

3) Heat any remaining sauce mixture to boiling; serve with pork chops.

HIGH ALTITUDE (3500-6500 FT.): Cook pork chops on covered grill over medium-low heat. Continue as directed above.

You'll find chili sauce in the condiment section of the store (near ketchup, mustard, etc.). Pick up some deli coleslaw to serve with the pork.

Easy Microwave Jammin' Jambalaya

PREP TIME: 20 MINUTES (READY IN 20 MINUTES)
SERVINGS: 3 (1-1/3 CUPS EACH)

 EASY

1 cup frozen bell pepper and onion stir-fry (from 16-oz. bag)

1/2 cup Old El Paso® Thick 'n Chunky salsa

1 can (14.5 oz.) Mexican-style stewed tomatoes, undrained

3/4 cup uncooked instant white rice

1/4 lb. cooked kielbasa or Polish sausage, cut into 1/2-inch-thick slices

1 cup chopped cooked chicken

Nutrition Information Per Serving:	
Calories: 370	From Fat: 130
Total Fat	14g
Saturated	5g
Cholesterol	65mg
Sodium	1100mg
Total Carbohydrate	39g
Dietary Fiber	3g
Sugars	9g
Protein	22g

1) In 1-quart microwavable casserole, mix bell pepper and onion stir-fry, salsa and tomatoes. Cover; microwave on High 3 to 5 minutes, stirring once or twice, until mixture boils, and bell pepper and onion are crisp-tender.

2) Stir in rice. Cover; microwave on High 2 minutes, stirring once halfway through cooking.

3) Gently stir in kielbasa and chicken. Cover; microwave on High 2 to 3 minutes, stirring once or twice, until kielbasa and chicken are thoroughly heated.

HIGH ALTITUDE (3500-6500 FT.): In Step 1, add 1/4 cup water to other ingredients in casserole. Cover; microwave on High 5 to 7 minutes. In Step 3, cover; microwave on High 3 to 4 minutes.

Lemon Halibut

PREP TIME: 25 MINUTES (READY IN 6 HOURS 25 MINUTES)
SERVINGS: 4

EASY

1/2 cup creamy Italian dressing

2 teaspoons grated lemon peel

1/4 cup fresh lemon juice

4 halibut steaks (6 to 8 oz. each)

4 lemon slices

Nutrition Information Per Serving:	
Calories: 280	From Fat: 130
Total Fat	14g
Saturated	1.5g
Cholesterol	95mg
Sodium	410mg
Total Carbohydrate	5g
Dietary Fiber	0g
Sugars	3g
Protein	33g

1) In 1-gallon resealable food-storage plastic bag, mix dressing, lemon peel and lemon juice. Add halibut; seal bag and turn to coat. Refrigerate no more than 6 hours to marinate, turning bag once or twice.

2) When ready to cook halibut, heat gas or charcoal grill. When grill is heated, lightly oil grill rack. Remove halibut from marinade; discard marinade. Place halibut on gas grill over medium heat or on charcoal grill over medium coals; cover grill. Cook 10 to 14 minutes, turning once, until fish flakes easily with fork. Garnish with lemon slices and fresh greens, if desired.

HIGH ALTITUDE (3500-6500 FT.): No change.

Canadian Bacon and Pineapple Pizza

PREP TIME: 15 MINUTES (READY IN 30 MINUTES)
SERVINGS: 8

 EASY   LOW FAT

- 1 can (13.8 oz.) Pillsbury® refrigerated pizza crust
- 8 slices ($^3/4$ oz. each) mozzarella cheese
- 1 package (5 to 6 oz.) sliced Canadian bacon
- 1 can (8 oz.) pineapple chunks in juice, well drained on paper towels
- $^1/2$ cup thinly sliced red onion
- $^1/2$ cup chopped green bell pepper ($^1/2$ medium)
- $^1/2$ cup shredded Cheddar cheese (2 oz.)

1) Heat oven to 425°F. Spray 12-inch pizza pan or 13x9-inch pan with cooking spray. Unroll dough; place in pan. Starting at center, press out dough to edge of pan to form crust. Bake 6 to 8 minutes or until set and dry.

2) Remove partially baked crust from oven. Top with mozzarella cheese, cutting to fit. Arrange Canadian bacon, pineapple, onion and bell pepper over cheese to within $^1/2$ inch of edge. Sprinkle with Cheddar cheese.

3) Return to oven; bake 12 to 16 minutes longer or until crust is deep golden brown.

HIGH ALTITUDE (3500-6500 FT.): No change.

Nutrition Information Per Serving:	
Calories: 260	From Fat: 80
Total Fat	9g
Saturated	5g
Cholesterol	25mg
Sodium	730mg
Total Carbohydrate	29g
Dietary Fiber	1g
Sugars	8g
Protein	15g

tip

If you'd like, feel free to use 1 cup chopped cooked ham in place of the Canadian bacon.

Chili Shrimp with Honey Salsa

PREP TIME: 30 MINUTES (READY IN 30 MINUTES)
SERVINGS: 4

 EASY   LOW FAT

3/4 cup Old El Paso® Thick 'n Chunky salsa

1 tablespoon honey

1/2 teaspoon ground cumin

1 teaspoon chili powder

1 1/2 lb. uncooked deveined peeled large shrimp, tails removed if desired

1 tablespoon butter, melted

1/2 teaspoon seasoned salt

Nutrition Information Per Serving:

Calories:	180	From Fat:	40
Total Fat			4.5g
Saturated			2g
Cholesterol			250mg
Sodium			820mg
Total Carbohydrate			9g
Dietary Fiber			0g
Sugars			6g
Protein			26g

1) Heat gas or charcoal grill. To make foil tray for shrimp, cut 18x12-inch sheet of heavy-duty (or nonstick) foil. Fold up sides and corners to create pan with sides. If using heavy-duty foil, spray foil with cooking spray.

2) In small bowl, mix salsa, honey, cumin and 1/2 teaspoon of the chili powder; set aside. In foil tray, toss shrimp with butter, remaining 1/2 teaspoon chili powder and the seasoned salt.

3) When grill is heated, place foil tray with shrimp on gas grill over medium heat or on charcoal grill over medium coals; cover grill. Cook 8 to 10 minutes, stirring shrimp or shaking tray occasionally to turn shrimp, until shrimp turn pink. Serve shrimp with salsa mixture.

HIGH ALTITUDE (3500-6500 FT.): Cook shrimp in foil tray on covered grill over medium-low heat.

So-Simple Flank Steak

PREP TIME: 35 MINUTES (READY IN 6 HOURS 35 MINUTES)
SERVINGS: 4

e EASY

¹⁄₄ cup soy sauce

¹⁄₄ cup water

2 tablespoons vegetable oil

1 teaspoon sugar

1 clove garlic, minced

1 beef flank steak (about 1¹⁄₄ lb.)

Nutrition Information Per Serving:		
Calories: 290	From Fat:	150
Total Fat		17g
Saturated		5g
Cholesterol		80mg
Sodium		980mg
Total Carbohydrate		3g
Dietary Fiber		0g
Sugars		1g
Protein		31g

1) In 2-gallon resealable food-storage plastic bag, mix all ingredients except steak. Add steak; seal bag and turn to coat. Refrigerate at least 6 hours or overnight to marinate, turning bag once or twice.

2) When ready to cook steak, heat gas or charcoal grill. When grill is heated, remove steak from marinade; pour marinade into measuring cup. Place steak on gas grill over medium heat or on charcoal grill over medium coals; cover grill. Cook 15 to 20 minutes, turning occasionally and brushing with marinade, until steak is desired doneness. Discard any remaining marinade. Let steak stand on platter 5 minutes; cut diagonally across grain into slices. If desired, garnish with cherry tomatoes and red onion slices.

HIGH ALTITUDE (3500-6500 FT.): Cook steak on covered grill over medium-low heat. Continue as directed above.

An alternative to the plastic bag for marinating the steak would be to use a 13x9-inch (3-quart) glass baking dish. Cover with a lid or plastic wrap.

Roasted Herb Pork Tenderloins

PREP TIME:	15 MINUTES (READY IN 50 MINUTES)
SERVINGS:	6

 EASY   LOW FAT

¹/₂ teaspoon garlic pepper blend

¹/₂ teaspoon dried rosemary leaves, crushed

¹/₂ teaspoon dried thyme leaves, crushed

¹/₂ teaspoon paprika

¹/₄ teaspoon salt

2 pork tenderloins (³/₄ lb. each)

2 teaspoons olive or vegetable oil

Nutrition Information Per Serving:

Calories:	160	From Fat:	50
Total Fat			6g
Saturated			1.5g
Cholesterol			70mg
Sodium			150mg
Total Carbohydrate			0g
Dietary Fiber			0g
Sugars			0g
Protein			26g

tip

If you don't have garlic pepper blend on hand, make your own with equal parts of garlic powder and black pepper.

1) Heat oven to 425°F. In small bowl, mix garlic pepper blend, rosemary, thyme, paprika and salt.

2) Brush pork tenderloins with oil. Sprinkle with seasoning mixture; rub in with fingers. In ungreased shallow roasting pan, place pork tenderloins.

3) Roast 25 to 35 minutes or until pork has slight blush of pink and meat thermometer inserted in center reads 160°F. Let stand 5 minutes before slicing.

HIGH ALTITUDE (3500-6500 FT.): No change.

Chicken Carbonara

PREP TIME: 15 MINUTES (READY IN 30 MINUTES)
SERVINGS: 4

 EASY

8 oz. uncooked spaghetti

1 cup Green Giant Select® LeSueur® frozen baby sweet peas (from 1-lb. bag)

3 slices bacon

1/2 deli rotisserie chicken, skin and bone removed, chopped (about 2 cups)

1 jar (16 oz.) Alfredo sauce

1/4 cup grated Parmesan cheese

Nutrition Information Per Serving:		
Calories: 580	From Fat: 220	
Total Fat		24g
Saturated		12g
Cholesterol		110mg
Sodium		1120mg
Total Carbohydrate		56g
Dietary Fiber		4g
Sugars		5g
Protein		38g

1) In 3-quart saucepan, cook spaghetti as directed on package, adding peas during last 2 minutes of cooking time. Drain; return to saucepan.

2) Meanwhile, place bacon on 2 microwave-safe paper towels and lay on microwave-safe plate. Microwave on High for 2 to 3 minutes or until crisp; crumble.

3) Stir bacon, chicken and Alfredo sauce into cooked spaghetti and peas. Cook over low heat about 5 minutes, stirring occasionally, until thoroughly heated. Sprinkle with cheese.

HIGH ALTITUDE (3500-6500 FT.): No change.

Chili-Lime Salmon

PREP TIME: 25 MINUTES (READY IN 55 MINUTES)
SERVINGS: 4

EASY

2 tablespoons butter, melted

2 tablespoons fresh lime juice

1/2 teaspoon chili powder

1/8 teaspoon salt

4 salmon fillets (4 oz. each)

Nutrition Information Per Serving:		
Calories: 210	From Fat: 110	
Total Fat		12g
Saturated		5g
Cholesterol		90mg
Sodium		180mg
Total Carbohydrate		0g
Dietary Fiber		0g
Sugars		0g
Protein		24g

1) In 1-gallon resealable food-storage plastic bag, mix all ingredients except salmon. Add salmon; seal bag and turn to coat. Let stand at room temperature 30 minutes to marinate, turning bag once or twice.

2) Meanwhile, heat gas or charcoal grill. When grill is heated, carefully oil grill rack. Remove salmon from marinade; discard marinade. Place salmon, skin side down, on gas grill over medium heat or on charcoal grill over medium coals; cover grill. Cook 10 to 14 minutes, without turning, until fish flakes easily with fork. If desired, garnish with fresh lime slices.

HIGH ALTITUDE (3500-6500 FT.): No change.

Pot Roast with Sweet Potatoes and Parsnips

PREP TIME: 35 MINUTES (READY IN 2 HOURS 50 MINUTES)
SERVINGS: 8

1 tablespoon vegetable oil

1 boneless beef chuck roast
(3 to 3¹/₂ lb.)

¹/₂ teaspoon salt

¹/₄ teaspoon pepper

1 medium onion, chopped (¹/₂ cup)

1 can (14 oz.) beef broth

2 tablespoons molasses

1 teaspoon dried thyme leaves

2 medium dark-orange sweet potatoes
(about 1 lb.), peeled, cut into 2-inch
pieces (3 cups)

3 medium parsnips, peeled, cut into
1-inch-thick slices (2 cups)

¹/₄ cup all-purpose flour

¹/₄ cup water

1) Heat oven to 350°F. In 12-inch nonstick skillet, heat oil over medium-high heat. Add beef roast; cook until browned on both sides. Place roast in center of ungreased shallow roasting pan or 13x9-inch (3-quart) glass baking dish. Sprinkle with salt and pepper.

2) In same skillet, cook onion over medium-high heat 4 to 6 minutes, stirring occasionally, until tender. Stir in broth, molasses and thyme. Heat to boiling. Boil 5 minutes, stirring occasionally. Pour broth mixture over roast. Cover tightly with foil.

3) Bake 1 hour. Place sweet potatoes and parsnips around roast; bake 1 to 1¹/₄ hours longer or until roast and vegetables are fork-tender.

4) Remove roast and vegetables from pan, reserving juices. Pour juices into 2-quart saucepan. In small bowl, mix flour and water until smooth. Place saucepan with drippings over medium heat; gradually stir in flour mixture, cooking and stirring, until mixture comes to a full boil. Boil 1 minute, stirring constantly, until thickened. Cut roast into slices; serve with vegetables and gravy.

HIGH ALTITUDE (3500-6500 FT.): No change.

Nutrition Information Per Serving:		
Calories: 450	From Fat:	190
Total Fat		22g
Saturated		8g
Cholesterol		105mg
Sodium		450mg
Total Carbohydrate		27g
Dietary Fiber		3g
Sugars		13g
Protein		37g

Stuffed Cabbage Rolls

PREP TIME: 1 HOUR 15 MINUTES (READY IN 2 HOURS 15 MINUTES)
SERVINGS: 8 (2 CABBAGE ROLLS EACH)

1 cup water

1/2 cup uncooked regular long-grain white rice

1 medium head cabbage, core removed

2 eggs

1 lb. lean (at least 80%) ground beef

1/3 cup chopped onion

1/2 teaspoon salt

1/4 teaspoon dried oregano leaves

1/4 teaspoon pepper

1 can (15 oz.) tomato sauce

3/4 cup grated Parmesan cheese

1) Heat oven to 375°F. Spray 13x9-inch (3-quart) glass baking dish with cooking spray. In 2-quart saucepan, heat water and rice to boiling. Reduce heat to low; cover and cook 12 to 14 minutes or until rice is tender. Remove from heat.

2) Meanwhile, in 6-quart Dutch oven, cook whole head of cabbage in enough boiling water to cover about 3 minutes or just until outer leaves are softened. Remove cabbage from water; remove as many leaves as can easily be removed. Return cabbage to water; repeat process until 16 leaves are removed.

3) In large bowl, beat eggs. Stir in ground beef, onion, salt, oregano, pepper and cooked rice. For each roll, place about 3 tablespoons beef mixture in cooked cabbage leaf; roll up, tucking in ends to completely cover mixture. Place seam side down in baking dish. Pour tomato sauce over rolls. Sprinkle with Parmesan cheese.

4) Cover tightly with foil; bake 50 to 60 minutes or until bubbly around edges, cheese is melted and beef is thoroughly cooked.

HIGH ALTITUDE (3500-6500 FT.): Heat oven to 400°F.

Nutrition Information Per Serving:	
Calories: 260	From Fat: 100
Total Fat	11g
Saturated	4.5g
Cholesterol	95mg
Sodium	710mg
Total Carbohydrate	21g
Dietary Fiber	4g
Sugars	7g
Protein	19g

Piñata Pork Roast

MARY EDWARDS | LONG BEACH, CALIFORNIA

PREP TIME: 30 MINUTES (READY IN 2 HOURS 10 MINUTES)
SERVINGS: 12

6 Old El Paso® taco shells (from 4.6-oz. box), crushed to 1/2-inch pieces (about 1 1/2 cups)

2 cups Green Giant Select® frozen gold & white corn (from 1-lb. bag)

1 1/2 cups shredded Mexican 4-cheese blend (6 oz.)

2 tablespoons chopped fresh cilantro

2 tablespoons chopped green onions (2 medium)

1 boneless pork loin roast (about 4 lb.), trimmed of fat, butterflied by butcher to be flattened and rolled*

Salt and freshly cracked pepper, if desired

1 package (1.25 oz.) Old El Paso® taco seasoning mix

1/2 teaspoon garlic salt

1/2 teaspoon ground cumin

1/2 cup chicken broth

1 1/2 teaspoons grated lime peel

1 tablespoon fresh lime juice

1/2 cup grape tomatoes or cherry tomatoes, cut in half

1 ripe avocado, pitted, peeled and cut into bite-size pieces

Lime slices, if desired

Additional fresh cilantro, if desired

1) Heat oven to 350°F. In medium bowl, mix crushed taco shells, 1 cup of the frozen corn, the cheese, chopped cilantro and onions.

2) Open pork roast to lay flat; sprinkle with salt and pepper. Press taco shell mixture evenly onto pork to within about 3/4 inch of edge.

3) Starting with one long side, tightly roll up pork jelly-roll fashion; tie with kitchen string at 1 1/2-inch intervals. Rub taco seasoning mix evenly over rolled pork. Place seam side down on rack in ungreased large heavy ovenproof roasting pan. Insert ovenproof meat thermometer so tip is in center of thickest part of pork.

4) Roast uncovered 1 hour 15 minutes to 1 hour 30 minutes or until meat thermometer inserted into center of pork reads 155°F. Remove pork from pan; place on cutting board or serving platter. Cover with foil; let stand 10 minutes until thermometer reads 160°F.

5) If necessary, drain off any excess fat from roasting pan; place pan over medium-high heat. Stir in garlic salt, cumin, broth and remaining 1 cup corn. Cook 2 to 3 minutes, stirring occasionally, just until corn is tender. Stir in lime peel, lime juice, tomatoes and avocado. Cook just until thoroughly heated. Remove string from pork; cut across grain into slices. Serve pork with corn-avocado salsa; garnish with lime and cilantro.

*NOTE: To cut pork roast so it can be filled and rolled, cut horizontally down length of pork, about 1/2 inch from top of pork, to within 1/2 inch of opposite side; open flat. Turn pork so you can cut other side. Repeat with other side of pork, cutting from the inside edge to within 1/2 inch of outer edge; open flat. Sprinkle with salt and pepper. Fill and roll as directed above.

HIGH ALTITUDE (3500-6500 FT.): No change.

Nutrition Information Per Serving:		
Calories: 380	From Fat:	180
Total Fat		20g
Saturated		7g
Cholesterol		110mg
Sodium		530mg
Total Carbohydrate		12g
Dietary Fiber		2g
Sugars		1g
Protein		38g

Cheesy Italian Chicken Bake

PREP TIME: 20 MINUTES (READY IN 40 MINUTES)
SERVINGS: 4

⊝ EASY

2 cups tomato pasta sauce

1 package (14 to 16 oz.) chicken breast tenders (not breaded)

1½ cups shredded Italian cheese blend (6 oz.)

8 oz. uncooked spaghetti

Nutrition Information Per Serving:	
Calories: 600	From Fat: 170
Total Fat	19g
Saturated	8g
Cholesterol	100mg
Sodium	1210mg
Total Carbohydrate	70g
Dietary Fiber	5g
Sugars	11g
Protein	40g

1) Heat oven to 350°F. Into ungreased 8-inch square (2-quart) glass baking dish, spoon and spread 1 cup of the pasta sauce. Top with chicken tenders in single layer. Spoon remaining 1 cup sauce over chicken. Sprinkle with cheese.

2) Bake uncovered 30 to 35 minutes or until mixture is bubbly and chicken is no longer pink in center.

3) Meanwhile, cook spaghetti as directed on package; drain.

4) Serve chicken and sauce over spaghetti.

HIGH ALTITUDE (3500-6500 FT.): Do not add cheese in Step 1. In Step 2, bake uncovered 35 to 40 minutes, sprinkling with cheese during last 5 minutes of baking.

Corny Sloppy Joe Pizza

PREP TIME: 15 MINUTES (READY IN 25 MINUTES)
SERVINGS: 6

⊝ EASY

1 lb. lean (at least 80%) ground beef

1 can (15.5 oz.) sloppy joe sandwich sauce

1 cup Green Giant® Niblets® frozen corn (from 1-lb. bag)

1 package (10 oz.) prebaked thin Italian pizza crust (12 inch)

2 cups Colby-Monterey Jack shredded cheese blend (8 oz.)

Nutrition Information Per Serving:	
Calories: 460	From Fat: 210
Total Fat	23g
Saturated	12g
Cholesterol	90mg
Sodium	930mg
Total Carbohydrate	33g
Dietary Fiber	3g
Sugars	6g
Protein	29g

1) Heat oven to 450°F. In 10-inch skillet, cook ground beef over medium-high heat 5 to 7 minutes, stirring frequently, until thoroughly cooked; drain. Stir in sandwich sauce and corn. Cook until thoroughly heated, stirring occasionally.

2) Place pizza crust on ungreased cookie sheet. Spoon beef mixture evenly onto crust. Sprinkle with cheese.

3) Bake 8 to 10 minutes or until cheese is melted and bubbly.

HIGH ALTITUDE (3500-6500 FT.): No change.

Stuffed Chicken Breasts Cordon Bleu

PREP TIME: 15 MINUTES (READY IN 45 MINUTES)
SERVINGS: 4

 EASY

4 large boneless skinless chicken breasts (1¼ to 1½ lb.)

¼ cup finely shredded Swiss cheese (1 oz.)

¼ cup finely chopped ham (1 oz.)

2 tablespoons real bacon pieces (from 2.8-oz. package)

2 tablespoons butter, melted

⅓ cup Progresso® plain dry bread crumbs

1) Heat oven to 350°F. To form pocket in each chicken breast, cut 3-inch-long slit in thick side of each breast, cutting into breast about 2 inches and to within ½ inch of opposite side.

2) In small bowl, mix cheese, ham and bacon. Spoon evenly into pockets in chicken; secure openings with toothpicks.

3) Place melted butter in shallow dish. Place bread crumbs on sheet of waxed paper. Dip each stuffed chicken breast in butter; roll in bread crumbs to coat. Place in ungreased 8-inch square (2-quart) glass baking dish. Sprinkle any remaining bread crumbs over chicken.

4) Bake 30 minutes or until juice of chicken is clear when center of thickest part is cut (170°F.). Remove toothpicks before serving.

HIGH ALTITUDE (3500-6500 FT.): Heat oven to 375°F. Bake 40 minutes.

Nutrition Information Per Serving:

Calories:	300	From Fat:	130
Total Fat			15g
Saturated			6g
Cholesterol			115mg
Sodium			360mg
Total Carbohydrate			7g
Dietary Fiber			0g
Sugars			0g
Protein			37g

To quickly melt butter, place it in a microwave-safe pie plate and microwave 30 seconds.

Polka Dot Meat Loaf

PREP TIME: 10 MINUTES (READY IN 1 HOUR 55 MINUTES)
SERVINGS: 6

EASY

1½ lb. lean (at least 80%) ground beef

½ cup ketchup

¼ cup Progresso® plain bread crumbs

2 tablespoons Worcestershire sauce

½ teaspoon salt

1 egg

6 sticks (1 oz. each) string cheese

1 teaspoon prepared yellow mustard

1 tablespoon packed brown sugar

1) Heat oven to 375°F. In large bowl, mix ground beef, ¼ cup of the ketchup, the bread crumbs, Worcestershire sauce, salt and egg. Press ⅓ of mixture in bottom of ungreased 8x4-inch loaf pan.

2) Place 2 pieces of the string cheese lengthwise and evenly spaced over beef mixture, with one end of the cheese about ½ inch from one end of pan. Cut 2 pieces of string cheese in half crosswise. Place 2 half pieces on beef mixture so cheese extends full length of pan. Press cheese into beef mixture.

3) Top with half of remaining beef mixture; pat evenly in place. Top with remaining string cheese in 2 rows; press in. Press remaining beef mixture over cheese. Press ends and edges of beef mixture well to seal in cheese; smooth top.

4) Bake 45 minutes. Meanwhile, in small bowl, mix remaining ¼ cup ketchup, the mustard and brown sugar.

5) Remove meat loaf from oven. Spoon juices from meat loaf; spoon ketchup mixture evenly over top.

6) Return to oven; bake 30 to 45 minutes longer or until thermometer inserted in center of meat loaf reads 160°F. Let stand 15 minutes before cutting into slices.

HIGH ALTITUDE (3500-6500 FT.): No change.

Nutrition Information Per Serving:

Calories:	340	From Fat:	180
Total Fat			20g
Saturated			9g
Cholesterol			120mg
Sodium			750mg
Total Carbohydrate			13g
Dietary Fiber			0g
Sugars			8g
Protein			29g

Stagger the placement of the cheese on the second layer so it is not directly above the first layer. Press ends and edges of beef mixture well to seal in the cheese.

Roasted Chicken with Peach Glaze

PREP TIME: 20 MINUTES (READY IN 2 HOURS 5 MINUTES)
SERVINGS: 6

 EASY

1 whole chicken (5 to 5$^1/_2$ lb.)

1 teaspoon garlic-pepper blend

$^1/_2$ cup peach or apricot preserves

Nutrition Information Per Serving:

Calories:	450	From Fat:	200
Total Fat			22g
Saturated			6g
Cholesterol			145mg
Sodium			140mg
Total Carbohydrate			19g
Dietary Fiber			0g
Sugars			13g
Protein			44g

1) Heat oven to 375°F. Spray rack in shallow roasting pan with cooking spray. Rinse chicken inside and out with cold water; drain and pat dry with paper towels.

2) Sprinkle garlic-pepper blend over chicken; place breast side up on rack in pan. Insert ovenproof meat thermometer so tip is in thickest part of inside thigh and does not touch bone.

3) Bake uncovered 1 hour. Brush chicken with preserves; bake 35 to 45 minutes longer or until thermometer reads 180°F. and legs move easily when lifted or twisted. Let stand 5 to 10 minutes before serving.

HIGH ALTITUDE (3500-6500 FT.): No change.

Roasted Pork Tenderloins and Vegetables

PREP TIME: 20 MINUTES (READY IN 1 HOUR 15 MINUTES)
SERVINGS: 6

⊝ EASY   **⑪ LOW FAT**

VEGETABLES AND PORK

- 6 ears Green Giant® Nibblers® frozen corn-on-the-cob

- 3 medium-size dark-orange sweet potatoes, peeled, cut into 1½-inch pieces

- 1 large onion, cut into 8 to 12 wedges

- 2 pork tenderloins (³⁄₄ lb. each)

GLAZE

- ²⁄₃ cup apple jelly

- 2 tablespoons vegetable oil

- 2 teaspoons ground dry mustard

- 1 teaspoon dried marjoram leaves

- ½ teaspoon salt

- ¼ teaspoon pepper

GARNISH

Italian parsley, if desired

1) Heat oven to 450°F. Place corn in large bowl of warm water to partially thaw. In ungreased 15x10x1-inch pan, arrange sweet potatoes and onion around sides.

2) In 1-quart saucepan, mix glaze ingredients. Cook over low heat, stirring constantly, until melted and smooth. Brush about half of glaze over vegetables. Roast uncovered 25 minutes.

3) Remove vegetables from oven. Turn vegetables in pan. Remove corn from water; place in pan with vegetables. Place pork tenderloins in center of pan. Brush pork and all vegetables with remaining glaze.

4) Return to oven; roast uncovered 25 to 30 minutes longer or until vegetables are tender, and pork has slight blush of pink in center and meat thermometer inserted in center reads 160°F. Slice pork. Arrange pork and vegetables on platter. Garnish with Italian parsley.

HIGH ALTITUDE (3500-6500 FT.): In Step 2, cook glaze ingredients over medium heat.

Nutrition Information Per Serving:	
Calories: 420 From Fat: 90	
Total Fat	10g
Saturated	2.5g
Cholesterol	70mg
Sodium	270mg
Total Carbohydrate	54g
Dietary Fiber	5g
Sugars	28g
Protein	29g

tip

One whole pork tenderloin is usually about ½ to ³⁄₄ pound. For this recipe, 2 large or 3 small tenderloins will yield the 1½ pounds necessary. There's no waste with pork tenderloin; it's very lean and tender.

Beef Pot Pie

PREP TIME: 15 MINUTES (READY IN 1 HOUR)
SERVINGS: 8

e EASY

- 1 box (15 oz.) Pillsbury® refrigerated pie crusts, softened as directed on box
- 1 jar (12 oz.) beef gravy
- 1 tablespoon cornstarch
- 1 tablespoon Worcestershire sauce
- 2 cups Green Giant® frozen mixed vegetables (from 1-lb. bag)
- 1 jar (4.5 oz.) Green Giant® sliced mushrooms, drained
- 1 lb. sliced ($\frac{1}{2}$ inch thick) cooked roast beef (from deli), cubed

1) Heat oven to 425°F. Make pie crusts as directed on box for Two-Crust Pie using 9-inch glass pie pan.

2) In 3-quart saucepan, mix gravy and cornstarch until well blended. Stir in Worcestershire sauce, frozen vegetables and mushrooms. Cook over medium-high heat, stirring occasionally, until bubbly. Stir in roast beef. Pour into crust-lined pan.

3) Top with second pie crust; seal edge and flute. Cut decorative slits in several places in top crust to allow steam to escape.

4) Bake 15 minutes. Cover crust edge with strips of foil to prevent excessive browning; bake 15 to 30 minutes longer or until crust is golden brown and filling is bubbly.

HIGH ALTITUDE (3500-6500 FT.): Increase cornstarch to 1 tablespoon plus 1 teaspoon. In Step 2, continue cooking vegetable mixture 1 to 2 minutes after mixture is bubbly. Bake pie 15 minutes. Cover crust edge with foil; bake 20 to 25 minutes longer.

Nutrition Information Per Serving:

Calories:	360	From Fat:	150
Total Fat		17g	
Saturated		6g	
Cholesterol		35mg	
Sodium		1150mg	
Total Carbohydrate		37g	
Dietary Fiber		3g	
Sugars		5g	
Protein		14g	

tip Use tiny cookie cutters to cut out decorative shapes from the top crust before placing it over the beef mixture. Brush the crust with beaten egg, and press the cutouts back onto the crust and brush them with egg.

Caesar Pork Chops

PREP TIME: 10 MINUTES (READY IN 50 MINUTES)
SERVINGS: 4

 EASY

1/4 cup all-purpose flour

1/2 teaspoon Italian seasoning

1/2 cup creamy Caesar dressing

4 bone-in pork loin chops (1/2 inch thick)

1/4 cup shredded Parmesan cheese (1 oz.)

Nutrition Information Per Serving:	
Calories: 400	From Fat: 250
Total Fat	28g
Saturated	7g
Cholesterol	80mg
Sodium	480mg
Total Carbohydrate	7g
Dietary Fiber	0g
Sugars	0g
Protein	30g

1) Heat oven to 375°F. Spray 12x8-inch (2-quart) glass baking dish with cooking spray. In pie pan or shallow dish, mix flour and Italian seasoning. Pour dressing into another pie pan or shallow dish.

2) Coat both sides of each pork chop with flour mixture; dip into dressing, coating both sides well. Place in baking dish. Sprinkle with cheese. Discard any remaining flour mixture and dressing.

3) Bake uncovered 35 to 40 minutes or until pork is no longer pink in center.

HIGH ALTITUDE (3500-6500 FT.): No change.

Veggie Macaroni and Cheese with Meatballs

PREP TIME: 25 MINUTES (READY IN 25 MINUTES)
SERVINGS: 6 (1-1/3 CUPS EACH)

 EASY

3 cups water

1 1/2 cups uncooked elbow macaroni (6 oz.)

1 bag (24 oz.) Green Giant® frozen broccoli, carrots, cauliflower & cheese flavored sauce

18 frozen cooked Italian meatballs (about 9 oz.), thawed

1 cup shredded Cheddar cheese (4 oz.)

Nutrition Information Per Serving:	
Calories: 350	From Fat: 130
Total Fat	14g
Saturated	7g
Cholesterol	70mg
Sodium	770mg
Total Carbohydrate	35g
Dietary Fiber	4g
Sugars	6g
Protein	19g

1) In 4-quart Dutch oven, heat water to boiling. Add macaroni; return to boiling. Cook 5 minutes over medium-high heat, stirring occasionally. Do not drain.

2) Stir in frozen vegetables with sauce chips and meatballs. Reduce heat to medium; cover and cook 11 to 13 minutes, stirring frequently to prevent sticking, until sauce chips are melted. Stir in Cheddar cheese until melted.

HIGH ALTITUDE (3500-6500 FT.): In Step 2, heat mixture to boiling before reducing heat to medium.

Roast Turkey with Sausage-Apple Stuffing

PREP TIME: 30 MINUTES (READY IN 5 HOURS)
SERVINGS: 12

½ lb. bulk pork sausage

½ cup chopped onion (1 medium)

½ cup chopped celery (1 medium stalk)

8 cups unseasoned stuffing cubes (about 14 oz.)

2 tablespoons finely chopped fresh parsley

2 teaspoons poultry seasoning

1 teaspoon salt

¼ teaspoon pepper

¼ cup butter or margarine, melted

2 cups chopped peeled apples (2 medium)

⅔ cup raisins

2 cups chicken broth or water

1 whole turkey (10 to 12 lb.)

1) Heat oven to 325°F. In 8-inch skillet, cook pork sausage, onion and celery over medium-high heat, stirring frequently, until sausage is no longer pink; do not drain.

2) In large bowl, mix stuffing cubes, parsley, poultry seasoning, salt, pepper and butter. Stir in apples, raisins, broth and sausage mixture with drippings.

3) Remove and discard giblets and neck from turkey. Rinse turkey inside and out with cold water; pat dry with paper towels. Spoon stuffing loosely into neck and body cavities of turkey; do not pack tightly. Cover and refrigerate remaining stuffing. Turn wings back and tuck tips over shoulder joints. Refasten drumsticks with metal piece or tuck under skin at tail. Fasten neck skin to back with skewers.

4) Place stuffed turkey, breast side up, in shallow roasting pan. Insert ovenproof meat thermometer so tip is in thickest part of inside thigh and does not touch bone.

5) Tent sheet of foil loosely over turkey; roast 3 hours 30 minutes to 4 hours 30 minutes, removing foil during last 30 to 60 minutes of roasting to allow browning, until thermometer reads 180°F. and legs move easily when lifted or twisted. Spoon or brush drippings over turkey several times during roasting. Remove from oven. Cover turkey with foil and allow to stand 10 to 15 minutes before carving.

6) Meanwhile, mix remaining stuffing with additional chicken broth or water to moisten. Spoon into microwavable casserole. Microwave on High 5 minutes, turning halfway through cooking until thoroughly heated.

HIGH ALTITUDE (3500-6500 FT.): No change.

Nutrition Information Per Serving:	
Calories: 560	From Fat: 240
Total Fat	27g
Saturated	8g
Cholesterol	140mg
Sodium	1150mg
Total Carbohydrate	36g
Dietary Fiber	2g
Sugars	9g
Protein	44g

Chicken Chimichanga with Jalapeño Cream

LORETTA TORRENS | GILBERT, ARIZONA

Pillsbury Bake-Off

PREP TIME: 30 MINUTES (READY IN 30 MINUTES)
SERVINGS: 4

2 tablespoons extra-virgin olive oil

2 boneless skinless chicken breasts (^{1}/$_2$ lb.), cut into 1-inch pieces

1 can (19 oz.) Progresso® Traditional southwestern-style chicken soup

1 package (3 oz.) cream cheese, softened

1 tablespoon whipping cream

1 jalapeño chile (from jar), finely chopped

1 tablespoon jalapeño liquid (from jar)

2 cups canola oil

4 Old El Paso® flour tortillas for burritos, 8 inch (from 11.5-oz. package)

1 cup shredded Cheddar-Monterey Jack cheese (4 oz.)

2 medium green onions, sliced (2 tablespoons)

1) In deep 12-inch skillet or wok, heat olive oil over medium heat. Add chicken; cook, stirring occasionally, until browned. Add soup; cook over high heat 8 to 12 minutes, stirring frequently, until mixture is thick.

2) Meanwhile, in 1-quart saucepan, melt cream cheese with whipping cream over low heat, stirring frequently. Stir in chile and chile liquid until well blended. Remove from heat; cover to keep warm. In 5-quart Dutch oven, heat canola oil over medium-high heat or to 350°F.

3) Onto each tortilla, spoon ^{1}/$_2$ cup chicken mixture. Fold sides of each tortilla up over filling; fold over remaining sides. Secure each with 2 or 3 toothpicks. Place in hot oil; fry 1 to 2 minutes, turning once, until tortillas are browned. Remove from oil; drain on paper towels.

4) Remove toothpicks; place chimichangas on individual plates. Top each with heaping 1 tablespoon cream cheese sauce, ^{1}/$_4$ cup Cheddar-Monterey Jack cheese and ^{1}/$_2$ tablespoon onions.

HIGH ALTITUDE (3500-6500 FT.): No change.

Nutrition Information Per Serving:

Calories:	630	From Fat:	380
Total Fat			43g
Saturated			15g
Cholesterol			95mg
Sodium			1120mg
Total Carbohydrate			33g
Dietary Fiber			1g
Sugars			2g
Protein			28g

Cornish Hens with Apple-Raisin Stuffing

PREP TIME: 30 MINUTES (READY IN 1 HOUR 45 MINUTES)
SERVINGS: 8

STUFFING

- 3 tablespoons butter or margarine
- ½ cup chopped green onions (8 medium)
- 1 red baking apple, unpeeled, chopped
- 4 cups unseasoned dry bread cubes
- ½ cup raisins
- ¼ teaspoon salt
- ¼ teaspoon ground allspice
- ¼ cup apple juice

CORNISH HENS

- 4 Cornish game hens (24 oz. each), thawed if frozen
- ¼ teaspoon salt
- ⅛ teaspoon pepper
- ¼ cup apple jelly
- 2 tablespoons butter or margarine

1) Heat oven to 350°F. In 10-inch skillet, melt 3 tablespoons butter over medium-high heat. Add onions and apple; cook and stir until tender. Stir in remaining stuffing ingredients. In ungreased 15x10x1-inch pan, spread stuffing.

2) Split each game hen in half. Sprinkle lightly with salt and pepper. Place hen halves, skin side up, over stuffing. In 1-quart saucepan, melt jelly with 2 tablespoons butter over low heat; brush over hens.

3) Bake uncovered 1 hour to 1 hour 15 minutes or until hens are fork-tender and juice is clear when thickest part is cut to bone (180°F.).

HIGH ALTITUDE (3500-6500 FT.): No change.

Nutrition Information Per Serving:

Calories:	810	From Fat:	390
Total Fat			44g
Saturated			14g
Cholesterol			260mg
Sodium			780mg
Total Carbohydrate			57g
Dietary Fiber			2g
Sugars			16g
Protein			48g

To split game hens, use a heavy-duty kitchen scissors or place the hens on a cutting board and use a large knife to cut through the birds.

Alfredo Chicken Pasta Toss

PREP TIME: 25 MINUTES (READY IN 25 MINUTES)
SERVINGS: 5 (1-1/3 CUPS EACH)

 EASY

4 cups uncooked rotini, penne or
bow-tie (farfalle) pasta (8 oz.)

1½ cups Green Giant® frozen sweet peas
(from 1-lb. bag)

1 cup shredded carrots (2 small)

1 tablespoon vegetable oil

1 lb. boneless skinless chicken breasts,
cut into thin bite-size strips

1 jar (16 oz.) Alfredo pasta sauce

2 teaspoons dried basil leaves

Nutrition Information Per Serving:

Calories:	530	From Fat:	220
Total Fat			24g
Saturated			9g
Cholesterol			135mg
Sodium			690mg
Total Carbohydrate			48g
Dietary Fiber			5g
Sugars			5g
Protein			31g

1) In 4-quart Dutch oven, cook and drain pasta as directed on package, adding
peas and carrots during last 5 minutes of cooking. Drain; return to Dutch oven.

2) Meanwhile, in 10-inch nonstick skillet, heat oil over medium heat. Add
chicken; cook 9 to 11 minutes, stirring frequently, until chicken is no longer
pink in center.

3) Stir chicken, Alfredo sauce and basil into pasta mixture in Dutch oven.
Cook and stir over medium heat until thoroughly heated.

HIGH ALTITUDE (3500-6500 FT.): No change.

Pizza-by-the-Yard

PREP TIME: 15 MINUTES (READY IN 15 MINUTES)
SERVINGS: 8

 EASY

1 bag (16 oz.) frozen cooked Italian-
style meatballs (about 32 meatballs)

1 jar (26 oz.) marinara or tomato
pasta sauce

1 loaf French bread (1 lb.)

2 cups shredded mozzarella cheese
(8 oz.)

Nutrition Information Per Serving:

Calories:	470	From Fat:	170
Total Fat			19g
Saturated			7g
Cholesterol			75mg
Sodium			1270mg
Total Carbohydrate			53g
Dietary Fiber			3g
Sugars			8g
Protein			25g

1) In large microwavable bowl, place meatballs. Microwave on High 3 minutes.
Cut meatballs in half; return to bowl. Stir in marinara sauce. Cover with
waxed paper. Microwave on High 6 to 8 minutes, stirring once or twice,
until hot.

2) Meanwhile, set oven control to broil. Cut bread in half crosswise; cut each
in half lengthwise, making 4 pieces. Place bread, cut side up, on ungreased
large cookie sheet. If desired, toast lightly under broiler.

3) Spoon hot meatballs and sauce evenly onto bread. Sprinkle with cheese. Broil
4 to 6 inches from heat 1 to 2 minutes or until cheese is melted and bubbly.

HIGH ALTITUDE (3500-6500 FT.): No change.

Layered Italian Meat Loaf

PREP TIME: 15 MINUTES (READY IN 1 HOUR 30 MINUTES)
SERVINGS: 6

 EASY

1½ lb. lean (at least 80%) ground beef

1 can (8 oz.) tomato sauce with basil, garlic and oregano

1 egg

¾ cup Progresso® Italian style bread crumbs

1 teaspoon garlic powder

¼ teaspoon pepper

1 cup shredded Italian cheese blend (4 oz.)

1 box (9 oz.) Green Giant® frozen spinach, thawed, well drained

1) Heat oven to 350°F. Spray 9x5-inch loaf pan with cooking spray or grease with shortening. In large bowl, mix ground beef, ½ cup of the tomato sauce, the egg, bread crumbs, garlic powder and pepper. Pat half of meat mixture in pan.

2) Sprinkle ½ cup of the cheese over meat mixture. Spread spinach over cheese; sprinkle with remaining ½ cup cheese. Pat remaining meat mixture on top of cheese. Insert ovenproof meat thermometer so tip is in center of loaf.

3) Bake uncovered 1 hour to 1 hour 15 minutes or until thoroughly cooked in center and thermometer reads 160°F. Run knife around edges of pan. Place serving platter upside down over pan; turn platter and pan over. Remove pan.

4) In small microwavable bowl, microwave remaining tomato sauce, loosely covered, on High 30 to 60 seconds or until hot; pour over top of meat loaf.

HIGH ALTITUDE (3500-6500 FT.): No change.

Nutrition Information Per Serving:

Calories:	350	From Fat:	180
Total Fat			19g
Saturated			8g
Cholesterol			120mg
Sodium			700mg
Total Carbohydrate			15g
Dietary Fiber			2g
Sugars			2g
Protein			29g

Red Wine Beef and Mushrooms

PREP TIME: 1 HOUR (READY IN 2 HOURS 15 MINUTES)
SERVINGS: 6

- 6 slices bacon, cut into $\frac{1}{2}$-inch pieces
- 2 lb. lean boneless beef stew meat
- 1 cup dry red wine
- 1 can (14 oz.) chicken broth
- $1\frac{1}{4}$ cups water
- 2 packages (8 oz. each) fresh whole mushrooms, quartered
- 4 cloves garlic, chopped
- 1 teaspoon dried thyme leaves
- $\frac{3}{4}$ teaspoon each salt and pepper
- 2 dried bay leaves
- $\frac{1}{4}$ cup all-purpose flour
- 1 package (12 oz.) uncooked fettuccine
- 1 tablespoon butter
- 1 jar (15 oz.) whole pearl onions in water, drained
- 2 tablespoons sugar

1) In 6-quart Dutch oven, cook bacon until lightly browned. Remove bacon; set aside. Reserve 1 tablespoon drippings in pan. Add beef; cook and stir until browned. Remove beef from Dutch oven.

2) In same Dutch oven, heat wine to boiling. Add broth and 1 cup of the water; cook and stir 2 minutes. Stir in bacon, beef, mushrooms, garlic, thyme, salt, pepper and bay leaves. Over medium-low heat, cover and simmer about 1 hour, stirring occasionally, until beef is tender.

3) Remove bay leaves. In small bowl, mix flour and remaining $\frac{1}{4}$ cup water until smooth. Add to beef mixture; cook and stir about 1 minute or until sauce is slightly thickened.

4) Cook fettuccine as directed on package. In 8-inch skillet, melt butter over medium-low heat. Stir in onions and sugar; cook about 15 minutes, stirring occasionally, until onions are lightly browned. Stir onion mixture into beef mixture. Serve over fettuccine; if desired sprinkle with parsley.

HIGH ALTITUDE (3500-6500 FT.): In Step 3, after adding flour-water mixture, cook 2 to 3 minutes. If mixture is too thick, add up to 1/4 cup additional water.

Nutrition Information Per Serving:

Calories:	650	From Fat:	260
Total Fat			28g
Saturated			10g
Cholesterol			155mg
Sodium			1060mg
Total Carbohydrate			54g
Dietary Fiber			3g
Sugars			7g
Protein			45g

Creamy Turkey and Broccoli Cobbler

PREP TIME:	20 MINUTES (READY IN 50 MINUTES)
SERVINGS:	6

 EASY

1 can (10³/₄ oz.) condensed cream of chicken soup

1 cup milk

6 cups Green Giant Select® frozen broccoli florets (from two 14-oz. bags), thawed

3¹/₂ cups cubed cooked turkey breast (about 1 lb.)

2 cups shredded sharp Cheddar cheese (8 oz.)

1 can (12 oz.) Pillsbury® Golden Layers® refrigerated buttermilk biscuits

1) Heat oven to 375°F. Spray 13x9-inch (3-quart) glass baking dish with cooking spray. In 12-inch skillet, mix soup and milk until well blended. Stir in thawed broccoli, turkey and cheese. Cook, stirring occasionally, until mixture is hot and bubbly. Pour into baking dish.

2) Separate dough into 10 biscuits; arrange on hot turkey mixture.

3) Bake uncovered 20 to 28 minutes or until biscuits are deep golden brown.

HIGH ALTITUDE (3500-6500 FT.): Add 1/4 cup water to skillet with soup and milk.

Nutrition Information Per Serving:

Calories:	560	From Fat:	250
Total Fat			28g
Saturated			12g
Cholesterol			115mg
Sodium			1260mg
Total Carbohydrate			35g
Dietary Fiber			4g
Sugars			9g
Protein			42g

Baked Ham with Orange-Mustard Glaze

PREP TIME: 20 MINUTES (READY IN 3 HOURS)
SERVINGS: 16

 EASY   LOW FAT

1 fully cooked bone-in ham (6 to 8 lb.)

1 cup water

1 cup orange juice

$^2/_3$ cup orange marmalade

$^1/_3$ cup stone-ground mustard

3 teaspoons dry mustard

1) Heat oven to 325°F. Place ham, fat side up, in disposable roasting pan (placed on baking pan) or on rack in shallow roasting pan. Pour water into pan. Bake 1 hour.

2) Remove ham from oven. Add orange juice to roasting pan. If necessary, trim fat from ham. Score ham diagonally at 1-inch intervals, cutting about $^1/_4$ inch deep; score in opposite direction to form diamond shapes. Insert meat thermometer so bulb reaches center of thickest part of ham but does not rest in fat or on bone.

3) In small bowl, combine marmalade and mustards; mix well. Brush half of marmalade mixture over ham; baste with pan juices. Return to oven; bake 1 to $1^1/_2$ hours or until meat thermometer registers 140°F., basting frequently with pan juices and brushing with remaining marmalade mixture.

4) Let ham stand in roasting pan for 15 minutes before slicing, basting frequently with pan juices.

Place ham, fat side up, in disposable roasting pan (placed on baking pan) or on a rack in a shallow roasting pan. Pour 1 cup of water into the pan. Bake at 325°F. for 1 hour.

Remove ham from the oven and score the top diagonally at 1-inch intervals, cutting about 1/4 inch deep to form diamond shapes. Brush ham with half of marmalade mixture and baste with pan juices. Bake until a meat thermometer registers 140°F.

Nutrition Information Per Serving:

Calories:	210	From Fat:	60
Total Fat		7g	
Saturated		2g	
Cholesterol		70mg	
Sodium		1770mg	
Total Carbohydrate		3g	
Dietary Fiber		0g	
Sugars		2g	
Protein		33g	

Calabacita Chicken Stew

LINDA S. BROWN | DALLAS, TEXAS

Pillsbury Bake-Off

PREP TIME:	50 MINUTES (READY IN 50 MINUTES)
SERVINGS:	6 (1-2/3 CUPS EACH)

1 tablespoon extra-virgin olive oil

1½ lb. uncooked chicken breast tenders (not breaded)

8 to 10 small to medium zucchini (2½ lb.), peeled, thinly sliced (8 cups)

1 medium white onion, chopped (½ cup)

1 can (15.25 oz.) Green Giant® whole kernel corn, undrained

1 can (14.5 oz.) diced tomatoes with green pepper and onion, undrained

1 can (4.5 oz.) Old El Paso® chopped green chiles, undrained

1½ teaspoons garlic powder

½ teaspoon ground cumin

Salt and pepper, if desired

½ cup chopped fresh cilantro

1) In 5- to 6-quart saucepan or Dutch oven, heat oil over medium heat. Add chicken; cover and cook 4 to 6 minutes, stirring occasionally, until no longer pink in center.

2) Stir in remaining ingredients except cilantro. Heat to boiling. Reduce heat to medium-low; cover and simmer about 20 minutes, stirring occasionally, until zucchini is tender.

3) Stir in cilantro; cook 3 minutes longer, stirring occasionally.

HIGH ALTITUDE (3500-6500 FT.): No change.

Nutrition Information Per Serving:

Calories:	270	From Fat:	60
Total Fat		7g	
Saturated		1.5g	
Cholesterol		70mg	
Sodium		470mg	
Total Carbohydrate		24g	
Dietary Fiber		4g	
Sugars		9g	
Protein		28g	

Pizza Bubbles

PREP TIME: 5 MINUTES (READY IN 30 MINUTES)
SERVINGS: 9

 EASY

1 can (7.5 oz.) Pillsbury® refrigerated buttermilk biscuits (from 4-can pack)

1 cup pizza sauce

1 cup shredded mozzarella cheese or pizza cheese blend (4 oz.)

Additional pizza sauce, if desired

Nutrition Information Per Serving:	
Calories: 130 From Fat: 60	
Total Fat	7g
Saturated	3g
Cholesterol	5mg
Sodium	420mg
Total Carbohydrate	11g
Dietary Fiber	0g
Sugars	2g
Protein	5g

1) Heat oven to 375°F. Spray 8-inch square (2-quart) glass baking dish with cooking spray. Separate dough into 10 biscuits. Cut each into quarters; place in medium bowl. Stir in 1 cup pizza sauce to coat. Spoon biscuit mixture evenly into dish.

2) Bake 15 to 20 minutes or until light golden brown and center biscuits are no longer doughy.

3) Sprinkle with cheese; bake 5 minutes longer or until cheese is melted. Cut into squares; serve warm with additional pizza sauce for dipping.

HIGH ALTITUDE (3500-6500 FT.): Bake 20 minutes. Sprinkle with cheese; bake 5 minutes longer.

Tex-Mex Beef-Topped Potatoes

PREP TIME: 20 MINUTES (READY IN 20 MINUTES)
SERVINGS: 4

 EASY

4 medium baking potatoes

1 lb. lean (at least 80%) ground beef

2 chipotle chiles in adobo sauce, chopped, if desired

1 can (8 oz.) tomato sauce

1 can (4.5 oz.) Old El Paso® chopped green chiles

1/4 cup water

1 1/2 cups shredded Mexican cheese blend (6 oz.)

Nutrition Information Per Serving:	
Calories: 500 From Fat: 240	
Total Fat	26g
Saturated	13g
Cholesterol	110mg
Sodium	850mg
Total Carbohydrate	33g
Dietary Fiber	4g
Sugars	5g
Protein	33g

1) Pierce potatoes several times with fork; place on microwavable paper towel in microwave oven. Microwave on High 11 to 14 minutes or until tender, turning potatoes over and rearranging halfway through cooking. Let stand 3 minutes.

2) Meanwhile, in 10-inch skillet, cook ground beef over medium-high heat, stirring frequently, until thoroughly cooked; drain. Stir in chipotle chiles, tomato sauce, green chiles, water and 1 cup of the cheese. Cook uncovered 2 to 3 minutes, stirring occasionally, until thoroughly heated.

3) Cut potatoes in half lengthwise; place on plates. Mash potatoes slightly with fork. Spoon beef mixture over potatoes; sprinkle with remaining 1/2 cup cheese.

HIGH ALTITUDE (3500-6500 FT.): No change.

Chicken Salad Crescent Cannoli

SUSAN SCARBOROUGH | FERNANDINA BEACH, FLORIDA

Bake-Off

PREP TIME: 20 MINUTES (READY IN 45 MINUTES)
SERVINGS: 4

2 cups $^3/_4$-inch pieces skinned lemon-pepper or regular deli rotisserie chicken breast (from 2- to 2$^1/_2$-lb. chicken)

$^1/_4$ cup mango chutney

$^1/_2$ teaspoon ground mustard

4 green onions, sliced ($^1/_4$ cup)

1 container (6 oz.) Yoplait® Original 99% Fat Free piña colada yogurt

1 can (8 oz.) Pillsbury® refrigerated reduced-fat crescent dinner rolls

$^1/_2$ teaspoon lemon-dill salt-free seasoning

$^1/_4$ teaspoon coarse ground black pepper

4 medium green onions

4 teaspoons mango chutney

1) Heat oven to 350°F. In medium bowl, mix chicken, $^1/_4$ cup chutney, the mustard, sliced onions and yogurt with fork until well blended. Refrigerate until needed.

2) Cut 4 (12-inch) squares of heavy-duty foil. Place 1 foil square on work surface; fold into thirds to make a triple-thick 12x4-inch strip. Starting with one 4-inch end, roll foil strip into tube with 1$^1/_4$-inch inside diameter. Repeat with remaining foil squares.

3) Unroll dough; separate into 4 rectangles, pressing perforations to seal. Place 1 foil tube on one short side of each rectangle; roll dough around tube. Place seam side down 2 inches apart on ungreased cookie sheet. Sprinkle each evenly with lemon-dill seasoning and pepper.

4) Bake 12 to 15 minutes or until golden brown. Remove from cookie sheet; place on wire rack. Cool 5 minutes. To remove foil from each crescent cannoli, grasp inside corner of foil and pull to uncoil foil from dough. Cool 5 minutes longer.

5) Fill each crescent cannoli with $^1/_2$ cup chicken mixture; place on individual plate. Place any extra chicken mixture near open ends of each cannoli. To garnish, cut off white ends from 4 green onions; save for later use. Cut each green portion lengthwise into 2 strips; tie ends of each pair to form a knot. Place knot on top of each cannoli, tucking ends under sides. Spoon 1 teaspoon chutney onto plate at side of each cannoli.

HIGH ALTITUDE (3500-6500 FT.): No change.

Nutrition Information Per Serving:

Calories:	400	From Fat:	130
Total Fat			15g
Saturated			3.5g
Cholesterol			60mg
Sodium			840mg
Total Carbohydrate			41g
Dietary Fiber			2g
Sugars			18g
Protein			26g

Herbed Pork Roast with Mushroom Gravy

PREP TIME: 15 MINUTES (READY IN 1 HOUR 25 MINUTES)
SERVINGS: 8

 EASY   LOW FAT

1 boneless pork loin roast (2$\frac{1}{2}$ to 3 lb.)

1 tablespoon finely chopped fresh parsley or 1 teaspoon parsley flakes

1 tablespoon finely chopped fresh rosemary or 1 teaspoon dried rosemary leaves, crushed

1 tablespoon finely chopped fresh thyme or 1 teaspoon dried thyme leaves

2 cloves garlic, finely chopped

1 can (10$\frac{3}{4}$ oz.) condensed golden mushroom soup

$\frac{1}{2}$ cup milk

1 jar (2.5 oz.) Green Giant® sliced mushrooms, drained

1) Heat oven to 350°F. In shallow roasting pan, place pork roast. In small bowl, mix parsley, rosemary, thyme and garlic; rub mixture evenly over pork. Insert meat thermometer so tip is in thickest part of pork and not resting in fat.

2) Roast uncovered about 1 hour 5 minutes to 1 hour 10 minutes or until thermometer reads 155°F. Remove pork from pan; place on cutting board. Cover with foil; let stand 10 minutes or until thermometer reads 160°F.

3) Meanwhile, in same roasting pan, stir soup into pan drippings. Stir in milk until smooth. Add mushrooms; cook and stir over medium-low heat until mixture boils. Cut pork into slices; serve with gravy.

HIGH ALTITUDE (3500-6500 FT.): No change.

Nutrition Information Per Serving:

Calories:	180	From Fat:	80
Total Fat			9g
Saturated			3g
Cholesterol			65mg
Sodium			190mg
Total Carbohydrate			3g
Dietary Fiber			0g
Sugars			1g
Protein			24g

Grilled Herbed Chicken

PREP TIME: 50 MINUTES (READY IN 50 MINUTES)
SERVINGS: 4

1 teaspoon seasoned salt

1 teaspoon dried oregano leaves

$^1/_2$ teaspoon garlic powder

$^1/_2$ teaspoon pepper

$^1/_2$ teaspoon paprika

$^1/_4$ teaspoon ground red pepper (cayenne)

3 to 3$^1/_2$ lb. cut-up broiler-fryer chicken, skin removed

2 tablespoons olive oil

1) Heat gas or charcoal grill. In small bowl, mix seasoned salt, oregano, garlic powder, pepper, paprika and ground red pepper. Brush chicken pieces with oil; sprinkle with seasoning mix.

2) When grill is heated, place chicken on gas grill over medium heat or on charcoal grill over medium coals; cover grill. Cook 35 to 50 minutes, turning occasionally, until thermometer inserted in center of chicken breasts reads 170°F. and in center of thighs, legs and wings reads 180°F. (move breasts to outer edges of grill when done).

HIGH ALTITUDE (3500-6500 FT.): Cook chicken on covered grill over medium-low heat 40 to 50 minutes.

Nutrition Information Per Serving:

Calories:	310	From Fat:	150
Total Fat			17g
Saturated			3.5g
Cholesterol			120mg
Sodium			460mg
Total Carbohydrate			0g
Dietary Fiber			0g
Sugars			0g
Protein			38g

Serve grilled vegetables with the chicken. Toss the cut-up veggies with a teaspoon of olive oil and season them to taste with salt and pepper. Cook them in a grill basket, stirring frequently.

Apple-Glazed Stuffed Pork Chops

PREP TIME: 30 MINUTES (READY IN 1 HOUR 35 MINUTES)
SERVINGS: 4

PORK CHOPS

4 pork rib or loin chops, 1 inch thick (about 2$\frac{1}{2}$ lb.)

STUFFING

2 slices cinnamon raisin bread, toasted, cut into cubes (about 1 cup)

$\frac{1}{2}$ cup chopped apple ($\frac{1}{2}$ medium)

$\frac{1}{2}$ cup chopped pecans

$\frac{1}{2}$ teaspoon salt

$\frac{1}{4}$ teaspoon grated orange peel

$\frac{1}{8}$ teaspoon ground cinnamon

Dash pepper

3 tablespoons orange juice

GLAZE

2 tablespoons sugar

1 tablespoon cornstarch

1 cup apple juice

2 tablespoons butter or margarine

1) Heat oven to 350°F. With sharp knife, make pocket in each pork chop by cutting into side of chop toward bone.

2) In medium bowl, mix stuffing ingredients. Stuff each pocket with $\frac{1}{4}$ of stuffing mixture; place chops in ungreased 13x9-inch pan. Bake uncovered 30 minutes.

3) Meanwhile, in 1-quart saucepan, mix sugar and cornstarch; stir in apple juice. Cook over medium-low heat, stirring frequently, until mixture boils and thickens. Remove from heat; stir in butter.

4) Pour glaze evenly over chops; bake uncovered 30 to 35 minutes longer or until pork is no longer pink in center.

HIGH ALTITUDE (3500-6500 FT.): Heat oven to 375°F. In Step 2, cover tightly with foil; bake 45 minutes. In Step 3, uncover; pour glaze over chops. Bake uncovered 10 to 15 minutes longer.

Nutrition Information Per Serving:

Calories:	540	From Fat:	270
Total Fat			29g
Saturated			9g
Cholesterol			125mg
Sodium			450mg
Total Carbohydrate			28g
Dietary Fiber			2g
Sugars			18g
Protein			40g

tip

Pork chops need to be at least 1 inch thick to cut a pocket in them for stuffing. If the chops are thicker, they may need to bake a bit longer.

Sausage Ratatouille with Couscous

JUDY MORTENSEN | CITRUS HEIGHTS, CALIFORNIA

PREP TIME: 45 MINUTES (READY IN 45 MINUTES)
SERVINGS: 5

1 to 2 tablespoons extra-virgin olive oil

5 uncooked mild Italian pork sausage links (about 1¹/₂ lb.)

¹/₂ cup finely chopped onion (1 medium)

¹/₂ cup finely chopped carrot

1 clove garlic, finely chopped

¹/₂ cup finely chopped zucchini

2 tablespoons finely chopped fresh parsley

¹/₂ teaspoon dried basil leaves

¹/₂ teaspoon salt

¹/₄ teaspoon pepper

1 can (28 oz.) Progresso® whole peeled tomatoes Italian style (with basil), undrained, cut up

1 can (15 oz.) Progresso® cannellini (white kidney) beans, undrained

1 box (5.9 oz.) Parmesan-flavor couscous mix

Butter

Water

2 tablespoons freshly grated Parmesan cheese

1) In 12-inch skillet, heat oil over medium heat. Add sausage links; cook and stir until browned on all sides. Remove from skillet; set aside. Add onion, carrot and garlic to skillet; cook and stir until onion becomes translucent. Stir in zucchini, parsley and basil. Cook 2 to 3 minutes, stirring occasionally. Stir in salt, pepper and tomatoes.

2) Return sausages to skillet. Heat to boiling. Reduce heat to medium-low; simmer uncovered 20 to 25 minutes, stirring occasionally, until liquid is reduced by half and meat thermometer inserted in center of sausages reads 160°F. Stir in beans. Cook until thoroughly heated.

3) Meanwhile, in 2-quart saucepan, make couscous with amounts of butter and water as directed on box.

4) To serve, fluff couscous; spoon around sides of large serving dish. Spoon tomato-vegetable mixture into center; arrange sausages over top. Sprinkle with Parmesan cheese.

HIGH ALTITUDE (3500-6500 FT.): In Step 1, cook over medium-high heat. In Step 2, reduce heat to medium.

Nutrition Information Per Serving:		
Calories: 540	From Fat:	210
Total Fat		24g
Saturated		8g
Cholesterol		60mg
Sodium		1220mg
Total Carbohydrate		54g
Dietary Fiber		9g
Sugars		7g
Protein		27g

Grilled Marinated Salmon with Cucumber Sauce

PREP TIME: 30 MINUTES (READY IN 1 HOUR)
SERVINGS: 8

SALMON

- ¼ cup soy sauce
- 3 tablespoons lemon juice
- 2 tablespoons water
- 1½ teaspoons garlic powder
- ½ teaspoon onion powder
- 1 salmon fillet, about 1 inch thick (2 to 2¼ lb.)
- 2 teaspoons vegetable oil

SAUCE

- ½ cup sour cream
- 1½ teaspoons chopped fresh or ½ teaspoon dried dill weed
- 1 teaspoon cider vinegar
- ¼ teaspoon onion powder
- ¼ teaspoon salt
- ⅔ cup chopped unpeeled cucumber

1) In shallow nonmetal dish, mix soy sauce, lemon juice, water, garlic powder and onion powder. Add salmon, skin side up. Let stand at room temperature 30 minutes to marinate.

2) Meanwhile, in small bowl, mix sauce ingredients. Cover; refrigerate until serving time.

3) Heat gas or charcoal grill. Brush skin side of salmon with oil. Place salmon, skin side down, on grill. Cover grill; cook over medium heat 13 to 18 minutes or until fish flakes easily with fork. To serve, cut into 8 pieces. Serve with sauce.

HIGH ALTITUDE (3500-6500 FT.): Cook over medium-low heat.

Nutrition Information Per Serving:	
Calories: 220	From Fat: 110
Total Fat	12g
Saturated	4.5g
Cholesterol	85mg
Sodium	780mg
Total Carbohydrate	3g
Dietary Fiber	0g
Sugars	2g
Protein	25g

Southwestern Chicken-Biscuit Pot Pie

DIANE LEIGH KEREKES | SAPULPA, OKLAHOMA

PREP TIME: 20 MINUTES (READY IN 1 HOUR 10 MINUTES)
SERVINGS: 2

1 can (18.5 oz.) Progresso® Traditional southwestern-style chicken soup

¼ teaspoon onion powder

¼ teaspoon garlic powder

¼ teaspoon ground chipotle chiles

   Cooking spray

½ cup frozen extra-sweet whole kernel corn (from 1-lb. bag)

1 package (3 oz.) frozen diced cooked chicken (²/₃ cup)

2 oz. Monterey Jack cheese, cut into 4 (3x1x⅛-inch) slices

3 tablespoons chopped roasted red bell peppers (from jar)

2 Pillsbury® Oven Baked frozen southern-style biscuits (from 25-oz. bag)

2 to 4 tablespoons sour cream

1 to 2 tablespoons finely chopped fresh chives or green onions

1) Heat oven to 350°F. Pour soup into 2-cup measuring cup or bowl. Stir in onion powder, garlic powder and ground chipotle chiles.

2) Spray insides of 2 ovenproof 2-cup bowls with cooking spray. Place ¼ cup corn and ⅓ cup chicken in each bowl. Pour about 1 cup soup mixture evenly into bowls. Carefully place 2 cheese slices in center on top of soup in each bowl. Sprinkle 1 tablespoon roasted peppers evenly around cheese in each. Place biscuits over cheese; spray biscuits with cooking spray.

3) Place bowls on cookie sheet; bake 38 to 43 minutes or until biscuits are golden brown and soup bubbles around edges. Cool 5 minutes before serving. Serve topped with sour cream, chives and remaining tablespoon roasted peppers.

HIGH ALTITUDE (3500-6500 FT.): Bake 43 to 48 minutes.

Nutrition Information Per Serving:	
Calories: 570	From Fat: 230
Total Fat	26g
Saturated	11g
Cholesterol	75mg
Sodium	1900mg
Total Carbohydrate	54g
Dietary Fiber	4g
Sugars	7g
Protein	31g

Lemony Fish and Tomatoes

PREP TIME: 15 MINUTES (READY IN 35 MINUTES)
SERVINGS: 4

 EASY   LOW FAT

1 lb. cod fillets

½ teaspoon salt

¼ teaspoon pepper

2 medium lemons, each cut into quarters

1 medium tomato, thinly sliced

2 tablespoons olive oil

1 medium onion, chopped (½ cup)

2 cloves garlic, minced

1 teaspoon parsley flakes

1) Heat oven to 400°F. Sprinkle both sides of each cod fillet with salt and pepper. In ungreased 13x9-inch (3-quart) glass baking dish, arrange fish in single layer.

2) Squeeze juice of 3 lemon quarters over fish. Arrange tomato slices on fish to cover, overlapping as necessary.

3) In 8-inch skillet, heat oil over medium heat. Add onion; cook 3 to 4 minutes, stirring frequently, until tender. Add garlic; cook and stir 1 to 2 minutes longer.

4) Remove from heat; stir in parsley. Sprinkle onion mixture evenly over tomatoes. Squeeze juice of 1 lemon quarter over onion mixture.

5) Bake uncovered 15 to 20 minutes or until fish flakes easily with fork. Serve fish with remaining lemon quarters.

HIGH ALTITUDE (3500-6500 FT.): No change.

Nutrition Information Per Serving:		
Calories: 190	From Fat:	80
Total Fat		8g
Saturated		1.5g
Cholesterol		60mg
Sodium		390mg
Total Carbohydrate		6g
Dietary Fiber		2g
Sugars		2g
Protein		22g

Enchilada Chicken Tart

PREP TIME: 35 MINUTES (READY IN 1 HOUR)
SERVINGS: 8

1 tablespoon vegetable oil

1/2 cup chopped onion (1 medium)

1 cup Green Giant® frozen corn (from 1-lb. bag)

2 cups cubed cooked chicken or turkey

1 can (4.5 oz.) Old El Paso® chopped green chiles

1/2 cup sour cream

1 1/2 cups shredded Colby-Monterey Jack cheese (6 oz.)

1 can (10 oz.) Old El Paso® enchilada sauce

1 can (13.8 oz.) Pillsbury® refrigerated pizza crust

3 large plum (Roma) tomatoes, chopped

1) Heat oven to 400°F. Spray 15x10x1-inch pan with cooking spray. In 10-inch skillet, heat oil over medium-high heat. Add onion; cook 2 to 3 minutes, stirring occasionally, until tender. Add corn; cook 3 to 4 minutes, stirring frequently, until corn is thawed and crisp-tender.

2) Stir in chicken and chiles. Remove from heat. Stir in sour cream and 1/2 cup of the cheese. Cool 5 minutes.

3) Unroll dough into pan. Starting at center, gently press dough into 10-inch square. Spread about 2 tablespoons of the enchilada sauce over dough. Spoon chicken mixture evenly over sauce to within 2 inches of each edge.

4) Drizzle 1/4 cup enchilada sauce over chicken mixture. Sprinkle with remaining 1 cup cheese. Fold edge of dough up over filling, rounding corners and pleating dough as necessary. (Tart should be 8 1/2 to 9 inches in diameter.)

5) Bake 20 to 25 minutes or until crust is deep golden brown and filling is bubbly. Let tart stand 10 minutes before serving. Meanwhile, heat remaining enchilada sauce.

6) To serve, top tart with tomatoes and lettuce. Cut into wedges; serve with warm enchilada sauce.

HIGH ALTITUDE (3500-6500 FT.): Bake 25 to 30 minutes.

Nutrition Information Per Serving:

Calories:	350	From Fat:	140
Total Fat			16g
Saturated			7g
Cholesterol			60mg
Sodium			720mg
Total Carbohydrate			32g
Dietary Fiber			2g
Sugars			6g
Protein			20g

Easy Ham and Noodles

PREP TIME: 20 MINUTES (READY IN 20 MINUTES)
SERVINGS: 4 (1-3/4 CUPS EACH)

 EASY   LOW FAT

1 can (14 oz.) chicken broth

1 cup water

3 cups uncooked dumpling egg noodles (5 oz.)

2 boxes (10 oz. each) Green Giant® frozen broccoli, cauliflower, carrots and cheese flavored sauce

2 cups cubed ($^1/_2$ inch) cooked ham

Nutrition Information Per Serving:	
Calories: 350	From Fat: 90
Total Fat	10g
Saturated	3.5g
Cholesterol	85mg
Sodium	1960mg
Total Carbohydrate	38g
Dietary Fiber	4g
Sugars	6g
Protein	25g

1) In 3-quart saucepan, heat broth and water to boiling. Add noodles; return to boiling. Reduce heat to medium-low; cook 8 to 10 minutes or until noodles are tender and most of liquid is absorbed, stirring occasionally (do not drain).

2) Meanwhile, cook vegetables as directed on box.

3) Gently stir vegetables in cheese sauce and ham into noodle mixture. Cook over medium-low heat 3 to 4 minutes or until hot, stirring occasionally.

HIGH ALTITUDE (3500-6500 FT.): In Step 1, cook 10 to 12 minutes. In Step 3, heat mixture to boiling; reduce heat and simmer 4 to 5 minutes.

Smoked Sausage and Cabbage Supper

PREP TIME: 20 MINUTES (READY IN 55 MINUTES)
SERVINGS: 4

 EASY

1 tablespoon olive oil

1 medium onion, chopped ($^1/_2$ cup)

1 small cabbage, cored, cut into 12 pieces

1 cup chicken broth

1 can (14.5 oz.) diced tomatoes with Italian herbs, undrained

$^1/_4$ teaspoon pepper

1 ring (1 lb.) smoked beef sausage

Nutrition Information Per Serving:	
Calories: 510	From Fat: 340
Total Fat	38g
Saturated	14g
Cholesterol	60mg
Sodium	1980mg
Total Carbohydrate	25g
Dietary Fiber	4g
Sugars	18g
Protein	18g

1) In 4-quart Dutch oven or 12-inch skillet, heat oil over medium heat. Add onion; cook about 4 minutes, stirring frequently, until lightly browned.

2) Stir in cabbage, broth, tomatoes and pepper. Heat to boiling. Reduce heat to low; cover and cook 20 minutes.

3) Add sausage; spoon cabbage mixture over sausage. Cover; cook over low heat 10 to 15 minutes longer or until sausage is thoroughly heated and cabbage is tender. Cut sausage into pieces to serve.

HIGH ALTITUDE (3500-6500 FT.): No change.

Picnics & Potlucks

These crowd-pleasing favorites serve 12 or more—
great choices for when the gang's all here!

LIGHTLY LIME FRUIT SALAD
PG. 253

SPICY HONEYED
CHICKEN DRUMMETTES
PG. 261

PEANUT BUTTER CRUNCH BROWNIES
PG. 264

HONEY-DIJON HAM SANDWICHES
PG. 246

Caesar Coleslaw

PREP TIME: 10 MINUTES (READY IN 10 MINUTES)
SERVINGS: 14 (1/2 CUP EACH)

 EASY

1 bag (16 oz.) coleslaw blend

1 can (2¼ oz.) sliced ripe olives, drained, if desired

½ cup slivered red onion

1 cup creamy Caesar dressing

1 cup croutons

Nutrition Information Per Serving:	
Calories: 110	From Fat: 90
Total Fat	10g
Saturated	1.5g
Cholesterol	0mg
Sodium	220mg
Total Carbohydrate	4g
Dietary Fiber	0g
Sugars	2g
Protein	1g

1) In large bowl, mix coleslaw blend, olives and onion. Pour dressing over salad; toss to coat. Serve immediately, or cover and refrigerate up to 8 hours.

2) Before serving, top with croutons.

HIGH ALTITUDE (3500-6500 FT.): No change.

Coleslaw is a great make-ahead salad to serve with sandwiches or hamburgers.

Garden Pizza Bites

PREP TIME: 40 MINUTES (READY IN 1 HOUR 40 MINUTES)
SERVINGS: 30

 EASY   LOW FAT

1 can (12 oz.) Pillsbury® Golden Layers® refrigerated flaky biscuits

2 teaspoons cornmeal

1 container (8 oz.) refrigerated spinach dip

½ cup shredded carrots

½ cup finely chopped red bell pepper

4 green onions, chopped

Nutrition Information Per Serving:	
Calories: 50	From Fat: 25
Total Fat	3g
Saturated	0.5g
Cholesterol	0mg
Sodium	170mg
Total Carbohydrate	6g
Dietary Fiber	0g
Sugars	1g
Protein	0g

1) Heat oven to 400°F. Separate dough into 10 biscuits; separate each into 3 layers. Arrange biscuit rounds on 2 ungreased cookie sheets. Sprinkle rounds with cornmeal.

2) Bake 7 to 11 minutes or until golden brown, switching position of cookie sheets halfway through baking. Remove from cookie sheets; place on wire rack. Cool completely, about 10 minutes.

3) Spread each baked biscuit round with 1½ teaspoons spinach dip. Sprinkle each evenly with carrots, bell pepper and onions. Cover; refrigerate at least 1 hour or until serving time.

HIGH ALTITUDE (3500-6500 FT.): No change.

Mexican Chili Cheese Dogs

| PREP TIME: | 15 MINUTES (READY IN 6 HOURS 15 MINUTES) |
| SERVINGS: | 36 |

 EASY

8 oz. mild Mexican pasteurized prepared cheese product with jalapeño peppers, cut into cubes (1½ cups)

½ cup mild taco sauce

1 can (15 oz.) chili without beans

3 lb. cocktail-size hot dogs or smoked link sausages

¼ cup chopped fresh cilantro

Nutrition Information Per Serving:		
Calories: 150	From Fat:	110
Total Fat		13g
Saturated		5g
Cholesterol		30mg
Sodium		600mg
Total Carbohydrate		3g
Dietary Fiber		0g
Sugars		2g
Protein		6g

If your family does not like cilantro, omit the cilantro from this recipe or use chopped fresh parsley in its place.

1) In 3- to 4-quart slow cooker, place cheese, taco sauce, chili and hot dogs; stir to coat well.

2) Cover; cook on Low heat setting 5 to 6 hours, stirring once halfway through cooking. Before serving, sprinkle with cilantro. Serve hot dogs with tortilla chips, if desired.

HIGH ALTITUDE (3500-6500FT.): No change.

Layered Picnic Salad

PREP TIME: 30 MINUTES (READY IN 30 MINUTES)
SERVINGS: 12 (1 CUP EACH)

 EASY

4 cups shredded lettuce

1 bag (16 oz.) broccoli slaw mix (shredded broccoli)

2 cups shredded carrots (3 medium)

1 medium yellow bell pepper, chopped (1 cup)

1 can (15 oz.) Green Giant® garbanzo beans, drained, rinsed

8 oz. mozzarella cheese, cut into $1/2$-inch cubes ($1^3/4$ cups)

2 cups chopped plum (Roma) tomatoes (about 6 medium)

$1/2$ cup mayonnaise

$1/2$ cup ranch dressing

$1/2$ teaspoon Italian seasoning

2 tablespoons chopped fresh parsley

1) In 5- to 6-quart clear glass or plastic bowl, layer lettuce, broccoli slaw mix, carrots, bell pepper, beans, cheese and tomatoes.

2) In small bowl, mix mayonnaise, dressing and Italian seasoning. Spread over top of salad. Sprinkle with parsley. Serve immediately, or cover and refrigerate up to 8 hours before serving. If desired, toss before serving.

HIGH ALTITUDE (3500-6500 FT.): No change.

Nutrition Information Per Serving:	
Calories: 240	From Fat: 160

Total Fat	17g
Saturated	4.5g
Cholesterol	20mg
Sodium	300mg
Total Carbohydrate	17g
Dietary Fiber	5g
Sugars	3g
Protein	10g

Party Chicken and Pasta Salad

PREP TIME: 40 MINUTES (READY IN 40 MINUTES)
SERVINGS: 12 (1-1/3 CUPS EACH)

SALAD

5 cups uncooked rotini pasta (16 oz.)

4 cups cubed cooked chicken

1 cup thinly sliced celery

1/2 cup chopped green onions

12 oz. fresh snow pea pods, trimmed, halved crosswise

2 cups seedless red and/or green grapes, halved

1 can (8 oz.) pineapple tidbits in unsweetened juice, drained, reserving liquid

1 cup slivered almonds, toasted if desired

6 to 8 leaves leaf lettuce

DRESSING

1 cup mayonnaise or salad dressing

2 tablespoons finely chopped fresh gingerroot

1 teaspoon garlic salt

2 tablespoons reserved pineapple liquid

2 tablespoons soy sauce

2 tablespoons honey

1) Cook pasta as directed on package. Drain; rinse with cold water to cool. Drain well.

2) Meanwhile, in large bowl, mix remaining salad ingredients except almonds and lettuce. In small bowl, mix dressing ingredients.

3) Add pasta and 1/2 cup of the almonds to salad; stir gently to mix. Add dressing; toss to coat. Line serving bowl or platter with lettuce. Spoon salad over lettuce. Sprinkle with remaining almonds.

HIGH ALTITUDE (3500-6500 FT.): No change.

Nutrition Information Per Serving:

Calories: 520	From Fat: 210
Total Fat	23g
Saturated	3.5g
Cholesterol	45mg
Sodium	580mg
Total Carbohydrate	54g
Dietary Fiber	5g
Sugars	13g
Protein	23g

Grapefruit Citrus Cooler

PREP TIME: 10 MINUTES (READY IN 10 MINUTES)
SERVINGS: 16 (1/2 CUP EACH)

 EASY    LOW FAT

3 1/2 cups ruby red grapefruit juice, chilled

1/4 cup lemon juice

3 tablespoons lime juice

1/2 cup sugar

4 cups club soda, chilled

Nutrition Information Per Serving:

Calories: 50	From Fat: 0
Total Fat	0g
Saturated	0g
Cholesterol	0mg
Sodium	15mg
Total Carbohydrate	12g
Dietary Fiber	0g
Sugars	10g
Protein	0g

1) In large punch bowl or pitcher, combine juices and sugar; mix well.

2) Just before serving, add club soda; stir gently. Serve over ice.

HIGH ALTITUDE (3500-6500 FT.): No change.

Chocolaty Caramel Layer Bars

PREP TIME: 20 MINUTES (READY IN 1 HOUR 20 MINUTES)
SERVINGS: 36

⟳ EASY

1 roll (18 oz.) Pillsbury® refrigerated chocolate chip cookies

1 package (11.5 oz.) milk chocolate chips

1 container (18 oz.) caramel apple dip (1¹/₂ cups)

3 cups Rice Chex® Cereal

1 cup chopped peanuts

Nutrition Information Per Serving:		
Calories: 190	From Fat:	70
Total Fat		8g
Saturated		3g
Cholesterol		0mg
Sodium		140mg
Total Carbohydrate		26g
Dietary Fiber		1g
Sugars		17g
Protein		3g

1) Heat oven to 350°F. Into ungreased 13x9-inch pan, break up cookie dough. With floured fingers, press dough evenly in bottom of pan to form crust.

2) Bake 15 to 18 minutes or until light golden brown. Cool 15 minutes.

3) Meanwhile, in 2-quart saucepan, place 1 cup of the chips and 1 cup of the dip. Cook over medium heat, stirring constantly, until melted and smooth. Remove from heat. Stir in cereal and peanuts.

4) Spread cereal mixture over cooled crust. In 1-quart saucepan, place remaining chips and dip. Cook over medium heat, stirring constantly, until melted and smooth. Spread over cereal mixture. Refrigerate until chocolate mixture is set, about 30 minutes. Cut into bars.

HIGH ALTITUDE (3500-6500 FT.): Bake crust at 350°F. 16 to 19 minutes. Continue as directed above.

4-Can Baked Beans

PREP TIME: 5 MINUTES (READY IN 1 HOUR 5 MINUTES)
SERVINGS: 12 (1/2 CUP EACH)

⟳ EASY   ⓕ LOW FAT

1 can (16 oz.) baked beans, undrained

1 can (15 oz.) spicy chili beans, undrained

1 can (15 oz.) Progresso® black beans, drained, rinsed

1 can (10 oz.) diced tomatoes with green chiles, undrained

Nutrition Information Per Serving:		
Calories: 110	From Fat:	5
Total Fat		0.5g
Saturated		0g
Cholesterol		0mg
Sodium		490mg
Total Carbohydrate		23g
Dietary Fiber		6g
Sugars		5g
Protein		7g

1) Heat oven to 350°F. Spray 2-quart casserole with cooking spray. In large bowl, mix all ingredients. Pour into casserole.

2) Bake 1 hour or until thoroughly heated and flavors are blended.

HIGH ALTITUDE (3500-6500 FT.): Bake at 375°F. 1 hour.

Shrimp-Salsa Dip

PREP TIME: 20 MINUTES (READY IN 20 MINUTES)
SERVINGS: 16 (3 TABLESPOONS DIP AND 2 CRACKERS EACH)

EASY

1 package (8 oz.) cream cheese, softened

1/2 teaspoon garlic powder

1/4 teaspoon onion powder

1/2 cup Old El Paso® Thick 'n Chunky salsa

2 tablespoons cocktail sauce

1 bag (7 oz.) frozen cooked salad shrimp, thawed

2 tablespoons sliced green onions (2 medium)

Crackers or tortilla chips

Nutrition Information Per Serving:

Calories: 110	From Fat: 70
Total Fat	7g
Saturated	3.5g
Cholesterol	40mg
Sodium	220mg
Total Carbohydrate	6g
Dietary Fiber	0g
Sugars	1g
Protein	4g

tip

Instead of crackers, feel free to enjoy Shrimp-Salsa Dip with lime-flavored tortilla chips.

1) In medium bowl, beat cream cheese, garlic powder and onion powder with electric mixer on medium speed until smooth. On dinner plate, spread cheese mixture into flat, round shape.

2) In another medium bowl, gently mix salsa, cocktail sauce and shrimp. Gently spoon over cream cheese to within 1/2 inch of edge. Sprinkle with onions. Serve with crackers.

HIGH ALTITUDE (3500-6500 FT.): No change.

Garden Party Salad

PREP TIME: 30 MINUTES (READY IN 30 MINUTES)
SERVINGS: 15 (1-1/3 CUPS EACH)

 EASY

6$\frac{1}{2}$ cups uncooked medium pasta shells (1 lb.)

4 cups small fresh broccoli florets (about 10 oz.)

3 cups thinly sliced carrots (about 6 medium)

1 lb. smoked turkey breast (from deli), cut into $\frac{1}{2}$-inch cubes

2 medium yellow bell peppers, coarsely chopped (2 cups)

$\frac{1}{2}$ cup chopped red onion

12 oz. Cheddar cheese, cut into $\frac{1}{2}$-inch cubes (3 cups)

1 cup Italian dressing

$\frac{1}{3}$ cup chopped fresh chives

1) Cook pasta as directed on package, adding broccoli and carrots during last 2 minutes of cooking. Drain; rinse with cold water to cool. Drain well.

2) Meanwhile, in large bowl, place turkey, bell peppers, onion and cheese.

3) Gently stir cooked cooled pasta with broccoli and carrots into turkey mixture. Pour dressing over salad and add chives; toss gently to coat. If desired, garnish with additional chives.

HIGH ALTITUDE (3500-6500 FT.): No change.

Nutrition Information Per Serving:		
Calories: 330	From Fat:	140
Total Fat		15g
Saturated		5g
Cholesterol		50mg
Sodium		430mg
Total Carbohydrate		31g
Dietary Fiber		4g
Sugars		5g
Protein		20g

Italian Marinated Pork Tenderloins

PREP TIME: 40 MINUTES (READY IN 2 HOURS 40 MINUTES)
SERVINGS: 12

 EASY

3 pork tenderloins (1 lb. each)

1 cup Italian dressing

1 teaspoon garlic powder

1 teaspoon coarse ground black pepper

4 medium bell peppers (any color), halved

Nutrition Information Per Serving:

Calories:	240	From Fat:	110
Total Fat			13g
Saturated			2g
Cholesterol			75mg
Sodium			230mg
Total Carbohydrate			5g
Dietary Fiber			0g
Sugars			3g
Protein			26g

1) In shallow glass or nonmetal container or large resealable food-storage plastic bag, place pork. Pour dressing over pork; turn to coat. Cover container or seal bag; refrigerate 1 to 2 hours to marinate.

2) Heat gas or charcoal grill. When grill is heated, remove pork from marinade; reserve marinade. Sprinkle pork with garlic powder and pepper; place on gas grill over medium heat or on charcoal grill over medium coals. Add bell peppers to marinade; turn to coat, then place on grill. Cover grill.

3) Cook pork and peppers 20 to 25 minutes, turning occasionally and brushing with marinade occasionally up to last 5 minutes of grilling, until pork has slight blush of pink in center and meat thermometer inserted in center reads 160°F. (if peppers begin to overcook, remove from grill). Discard any remaining marinade.

4) Cut pepper halves into lengthwise strips; cut pork into slices. Serve pork with peppers.

HIGH ALTITUDE (3500-6500 FT.): Cook pork and peppers on covered grill over medium-low heat. Continue as directed above.

Ham and Dill Pickle Deviled Eggs

PREP TIME:	20 MINUTES (READY IN 45 MINUTES)	EASY
SERVINGS:	16	

8 eggs

¼ cup mayonnaise

2 teaspoons prepared mustard

¼ cup finely chopped cooked ham

1 tablespoon dill pickle relish

Dash pepper

Fresh parsley, if desired

Nutrition Information Per Serving:	
Calories: 70	From Fat: 50
Total Fat	5g
Saturated	1.5g
Cholesterol	110mg
Sodium	120mg
Total Carbohydrate	0g
Dietary Fiber	0g
Sugars	0g
Protein	4g

1) In 3-quart saucepan, place eggs in single layer. Add enough water to cover eggs by 1 inch. Heat to boiling. Immediately remove from heat; cover and let stand 15 minutes. Drain; rinse with cold water. Place eggs in bowl of ice water; let stand 10 minutes. Drain.

2) Peel eggs; cut lengthwise in half. Remove yolks; place in medium bowl. Add mayonnaise and mustard; blend well, mashing yolks just until smooth. Stir in ham, relish and pepper.

3) Spoon yolk mixture into egg white halves. Serve immediately, or cover and refrigerate until serving time. Just before serving, garnish with fresh parsley.

HIGH ALTITUDE (3500-6500 FT.): When cooking eggs, after heating water with eggs to boiling, boil gently 5 minutes. Remove from heat; cover and let stand 15 minutes. Continue as directed above.

Jelly-Filled Thumbprints

PREP TIME:	1 HOUR (READY IN 1 HOUR)	EASY
SERVINGS:	3 DOZEN COOKIES	

1 roll (18 oz.) Pillsbury® refrigerated sugar cookies

1 cup flaked or shredded coconut

½ cup seedless raspberry jam or red currant jelly

⅓ cup white vanilla chips

Nutrition Information Per Serving:	
Calories: 90	From Fat: 35
Total Fat	4g
Saturated	1.5g
Cholesterol	0mg
Sodium	45mg
Total Carbohydrate	13g
Dietary Fiber	0g
Sugars	8g
Protein	0g

1) Heat oven to 350°F. Into large bowl, break up cookie dough. Stir in coconut.

2) Shape dough into 1-inch balls; place 2 inches apart on ungreased cookie sheets. With thumb or handle of wooden spoon, make indentation in center of each cookie. Spoon about ½ teaspoon jam into each indentation.

3) Bake 10 to 13 minutes or until edges are light golden brown. Immediately remove from cookie sheets; place on wire racks. Cool 5 minutes.

4) Into small resealable food-storage plastic bag, place vanilla chips; partially seal bag. Microwave on High 45 to 60 seconds. Squeeze bag until chips are smooth. If necessary, microwave 10 seconds longer. Cut small hole in bottom corner of bag. Squeeze bag gently to drizzle melted chips over cookies.

HIGH ALTITUDE (3500-6500 FT.): No change.

Red, White and Blue Poke Cake

PREP TIME: 15 MINUTES (READY IN 4 HOURS 50 MINUTES)
SERVINGS: 16

e EASY

1 box (18.25 oz.) white cake mix with pudding in the mix

Water, oil and egg whites

1 box (4-serving size) strawberry gelatin

1 cup boiling water

1/2 cup cold water

1 box (4-serving size) white chocolate instant pudding and pie filling mix

1/3 cup milk

1 container (8 oz.) frozen whipped topping, thawed

1 cup sliced fresh strawberries

1/2 cup fresh blueberries

Nutrition Information Per Serving:			
Calories:	270	From Fat:	90
Total Fat		10g	
Saturated		4g	
Cholesterol		0mg	
Sodium		350mg	
Total Carbohydrate		41g	
Dietary Fiber		1g	
Sugars		26g	
Protein		3g	

1) Heat oven to 350°F. Prepare cake mix as directed on box using water, oil and egg whites; bake in 13x9-inch pan. Cool completely in pan on wire rack 1 hour.

2) Pierce cooled cake with fork at 1/2-inch intervals. In medium bowl, stir gelatin and boiling water until dissolved. Stir in cold water. Carefully pour mixture over entire surface of cake. Refrigerate at least 3 hours or until serving time.

3) In large bowl, mix pudding mix and milk until well blended. Gently stir in whipped topping. Spread over cake. Arrange strawberries and blueberries on top of cake to resemble flag. Store in refrigerator.

HIGH ALTITUDE (3500-6500 FT.): Make cake following High Altitude Directions on box. Continue as directed above.

Honey-Dijon Ham Sandwiches

PREP TIME: 15 MINUTES (READY IN 8 HOURS 15 MINUTES)
SERVINGS: 24

 EASY   LOW FAT

1	bone-in cooked ham (5 lb.)
1/3	cup apple juice
1/4	cup packed brown sugar
1	tablespoon honey
1	tablespoon Dijon mustard
24	sandwich buns, split
	Small lettuce leaves
	American cheese slices
	Additional Dijon mustard, if desired

Nutrition Information Per Serving:

Calories: 170	From Fat: 50
Total Fat	6g
Saturated	2g
Cholesterol	55mg
Sodium	1260mg
Total Carbohydrate	8g
Dietary Fiber	0g
Sugars	8g
Protein	21g

1) In 4- to 6-quart slow cooker, place ham and apple juice. In small bowl, mix brown sugar, honey and mustard. Spread mixture over ham.

2) Cover; cook on Low heat setting 6 to 8 hours.

3) At serving time, place buns in serving basket, place lettuce leaves in serving bowl, arrange cheese slices on plate or tray, and set out Dijon mustard with spreader. Cut ham into small slices; arrange on serving platter. Let guests assemble sandwiches.

HIGH ALTITUDE (3500-6500 FT.): No change.

This glazed ham is also a perfect make-ahead for a company dinner. Serve with scalloped potatoes, buttered green beans, a fruit salad and warm dinner rolls.

Crunchy Trail Mix Bars

PREP TIME: 20 MINUTES (READY IN 50 MINUTES)
SERVINGS: 36

 EASY

4 cups Cheerios® cereal

3 cups trail mix (seeds, nuts and dried fruits)

1/4 cup butter or margarine

1 cup packed brown sugar

2 tablespoons all-purpose flour

1/2 cup light corn syrup

Nutrition Information Per Serving:		
Calories: 130	From Fat:	45
Total Fat		5g
Saturated		1.5g
Cholesterol		0mg
Sodium		70mg
Total Carbohydrate		18g
Dietary Fiber		1g
Sugars		12g
Protein		2g

1) Grease 13x9-inch pan with shortening or cooking spray. In large bowl, mix cereal and trail mix; set aside.

2) In 2-quart saucepan, melt butter over medium heat. Stir in brown sugar, flour and corn syrup. Cook, stirring occasionally, until mixture comes to a full boil. Boil 1 minute, stirring constantly.

3) Pour mixture evenly over cereal mixture; toss to coat. Press mixture in pan. Cool completely, about 30 minutes. Cut into 6 rows by 6 rows.

HIGH ALTITUDE (3500-6500 FT.): No change.

 If you plan to bring these to a gathering, cut them into bars and place on a large plastic or paper plate, then cover with plastic wrap or foil for toting. You won't need to carry the pan home!

Salami Roll-Ups

PREP TIME: 20 MINUTES (READY IN 50 MINUTES)
SERVINGS: 48

 EASY   LOW FAT

2 tablespoons mayonnaise

4 oz. cream cheese, softened

1/2 teaspoon prepared yellow mustard

1 can (4.5 oz.) Old El Paso® chopped green chiles

6 Old El Paso® flour tortillas for burritos, 8 inch (from 11.5-oz. package)

1/2 lb. thinly sliced salami

6 leaves leaf lettuce

Nutrition Information Per Serving:		
Calories: 40	From Fat:	25
Total Fat		2.5g
Saturated		1g
Cholesterol		5mg
Sodium		110mg
Total Carbohydrate		3g
Dietary Fiber		0g
Sugars		0g
Protein		1g

1) In small bowl, mix mayonnaise, cream cheese, mustard and chiles until smooth.

2) Heat tortillas as directed on package. On each warm tortilla, spread 1 1/2 teaspoons mayonnaise mixture and top evenly with salami; spread 1 1/2 teaspoons mayonnaise mixture over salami and top with lettuce leaf.

3) Roll up each tortilla tightly; trim ends. Wrap each roll in plastic wrap. Refrigerate at least 30 minutes or until serving time.

4) To serve, cut each roll into 8 pieces; secure each piece with cocktail toothpick.

HIGH ALTITUDE (3500-6500 FT.): No change.

Tomato, Basil and Cheese Sticks

| PREP TIME: | 10 MINUTES (READY IN 10 MINUTES) |
| SERVINGS: | 12 |

 EASY

12 toothpicks (2¹/₂ inch)

12 grape tomatoes

12 small fresh basil leaves

3 pieces (1 oz. each) mozzarella string cheese, each cut into 4 pieces

¹/₄ cup Italian dressing

Nutrition Information Per Serving:	
Calories: 50	From Fat: 30
Total Fat	3.5g
Saturated	1g
Cholesterol	0mg
Sodium	85mg
Total Carbohydrate	2g
Dietary Fiber	0g
Sugars	1g
Protein	2g

1) Onto each toothpick, thread 1 tomato, 1 basil leaf and 1 piece of cheese; place on serving plate.

2) Just before serving, drizzle kabobs with dressing.

HIGH ALTITUDE (3500-6500 FT.): No change.

Creamy Spinach Dip

| PREP TIME: | 20 MINUTES (READY IN 2 HOURS 20 MINUTES) |
| SERVINGS: | 28 (2 TABLESPOONS DIP AND 2 CRACKERS EACH) |

 EASY

1 package (10 oz.) Green Giant® frozen spinach

1 container (8 oz.) sour cream

1 cup mayonnaise

¹/₂ teaspoon celery salt

¹/₂ teaspoon dried dill

¹/₄ teaspoon onion salt

¹/₄ cup chopped green onions

1 can (8 oz.) water chestnuts, drained, finely chopped

1 jar (2 oz.) diced pimientos, drained

Crackers or cut-up fresh vegetables

Nutrition Information Per Serving:	
Calories: 120	From Fat: 90
Total Fat	10g
Saturated	2.5g
Cholesterol	10mg
Sodium	160mg
Total Carbohydrate	7g
Dietary Fiber	0g
Sugars	1g
Protein	1g

1) Cook spinach as directed on package. Cool slightly; squeeze to drain well.

2) Meanwhile, in medium bowl, mix sour cream, mayonnaise, celery salt, dill and onion salt; blend well. Stir in cooked spinach, onions, water chestnuts and pimientos. Cover; refrigerate at least 2 hours to blend flavors. Serve dip with crackers.

HIGH ALTITUDE (3500-6500 FT.): No change.

Chocolate Candy Cookie Bars

PREP TIME: 15 MINUTES (READY IN 1 HOUR 10 MINUTES)
SERVINGS: 36

 EASY

¾ cup packed brown sugar

½ cup granulated sugar

½ cup butter or margarine, softened

½ cup shortening

1½ teaspoons vanilla

1 egg

1¾ cups all-purpose flour

1 teaspoon baking soda

½ teaspoon salt

1 cup candy-coated chocolate candies or semisweet chocolate chips

½ cup chopped nuts, if desired

1) Heat oven to 375°F. In large bowl, beat brown sugar, granulated sugar, butter and shortening with electric mixer on medium speed until light and fluffy, scraping bowl occasionally. Beat in vanilla and egg until well blended.

2) On low speed, beat in flour, baking soda and salt until dough forms. With spoon, stir in chocolate candies and nuts. Spread dough in ungreased 13x9-inch pan.

3) Bake 15 to 25 minutes or until light golden brown. Cool completely, about 30 minutes. Cut into 6 rows by 6 rows.

HIGH ALTITUDE (3500-6500 FT.): Decrease granulated sugar to 1/4 cup, butter to 1/4 cup and baking soda to 3/4 teaspoon. Bake 18 to 23 minutes.

Nutrition Information Per Serving:		
Calories: 130	From Fat:	60
Total Fat		7g
Saturated		3g
Cholesterol		15mg
Sodium		90mg
Total Carbohydrate		16g
Dietary Fiber		0g
Sugars		11g
Protein		1g

tip Italian plum tomatoes, also known as Roma tomatoes, were chosen for this recipe because they are not as juicy as regular tomatoes.

Poolside Crostini

PREP TIME: 25 MINUTES (READY IN 45 MINUTES)
SERVINGS: 20 (2 TABLESPOONS MIXTURE AND 2 BREAD SLICES EACH)

 EASY   LOW FAT

40 slices baguette-style French bread
(¹⁄₄ inch thick slices)

Cooking spray

1 jar (6 oz.) marinated artichoke
hearts, drained

2 cups finely chopped, seeded plum
(Roma) tomatoes (6 to 7 medium)

2 tablespoons chopped fresh basil

¹⁄₂ teaspoon salt

¹⁄₈ teaspoon coarse ground black
pepper

1) Heat oven to 325°F. Line cookie sheet with foil. Place bread slices on cookie sheet; lightly spray bread with cooking spray.

2) Bake 6 to 9 minutes or until crisp. Remove bread slices from cookie sheet; place on wire rack. Cool completely, about 20 minutes.

3) Meanwhile, finely chop artichokes. In medium bowl, mix artichokes and remaining ingredients.

4) Serve artichoke mixture with toasted bread slices.

HIGH ALTITUDE (3500-6500 FT.): No change.

Nutrition Information Per Serving:		
Calories: 180	From Fat:	25
Total Fat		2.5g
Saturated		0.5g
Cholesterol		0mg
Sodium		440mg
Total Carbohydrate		34g
Dietary Fiber		2g
Sugars		0g
Protein		6g

Tropical Sherbet Punch

PREP TIME: 20 MINUTES (READY IN 20 MINUTES)
SERVINGS: 36 (1/2 CUP EACH)

 EASY   LOW FAT

1 quart (4 cups) lemon sherbet, softened

2 bottles (33.8 oz. each) lemon-lime carbonated beverage, chilled

1/2 cup fresh lime juice

Ice

2 medium star fruit, cut into thin slices

Nutrition Information Per Serving:	
Calories: 45	From Fat: 0
Total Fat	0g
Saturated	0g
Cholesterol	0mg
Sodium	15mg
Total Carbohydrate	10g
Dietary Fiber	0g
Sugars	9g
Protein	0g

1) In 5¹/₂- to 6-quart punch bowl, place sherbet. Gently stir in carbonated beverage and lime juice. Serve over ice in glasses garnished with star fruit.

HIGH ALTITUDE (3500-6500 FT.): No change.

Slow-Cooked Barbecued Pork on Buns

PREP TIME: 20 MINUTES (READY IN 8 HOURS 20 MINUTES)
SERVINGS: 18

 EASY   LOW FAT

1 boneless pork roast (3 lb.), trimmed of fat, cut into thin strips

³/4 cup chopped onion (1 large)

¹/4 cup cornstarch

¹/4 cup packed brown sugar

2 teaspoons ground mustard

¹/2 teaspoon salt

¹/4 teaspoon garlic powder

¹/4 teaspoon ground red pepper (cayenne)

1¹/2 cups ketchup

2 tablespoons Worcestershire sauce

18 sandwich buns, split

Nutrition Information Per Serving:	
Calories: 290	From Fat: 70
Total Fat	8g
Saturated	3g
Cholesterol	50mg
Sodium	590mg
Total Carbohydrate	33g
Dietary Fiber	1g
Sugars	10g
Protein	21g

1) In 3¹/2- to 4-quart slow cooker, mix all ingredients except buns.

2) Cover; cook on Low heat setting 6 to 8 hours.

3) Spoon about ¹/3 cup pork mixture into each bun.

HIGH ALTITUDE (3500-6500 FT.): No change.

Barbecue Cola Chicken

PREP TIME: 35 MINUTES (READY IN 6 HOURS 35 MINUTES)
SERVINGS: 12

 EASY   LOW FAT

1½ cups barbecue sauce

2 tablespoons dried minced onion

1 can (12 oz.) cola carbonated beverage

12 boneless skinless chicken breasts

Nutrition Information Per Serving:

Calories:	200	From Fat:	35
Total Fat			4g
Saturated			1g
Cholesterol			75mg
Sodium			380mg
Total Carbohydrate			15g
Dietary Fiber			0g
Sugars			12g
Protein			27g

1) In medium bowl, mix barbecue sauce, minced onion and cola beverage. Divide barbecue sauce mixture evenly into 2 (1-gallon) resealable food-storage plastic bags. Add 6 chicken breasts to each bag; seal bags and turn to coat. Refrigerate at least 6 hours or overnight to marinate, turning bags once or twice.

2) When ready to cook chicken, heat gas or charcoal grill. When grill is heated, carefully oil grill rack. Remove chicken from marinade; reserve marinade. Place chicken on gas grill over medium heat or on charcoal grill over medium coals; cover grill. Cook 12 to 15 minutes, turning occasionally, until juice is no longer pink when centers of thickest pieces are cut and thermometer inserted in centers reads 170°F.

3) In 1-quart saucepan, heat remaining marinade to boiling. Serve chicken with sauce.

HIGH ALTITUDE (3500-6500 FT.): Cook chicken on covered grill over medium heat 15 to 18 minutes. Continue as directed above.

Lightly Lime Fruit Salad

PREP TIME: 25 MINUTES (READY IN 25 MINUTES)
SERVINGS: 12 (3/4 CUP EACH)

 EASY   LOW FAT

SALAD

1³/₄ cups uncooked small pasta shells (7 oz.)

1¹/₂ cups seedless green grapes

1¹/₂ cups cantaloupe cubes

2 bananas, sliced

2 cups halved fresh strawberries

Lettuce leaves, if desired

DRESSING

¹/₂ cup sour cream

3 tablespoons frozen (thawed) limeade concentrate

¹/₈ teaspoon salt

Nutrition Information Per Serving:	
Calories: 140	From Fat: 25
Total Fat	2.5g
Saturated	1.5g
Cholesterol	5mg
Sodium	95mg
Total Carbohydrate	27g
Dietary Fiber	2g
Sugars	11g
Protein	3g

1) Cook pasta as directed on package. Drain; rinse with cold water to cool. Drain well.

2) Meanwhile, in large bowl, mix grapes, cantaloupe and bananas. In small bowl, mix dressing ingredients until well blended.

3) Gently stir cooled cooked pasta and dressing into salad. Gently stir in strawberries. Serve in lettuce-lined cups.

HIGH ALTITUDE (3500-6500 FT.): No change.

Minestrone Salad

PREP TIME: 20 MINUTES (READY IN 20 MINUTES)
SERVINGS: 12

 EASY

12 oz. (5 cups) uncooked bow tie pasta (farfalle)

1 can (15.5 or 15 oz.) Green Giant®, Joan of Arc® or Progresso® red kidney beans, drained, rinsed

1 package (3.5 oz.) sliced pepperoni

4 Italian plum tomatoes, coarsely chopped

¹/₂ cup chopped green bell pepper

¹/₄ cup chopped fresh parsley

¹/₄ cup shredded fresh Parmesan cheese (1 oz.)

Freshly ground black pepper, if desired

1 bottle (8 oz.) Italian salad dressing (³/₄ cup)

1) Cook pasta to desired doneness as directed on package. Drain; rinse with cold water to cool.

2) In large bowl, combine cooked pasta and all remaining ingredients; mix well. Serve immediately, or cover and refrigerate until serving time.

HIGH ALTITUDE (3500-6500 FT.): No change.

Nutrition Information Per Serving:	
Calories: 270	From Fat: 130
Total Fat	14g
Saturated	3g
Cholesterol	10mg
Sodium	400mg
Total Carbohydrate	29g
Dietary Fiber	2g
Sugars	4g
Protein	8g

Reese's® Puffs® Sticky Balls

PREP TIME: 30 MINUTES (READY IN 1 HOUR)
SERVINGS: 30

 EASY

¹/₄ cup butter or margarine

1 bag (10 oz.) regular marshmallows

1 box (14.25 oz.) Reese's® Puffs® cereal

¹/₄ cup semisweet chocolate chips

1 teaspoon shortening

1) Cut 18x12-inch sheet of waxed paper; place on work surface. In 4-quart Dutch oven, melt butter and marshmallows over low heat, stirring frequently, until smooth. Stir in cereal. Spread cereal mixture on waxed paper; cool 5 minutes.

2) Cut 34x12-inch sheet of waxed paper; place on work surface. Lightly spray hands with cooking spray. With hands, shape cereal mixture into about 2¹/₂-inch balls.

3) In small microwavable dish, microwave chocolate chips and shortening on High 1 to 1¹/₂ minutes, stirring until smooth. Drizzle chocolate over cereal balls. Let stand at least 30 minutes until chocolate is set before serving.

HIGH ALTITUDE (3500-6500 FT.): No change.

Nutrition Information Per Serving:		
Calories: 110	From Fat:	30
Total Fat		3.5g
Saturated		1.5g
Cholesterol		0mg
Sodium		90mg
Total Carbohydrate		19g
Dietary Fiber		0g
Sugars		11g
Protein		1g

Peppy-Mex Popcorn Snack

PREP TIME: 10 MINUTES (READY IN 55 MINUTES)
SERVINGS: 22 (1/2 CUP EACH)

 EASY

8 cups popped popcorn

2½ cups pretzel sticks

2½ cups crunchy cheese-flavored snacks

⅓ cup butter or margarine

1 teaspoon lemon-pepper seasoning

½ teaspoon dried oregano leaves

¼ to ½ teaspoon chili powder

¼ teaspoon garlic powder

¼ teaspoon onion powder

1) Heat oven to 325°F. In large bowl, mix popcorn, pretzels and cheese-flavored snacks.

2) In small saucepan, melt butter over low heat. Stir in lemon-pepper seasoning, oregano, chili powder, garlic powder and onion powder. Pour butter mixture over popcorn mixture; stir gently to coat. Spread mixture in ungreased 15x10x1-inch pan.

3) Bake 10 to 15 minutes, stirring once. Cool completely, about 30 minutes. Store in airtight container.

HIGH ALTITUDE (3500-6500 FT.): Bake 15 to 20 minutes, stirring once.

Nutrition Information Per Serving:		
Calories: 90	From Fat:	60
Total Fat		6g
Saturated		2.5g
Cholesterol		5mg
Sodium		150mg
Total Carbohydrate		8g
Dietary Fiber		0g
Sugars		0g
Protein		1g

Asian Coleslaw Salad

PREP TIME: 10 MINUTES (READY IN 1 HOUR 10 MINUTES)
SERVINGS: 14 (1/2 CUP EACH)

 EASY   LOW FAT

- 1 box (9 oz.) Green Giant® frozen sugar snap peas
- 1 bag (16 oz.) coleslaw mix (shredded cabbage and carrots)
- 1 cup thin bite-size red bell pepper strips
- 1 cup shredded carrots (1½ medium)
- 1 package (3 oz.) Oriental-flavor ramen noodle soup mix
- 1 cup sweet-and-sour sauce
- 2 tablespoons soy sauce

Nutrition Information Per Serving:

Calories:	50	From Fat:	5
Total Fat			1g
Saturated			0g
Cholesterol			0mg
Sodium			220mg
Total Carbohydrate			10g
Dietary Fiber			2g
Sugars			6g
Protein			1g

tip

If the sweet-and-sour sauce that you are using is not sweet enough for your taste, go ahead and add 1 to 2 teaspoons honey to the dressing mixture.

1) Cook and drain sugar snap peas as directed on box. Cool 1 minute.

2) Meanwhile, in large serving bowl, toss coleslaw mix, bell pepper and carrots. Discard seasoning packet from soup mix; break noodles into bite-size pieces and add to salad.

3) Add sugar snap peas to salad. In small bowl, mix sweet-and-sour sauce and soy sauce; pour over salad and toss gently. Cover; refrigerate at least 1 hour to soften noodles before serving.

HIGH ALTITUDE (3500-6500 FT.): No change.

Bacon and Green Chile Spiral Snacks

PREP TIME: 20 MINUTES (READY IN 2 HOURS 20 MINUTES)
SERVINGS: 24 (2 SNACKS EACH)

 EASY   LOW FAT

8 slices bacon

1 container (9 oz.) bean dip (about 1 cup)

4 oz. cream cheese, softened

6 Old El Paso® flour tortillas for burritos (8-inch)

¼ cup finely chopped red bell pepper

1 can (4.5 oz.) Old El Paso® chopped green chiles

1) Cook bacon until crisp. Drain on paper towels. Crumble bacon; set aside.

2) In medium bowl, mix bean dip and cream cheese. Spread each tortilla with bean dip mixture. Sprinkle each with bell pepper, green chiles and bacon. Roll up each tortilla. Wrap each in plastic wrap. Refrigerate at least 2 hours or until ready to serve.

3) To serve, cut each roll into 8 pieces. If desired, secure each piece with toothpick.

HIGH ALTITUDE (3500-6500 FT.): No change.

Nutrition Information Per Serving:		
Calories: 80	From Fat:	40
Total Fat		4g
Saturated		1.5g
Cholesterol		10mg
Sodium		240mg
Total Carbohydrate		7g
Dietary Fiber		0g
Sugars		0g
Protein		3g

Praline Brookies

JOANNA CRUMLEY | HUBBARD, OREGON

PREP TIME: 20 MINUTES (READY IN 1 HOUR 30 MINUTES)
SERVINGS: 24 BARS

1 box (19.5 oz.) Pillsbury®
  Brownie Classics Traditional
  fudge brownie mix

½ cup vegetable oil

¼ cup water

2 eggs

¼ cup butter

¼ cup milk

½ cup granulated sugar

½ cup packed brown sugar

½ cup coarsely chopped pecans

½ teaspoon vanilla

1 roll (18 oz.) Pillsbury® refrigerated
  chocolate chip cookies

  Vanilla ice cream, if desired

1) Heat oven to 350°F. (325°F. for dark pan).
   Spray 13x9-inch pan with cooking spray.
   Make brownie mix as directed on box
   using oil, water and eggs. Spread batter
   evenly in pan. Bake 25 minutes.

2) Meanwhile, in 2-quart saucepan, heat
   butter, milk, granulated sugar, brown
   sugar, pecans and vanilla to boiling over
   medium heat, stirring constantly. Reduce
   heat to medium-low; simmer 3 minutes,
   stirring occasionally. Remove from heat; set aside until brownies are baked.

3) Immediately pour praline mixture evenly over partially baked brownies. Cut
   cookie dough crosswise into 4 equal pieces; cut each piece into 4 slices.
   Carefully place slices in 3 rows of 5 slices each, using last slice to fill in
   spaces. (Spaces between cookie dough pieces will spread during baking to
   cover top.)

4) Bake 23 to 28 minutes longer or until cookie topping is deep golden brown.
   If serving as bars, cool 2 hours; cut into 6 rows by 4 rows. If serving with
   ice cream as dessert, cool 20 to 30 minutes; cut into 4 rows by 3 rows.

HIGH ALTITUDE (3500-6500 FT.): Follow High Altitude brownie mix directions for 13x9-inch pan. Bake
26 to 31 minutes.

Nutrition Information Per Bar:		
Calories:	320	From Fat: 140
Total Fat		16g
Saturated		4g
Cholesterol		25mg
Sodium		150mg
Total Carbohydrate		41g
Dietary Fiber		2g
Sugars		30g
Protein		2g

Layered Salad Supreme

PREP TIME: 25 MINUTES (READY IN 25 MINUTES)
SERVINGS: 12

 EASY

SALAD

- 5 cups torn lettuce
- 2½ cups broccoli florets
- 2 cups julienne-cut carrots
- 1 can (15 oz.) chick peas or garbanzo beans, drained, rinsed
- 1 small red onion, thinly sliced

DRESSING

- ¾ cup mayonnaise or salad dressing
- ⅓ cup milk
- ½ cup grated Parmesan cheese
- 2 tablespoons chopped fresh parsley

1) In 3-quart glass bowl with straight sides, layer lettuce, broccoli, carrots, beans and onion slices.

2) In small bowl, mix all dressing ingredients except parsley until well blended. Spread dressing evenly over salad. Sprinkle with parsley. Serve immediately or cover and refrigerate several hours or overnight.

HIGH ALTITUDE (3500-6500 FT.): No change.

Nutrition Information Per Serving:

Calories: 190	From Fat: 120
Total Fat	13g
Saturated	2.5g
Cholesterol	10mg
Sodium	170mg
Total Carbohydrate	13g
Dietary Fiber	3g
Sugars	3g
Protein	6g

tip

If you don't have the large glass bowl, the salad can be layered in a 13x9-inch (3-quart) glass baking dish instead.

Dilled Potato Salad

PREP TIME: 30 MINUTES (READY IN 1 HOUR 30 MINUTES)
SERVINGS: 12 (1/2 CUP EACH)

SALAD

4 medium red potatoes (about 2 lb.), peeled and diced

4 hard-cooked eggs, chopped

1/2 cup sliced green onions

3 tablespoons chopped fresh dill

1/2 teaspoon salt

1/4 teaspoon pepper

DRESSING

3/4 cup mayonnaise

1/3 cup milk

1 teaspoon white wine vinegar

1/2 teaspoon yellow mustard

1) Place potatoes in large saucepan. Add enough water to cover potatoes. Bring to a boil. Cook 5 to 8 minutes or just until potatoes are fork-tender. Drain; rinse with cold water until cool.

2) In large bowl, mix potatoes and remaining salad ingredients. In medium bowl, mix dressing ingredients. Pour dressing over salad; mix gently. Refrigerate 1 hour to blend flavors.

HIGH ALTITUDE (3500-6500 FT.): No change.

Nutrition Information Per Serving:

Calories:	190	From Fat:	110
Total Fat			13g
Saturated			2.5g
Cholesterol			75mg
Sodium			210mg
Total Carbohydrate			15g
Dietary Fiber			2g
Sugars			2g
Protein			4g

In this recipe, the potatoes are peeled and diced before cooking to shorten the preparation time.

Spicy Honeyed Chicken Drummettes

PREP TIME: 15 MINUTES (READY IN 1 HOUR 5 MINUTES)
SERVINGS: 20 DRUMMETTES

 EASY

2 packages (16 oz. each) chicken drummettes (about 20 drummettes)

½ cup chili sauce

¼ cup honey

2 tablespoons soy sauce or teriyaki sauce

½ teaspoon crushed red pepper flakes

1) Heat oven to 375°F. In 13x9-inch (3-quart) glass baking dish, arrange drummettes in single layer.

2) In small bowl, mix remaining ingredients; pour over drummettes to cover.

3) Bake 30 minutes. Turn drummettes; bake 15 to 20 minutes longer or until drummettes are glazed and juice of chicken is clear when thickest part is cut to bone (180°F.).

HIGH ALTITUDE (3500-6500 FT.): No change.

Nutrition Information Per Serving:		
Calories: 70	From Fat:	30
Total Fat		3.5g
Saturated		1g
Cholesterol		15mg
Sodium		200mg
Total Carbohydrate		5g
Dietary Fiber		0g
Sugars		4g
Protein		5g

Big Bean Pot

PREP TIME: 15 MINUTES (READY IN 1 HOUR 25 MINUTES)
SERVINGS: 12 (1/2 CUP EACH)

 EASY

12 slices bacon (about $3/4$ lb.), diced

3 medium onions, chopped

1 teaspoon garlic powder

$1/2$ teaspoon ground mustard

$1/2$ cup packed brown sugar

$1/3$ cup cider vinegar

$1/4$ cup ketchup

2 cans (16 oz. each) baked beans

1 can (15 oz.) red kidney beans, drained, rinsed

1 can (15 oz.) lima beans, drained, rinsed

Nutrition Information Per Serving:		
Calories: 260	From Fat:	40
Total Fat	4.5g	
Saturated	1.5g	
Cholesterol	15mg	
Sodium	580mg	
Total Carbohydrate	41g	
Dietary Fiber	9g	
Sugars	16g	
Protein	12g	

1) Heat oven to 350°F. In Dutch oven or large saucepan over medium heat, cook and stir bacon and onions until bacon is crisp and onions are tender. Drain. Stir in remaining ingredients.

2) Bake uncovered 60 to 70 minutes or until hot and bubbly.

HIGH ALTITUDE (3500-6500 FT.): No change.

tip

You can vary the beans in this tasty picnic side dish to suit your taste. Why not try substituting pinto or black beans for the kidney and lima beans?

Butterscotch Crackles

KATE SEVERANCE | GLOUCESTER CITY, NEW JERSEY

Pillsbury Bake-Off

PREP TIME: 1 HOUR 10 MINUTES (READY IN 1 HOUR 30 MINUTES)
SERVINGS: 4 DOZEN COOKIES

2 rolls (18 oz. each) Pillsbury®
  refrigerated sugar cookies,
  softened at room temperature
  about 20 minutes

2 cups Wheaties® cereal, crushed
  (1 cup)

1 cup Hershey®'s butterscotch chips
  (6 oz.)

1 cup Mounds® coconut flakes

½ cup powdered sugar

1) Heat oven to 350°F. Spray cookie sheets
   with cooking spray. In large bowl, break
   up cookie dough. Stir or knead in
   crushed cereal, butterscotch chips and
   coconut until well blended.

2) Shape dough into about 1-inch balls; roll
   in powdered sugar and place 2 inches
   apart on cookie sheets.

3) Bake 11 to 15 minutes or until edges are
   golden brown. Cool 1 minute; remove
   from cookie sheets.

HIGH ALTITUDE (3500-6500 FT.): No change.

Nutrition Information Per Cookie:		
Calories: 130	From Fat:	50
Total Fat		6g
Saturated		2.5g
Cholesterol		5mg
Sodium		75mg
Total Carbohydrate		18g
Dietary Fiber		0g
Sugars		11g
Protein		0g

Peanut Butter Crunch Brownies

CINDY EGERSDORFER | CUYAHOGA FALLS , OHIO

PREP TIME: 30 MINUTES (READY IN 4 HOURS 10 MINUTES)
SERVINGS: 24 BROWNIES

- 1 box (19.5 oz.) Pillsbury® Brownie Classics Traditional fudge brownie mix
- ½ cup vegetable oil
- ¼ cup water
- 2 eggs
- 3 cups Hershey's® semi-sweet chocolate chips
- 1 bag (14 oz.) caramels, unwrapped
- ¼ cup water
- 2 cups slightly broken pretzels (4 ½ oz.)*
- ¼ cup butter or margarine, melted
- 1 cup powdered sugar
- 1 jar (18 oz.) crunchy peanut butter
- 2 cups Reese's® Puffs® cereal, slightly broken*

1) Heat oven to 350°F. (325°F. for dark pan). Grease 13x9-inch pan with cooking spray or shortening.** In large bowl, make brownie mix as directed on box using oil, water and eggs. Stir in 1 cup of the chocolate chips. Spread batter evenly in pan. Bake 28 to 30 minutes. Cool on wire rack while making topping.

2) In medium microwavable bowl, microwave caramels and water on High 1 minute. Stir; continue to microwave in 15-second increments, stirring after each, until caramels are completely melted and mixture is smooth. Stir in crushed pretzels until well coated. Spoon and spread carefully over cooled brownie layer.

3) In large bowl, mix melted butter and powdered sugar until smooth. Stir in peanut butter. Stir in crushed cereal until well blended. Spread or pat over caramel layer.

4) In small microwavable bowl, microwave remaining 2 cups chocolate chips on High 1 minute. Stir; continue to microwave in 15-second increments, stirring after each, until chocolate is melted. Spread over cereal layer. Refrigerate until chocolate is set and caramel mixture in center is firm, 2 to 3 hours. Let stand at room temperature 10 minutes before cutting. Cut into 6 rows by 4 rows.

*NOTE: To slightly break pretzels and cereal, place in separate resealable food-storage plastic bags; seal bags and break with rolling pin.

**NOTE: To easily cut brownies, line pan with foil so foil extends over sides of pan; spray foil with cooking spray. When ready to cut, lift brownies from pan using foil.

HIGH ALTITUDE (3500-6500 FT.): Follow High Altitude brownie mix directions for 13x9-inch pan.

Nutrition Information Per Bar:	
Calories: 530	From Fat: 250
Total Fat	28g
Saturated	9g
Cholesterol	25mg
Sodium	340mg
Total Carbohydrate	61g
Dietary Fiber	4g
Sugars	41g
Protein	9g

Easy Mustard Potato Salad

PREP TIME: 30 MINUTES (READY IN 1 HOUR 30 MINUTES)
SERVINGS: 12 (3/4 CUP EACH)

SALAD

4 eggs

2 packages (20 oz. each) refrigerated red-skinned potato wedges or diced potatoes with onions

1 cup sliced celery (1^1/$_2$ to 2 stalks)

1 cup chopped red bell pepper (1 medium)

DRESSING

1^1/$_2$ cups mayonnaise or salad dressing

2 tablespoons chopped fresh dill

^{1}/$_4$ cup prepared yellow mustard

2 teaspoons sugar

1 teaspoon salt

1) In 1^1/$_2$-quart saucepan, place eggs; add enough water to cover by 1 inch. Heat to boiling. Immediately remove from heat; cover and let stand 15 minutes. Drain; rinse with cold water. Place eggs in bowl of ice water; let stand 10 minutes. Drain. Peel eggs; coarsely chop.

2) Meanwhile, in 3-quart saucepan, heat 4 cups water to boiling. Reduce heat to medium. Add potatoes; cook 5 to 8 minutes or until tender. Drain; rinse with cold water to cool. Drain well.

3) In large bowl, mix cooled cooked potatoes, the celery, bell pepper and chopped hard-cooked eggs. In small bowl, mix dressing ingredients until well blended. Add dressing to salad; toss gently to coat. Cover; refrigerate at least 1 hour before serving.

HIGH ALTITUDE (3500-6500 FT.): When cooking eggs, after heating water with eggs to boiling, boil gently 5 minutes. Remove from heat; cover and let stand 15 minutes. Continue as directed above.

Nutrition Information Per Serving:		
Calories: 270	From Fat: 210	
Total Fat		24g
Saturated		4g
Cholesterol		85mg
Sodium		440mg
Total Carbohydrate		12g
Dietary Fiber		2g
Sugars		3g
Protein		4g

Slow Cooker Favorites

Gone all day? No problem!
It's easier than ever to come home
to heartwarming flavor.

EASY SLOW COOKER POT-ROASTED
STEAK
PG. 273

SPICY CHEESEBURGER NACHOS
PG. 272

SLOW COOKER SWEET-AND-SOUR
PORK
PG. 281

BEEF AND VEGETABLE CHILI
PG. 278

Texas-Style Cowboy Beans

PREP TIME: 20 MINUTES (READY IN 5 HOURS 20 MINUTES)
SERVINGS: 12 (1/2 CUP EACH)

 EASY

Serve these tasty beans as a side dish for grilled hamburgers and bratwurst or use as a coney-dog topping for hot dogs.

1 lb. lean (at least 80%) ground beef

1 large onion, chopped (1 cup)

1/2 lb. bacon, cut into small pieces

1 can (14 1/2 oz.) stewed tomatoes with jalapeño chiles, garlic and cumin, undrained

1 can (28 oz.) baked beans with onion

Nutrition Information Per Serving:	
Calories: 170	From Fat: 70
Total Fat	8g
Saturated	3g
Cholesterol	35mg
Sodium	490mg
Total Carbohydrate	16g
Dietary Fiber	4g
Sugars	6g
Protein	12g

1) In 10-inch skillet, cook ground beef and onion over medium heat 8 to 10 minutes, stirring frequently, until beef is thoroughly cooked; drain. Into 3 1/2- to 4-quart slow cooker, spoon ground beef.

2) In same skillet, cook bacon over medium heat, stirring frequently, until bacon is brown and crisp; do not drain off drippings. Add tomatoes; heat to boiling. With spoon, break up large pieces of tomato. Spoon bacon mixture into slow cooker. Stir in baked beans.

3) Cover; cook on Low heat setting 4 to 5 hours.

HIGH ALTITUDE (3500-6500 FT.): No change.

Smoky BBQ Pork Sandwiches

PREP TIME: 20 MINUTES (READY IN 10 HOURS 50 MINUTES)
SERVINGS: 12 (1/2 CUP EACH)

 EASY

1 boneless pork shoulder roast (3 1/2 lb.)

1/2 teaspoon salt

1/2 teaspoon pepper

2 cups barbecue sauce

1 tablespoon honey

1 teaspoon liquid smoke

Nutrition Information Per Serving:	
Calories: 350	From Fat: 180
Total Fat	20g
Saturated	7g
Cholesterol	90mg
Sodium	570mg
Total Carbohydrate	16g
Dietary Fiber	0g
Sugars	12g
Protein	25g

1) Heat 12-inch nonstick skillet over medium heat. Sprinkle pork roast with salt and pepper. Add roast to skillet; cook 8 to 10 minutes or until browned on all sides. Place roast in 4- to 5-quart slow cooker.

2) Cover; cook on Low heat setting 8 to 10 hours.

3) About 40 minutes before serving, remove roast from slow cooker and place on cutting board; discard liquid in slow cooker. In slow cooker, stir together all remaining ingredients. With 2 forks, shred pork roast. Return pork to slow cooker; stir gently to mix with sauce.

4) Increase heat setting to High; cover and cook 30 minutes longer or until thoroughly heated. Serve on buns.

HIGH ALTITUDE (3500-6500 FT.): No change.

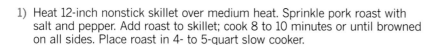

Tuscan Pork Roast

PREP TIME: 30 MINUTES (READY IN 8 HOURS 30 MINUTES)
SERVINGS: 8

4 slices bacon, cut into 1-inch pieces

2 teaspoons finely chopped garlic (about 4 medium cloves)

1 teaspoon dried rosemary leaves, crushed

1/2 teaspoon salt

1/2 teaspoon ground sage

1 boneless pork loin roast (3 to 4 lb.)

1/3 cup dry white wine or chicken broth

3 tablespoons all-purpose flour

3 tablespoons water

Nutrition Information Per Serving:

Calories: 310	From Fat: 140
Total Fat	15g
Saturated	5g
Cholesterol	110mg
Sodium	280mg
Total Carbohydrate	3g
Dietary Fiber	0g
Sugars	0g
Protein	39g

1) Spray inside of 3½- to 4-quart slow cooker with cooking spray. In 10-inch skillet, cook bacon over medium heat 6 to 8 minutes, stirring occasionally, until crisp. Remove from skillet; place in slow cooker.

2) In small bowl, mix garlic, rosemary, salt and sage. Rub all sides of pork roast with garlic mixture. Add roast to skillet; cook 4 to 6 minutes, turning occasionally, until browned on all sides.

3) Remove roast from skillet; place in slow cooker. Pour wine over roast.

4) Cover; cook on Low heat setting 6 to 8 hours.

5) In small bowl, mix flour and water until smooth. Remove roast from slow cooker. Strain juices from slow cooker into 4-cup microwavable measuring cup or medium microwavable bowl. Stir flour mixture into juices until smooth. Microwave on High 3 minutes or until thickened; stir. Cut roast into slices; serve with gravy.

HIGH ALTITUDE (3500-6500 FT.): No change.

Scalloped Potatoes and Ham

PREP TIME: 15 MINUTES (READY IN 6 HOURS 20 MINUTES)
SERVINGS: 4 (1-1/2 CUPS EACH)

 EASY

2 lb. unpeeled medium-size red potatoes, cut into quarters (about 6 cups)

$^1/_3$ cup chopped green bell pepper (1 small)

2 cups cubed ($^1/_2$ inch) cooked ham

1 tablespoon dried minced onion

1 jar (16 oz.) Alfredo pasta sauce

$^1/_2$ cup milk

$^1/_4$ teaspoon pepper

$^1/_3$ cup shredded Parmesan cheese (1$^1/_3$ oz.), if desired

Chopped fresh parsley, if desired

1) Spray 3$^1/_2$- to 4-quart slow cooker with cooking spray. Layer half each of the potatoes, bell pepper and ham in slow cooker. Sprinkle with half of the onion.

2) In medium bowl, mix pasta sauce, milk and pepper; spoon half of mixture over ham. Layer with remaining potatoes, bell pepper, ham, onion and sauce (do not stir).

3) Cover; cook on Low heat setting 6 to 8 hours.

4) About 5 minutes before serving, stir mixture gently; sprinkle Parmesan cheese over top. Cover; cook on Low heat setting until cheese is melted. Top each serving with parsley.

HIGH ALTITUDE (3500-6500 FT.): No change.

Nutrition Information Per Serving:

Calories: 550	From Fat: 260
Total Fat	29g
Saturated	12g
Cholesterol	140mg
Sodium	1800mg
Total Carbohydrate	48g
Dietary Fiber	5g
Sugars	7g
Protein	25g

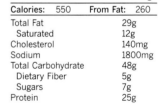

Although other potatoes can be used, red potatoes have a firm, waxy texture and hold their shape well during the long cooking process—they are ideal to use in slow cooker recipes.

French Onion Meatballs

PREP TIME:	10 MINUTES (READY IN 4 HOURS 40 MINUTES)	
SERVINGS:	18	EASY

2 bags (18 oz. each) frozen cooked meatballs

1 jar (12 oz.) beef gravy

1 package (1 oz.) dry onion soup mix

1 tablespoon dry sherry, if desired

Nutrition Information Per Serving:

Calories: 160	From Fat: 70
Total Fat	8g
Saturated	3g
Cholesterol	60mg
Sodium	570mg
Total Carbohydrate	8g
Dietary Fiber	0g
Sugars	2g
Protein	12g

1) In 4- to 5-quart slow cooker, place meatballs. In medium bowl, mix gravy, soup mix and sherry; gently stir into meatballs.

2) Cover; cook on Low heat setting $3^1/2$ to $4^1/2$ hours. Serve meatballs with fondue forks or long toothpicks.

HIGH ALTITUDE (3500-6500 FT.): No change.

Favorite Ground Beef and Beans

PREP TIME:	20 MINUTES (READY IN 4 HOURS 20 MINUTES)		
SERVINGS:	10 (1 CUP EACH)	EASY	LOW FAT

2 lb. lean (at least 80%) ground beef

1 large onion, chopped (about $3/4$ cup)

1 can (28 oz.) baked beans, undrained

1 can (15.5 oz.) butter beans, drained, rinsed

1 can (15 oz.) Progresso® kidney beans, drained, rinsed

1 bottle (12 oz.) chili sauce

2 cans (4.5 oz. each) Old El Paso® chopped green chiles

2 tablespoons packed brown sugar

3 teaspoons chili powder

Shredded Cheddar cheese, if desired

Nutrition Information Per Serving:

Calories: 340	From Fat: 80
Total Fat	9g
Saturated	3.5g
Cholesterol	60mg
Sodium	950mg
Total Carbohydrate	43g
Dietary Fiber	12g
Sugars	11g
Protein	29g

1) In 10-inch nonstick skillet, cook ground beef and onion over medium-high heat, stirring frequently, until beef is thoroughly cooked; drain.

2) In $3^1/2$- to 4-quart slow cooker, mix cooked ground beef mixture and remaining ingredients except cheese.

3) Cover; cook on Low heat setting 4 hours. Top individual servings with Cheddar cheese.

HIGH ALTITUDE (3500-6500 FT.): No change.

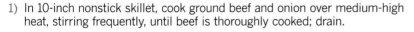

Buffalo Chicken Wraps

PREP TIME: 20 MINUTES (READY IN 7 HOURS 20 MINUTES)
SERVINGS: 8

 EASY

2 lb. boneless skinless chicken thighs

1/2 teaspoon salt

3/4 cup buffalo wing sauce (from 12-oz. jar)

3/4 cup ranch dressing

1 package (11.5 oz.) Old El Paso® flour tortillas for burritos (8 tortillas)

3 cups shredded lettuce

Nutrition Information Per Serving:

Calories: 450	From Fat: 220
Total Fat	24g
Saturated	6g
Cholesterol	80mg
Sodium	940mg
Total Carbohydrate	31g
Dietary Fiber	0g
Sugars	7g
Protein	27g

1) In 1 1/2-quart slow cooker, place chicken; sprinkle with salt.

2) Cover; cook 6 to 7 hours (if slow cooker has heat settings, use Low).

3) With slotted spoon, remove chicken from slow cooker and place on cutting board; discard liquid in slow cooker. In slow cooker, mix buffalo wing sauce and 1/4 cup of the ranch dressing. With 2 forks, shred chicken. Return chicken to slow cooker; stir gently to mix with sauce.

4) To serve, spread each tortilla with 1 tablespoon remaining ranch dressing; top each with about 1/2 cup chicken mixture and about 1/3 cup lettuce. Roll up tortilla; secure with toothpicks.

HIGH ALTITUDE (3500-6500 FT.): No change.

Spicy Cheeseburger Nachos

PREP TIME: 20 MINUTES (READY IN 4 HOURS 20 MINUTES)
SERVINGS: 22

 EASY

1 lb. lean (at least 80%) ground beef

1 clove garlic, minced

2 boxes (16 oz. each) Mexican prepared cheese product with jalapeño peppers, cut into cubes

2 cans (10 oz. each) diced tomatoes with green chiles, drained

1/2 cup chopped green onions (8 medium)

22 oz. tortilla chips

Nutrition Information Per Serving:

Calories: 310	From Fat: 170
Total Fat	18g
Saturated	7g
Cholesterol	45mg
Sodium	870mg
Total Carbohydrate	24g
Dietary Fiber	1g
Sugars	6g
Protein	13g

1) In 10-inch skillet, cook ground beef and garlic, stirring frequently, until beef is thoroughly cooked; drain. Spoon into 3 1/2- to 4-quart slow cooker. Add cheese and tomatoes; mix well.

2) Cover; cook on Low heat setting 3 to 4 hours, stirring after 2 hours.

3) Before serving, stir in onions. Serve with tortilla chips.

HIGH ALTITUDE (3500-6500 FT.): No change.

Easy Slow Cooker Pot-Roasted Steak

PREP TIME: 10 MINUTES (READY IN 5 HOURS 10 MINUTES)
SERVINGS: 4

 EASY   LOW FAT

1½ lb. boneless beef top round steak
    (1 inch thick)

½   teaspoon paprika

¼   teaspoon pepper

1   cup julienne cut (2x⅛x⅛-inch)
    carrots

1   jar (4.5 oz.) Green Giant® sliced
    mushrooms, undrained

1   can (10¾ oz.) condensed cream of
    mushroom soup

2   tablespoons dry onion soup mix
    (from 1-oz. package)

1) Spray 3- to 3½-quart slow cooker with cooking spray. Sprinkle beef with paprika and pepper; cut into 4 serving pieces. Place in slow cooker.

2) In medium bowl, mix carrots, mushrooms, soup and soup mix; pour over beef.

3) Cover; cook on Low heat setting 5 to 6 hours.

4) Serve steak topped with gravy and vegetables.

HIGH ALTITUDE (3500-6500 FT.): No change.

Nutrition Information Per Serving:	
Calories: 280	From Fat: 90
Total Fat	10g
Saturated	3g
Cholesterol	95mg
Sodium	990mg
Total Carbohydrate	12g
Dietary Fiber	2g
Sugars	4g
Protein	36g

 tip

Serve this hearty beef dish with mashed potatoes or egg noodles and cooked green beans.

Turkey with Cranberry Stuffing

PREP TIME: 20 MINUTES (READY IN 8 HOURS 30 MINUTES)
SERVINGS: 4

 EASY

1 package (6 oz.) cubed herb-seasoned stuffing mix

1 cup sliced celery (2 medium stalks)

1/2 cup chopped onion (1 medium)

1/4 teaspoon poultry seasoning, if desired

1 cup chicken broth

1/2 cup sweetened dried cranberries

2 lb. bone-in turkey or chicken thighs, skin removed

1/4 teaspoon salt

1/4 teaspoon pepper

1 jar (12 oz.) turkey gravy

1) Spray 3 1/2- to 4-quart slow cooker with cooking spray. In medium bowl, mix stuffing mix, celery, onion and poultry seasoning. Stir in broth to moisten. Stir in cranberries.

2) Spoon half of stuffing into slow cooker. Sprinkle turkey with salt and pepper; place over stuffing. Spoon remaining stuffing around turkey.

3) Cover; cook on Low heat setting 8 to 9 hours.

4) About 15 minutes before serving, remove turkey from slow cooker; keep warm. Stir stuffing and cooking juices until mixed. Cover; let stand about 10 minutes. Meanwhile, in 1-quart saucepan, heat gravy.

5) Cut turkey into serving pieces. Serve with stuffing and gravy.

HIGH ALTITUDE (3500-6500 FT.): No change.

Nutrition Information Per Serving:

Calories:	500	From Fat:	110
Total Fat			12g
Saturated			3.5g
Cholesterol			145mg
Sodium			1700mg
Total Carbohydrate			53g
Dietary Fiber			3g
Sugars			14g
Protein			44g

Turkey drumsticks can be substituted for the thighs if they fit in your slow cooker. You'll find that an oval slow cooker will accommodate these larger pieces of meat better than a round one.

Pizza Dunkers

PREP TIME: 15 MINUTES (READY IN 2 HOURS 45 MINUTES)
SERVINGS: 10 (1/4 CUP DIP AND 1 BREAD STICK EACH)

 EASY

3 oz. turkey pepperoni (half
of 6-oz. package), chopped

4 medium green onions, chopped
($^{1}/_{4}$ cup)

1 jar (14 oz.) pizza sauce

2 cups shredded mozzarella cheese
(8 oz.)

10 soft bread sticks

Nutrition Information Per Serving:	
Calories: 200	From Fat: 70
Total Fat	8g
Saturated	3.5g
Cholesterol	20mg
Sodium	630mg
Total Carbohydrate	20g
Dietary Fiber	1g
Sugars	2g
Protein	11g

1) In 1$^{1}/_{2}$-quart slow cooker, mix pepperoni, onions and pizza sauce.

2) Cover; cook 2 hours (if slow cooker has heat settings, use Low).

3) Stir in cheese. Cover; cook on Low heat setting 30 minutes longer or until mixture is hot and cheese has begun to melt. Serve dip with bread sticks.

HIGH ALTITUDE (3500-6500 FT.): No change.

Caesar Artichoke Dip

PREP TIME: 10 MINUTES (READY IN 2 HOURS 10 MINUTES)
SERVINGS: 20 (2 TABLESPOONS DIP AND 2 BREAD SLICES EACH)

 EASY

1 can (14 oz.) quartered artichoke
hearts, drained, coarsely chopped

1 package (8 oz.) cream cheese, cut
into cubes

$^{1}/_{2}$ cup creamy Caesar dressing

$^{3}/_{4}$ cup shredded Parmesan cheese (3 oz.)

$^{1}/_{4}$ cup chopped green onions
(4 medium)

Dash red pepper sauce

Chopped green onions, if desired

1 loaf (8 oz.) baguette French bread
(about 22 inches long), cut into
$^{1}/_{2}$-inch slices, toasted if desired

Nutrition Information Per Serving:	
Calories: 130	From Fat: 80
Total Fat	9g
Saturated	4g
Cholesterol	15mg
Sodium	270mg
Total Carbohydrate	8g
Dietary Fiber	1g
Sugars	0g
Protein	4g

1) Spray inside of 1- to 1$^{1}/_{2}$-quart slow cooker with cooking spray. In slow cooker, mix all ingredients except bread and additional green onions.

2) Cover; cook on Low heat setting 2 to 3 hours.

3) Before serving, stir until dip is well blended and smooth. Top with green onions. Serve with bread slices. Dip can be held on Low heat setting up to 1 hour.

HIGH ALTITUDE (3500-6500 FT.): No change.

Slow-Cooked Hamburger Spaghetti

PREP TIME: 45 MINUTES (READY IN 6 HOURS 15 MINUTES)
SERVINGS: 6 (1-1/2 CUPS EACH)

1 lb. lean (at least 80%) ground beef

1 cup finely chopped onions
(2 medium)

2 tablespoons sugar

1 teaspoon dried basil leaves

1 teaspoon dried oregano leaves

$\frac{1}{2}$ teaspoon salt

2 cloves garlic, minced

1 can (28 oz.) Progresso® crushed
tomatoes, undrained

1 can (15 oz.) tomato sauce

1 can (12 oz.) tomato paste

1 package (16 oz.) spaghetti

Nutrition Information Per Serving:		
Calories: 560	From Fat:	90
Total Fat		11g
Saturated		3.5g
Cholesterol		45mg
Sodium		1610mg
Total Carbohydrate		89g
Dietary Fiber		10g
Sugars		14g
Protein		28g

1) In 10-inch skillet, cook ground beef and onions over medium-high heat, stirring frequently, until beef is thoroughly cooked; drain.

2) In 3$\frac{1}{2}$- to 4-quart slow cooker, mix ground beef mixture and remaining ingredients except spaghetti.

3) Cover; cook on Low heat setting 6 to 8 hours.

4) About 30 minutes before serving, cook spaghetti as directed on package; drain. Serve sauce over spaghetti.

HIGH ALTITUDE (3500-6500 FT.): No change.

Beans 'n Wieners

PREP TIME: 10 MINUTES (READY IN 5 HOURS 10 MINUTES)
SERVINGS: 8 (1 CUP EACH)

 EASY

1 lb. hot dogs, each cut into 4 pieces

3 cans (15 oz. each) pork and beans in
tomato sauce, undrained

$\frac{1}{2}$ cup ketchup

$\frac{1}{4}$ cup finely chopped onion ($\frac{1}{2}$ medium)

$\frac{1}{4}$ cup molasses

2 teaspoons yellow mustard

Nutrition Information Per Serving:		
Calories: 400	From Fat:	160
Total Fat		18g
Saturated		7g
Cholesterol		45mg
Sodium		1570mg
Total Carbohydrate		45g
Dietary Fiber		9g
Sugars		19g
Protein		15g

1) In 3$\frac{1}{2}$- to 4-quart slow cooker, mix ingredients.

2) Cover; cook on Low heat setting 5 to 6 hours.

HIGH ALTITUDE (3500-6500 FT.): No change.

Slow-Cooked Praline Apple Crisp

PREP TIME: 25 MINUTES (READY IN 4 HOURS 25 MINUTES)
SERVINGS: 10 (1/2 CUP EACH)

6 medium-size crisp tart apples (Granny Smith or Braeburn), peeled if desired, cut into 1/2-inch-thick slices (about 6 cups)

1 teaspoon ground cinnamon

1/2 cup quick-cooking rolled oats

1/3 cup packed brown sugar

1/4 cup all-purpose flour

1/2 cup cold butter, cut into small pieces

1/2 cup chopped pecans

1/2 cup toffee bits

Ice cream, if desired

Nutrition Information Per Serving:	
Calories: 280	From Fat: 160
Total Fat	17g
Saturated	7g
Cholesterol	30mg
Sodium	110mg
Total Carbohydrate	30g
Dietary Fiber	3g
Sugars	20g
Protein	2g

1) Spray 3- to 4-quart slow cooker with cooking spray. In large bowl, mix apples and cinnamon to coat. Place in slow cooker.

2) In medium bowl with pastry blender or fork, mix oats, brown sugar, flour and butter until crumbly. Stir in pecans and toffee bits. Sprinkle crumb mixture evenly over apples.

3) Cover; cook on Low heat setting 4 to 6 hours. Serve apple crisp with ice cream.

HIGH ALTITUDE (3500-6500 FT.): No change.

If you'd like the apple slices to retain their shape and have a slightly firm texture, use the low end of the cook time range.

Beef and Vegetable Chili

PREP TIME: 5 MINUTES (READY IN 8 HOURS 5 MINUTES)
SERVINGS: 6 (1-1/3 CUPS EACH)

 EASY LOW FAT

1 box (8.5 oz.) Slow Cooker Helper® beef stew

3½ cups hot water

1 lb. lean beef stew meat (¾-inch pieces)

1 can (16 oz.) red beans in chili sauce, undrained

1 can (14.5 oz.) diced tomatoes with zesty mild green chiles, undrained

Cheddar cheese, if desired

1) In 3½- to 4-quart slow cooker, mix vegetables plus sauce from box and hot water. Stir in remaining ingredients.

2) Cover; cook on Low heat setting 8 to 10 hours (or on High heat setting 4 to 5 hours). Stir stew before serving. Serve individual servings topped with cheese.

HIGH ALTITUDE (3500-6500 FT.): No change.

Nutrition Information Per Serving:

Calories:	350	From Fat:	90
Total Fat			10g
Saturated			3.5g
Cholesterol			45mg
Sodium			1550mg
Total Carbohydrate			43g
Dietary Fiber			8g
Sugars			9g
Protein			24g

Sauerbraten Beef

2 lb. beef stew meat (1-inch pieces)

1 cup chopped onions (2 medium)

1 cup beef broth

1 cup red wine vinegar or cider vinegar

2 dried bay leaves

6 cups uncooked medium egg noodles (12 oz.)

3/4 cup crushed gingersnap cookies (about 15)

2 tablespoons packed brown sugar

2 tablespoons chopped fresh parsley

Nutrition Information Per Serving:	
Calories: 590	From Fat: 190
Total Fat	21g
Saturated	7g
Cholesterol	140mg
Sodium	360mg
Total Carbohydrate	59g
Dietary Fiber	2g
Sugars	16g
Protein	39g

For the best results, purchase lean beef stew meat or trim any excess fat from the beef pieces.

1) In 3¹/₂- to 4-quart slow cooker, mix beef, onions, broth, vinegar and bay leaves.

2) Cover; cook on Low heat setting 7 to 9 hours.

3) About 15 minutes before serving, cook noodles as directed on package. Remove bay leaves from beef mixture. Stir in crushed cookies and brown sugar. Cover; cook on Low heat setting 15 minutes longer or until mixture is bubbly and thickened. Serve beef mixture over noodles; sprinkle with parsley.

HIGH ALTITUDE (3500-6500 FT.): No change.

Slow Cooker Tex-Mex Turkey Sandwiches

PREP TIME: 15 MINUTES (READY IN 9 HOURS 30 MINUTES)
SERVINGS: 8 SANDWICHES

 EASY

4 bone-in turkey thighs (about 3 lb.), skin removed

1/2 cup Old El Paso® Thick 'n Chunky salsa

1/4 cup water

1 package (1.25 oz.) Old El Paso® taco seasoning mix

8 kaiser rolls, split

8 slices (1 oz. each) Monterey Jack cheese

2 medium avocados, pitted, peeled and sliced

1 medium red or green bell pepper, cut into rings

1) In 3 1/2- to 4-quart slow cooker, place turkey thighs. In small bowl, mix salsa, water and taco seasoning mix; pour over turkey.

2) Cover; cook on Low heat setting 7 to 9 hours or until juice of turkey is clear when thickest part is cut to bone (180°F.).

3) Remove turkey from slow cooker; place on cutting board. With 2 forks, shred turkey; discard bones. Return turkey to slow cooker; mix well. Cover; cook on High heat setting 15 minutes longer or until mixture is hot.

4) With slotted spoon, spoon about 1/2 cup turkey mixture onto bottom half of each bun. Top with cheese, avocados, bell pepper and top halves of buns.

HIGH ALTITUDE (3500-6500 FT.): No change.

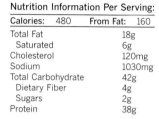

Nutrition Information Per Serving:		
Calories: 480	From Fat:	160
Total Fat		18g
Saturated		6g
Cholesterol		120mg
Sodium		1030mg
Total Carbohydrate		42g
Dietary Fiber		4g
Sugars		2g
Protein		38g

Slow Cooker Sweet-and-Sour Pork

PREP TIME:	20 MINUTES (READY IN 5 HOURS)
SERVINGS:	4

EASY

2 tablespoons butter or margarine

1 boneless pork shoulder blade roast (2 lb.)

1 jar (10 oz.) sweet-and-sour sauce

¼ cup chicken broth

1 can (20 oz.) pineapple chunks in juice, drained

¼ cup cold water

1 tablespoon cornstarch

Nutrition Information Per Serving:		
Calories: 660	From Fat:	340
Total Fat		38g
Saturated		14g
Cholesterol		170mg
Sodium		460mg
Total Carbohydrate		31g
Dietary Fiber		2g
Sugars		23g
Protein		50g

1) In 10-inch skillet, melt butter over medium heat. Add pork roast; cook 3 to 4 minutes on each side or until browned.

2) Into 3½- to 4-quart slow cooker, pour sweet-and-sour sauce. Add pork, broth and drained pineapple.

3) Cover; cook on Low heat setting 4 hours 30 minutes to 5 hours.

4) About 15 minutes before serving, in small bowl, mix water and cornstarch until smooth. Remove pork from slow cooker; place on cutting board or serving platter. Stir cornstarch mixture into juices in slow cooker. Return pork to slow cooker. Increase heat setting to High; cover and cook 10 minutes or until sauce has slightly thickened. Cut pork into slices; serve with sauce.

HIGH ALTITUDE (3500-6500 FT.): No change.

tip

Serve the sweet-and-sour pork with rice and a tossed green salad.

Easy Chicken and Rice Casserole

PREP TIME: 20 MINUTES (READY IN 4 HOURS 50 MINUTES)
SERVINGS: 4 (1-1/4 CUPS EACH)

1 lb. boneless skinless chicken thighs, each cut into 4 pieces

1 can (10³/₄ oz.) condensed cream of chicken soup

1 jar (4.5 oz.) Green Giant® sliced mushrooms, undrained

¹/₂ cup water

1¹/₂ cups Green Giant® frozen sweet peas (from 1-lb. bag), thawed

1¹/₂ cups uncooked instant white rice

1) In 3- to 4-quart slow cooker, place chicken. Top with soup, mushrooms and water; stir gently to mix and spread evenly over chicken.

2) Cover; cook on Low heat setting 4 hours 30 minutes to 5 hours 30 minutes.

3) About 15 minutes before serving, stir thawed peas and the rice into chicken mixture. Cover; cook on Low heat setting 10 to 15 minutes longer or until rice is tender. If desired, add salt and pepper to taste.

HIGH ALTITUDE (3500-6500 FT.): No change.

Nutrition Information Per Serving:	
Calories: 460	From Fat: 130
Total Fat	15g
Saturated	4.5g
Cholesterol	75mg
Sodium	780mg
Total Carbohydrate	50g
Dietary Fiber	3g
Sugars	3g
Protein	32g

Root Beer Barbecue Beef Sandwiches

PREP TIME: 30 MINUTES (READY IN 10 HOURS 30 MINUTES)
SERVINGS: 16 SANDWICHES

 EASY   LOW FAT

1 boneless beef rump roast (4 lb.)

2 cups barbecue sauce

1 cup root beer

  Dash salt and pepper, if desired

16 sandwich buns, split

Nutrition Information Per Serving:

Calories:	290	From Fat:	50
Total Fat			6g
Saturated			1.5g
Cholesterol			60mg
Sodium			600mg
Total Carbohydrate			34g
Dietary Fiber			0g
Sugars			11g
Protein			26g

1) In $3^1/_2$- to 4-quart slow cooker, place beef. In 4-cup measuring cup or bowl, mix $1^1/_2$ cups of the barbecue sauce and the root beer; pour over beef.

2) Cover; cook on Low heat setting 10 to 12 hours.

3) About 20 minutes before serving, remove beef from slow cooker; place on large plate. Pour juices from slow cooker into 12-inch skillet. Cook over medium-high heat about 15 minutes, stirring occasionally, until juices are thickened and reduced to about 3 cups. Meanwhile, shred beef with 2 forks; return to slow cooker.

4) Stir remaining $^1/_2$ cup barbecue sauce into reduced juices in skillet; pour over shredded beef in slow cooker. Stir in salt and pepper to taste. Spoon about $^1/_2$ cup beef mixture into each bun.

HIGH ALTITUDE (3500-6500 FT.): No change.

tip

Serve these hearty sandwiches with coleslaw from the deli and baked beans.

BROWNIE TRIFLE
PG. 309

Scrumptious Desserts

What's for dessert? Dozens of delectable
ways to satisfy your sweet tooth!

CANDY BAR CHEESECAKE
PG. 294

MINTY ICE CREAM SQUARES
PG. 297

RASPBERRY CREAM TARTS
PG. 303

Peanut Butter-Fudge-Ice Cream Pie

PREP TIME: 15 MINUTES (READY IN 2 HOURS 15 MINUTES)
SERVINGS: 8

 EASY

2 cups Reese's® Puffs® cereal

1 quart (4 cups) vanilla ice cream, softened

3/4 cup fudge ice cream topping

1/4 cup creamy peanut butter

Nutrition Information Per Serving:	
Calories: 340	From Fat: 140
Total Fat	16g
Saturated	7g
Cholesterol	30mg
Sodium	250mg
Total Carbohydrate	44g
Dietary Fiber	2g
Sugars	31g
Protein	6g

1) In ungreased 8-inch round cake pan, spread cereal evenly. Drop ice cream by small spoonfuls on top of cereal. Rinse metal spoon with hot water; wipe dry. With back of hot spoon, spread ice cream evenly in pan, pressing down firmly and reheating spoon as needed.

2) In small microwavable bowl, mix fudge topping and peanut butter until well blended. Microwave on High 20 seconds. Stir to blend; continue to microwave on High in 5-second increments until mixture can be stirred smooth and is pourable.

3) Pour topping mixture into small resealable food-storage plastic bag; seal bag. Cut small hole in bottom corner of bag. Drizzle mixture over ice cream. Freeze until firm, at least 2 hours. Cut into wedges to serve. Reheat and serve any remaining topping with pie.

HIGH ALTITUDE (3500-6500 FT.): No change.

Easy-as-Peach-Pie Wedges

PREP TIME: 10 MINUTES (READY IN 1 HOUR)
SERVINGS: 8

 EASY

1 box (15 oz.) Pillsbury® refrigerated pie crusts, softened as directed on box

1 can (21 oz.) peach pie filling with more fruit

1/8 teaspoon ground nutmeg

2 teaspoons sugar

Nutrition Information Per Serving:	
Calories: 310	From Fat: 130
Total Fat	14g
Saturated	5g
Cholesterol	5mg
Sodium	220mg
Total Carbohydrate	45g
Dietary Fiber	1g
Sugars	18g
Protein	1g

1) Heat oven to 450°F. Spray large cookie sheet with cooking spray. Remove pie crusts from pouches; unroll crusts onto opposite ends of cookie sheet (edges of crusts will hang over sides of small cookie sheet).

2) Spoon half of pie filling onto one half of each crust to within 1 inch of edge. Sprinkle with nutmeg. Fold other halves of crusts over filling; press 1/2-inch edge with fork to seal. Cut several slits in top crust of each. Sprinkle with sugar.

3) Bake 10 minutes. Cover edges of crusts with strips of foil. Bake 5 to 8 minutes longer or until crusts are golden brown. Cool at least 30 minutes. Cut into wedges to serve.

HIGH ALTITUDE (3500-6500 FT.): No change.

White Chocolate-Strawberry Yogurt Parfaits

JANELLE SPERRY | BUNKER HILL, WEST VIRGINIA

PREP TIME: 15 MINUTES (READY IN 15 MINUTES)
SERVINGS: 2

PARFAITS

4 Nature Valley® pecan crunch crunchy granola bars (2 pouches from 8.9-oz. box), crushed (3/4 cup)*

1/2 cup chopped pecans

1 package (3 oz.) cream cheese, softened

1/2 cup whipped topping

1/2 cup marshmallow creme (from 7-oz. jar)

1 oz. white chocolate baking bar, shaved

1 container (6 oz.) Yoplait® Light Fat Free white chocolate strawberry yogurt

1 cup sliced fresh strawberries

GARNISHES

Additional strawberry slices

White chocolate curls

Fresh mint leaves

Nutrition Information Per Serving:

Calories:	860	From Fat:	440
Total Fat			49g
Saturated			17g
Cholesterol			50mg
Sodium			370mg
Total Carbohydrate			89g
Dietary Fiber			7g
Sugars			64g
Protein			15g

1) In small bowl, mix crushed granola bars and pecans; set aside. In large bowl, beat cream cheese with electric mixer on medium speed until smooth. Beat in whipped topping, marshmallow creme, shaved white chocolate and yogurt until well blended.

2) In each of 2 (14-oz.) parfait glasses, layer 1/4 cup granola mixture, about 1/2 cup yogurt mixture and 1/4 cup sliced strawberries. Repeat layers. Top each parfait with 1 tablespoon remaining granola mixture. Garnish each with additional strawberry slices, white chocolate curls and mint leaves. Serve immediately.

*NOTE: To easily crush granola bars, do not unwrap; use rolling pin to crush bars.

HIGH ALTITUDE (3500-6500 FT.): No change.

Double-Strawberry Baked Alaska

CAROLYN VEAZEY SHLENS | SEYMOUR, ILLINOIS

PREP TIME: 15 MINUTES (READY IN 2 HOURS 45 MINUTES)
SERVINGS: 2

2 Pillsbury® Ready to Bake!™ Big Deluxe Classics® refrigerated white chunk macadamia nut cookies (from 18-oz. package)

1 cup strawberry ice cream

1 cup Cascadian Farm® Organic frozen strawberries (from 10-oz. bag), partially thawed

2 tablespoons seedless strawberry jam

2 egg whites (3 to 4 tablespoons)

¼ cup granulated sugar

⅛ teaspoon vanilla

1 tablespoon Hershey®'s chocolate syrup

2 Hershey®'s Kisses® milk chocolates (do not unwrap)

1) Heat oven to 350°F. Place cookie dough rounds 2 inches apart on ungreased cookie sheet. Bake 14 to 18 minutes or until edges are golden brown. Cool 3 minutes; remove from cookie sheet. Cool completely, about 15 minutes.

2) Place ½ cup ice cream on top of each cookie; place 4 to 5 inches apart on same cookie sheet. Cover loosely; freeze until hardened, at least 1 hour 30 minutes or until serving time. Meanwhile, in small bowl, mix strawberries and jam; refrigerate.

3) To serve, heat oven to 450°F. In small bowl, beat egg whites with electric mixer on high speed until foamy. Gradually beat in sugar until stiff peaks form. Beat in vanilla. Spread egg white mixture over ice cream on each cookie, covering ice cream and cookie edge completely.

4) Bake 4 to 6 minutes or just until meringue is lightly browned. Immediately remove from cookie sheet; place on individual dessert plates. Place strawberries from sauce on side of each dessert; spoon sauce over tops. Drizzle chocolate topping over each; place wrapped candy drop on each plate. Serve immediately.

HIGH ALTITUDE (3500-6500 FT.): No change.

Nutrition Information Per Serving:		
Calories: 620	From Fat:	190
Total Fat		21g
Saturated		9g
Cholesterol		45mg
Sodium		240mg
Total Carbohydrate		98g
Dietary Fiber		3g
Sugars		75g
Protein		10g

Black Bottom Strawberry Cream Pie

PREP TIME: 20 MINUTES (READY IN 2 HOURS 40 MINUTES)
SERVINGS: 8

 EASY

1 Pillsbury® refrigerated pie crust
(from 15-oz. box), softened as
directed on box

²/₃ cup hot fudge topping

1 package (8 oz.) cream cheese,
softened

1 cup powdered sugar

1 pint (2 cups) fresh strawberries,
quartered

½ cup strawberry pie glaze

½ cup whipping cream, whipped,
if desired

1) Heat oven to 450°F. Make pie crust as directed on box for One-Crust Baked Shell using 9-inch glass pie pan. Bake 9 to 11 minutes or until lightly browned. Cool completely, about 15 minutes.

2) Spread hot fudge topping in bottom of cooled baked shell. Refrigerate 1 hour.

3) In small bowl, beat cream cheese and powdered sugar with electric mixer on medium speed until smooth. Carefully spread over fudge layer in shell.

4) In medium bowl, gently mix strawberries and pie glaze. Spoon evenly over cream cheese layer. Refrigerate until firm, about 1 hour.

5) Just before serving, pipe or spoon whipped cream around edge of pie. Store in refrigerator.

HIGH ALTITUDE (3500-6500 FT.): No change.

Nutrition Information Per Serving:

Calories:	440	From Fat:	170
Total Fat			19g
Saturated			10g
Cholesterol			35mg
Sodium			290mg
Total Carbohydrate			62g
Dietary Fiber			2g
Sugars			41g
Protein			4g

Spicy Pumpkin Bars

PREP TIME: 30 MINUTES (READY IN 2 HOURS 30 MINUTES)
SERVINGS: 48

BARS

2 cups all-purpose flour

1½ cups packed brown sugar

2 teaspoons baking powder

1 teaspoon baking soda

2 teaspoons pumpkin pie spice

¼ teaspoon salt

½ cup vegetable oil

½ cup apple juice

1 can (15 oz.) pumpkin
(not pumpkin pie mix)

2 eggs

FROSTING

1 container (16 oz.) cream cheese
creamy ready-to-spread frosting

Nutrition Information Per Serving:

Calories:	110	From Fat:	45
Total Fat			5g
Saturated			1g
Cholesterol			10mg
Sodium			85mg
Total Carbohydrate			17g
Dietary Fiber			0g
Sugars			12g
Protein			0g

1) Heat oven to 350°F. Grease 15x10x1-inch pan with shortening; lightly flour. In large bowl with electric mixer, beat bar ingredients on low speed until moistened. Beat 2 minutes on medium speed. Spread batter in pan.

2) Bake 20 to 30 minutes or until toothpick inserted in center comes out clean. Cool completely, about 1 hour.

3) Spread frosting over cooled bars. Refrigerate until set, about 30 minutes. Cut into 8 rows by 6 rows. Store in refrigerator.

HIGH ALTITUDE (3500-6500 FT.): Increase all-purpose flour to 1-1/3 cups; reduce baking powder to 1 teaspoon. Bake as directed above.

Strawberry and Nectarine Shortcakes

PREP TIME: 45 MINUTES (READY IN 1 HOUR 10 MINUTES)
SERVINGS: 12

4 cups sliced strawberries

3 nectarines, thinly sliced

1/4 cup sugar

4 cups all-purpose flour

1/4 cup sugar

2 tablespoons baking powder

1 teaspoon salt

1 cup margarine or butter

1 1/2 cups milk

1 container (8 oz.) frozen whipped topping, thawed

Nutrition Information Per Serving:

Calories:	430	From Fat:	180
Total Fat			20g
Saturated			7g
Cholesterol			0mg
Sodium			640mg
Total Carbohydrate			55g
Dietary Fiber			3g
Sugars			18g
Protein			7g

1) In large bowl, combine strawberries, nectarines and 1/4 cup sugar; set aside.

2) Meanwhile, heat oven to 425°F. Grease two 8-inch round cake pans. In large bowl, combine flour, 1/4 cup sugar, baking powder and salt; mix well. Using pastry blender or fork, cut in margarine until consistency of coarse meal. Add milk; stir just until dry ingredients are moistened. Spread dough in greased pans.

3) Bake at 425°F. for 20 to 25 minutes or until golden brown. Cool 5 minutes; remove from pans.

4) To serve, split warm or cool shortcakes; cut each round into six wedges. Spoon fruit mixture and whipped topping between layers and over top of each shortcake.

HIGH ALTITUDE (3500-6500 FT.): No change.

Peanut Butter and Jelly Bars

PREP TIME: 10 MINUTES (READY IN 1 HOUR)
SERVINGS: 24

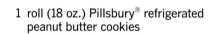 EASY

1 roll (18 oz.) Pillsbury® refrigerated peanut butter cookies

1/2 cup peanut butter chips

1/4 cup creamy peanut butter

1 container (16 oz.) creamy vanilla ready-to-spread frosting

1/4 cup strawberry jelly or seedless raspberry jam

Nutrition Information Per Serving:

Calories:	220	From Fat:	90
Total Fat			10g
Saturated			4.5g
Cholesterol			0mg
Sodium			115mg
Total Carbohydrate			31g
Dietary Fiber			0g
Sugars			24g
Protein			2g

1) Heat oven to 350°F. (325°F. for dark pan). Spray 13x9-inch pan with cooking spray. Break up cookie dough into pan; press evenly in pan. Press chips evenly into dough.

2) Bake 15 to 20 minutes or until golden brown. Cool completely, about 30 minutes.

3) In medium bowl, stir peanut butter until smooth. Stir in frosting until well blended. Spread over cooled bars.

4) In small bowl, stir jelly until smooth. Drop jelly by teaspoonfuls over frosting. With tip of knife, swirl jelly for a marbled design. Cut into 6 rows by 4 rows.

HIGH ALTITUDE (3500-6500 FT.): Stir 2 tablespoons flour into cookie dough before pressing into pan.

tip

To keep these bars moist and fresh, store them in the pan at room temperature, covered with foil.

Sugar Cookie-Chocolate Crunch Fudge

DICK BOULANGER | WILLISTON, VERMONT

PREP TIME: 15 MINUTES (READY IN 2 HOURS 15 MINUTES)
SERVINGS: 48 CANDIES

2 tablespoons light corn syrup

2 tablespoons butter or margarine

1/4 teaspoon salt

1 can (14 oz.) sweetened condensed milk (not evaporated)

1 roll (18 oz.) Pillsbury® refrigerated sugar cookies, cut into small chunks

2 bags (12 oz. each) Hershey®'s semi-sweet chocolate chips

5 teaspoons vanilla

6 Nature Valley® pecan crunch crunchy granola bars (3 pouches from 8.9-oz. box), coarsely crushed (heaping 1 cup)*

Fresh mint sprigs, if desired

1) In 3-quart heavy saucepan or deep 10-inch nonstick skillet, cook corn syrup, butter, salt and condensed milk over medium heat 2 to 3 minutes, stirring constantly with wooden spoon, until well blended. Reduce heat to medium-low; stir in cookie dough chunks. Cook 3 to 5 minutes, stirring constantly, until mixture is smooth and candy thermometer reads 160°F. Remove from heat.

2) Stir in chocolate chips and vanilla until chips are melted and mixture is smooth. Add crushed granola bars; stir until well blended. Cook over low heat 1 to 2 minutes, stirring constantly, until mixture is shiny. Spread in ungreased 12x8-inch or 13x9-inch pan.** Refrigerate uncovered at least 2 hours or until firm.

3) Cut into 8 rows by 6 rows. Serve in decorative candy cups or mini paper baking cups on platter; garnish platter with mint sprigs.

*NOTE: To easily crush granola bars, do not unwrap; use rolling pin to crush bars.

**NOTE: To easily cut fudge, line pan with foil so foil extends over sides of pan. Lift candy from pan using foil.

HIGH ALTITUDE (3500-6500 FT.): No change.

Nutrition Information Per Candy:		
Calories: 170	From Fat:	70
Total Fat		8g
Saturated		4g
Cholesterol		5mg
Sodium		65mg
Total Carbohydrate		22g
Dietary Fiber		1g
Sugars		17g
Protein		2g

Fudge-Strawberry Cream Torte

REBECCA KREMER | HUDSON, WISCONSIN

Pillsbury
Bake-Off

PREP TIME: 1 HOUR 15 MINUTES (READY IN 3 HOURS 35 MINUTES)
SERVINGS: 12

BROWNIE LAYERS

- 1 box (19.5 oz.) Pillsbury® Brownie Classics Traditional fudge brownie mix
- 1/2 cup vegetable oil
- 1/4 cup water
- 3 eggs

STRAWBERRY CREAM

- 3 tablespoons granulated sugar
- 1 package (8 oz.) cream cheese, softened
- 1 container (6 oz.) Yoplait® Thick & Creamy strawberry yogurt
- 1 1/2 cups finely chopped fresh strawberries

CHOCOLATE FUDGE

- 1/2 cup whipping cream
- 1 1/2 cups Hershey®'s semi-sweet chocolate chips (9 oz.)

GARNISH

- 1 teaspoon powdered sugar
- 6 small to medium fresh whole strawberries, halved

1) Heat oven to 350°F. Spray bottoms of 2 (9-inch) round cake pans with cooking spray.* Make brownie mix as directed on box for cake-like brownies using oil, water and eggs. Spread half of batter evenly in each pan. Bake 18 to 23 minutes. Cool on wire racks 10 minutes. Run knife around brownie layers to loosen. Place wire racks upside down over pans; turn racks and pans over. Remove pans. Cool completely, about 35 minutes.

2) Meanwhile, in small bowl, beat granulated sugar and cream cheese with electric mixer on medium speed until well blended. Beat in strawberry yogurt until smooth and creamy. Fold in chopped strawberries. Refrigerate while brownie layers cool.

3) In 1-quart saucepan, heat whipping cream over medium heat, stirring constantly, just until cream begins to boil. Remove from heat. Add chocolate chips; press into cream. Cover; let stand 3 minutes. Vigorously beat with wire whisk until smooth. Cool completely, about 30 minutes.

4) To assemble torte, place 1 brownie layer on serving plate. Spread half of strawberry cream evenly over brownie to within 1 inch of edge. Carefully spoon and spread half of chocolate fudge almost to edge of strawberry cream. Repeat layers, ending with chocolate fudge. Arrange halved strawberries in spoke fashion on top of torte. Refrigerate at least 1 hour before serving.

5) To serve,** sprinkle powdered sugar over top of torte and around plate. Carefully cut torte with hot knife into wedges to avoid "cracking" of chocolate fudge on top. Store loosely covered in refrigerator.

*NOTE: For easy pan removal, line bottoms of pans with waxed paper before spraying with cooking spray.

**NOTE: If stored for more than 3 hours, let torte stand at room temperature 10 minutes before cutting.

HIGH ALTITUDE (3500-6500 FT.): Stir 1/2 cup flour into dry brownie mix. Increase water to 1/3 cup. Bake 21 to 25 minutes.

Nutrition Information Per Serving:	
Calories: 550	From Fat: 280
Total Fat	31g
Saturated	13g
Cholesterol	85mg
Sodium	210mg
Total Carbohydrate	61g
Dietary Fiber	3g
Sugars	45g
Protein	7g

Mocha Bread Pudding with Caramel Topping

PREP TIME: 10 MINUTES (READY IN 1 HOUR 25 MINUTES)
SERVINGS: 16

 EASY

BREAD PUDDING

- 10 oz. day-old Italian or French bread, torn into pieces (about 8 cups)
- 1 cup chopped dates
- 1 cup chopped nuts
- 1/2 cup flaked coconut
- 1 teaspoon ground cinnamon
- 1/2 cup butter or margarine, melted
- 1/2 cup sugar
- 1/2 cup coffee-flavored liqueur or cold brewed coffee
- 3 eggs
- 2 cups half-and-half
- 1 cup milk

TOPPING

- 1 cup caramel ice cream topping, heated

1) Heat oven to 325°F. Spray 13x9-inch (3-quart) glass baking dish with cooking spray. In pan, gently mix bread pieces, dates, nuts, coconut and cinnamon.

2) In large bowl, mix butter, sugar and liqueur. Beat in eggs with spoon until well blended. Stir in half-and-half and milk. Pour over bread mixture in pan; toss to mix well. Let stand 10 to 15 minutes or until most of liquid has been absorbed.

3) Bake 1 hour or until set. Serve warm bread pudding with warm caramel topping. Store in refrigerator.

HIGH ALTITUDE (3500-6500 FT.): No change.

Nutrition Information Per Serving:	
Calories: 320	From Fat: 120
Total Fat	14g
Saturated	5g
Cholesterol	55mg
Sodium	240mg
Total Carbohydrate	44g
Dietary Fiber	2g
Sugars	30g
Protein	5g

Granola-Apple-Cherry Crisp

PREP TIME: 10 MINUTES (READY IN 55 MINUTES)
SERVINGS: 8 (1 CUP EACH)

 EASY

- 1 can (21 oz.) cinnamon and spice apple pie filling with more fruit
- 1 can (21 oz.) cherry pie filling with more fruit
- 12 Nature Valley® roasted almond crunchy granola bars (6 pouches from 8.9-oz. box), crushed (2 cups)
- 1/2 cup all-purpose flour
- 1/2 cup butter or margarine, melted
- 1/4 cup sliced almonds

Nutrition Information Per Serving:	
Calories: 460	From Fat: 170
Total Fat	18g
Saturated	7g
Cholesterol	30mg
Sodium	200mg
Total Carbohydrate	68g
Dietary Fiber	5g
Sugars	44g
Protein	6g

1) Heat oven to 350°F. In ungreased 11x7-inch (2-quart) glass baking dish, mix pie fillings.

2) In large bowl, mix crushed granola bars, flour and butter until crumbly. Stir in almonds. Sprinkle evenly over pie filling mixture.

3) Bake 25 to 30 minutes or until edges are bubbly and center is thoroughly heated. Cool slightly, about 15 minutes. Serve warm or cool.

HIGH ALTITUDE (3500-6500 FT.): Heat oven to 375°F. Bake 30 to 35 minutes.

Candy Bar Cheesecake

PREP TIME: 15 MINUTES (READY IN 6 HOURS 5 MINUTES)
SERVINGS: 12

🄔 EASY

CRUST

1¼ cups finely crushed shortbread cookies (about 25 cookies)

2 tablespoons butter or margarine, melted

FILLING

2 packages (8 oz. each) cream cheese, softened

½ cup sugar

¼ cup whipping cream

2 eggs

2 caramel and nougat-filled chocolate candy bars (2.05 oz. each), unwrapped, cut into ½-inch pieces

SAUCE AND GARNISH

1 caramel and nougat-filled chocolate candy bar (2.05 oz.), unwrapped, chopped

4 to 5 teaspoons milk

Whipped cream, if desired

1 caramel and nougat-filled chocolate candy bar (2.05 oz.), unwrapped, chopped, if desired

1) Heat oven to 325°F. Line 9- or 8-inch round cake pan with foil. In medium bowl, mix crushed cookies and butter; press firmly in bottom of pan. Bake 8 minutes.

2) Meanwhile, in large bowl with electric mixer, beat cream cheese on medium speed until smooth and creamy. Reserve 1 tablespoon of the sugar; place in small bowl. Gradually beat remaining sugar and the whipping cream into cream cheese. Add eggs 1 at a time, beating well after each addition. In reserved sugar, toss 2 chopped candy bars until coated.

3) Remove partially baked crust from oven. Sprinkle sugar-coated candy bar pieces over crust; press in lightly. Pour cream cheese mixture evenly over candy.

4) Return to oven; bake 40 to 50 minutes or until edges are set and center is almost set but jiggles slightly. Cool on wire rack 1 hour. Refrigerate at least 4 hours before serving.

5) Just before serving, in small microwavable bowl, microwave 1 chopped candy bar and enough milk on High 20 to 40 seconds, stirring every 20 seconds, until melted, smooth and drizzling consistency.

6) Use foil to lift cheesecake from pan. Remove foil; place cheesecake on serving plate. Cut into wedges; place on individual plates. Drizzle 1 teaspoon melted candy topping over each serving. Top with whipped cream and chopped candy. Store in refrigerator.

HIGH ALTITUDE (3500-6500 FT.): In Step 1, bake crust 10 minutes.

Nutrition Information Per Serving:		
Calories: 350	From Fat: 210	
Total Fat		24g
Saturated		13g
Cholesterol		95mg
Sodium		240mg
Total Carbohydrate		30g
Dietary Fiber		0g
Sugars		22g
Protein		6g

Fudgy-Peanut Butter Banana Parfaits

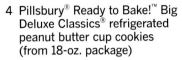

ROBIN WILSON | ALTAMONTE SPRINGS, FLORIDA

PREP TIME: 15 MINUTES (READY IN 1 HOUR 50 MINUTES)
SERVINGS: 2

4 Pillsbury® Ready to Bake!™ Big Deluxe Classics® refrigerated peanut butter cup cookies (from 18-oz. package)

¼ cup whipped cream cheese (from 8-oz. container)

3 tablespoons powdered sugar

2 tablespoons creamy peanut butter

1 container (6 oz.) Yoplait® Thick & Creamy banana yogurt

½ cup frozen (thawed) whipped topping

1 bar (2.1 oz.) chocolate-covered crispy peanut-buttery candy, unwrapped, finely crushed*

¼ cup Hershey®'s hot fudge topping

1) Heat oven to 350°F. Place cookie dough rounds 2 inches apart on ungreased cookie sheet. Bake 14 to 18 minutes or until edges are golden brown. Cool 3 minutes; remove from cookie sheet. Cool completely, about 15 minutes.

2) Meanwhile, in medium bowl, beat cream cheese, powdered sugar, peanut butter and yogurt with electric mixer on low speed until blended. Fold in whipped topping and crushed candy with rubber spatula.

3) In small microwavable bowl, microwave fudge topping on High 25 to 30 seconds or until melted and drizzling consistency. Crumble 1 cookie into each of 2 (12- to 14-oz.) parfait glasses.** Top each with about ⅓ cup yogurt mixture; drizzle each with 1 tablespoon fudge topping. Repeat layers. Refrigerate at least 1 hour but no longer than 4 hours before serving.

*NOTE: To easily crush candy bar, unwrap, break into pieces and place in mini food processor; process with on-and-off motions until crushed. Or place unwrapped candy bar in small resealable plastic bag; use rolling pin to crush bar.

**NOTE: Any 12- to 14-ounce tall parfait, dessert or wine glasses can be used.

HIGH ALTITUDE (3500-6500 FT.): No change.

Nutrition Information Per Serving:		
Calories: 1030	From Fat: 450	
Total Fat	50g	
Saturated	21g	
Cholesterol	40mg	
Sodium	740mg	
Total Carbohydrate	124g	
Dietary Fiber	4g	
Sugars	92g	
Protein	20g	

Fluffy Lemon-Raspberry Treat

KATHRYN FRIEDL | LAWTON, OKLAHOMA

PREP TIME: 20 MINUTES (READY IN 2 HOURS 25 MINUTES)
SERVINGS: 24

1 roll (18 oz.) Pillsbury® refrigerated sugar cookies

1 bag (12 oz.) Hershey®'s premier white chips (2 cups)

1 cup Cascadian Farm® Organic frozen raspberries (from 10-oz. bag), thawed

1 container (16 oz.) Pillsbury® Creamy Supreme® lemon frosting

1 package (8 oz.) cream cheese, softened

1 teaspoon lemon extract

1 container (8 oz.) frozen (thawed) whipped topping

1 teaspoon vegetable oil, if desired

1) Heat oven to 350°F. Grease 13x9-inch pan with shortening. Break up cookie dough into pan; press in bottom to form crust. Bake 13 to 18 minutes or until golden brown. Immediately sprinkle 1 cup of the white chips evenly over cookie crust. Let stand 5 minutes. Spread evenly with back of spoon. Cool completely, about 30 minutes.

2) Meanwhile, in small bowl, stir 1/2 cup of the raspberries with fork until broken up and slightly mashed. Refrigerate. In large bowl, beat frosting, cream cheese and lemon extract with electric mixer on medium-high speed about 2 minutes or until well blended. Fold in whipped topping. Refrigerate.

3) Spread mashed raspberries over cooled crust. Place in freezer for 15 minutes. Spread frosting mixture over raspberries. Refrigerate until set, about 1 hour.

4) To serve, in small bowl, mash remaining 1/2 cup raspberries with fork. Spread raspberries over frosting mixture. In small resealable freezer plastic bag, place remaining 1 cup white chips and the oil; seal bag. Microwave on High 1 minute. Squeeze bag to mix; microwave in 10-second increments, squeezing after each, until chips are melted and smooth. Cut small hole in one bottom corner of bag; squeeze bag to drizzle mixture over top of dessert. Cut into squares to serve. Store in refrigerator.

HIGH ALTITUDE (3500-6500 FT.): Break up cookie dough into bowl. Knead or stir 3 tablespoons flour into cookie dough before pressing into bottom of pan.

Nutrition Information Per Serving:		
Calories: 310	From Fat: 140	
Total Fat	16g	
Saturated	10g	
Cholesterol	20mg	
Sodium	115mg	
Total Carbohydrate	39g	
Dietary Fiber	1g	
Sugars	31g	
Protein	3g	

Two-Berry Crisp with Pecan Streusel Topping

PREP TIME: 15 MINUTES (READY IN 55 MINUTES)
SERVINGS: 6

 EASY

TOPPING

- ³/₄ cup quick-cooking oats
- ¹/₂ cup all-purpose flour
- ¹/₂ cup packed brown sugar
- ¹/₂ cup butter or margarine, cut into pieces
- ¹/₄ cup chopped pecans

FILLING

- 1 can (21 oz.) blueberry pie filling
- 2 cups fresh or frozen unsweetened raspberries
- 3 tablespoons granulated sugar
- 1 tablespoon all-purpose flour

1) Heat oven to 400°F. Spray 8-inch square (2-quart) glass baking dish with cooking spray. In large bowl, mix topping ingredients except butter and pecans.

2) Cut in butter with pastry blender (or by pulling 2 knives through ingredients in opposite directions) until crumbly. Stir in pecans.

3) In another large bowl, mix filling ingredients. Pour into baking dish. Sprinkle topping over filling.

4) Bake 30 to 40 minutes or until mixture is bubbly and topping is golden brown.

HIGH ALTITUDE (3500-6500 FT.): No change.

Nutrition Information Per Serving:	
Calories: 460	From Fat: 180
Total Fat	20g
Saturated	8g
Cholesterol	40mg
Sodium	110mg
Total Carbohydrate	74g
Dietary Fiber	9g
Sugars	52g
Protein	4g

Minty Ice Cream Squares

PREP TIME: 30 MINUTES (READY IN 3 HOURS 10 MINUTES)
SERVINGS: 16

- ¹/₂ cup butter or margarine
- ¹/₄ cup unsweetened baking cocoa
- 2 cups coarsely crushed chocolate or regular graham crackers (about 20 cracker squares)
- ¹/₂ cup powdered sugar
- 1 carton (¹/₂ gallon) green mint chocolate chip ice cream, slightly softened
- 1 cup semisweet chocolate chips
- ²/₃ cup whipping cream
- 16 thin rectangular creme de menthe chocolate candies, unwrapped

1) In 2-quart saucepan, heat butter and cocoa over medium heat, stirring frequently, until butter is melted and mixture is well blended. Remove from heat. Stir in graham cracker crumbs and powdered sugar. In bottom of ungreased 13x9-inch pan, press mixture to form crust.

2) Place heaping spoonfuls of ice cream on crust. With back of spoon, lightly press and smooth ice cream. Freeze 30 minutes.

3) Meanwhile, in 1-quart saucepan, heat chocolate chips and whipping cream over low heat 2 to 3 minutes, stirring constantly, until melted. Cool 15 minutes.

4) Drizzle chocolate mixture over ice cream. Arrange candies on top so each serving has 1 candy. Freeze until firm, about 2 hours. Let stand at room temperature 10 minutes before cutting into squares.

HIGH ALTITUDE (3500-6500 FT.): No change.

Nutrition Information Per Serving:	
Calories: 370	From Fat: 200
Total Fat	22g
Saturated	13g
Cholesterol	60mg
Sodium	150mg
Total Carbohydrate	38g
Dietary Fiber	2g
Sugars	28g
Protein	4g

Raspberry Cheesecake Bars

PREP TIME: 20 MINUTES (READY IN 1 HOUR 55 MINUTES)
SERVINGS: 25 BARS

 EASY

CRUST

- $\frac{1}{2}$ cup sugar
- $\frac{1}{2}$ cup butter, softened
- $1\frac{1}{4}$ cups all-purpose flour

FILLING

- 1 package (8 oz.) cream cheese, softened
- $\frac{1}{2}$ cup sugar
- $\frac{1}{2}$ teaspoon almond extract
- 1 egg

TOPPING

- 4 tablespoons seedless red raspberry jam

Nutrition Information Per Serving:

Calories:	130	From Fat:	60
Total Fat			7g
Saturated			4g
Cholesterol			30mg
Sodium			55mg
Total Carbohydrate			15g
Dietary Fiber			0g
Sugars			10g
Protein			2g

1) Heat oven to 350°F. Spray 9-inch square pan with cooking spray. In large bowl, mix $\frac{1}{2}$ cup sugar and the butter until well blended. Stir in flour until crumbly. Press mixture in bottom of pan.

2) Bake 15 to 18 minutes or until edges are light golden brown. Meanwhile, in large bowl with electric mixer, beat filling ingredients until well blended.

3) Remove partially baked crust from oven. Pour filling over crust. In small bowl, stir 2 tablespoons of the jam until softened. Spoon over cream cheese mixture. With tip of spoon, carefully swirl jam into top of filling (do not disturb crust).

4) Return to oven; bake 15 to 20 minutes longer or until filling is set. Cool 30 minutes.

5) Stir remaining 2 tablespoons jam until smooth; spread evenly over cooled bars. Refrigerate 30 minutes. Cut into 5 rows by 5 rows. Store in refrigerator.

HIGH ALTITUDE (3500-6500 FT.): In Step 2, bake 18 to 21 minutes.

Fudge Sundae Cake

PREP TIME: 30 MINUTES (READY IN 4 HOURS 30 MINUTES)
SERVINGS: 8

 EASY

- 1 package (10.75 oz.) frozen pound cake loaf, partially thawed
- $\frac{3}{4}$ cup thick fudge ice cream topping
- 1 quart (4 cups) cherry nut ice cream, slightly softened

Nutrition Information Per Serving:

Calories:	430	From Fat:	190
Total Fat			21g
Saturated			11g
Cholesterol			75mg
Sodium			190mg
Total Carbohydrate			53g
Dietary Fiber			2g
Sugars			36g
Protein			6g

1) Cut 20x18-inch sheet of heavy-duty foil. Cut frozen cake horizontally into 4 thin slices; place bottom layer lengthwise on foil.

2) Spread $\frac{1}{4}$ cup of the ice cream topping over bottom layer. Spoon $\frac{1}{3}$ of the ice cream over topping; smooth top. Repeat layers twice and top with remaining cake slice, pressing cake firmly.

3) Wrap tightly in foil; freeze until firm, about 4 hours. To serve, cut into slices.

HIGH ALTITUDE (3500-6500 FT.): No change.

Heavenly Chocolate-Raspberry Torte

PAT FREYMUTH | COLORADO SPRINGS, COLORADO

PREP TIME: 20 MINUTES (READY IN 1 HOUR 50 MINUTES)
SERVINGS: 12

1 bag (12 oz.) Hershey's® Special Dark® chips (2 cups)

1 container (6 oz.) Yoplait® Original 99% Fat Free raspberry yogurt

6 Nature Valley® roasted almond crunchy granola bars (3 pouches from 8.9-oz. box), finely crushed (heaping 1 cup)

1 cup egg whites (about 7)

2 tablespoons plus 1 teaspoon fat-free half-and-half

2 teaspoons raspberry-flavored syrup (for coffee drinks) or red raspberry syrup (for pancakes)

1/4 cup powdered sugar

Fresh raspberries, if desired

Fresh mint leaves, if desired

Nutrition Information Per Serving:

Calories:	240	From Fat:	90
Total Fat			10g
Saturated			5g
Cholesterol			0mg
Sodium			90mg
Total Carbohydrate			31g
Dietary Fiber			2g
Sugars			24g
Protein			5g

1) Heat oven to 350°F. Lightly spray bottom of 9-inch round cake pan with cooking spray; line bottom with parchment paper. Spray paper and side of pan with cooking spray.

2) Reserve 1/2 cup of the chocolate chips for glaze; place remaining chips in medium microwavable bowl (or place in top of double boiler). Stir in yogurt until chips are coated. Microwave on High in 1-minute increments, stirring after each, until chips are completely melted (or heat in double boiler over simmering water, stirring frequently, until melted). Stir in crushed granola bars and egg whites until well blended. Pour batter into pan.

3) Bake 20 to 30 minutes or until side of torte has risen and center is shiny but firm when touched (if center rises, torte has been overbaked). Cool in pan on wire rack, about 30 minutes (as torte cools, side will pull away from pan and torte will slightly sink). Refrigerate until chilled, about 1 hour.

4) In small microwavable bowl, microwave reserved 1/2 cup chocolate chips and the half-and-half on High in 30-second increments, stirring after each, until chips are melted. Cool slightly, about 2 minutes.

5) Place wire rack upside down over pan; turn rack and pan over. Remove pan and parchment paper. Pour chocolate mixture over torte; spread over top and side. Slide torte onto serving plate.

6) In small bowl, mix syrup and sugar. Place in small resealable food-storage plastic bag; seal bag and cut tiny hole in one bottom corner. Drizzle over top of torte in spiral pattern; gently run toothpick back and forth through spiral pattern to feather. Refrigerate until glaze is set and firm to the touch, about 20 minutes.

7) Before serving, garnish tray and/or individual dessert plates with raspberries and mint. Cut torte into wedges with warm, dry knife, cleaning knife between cuts. Store torte in refrigerator.

HIGH ALTITUDE (3500-6500 FT.): Bake 25 to 30 minutes.

Peanut Butter Custard Bars

NORITA SOLT | BETTENDORF, IOWA

Pillsbury
Bake-Off®

PREP TIME: 20 MINUTES (READY IN 2 HOURS 40 MINUTES)
SERVINGS: 36 BARS

1 roll (18 oz.) Pillsbury® refrigerated peanut butter cookies

1 bag (10 oz.) peanut butter chips

3 eggs

1/2 cup packed light brown sugar

3 tablespoons peanut butter

2 containers (6 oz. each) Yoplait® Thick & Creamy crème caramel yogurt

4 Nature Valley® peanut butter crunchy granola bars (2 pouches from 8.9-oz. box), crushed (3/4 cup)*

1) Heat oven to 350°F. Grease 13x9-inch pan with shortening or cooking spray. With fingers, press cookie dough evenly in bottom of pan. Sprinkle with peanut butter chips; press lightly into dough. Set aside.

2) In medium bowl, beat eggs, brown sugar, peanut butter and yogurt with wire whisk until thoroughly blended. Pour mixture over dough. Sprinkle crushed granola bars evenly over top of egg mixture.

3) Bake 40 to 50 minutes or until bars pull away from edges of pan and are set in center. Cool completely in pan, about 1 hour 30 minutes. Cut into 6 rows by 6 rows. Store in refrigerator.

*NOTE: To easily crush granola bars, do not unwrap; use rolling pin to crush bars.

HIGH ALTITUDE (3500-6500 FT.): Break up cookie dough into bowl; knead or stir 3 tablespoons flour into dough. Press dough in pan.

Nutrition Information Per Bar:		
Calories: 150	From Fat:	60
Total Fat		7g
Saturated		1.5g
Cholesterol		20mg
Sodium		120mg
Total Carbohydrate		19g
Dietary Fiber		0g
Sugars		13g
Protein		4g

Maple-Walnut-Pumpkin Pie

PREP TIME: 20 MINUTES (READY IN 3 HOURS)
SERVINGS: 8

 EASY

CRUST

1 Pillsbury® refrigerated pie crust (from 15-oz. box), softened as directed on box

FILLING

1 can (15 oz.) pumpkin (not pumpkin pie mix)

1 can (14 oz.) sweetened condensed milk (not evaporated)

2 eggs

2 tablespoons real maple syrup or maple-flavored syrup

$1^1/2$ teaspoons pumpkin pie spice

STREUSEL

$1/4$ cup packed brown sugar

$1/4$ cup finely chopped walnuts

2 tablespoons all-purpose flour

2 tablespoons cold butter or margarine

TOPPING

1 cup whipping (heavy) cream

2 tablespoons packed brown sugar

Chopped walnuts, if desired

1) Heat oven to 425°F. Place pie crust in 9-inch glass pie pan as directed on box for One-Crust Filled Pie. In large bowl with electric mixer, beat filling ingredients until smooth. Pour into crust-lined pan. Bake 10 minutes.

2) Meanwhile, in small bowl, mix $1/4$ cup brown sugar, the chopped walnuts and flour; cut in butter until crumbly. Set aside.

3) Remove pie from oven; reduce oven temperature to 350°F. Sprinkle streusel over pie. Cover crust edge with 3-inch-wide strips of foil to prevent excessive browning.

4) Return to oven; bake 30 to 35 minutes longer or until knife inserted 1 inch from edge comes out clean. Cool completely, about 2 hours. Serve or refrigerate until serving time.

5) To serve, in medium bowl with electric mixer, beat whipping cream and 2 tablespoons brown sugar on medium-high speed until soft peaks form. Serve pie with whipped cream; garnish with chopped walnuts. Store in refrigerator.

HIGH ALTITUDE (3500-6500 FT.): In Step 4, bake 40 to 45 minutes.

Nutrition Information Per Serving:		
Calories: 520	From Fat: 250	
Total Fat		27g
Saturated		13g
Cholesterol		115mg
Sodium		230mg
Total Carbohydrate		61g
Dietary Fiber		2g
Sugars		44g
Protein		8g

For this recipe, purchase plain pumpkin, not pumpkin pie mix which includes seasonings.

Chocolate Silk Raspberry Tart

PREP TIME: 35 MINUTES (READY IN 5 HOURS)
SERVINGS: 12

20 creme-filled golden sandwich cookies, crushed (2 cups)

$1/4$ cup butter or margarine, melted

$1^1/2$ cups semisweet chocolate chips

2 cups whipping (heavy) cream

1 teaspoon vanilla

1 package (8 oz.) cream cheese, softened

1 cup fresh raspberries

2 tablespoons seedless raspberry jam

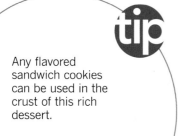

Any flavored sandwich cookies can be used in the crust of this rich dessert.

1) Heat oven to 375°F. In medium bowl, mix cookie crumbs and butter. In 9- or 10-inch springform pan, press mixture in bottom and 1 inch up side. Bake 7 to 9 minutes or until set. Cool completely, about 30 minutes.

2) Meanwhile, in 1-quart saucepan, heat chocolate chips and $1/2$ cup of the whipping cream over low heat, stirring frequently, until chocolate is melted. Stir in vanilla. Cool to room temperature, about 15 minutes.

3) In large bowl with electric mixer, beat cream cheese on medium speed until smooth. Beat in chocolate mixture until creamy. Set aside.

4) In another large bowl with electric mixer, beat remaining $1^1/2$ cups whipping cream on high speed until stiff peaks form. Fold half of whipped cream into cream cheese mixture until blended. Fold in remaining whipped cream. Spoon into cooled baked crust. Refrigerate until set, about 4 hours.

5) To serve, arrange raspberries around edge of tart. In small microwavable bowl, microwave jam on High 1 to 2 minutes, stirring every 30 seconds, until melted; lightly brush over raspberries. Remove side of pan. Cut tart into wedges. Store in refrigerator.

HIGH ALTITUDE (3500-6500 FT.): No change.

Nutrition Information Per Serving:	
Calories: 430	From Fat: 300
Total Fat	33g
Saturated	18g
Cholesterol	75mg
Sodium	160mg
Total Carbohydrate	29g
Dietary Fiber	2g
Sugars	19g
Protein	4g

Mock Lemon Meringue Bars

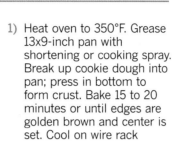

ROBIN JANINE PETERSON | PEORIA, ARIZONA

PREP TIME: 15 MINUTES (READY IN 2 HOURS 5 MINUTES)
SERVINGS: 24 BARS

1 roll (18 oz.) Pillsbury® refrigerated sugar cookies

1 cup lemon curd (from 11¼- to 12-oz. jar)

1 package (3 oz.) cream cheese (⅓ cup), softened

½ cup marshmallow creme

1 container (6 oz.) Yoplait® Original 99% Fat Free French vanilla yogurt

1 cup frozen (thawed) whipped topping

1) Heat oven to 350°F. Grease 13x9-inch pan with shortening or cooking spray. Break up cookie dough into pan; press in bottom to form crust. Bake 15 to 20 minutes or until edges are golden brown and center is set. Cool on wire rack 30 minutes.

2) Spread lemon curd over cooled baked crust. In large bowl, beat with wooden spoon, cream cheese, marshmallow creme and yogurt until well blended. Fold in whipped topping. Spread over lemon curd, swirling to resemble meringue topping. Refrigerate at least 1 hour or until serving time. Cut into 6 rows by 4 rows. Store in refrigerator.

HIGH ALTITUDE (3500-6500 FT.): Before pressing cookie dough in pan, knead or stir 3 tablespoons flour into dough.

Nutrition Information Per Bar:

Calories:	170	From Fat:	60
Total Fat			7g
Saturated			2.5g
Cholesterol			20mg
Sodium			85mg
Total Carbohydrate			26g
Dietary Fiber			0g
Sugars			18g
Protein			1g

Raspberry Cream Tarts

PREP TIME: 15 MINUTES (READY IN 15 MINUTES)
SERVINGS: 4

🄴 EASY

1 box (4-serving size) vanilla instant pudding and pie filling mix

¾ cup cold milk

1½ cups frozen (thawed) whipped topping

4 graham cracker tart shells (from 4-oz. package)

1 cup fresh raspberries

Nutrition Information Per Serving:

Calories:	320	From Fat:	110
Total Fat			12g
Saturated			6g
Cholesterol			0mg
Sodium			540mg
Total Carbohydrate			51g
Dietary Fiber			3g
Sugars			34g
Protein			3g

1) In medium bowl, beat pudding mix and milk with wire whisk until well blended. Stir in 1 cup of the whipped topping. Spoon mixture evenly into tart shells.

2) Spoon 2 tablespoons remaining whipped topping in center of each tart. Top with raspberries. Serve immediately, or refrigerate until serving time.

HIGH ALTITUDE (3500-6500 FT.): No change.

Choco-Peanut Butter Cups

RONNA FARLEY | ROCKVILLE, MARYLAND

Bake-Off

PREP TIME: 40 MINUTES (READY IN 1 HOUR 40 MINUTES)
SERVINGS: 24 COOKIE CUPS

1 roll (18 oz.) Pillsbury® refrigerated peanut butter cookies

1 cup Hershey®'s premier white chips (6 oz.)

1 1/2 cups creamy peanut butter

1 cup Hershey®'s semi-sweet chocolate chips (6 oz.)

4 Nature Valley® oats 'n honey crunchy granola bars (2 pouches from 8.9-oz. box), crushed (3/4 cup)*

Nutrition Information Per Cookie Cup:

Calories:	280	From Fat:	150
Total Fat			17g
Saturated			5g
Cholesterol			0mg
Sodium			210mg
Total Carbohydrate			27g
Dietary Fiber			2g
Sugars			17g
Protein			7g

1) Heat oven to 350°F. Grease 24 mini muffin cups with cooking spray or shortening. Cut cookie dough into 24 slices. Press 1 slice in bottom and up side of each mini muffin cup, forming 1/4-inch rim above top of cup (dust fingers with flour if necessary). Bake 10 to 15 minutes or until edges are deep golden brown. Cool in pans on wire racks 5 minutes. With tip of handle of wooden spoon, press dough down in center of each cup to make room for 2 tablespoons filling.

2) Meanwhile, in 2-quart saucepan, melt white chips and 3/4 cup of the peanut butter over low heat, stirring constantly. Spoon about 1 tablespoon mixture into each dough-lined cup. Refrigerate 10 minutes.

3) In another 2-quart saucepan, melt chocolate chips and remaining 3/4 cup peanut butter over low heat, stirring constantly. Spoon about 1 tablespoon chocolate mixture on top of peanut butter mixture in each cup. Sprinkle crushed granola bars over top of each. Refrigerate until set, about 1 hour. Remove from muffin cups before serving.

*NOTE: To easily crush granola bars, do not unwrap; use rolling pin to crush bars.

HIGH ALTITUDE (3500-6500 FT.): Break up cookie dough into bowl; knead or stir 1/4 cup flour into dough. Divide dough into 24 pieces; press 1 piece in each cup.

Brickle Bars

PREP TIME: 10 MINUTES (READY IN 1 HOUR 20 MINUTES)
SERVINGS: 36

 EASY

BARS

- 1/2 cup granulated sugar
- 1/2 cup packed brown sugar
- 1/2 cup butter or margarine, softened
- 2 teaspoons vanilla
- 2 eggs
- 1 1/2 cups all-purpose flour
- 2 teaspoons baking powder
- 1/4 teaspoon salt
- 1/2 cup toffee bits

TOPPING

- 3/4 cup semisweet chocolate chips
- 1/3 cup toffee bits

1) Heat oven to 350°F. Grease 13x9-inch pan with shortening. In large bowl with electric mixer, beat granulated sugar, brown sugar and butter on medium speed until well blended. Beat in vanilla and eggs until light and fluffy. On low speed, beat in flour, baking powder and salt until dough forms. With spoon, stir in 1/2 cup toffee bits. Spread in pan.

2) Bake 20 to 25 minutes or until golden brown and toothpick inserted in center comes out clean.

3) Remove pan from oven. Immediately sprinkle with chocolate chips; let stand 1 minute. Spread melted chips over bars. Sprinkle 1/3 cup toffee bits evenly over top. Cool completely, about 45 minutes. Cut into bars.

HIGH ALTITUDE (3500-6500 FT.): Decrease granulated sugar and brown sugar to 1/3 cup each. Bake as directed above.

Nutrition Information Per Serving:		
Calories: 110	From Fat:	45
Total Fat		5g
Saturated		3g
Cholesterol		20mg
Sodium		70mg
Total Carbohydrate		15g
Dietary Fiber		0g
Sugars		10g
Protein		1g

Raspberry-Cookie Parfaits

PREP TIME: 25 MINUTES (READY IN 55 MINUTES)
SERVINGS: 10

 EASY

1 roll (18 oz.) Pillsbury® refrigerated double chocolate chip & chunk cookies

1 box (4-serving size) chocolate instant pudding and pie filling mix

2 cups milk

1 container (8 oz.) frozen whipped topping, thawed

1 can (21 oz.) raspberry or cherry pie filling

Nutrition Information Per Serving:	
Calories: 350	From Fat: 130
Total Fat	14g
Saturated	7g
Cholesterol	10mg
Sodium	280mg
Total Carbohydrate	52g
Dietary Fiber	2g
Sugars	38g
Protein	4g

1) Bake cookies as directed on label. Cool completely, about 15 minutes.

2) Meanwhile, make pudding as directed on box using milk; do not refrigerate.

3) Crumble enough cookies to make 2$\frac{1}{2}$ cups; reserve remaining cookies for another use.

4) To assemble parfaits, in bottom of each of 10 (8-oz.) parfait glasses or clear plastic drinking cups, layer about 1 tablespoon raspberry pie filling, 3 tablespoons cookie crumbs, 3 tablespoons pudding, about $\frac{1}{4}$ cup whipped topping, 2 tablespoons pie filling and 1 tablespoon cookie crumbs. Top each with dollop of remaining whipped topping.

HIGH ALTITUDE (3500-6500 FT.): No change.

Double-Layer Mint Fudge

PREP TIME: 30 MINUTES (READY IN 1 HOUR 30 MINUTES)
SERVINGS: 117 SQUARES

FUDGE LAYER

1 bag (12 oz.) semisweet chocolate chips (2 cups)

1 can (16 oz.) creamy chocolate ready-to-spread frosting

PEPPERMINT LAYER

1 bag (12 oz.) white vanilla baking chips (2 cups)

1 can (16 oz.) creamy vanilla ready-to-spread frosting

2 drops red food color

$\frac{1}{2}$ cup finely crushed peppermint candy

2 milk chocolate candy bars (1.55 oz. each), chopped

1) Line 13x9-inch pan with foil so foil extends over sides of pan; lightly butter foil. In 3-quart saucepan, melt chocolate chips over low heat, stirring constantly, until smooth. Remove from heat. Stir in chocolate frosting. Spread in pan. Refrigerate 20 minutes.

2) Meanwhile, in 3-quart saucepan, melt vanilla baking chips over low heat, stirring constantly, until smooth. Remove from heat. Stir in vanilla frosting and food color until well blended. Fold in crushed peppermint candy.

3) Spread carefully over chilled chocolate layer. Sprinkle chopped candy bars over top; press in lightly. Refrigerate just until set, about 1 hour.

4) As soon as fudge is set, use foil to lift fudge from pan; remove foil. Cut into 13 rows by 9 rows. Store at room temperature.

HIGH ALTITUDE (3500-6500 FT.): No change.

Nutrition Information Per Serving:	
Calories: 70	From Fat: 30
Total Fat	3.5g
Saturated	2.5g
Cholesterol	0mg
Sodium	0mg
Total Carbohydrate	10g
Dietary Fiber	0g
Sugars	9g
Protein	0g

Black Forest Cheesecake Dessert Cups

KYLE O'MALLEY | BRIGANTINE BEACH, NEW JERSEY

PREP TIME: 55 MINUTES (READY IN 2 HOURS 50 MINUTES)
SERVINGS: 24 DESSERT CUPS

EASY

- 1 box (19.5 oz.) Pillsbury® Brownie Classics Traditional fudge brownie mix
- ½ cup vegetable oil
- ¼ cup water
- 4 eggs
- 1 cup Hershey®'s semi-sweet chocolate chips (6 oz.)
- 2 packages (8 oz. each) cream cheese, softened
- ½ cup granulated sugar
- 1 container (6 oz.) Yoplait® Thick & Creamy vanilla yogurt
- 1 can (21 oz.) cherry pie filling
- 1 aerosol can whipped cream topping
- 1 large sprig fresh mint, if desired

1) Heat oven to 350°F. Place paper baking cup in each of 24 large muffin cups (2 ³/₄ inches in diameter and 1¹/₄ inches deep). Make brownie mix as directed on box using oil, water and 2 of the eggs. Divide batter evenly among muffin cups (about 2 tablespoons per cup). Bake 15 minutes.

2) Meanwhile, in small microwavable bowl, microwave chocolate chips on High 1 minute. Stir and microwave in 15-second increments, stirring after each, until chips are melted and smooth; set aside. In large bowl, beat cream cheese with electric mixer on medium speed until smooth. Beat in sugar, remaining 2 eggs and the yogurt until blended. Add melted chocolate; beat until well blended.

3) Divide chocolate mixture evenly over warm brownie layer in cups (about 3 tablespoons per cup), filling each to top of cup. Cups will be full.

4) Bake 22 to 26 minutes longer or until set. Cool in pans 20 to 30 minutes. Carefully remove dessert cups from pan (cream cheese mixture will be soft); place on serving platter. Refrigerate at least 1 hour before serving.

5) To serve, remove paper; top each dessert cup with 1 tablespoon pie filling (including 2 or 3 cherries) and 1 tablespoon whipped cream topping. If desired, arrange cupcakes on pedestal cake plate covered with linen napkin. Garnish platter or plate with mint sprig. Store in refrigerator.

HIGH ALTITUDE (3500-6500 FT.): Stir 1/2 cup flour into dry brownie mix. Increase water to 1/3 cup. Makes 30 dessert cups.

Nutrition Information Per Dessert Cup:		
Calories: 330	From Fat:	160
Total Fat		18g
Saturated		8g
Cholesterol		65mg
Sodium		150mg
Total Carbohydrate		36g
Dietary Fiber		2g
Sugars		29g
Protein		4g

Peanut Butter Truffle Tart

LAURA STENSBERG | MARSHFIELD, WISCONSIN

PREP TIME: 25 MINUTES (READY IN 3 HOURS 25 MINUTES)
SERVINGS: 16

1 roll (18 oz.) Pillsbury® refrigerated peanut butter cookies

6 Nature Valley® peanut butter crunchy granola bars (3 pouches from 8.9-oz. box), crushed (1 heaping cup)*

2 bags (12 oz. each) Hershey®'s semi-sweet chocolate chips (4 cups)

1 cup whipping cream

1/2 cup crunchy peanut butter

1/3 cup chopped peanuts or 1 package (2 oz.) nut topping

Nutrition Information Per Serving:

Calories:	520	From Fat:	270
Total Fat			30g
Saturated			13g
Cholesterol			20mg
Sodium			240mg
Total Carbohydrate			54g
Dietary Fiber			4g
Sugars			36g
Protein			8g

1) Heat oven to 350°F. In large bowl, break up cookie dough. Stir or knead in crushed granola bars until well mixed. Press dough in bottom and up side of ungreased 10-inch tart pan with removable bottom or 13x9-inch pan. Bake 12 to 17 minutes or until light golden brown.

2) With back of spoon, press down crust on bottom and side; bake 3 to 5 minutes longer or until deep golden brown. Press down crust again with spoon. Cool 3 minutes.

3) Meanwhile, in large microwavable bowl, microwave chocolate chips and whipping cream on High 1 minute. Stir; microwave 1 to 2 minutes longer, stirring every 30 seconds to prevent chocolate from burning, until completely melted and smooth. In small microwavable bowl, microwave peanut butter on High 1 minute or until melted; stir.

4) Spread warm peanut butter in bottom of crust. Pour chocolate mixture over peanut butter mixture. Sprinkle peanuts evenly over top. Refrigerate at least 2 hours or until serving time. For easier cutting, let tart stand at room temperature 15 minutes before serving. Store in refrigerator.

*NOTE: To easily crush granola bars, do not unwrap; use rolling pin to crush bars.

HIGH ALTITUDE (3500-6500 FT.): No change.

Brownie Trifle

PREP TIME: 10 MINUTES (READY IN 1 HOUR 40 MINUTES)
SERVINGS: 6 (3/4 CUP EACH)

 EASY

1 pouch (10.25 oz.) fudge brownie mix

1/4 cup vegetable oil

2 tablespoons water

1/2 teaspoon almond extract

1 egg

2 cups frozen (thawed) whipped topping

1 1/2 cups fresh raspberries (6 oz.)

1/4 cup sliced almonds

Nutrition Information Per Serving:		
Calories: 390	From Fat:	170
Total Fat		19g
Saturated		6g
Cholesterol		35mg
Sodium		180mg
Total Carbohydrate		51g
Dietary Fiber		4g
Sugars		34g
Protein		4g

1) Heat oven to 325°F. Spray bottom only of 8-inch square pan with cooking spray or grease with shortening. In large bowl, stir brownie mix, oil, water, almond extract and egg with spoon about 50 times (batter may be lumpy). Spread in pan.

2) Bake 26 to 28 minutes or until toothpick inserted in center comes out almost clean. Cool completely, about 1 hour.

3) Break cooled brownies into bite-size pieces, placing half of pieces in 2-quart straight-sided serving bowl. Top with half of the whipped topping and half of the raspberries; repeat layers. Sprinkle almonds over top.

HIGH ALTITUDE (3500-6500 FT.): Follow High Altitude directions on brownie mix pouch.

Banana Cake with Browned Butter Frosting

PREP TIME: 30 MINUTES (READY IN 2 HOURS 5 MINUTES)
SERVINGS: 18

CAKE

1 package (18.25 oz.) yellow cake mix with pudding in the mix

1 large ripe banana, mashed (1/2 cup)

1 cup water

3 eggs

FROSTING

1/2 cup butter (do not use margarine)

4 cups powdered sugar

2 teaspoons vanilla

3 to 5 tablespoons milk

Nutrition Information Per Serving:		
Calories: 300	From Fat:	80
Total Fat		9g
Saturated		3.5g
Cholesterol		50mg
Sodium		240mg
Total Carbohydrate		52g
Dietary Fiber		0g
Sugars		44g
Protein		2g

1) Heat oven to 350°F. (325°F. for dark pan). Grease bottom only of 13x9-inch pan with shortening. Make cake mix as directed on box adding mashed banana with water and eggs. Pour batter into pan.

2) Bake 30 to 35 minutes or until toothpick inserted in center comes out clean. Cool completely, about 1 hour.

3) In 3-quart saucepan, melt butter over medium heat. Cook 4 to 6 minutes, stirring constantly and watching closely, until butter just begins to turn golden (butter will get foamy and bubble). Remove from heat. Cool 15 minutes.

4) With electric mixer on low speed, beat in powdered sugar, vanilla and enough milk until frosting is smooth and desired spreading consistency. Frost cooled cake.

HIGH ALTITUDE (3500-6500 FT.): Heat oven to 375°F. (350°F. for dark pan).

Pear-Cranberry Crisp

PREP TIME: 25 MINUTES (READY IN 1 HOUR 35 MINUTES)
SERVINGS: 12

 EASY

5 cups sliced peeled pears (5 medium)

1 1/2 cups fresh or frozen cranberries

1 cup sugar

2 tablespoons all-purpose flour

2 teaspoons grated orange peel

1 cup oats

1/2 cup packed brown sugar

1/3 cup all-purpose flour

1/4 cup butter or margarine

1/2 cup chopped nuts

Whipped cream, if desired

Nutrition Information Per Serving:	
Calories: 270	From Fat: 70
Total Fat	8g
Saturated	3g
Cholesterol	10mg
Sodium	30mg
Total Carbohydrate	47g
Dietary Fiber	4g
Sugars	33g
Protein	3g

1) Heat oven to 375°F. Spray 12x8-inch (2-quart) glass baking dish with cooking spray. In large bowl, toss pears, cranberries, sugar, 2 tablespoons flour and orange peel to coat. Spoon into baking dish.

2) In small bowl, mix oats, brown sugar and 1/3 cup flour. With fork or pastry blender, cut in butter until mixture is crumbly. Stir in nuts. Sprinkle evenly over fruit mixture.

3) Bake 30 to 40 minutes or until topping is golden brown and fruit is tender. Cool 30 minutes before serving. Serve warm with whipped cream.

HIGH ALTITUDE (3500-6500 FT.): No change.

Ice Cream-Strawberry Hearts

PREP TIME: 15 MINUTES (READY IN 50 MINUTES)
SERVINGS: 4

EASY

1 pint (2 cups) fresh strawberries, quartered

1/4 cup granulated sugar

1 Pillsbury® refrigerated pie crust (from 15-oz. box), softened as directed on box

1 tablespoon powdered sugar

1 cup vanilla ice cream

Nutrition Information Per Serving:	
Calories: 390	From Fat: 160
Total Fat	18g
Saturated	7g
Cholesterol	25mg
Sodium	250mg
Total Carbohydrate	54g
Dietary Fiber	2g
Sugars	27g
Protein	3g

1) Heat oven to 450°F. In medium bowl, gently mix strawberries and granulated sugar. Let stand at room temperature 30 minutes to sweeten strawberries.

2) Remove pie crust from pouch; unroll onto cutting board. With 4 1/2-inch and 3-inch heart-shaped cookie cutters, cut out 4 large heart shapes and 4 small heart shapes from crust. Place all hearts on ungreased cookie sheet.

3) Bake 5 to 7 minutes or until lightly browned.

4) For each serving, place 1 large heart crust on dessert plate; sprinkle powdered sugar over heart and plate. Place 1/4 cup ice cream on heart crust. Place small heart crust over ice cream; sprinkle powdered sugar over small heart. Serve with about 1/2 cup strawberries.

*NOTE: If heart-shaped cookie cutters are unavailable, cut out patterns for hearts from waxed paper; place the patterns on the pie crust and cut around them with a sharp knife.

HIGH ALTITUDE (3500-6500 FT.): No change.

Italian Cream Pie with Strawberry Sauce

JEAN GOTTFRIED | UPPER SANDUSKY, OHIO

PREP TIME: 50 MINUTES (READY IN 3 HOURS 50 MINUTES)
SERVINGS: 12

CRUST

1 Pillsbury® refrigerated pie crust (from 15-oz. box), softened as directed on box

FILLING

1 cup skim (fat-free) milk

1 package unflavored gelatin

1/4 cup SPLENDA® Sugar Blend for Baking

1 1/2 cups part-skim ricotta cheese (12 oz.)

1/2 teaspoon vanilla

1 cup frozen (thawed) fat-free whipped topping

2 containers (6 oz. each) Yoplait® Light Fat Free very vanilla yogurt

STRAWBERRY SAUCE

1/4 cup SPLENDA® Sugar Blend for Baking

1 tablespoon cornstarch

1 bag (10 oz.) Cascadian Farm® Organic frozen whole strawberries, thawed

1 tablespoon lemon juice

1) Heat oven to 450°F. Unroll pie crust; place in 8- or 9-inch springform pan, pressing crust up side of pan to top edge. (Do not overwork or let crust get too warm.) Prick bottom and side of crust with fork. Bake 9 to 11 minutes or until lightly browned. Cool completely, about 30 minutes.

2) Meanwhile, in 1-quart saucepan, place 1/2 cup of the milk. Sprinkle gelatin over milk; let stand 5 minutes to soften. Stir in remaining 1/2 cup milk and 1/4 cup SPLENDA. Cook on low heat, stirring frequently, until gelatin is completely dissolved (do not boil). Pour milk mixture into blender. Add ricotta cheese and vanilla; cover and blend until pureed. Pour into large bowl; stir in whipped topping and yogurt.

3) Remove side of pan; remove crust from pan and place crust on serving plate. To create collar for crust, wrap piece of string around outside of crust to measure; cut sheet of waxed paper length of string plus 3 inches. Fold waxed paper in half lengthwise; fold in half again. Wrap around outside of crust; staple collar together to secure around crust. Pour filling into cooled baked crust. Refrigerate until set, about 2 to 3 hours.

4) In 1 1/2-quart saucepan, mix 1/4 cup SPLENDA and the cornstarch. Stir in thawed strawberries. Cook over medium heat, stirring constantly, until slightly thickened. Remove from heat. Stir in lemon juice. Refrigerate until serving time.

5) To serve, remove waxed paper collar. Cut into wedges; place on individual dessert plates. Top servings with strawberry sauce. Store dessert and sauce in refrigerator.

HIGH ALTITUDE (3500-6500 FT.): No change.

Nutrition Information Per Serving:		
Calories: 210	From Fat:	70
Total Fat	7g	
Saturated	3.5g	
Cholesterol	15mg	
Sodium	140mg	
Total Carbohydrate	29g	
Dietary Fiber	0g	
Sugars	17g	
Protein	6g	

Coconut-Pecan-Fudge Bars

JENNA REYNOLDS | SILVERDALE, WASHINGTON

PREP TIME:	20 MINUTES (READY IN 3 HOURS)
SERVINGS:	16 BARS

BASE

- 1/2 cup Pillsbury® Fudge Supreme double chocolate premium brownie mix (from 15.8-oz. box), reserving remaining mix for filling
- 6 Nature Valley® pecan crunch crunchy granola bars (3 pouches from 8.9-oz. box), crushed (heaping 1 cup)*
- 1/4 cup packed brown sugar
- 1/4 cup chopped pecans or pecan pieces
- 1/4 cup butter or margarine, melted

FILLING

- Remaining dry brownie mix
- Chocolate Syrup (from mix)
- 1/4 cup vegetable oil
- 1/4 cup water
- 1 egg or 1/4 cup fat-free egg product or 1 egg white

TOPPING

- 1/4 cup packed brown sugar
- 1/4 cup chopped pecans or pecan pieces
- 1/4 cup butter or margarine, melted
- 3/4 cup Mounds® coconut flakes
- 1/4 teaspoon vanilla

GARNISH, IF DESIRED

- Whipped cream or ice cream
- Additional crushed Nature Valley® pecan crunch crunchy granola bars

Nutrition Information Per Bar:

Calories:	320	From Fat:	160
Total Fat			18g
Saturated			7g
Cholesterol			30mg
Sodium			160mg
Total Carbohydrate			37g
Dietary Fiber			2g
Sugars			27g
Protein			3g

1) Heat oven to 350°F. (325°F. for dark pan). Grease bottom only of 9- or 8-inch square pan with shortening or cooking spray. Set Chocolate Syrup aside. In medium bowl, mix all base ingredients. Spread mixture in pan, pressing down evenly with back of spoon or fork.

2) In large bowl, beat all filling ingredients 50 strokes with spoon. Spoon and spread batter evenly over base. In small bowl, mix all topping ingredients; sprinkle over filling.

3) Bake 35 to 40 minutes for 9-inch pan (45 to 50 minutes for 8-inch pan) or until coconut is golden brown and bars begin to pull away from sides of pan. Cool 1 hour 30 minutes to 2 hours before serving. Cut into 4 rows by 4 rows. Serve at room temperature topped with whipped cream and additional crushed granola bars.

*NOTE: To easily crush granola bars, do not unwrap; use rolling pin to crush bars.

HIGH ALTITUDE (3500-6500 FT.): Do not use 8-inch pan. Stir 1/4 cup flour into remaining dry brownie mix for filling. Bake 40 to 45 minutes.

Chocolate Malted Milk Cheesecake

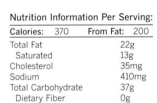

PREP TIME: 25 MINUTES (READY IN 5 HOURS 20 MINUTES)
SERVINGS: 18

5 packages (8 oz. each) cream cheese, softened

1½ cups sugar

1 cup malted milk powder

½ cup baking cocoa

1 container (8 oz.) sour cream

2 teaspoons vanilla

¼ teaspoon salt

5 eggs

1 cup whipping cream

½ cup chopped malted milk balls

Nutrition Information Per Serving:

Calories:	420	From Fat:	280
Total Fat			31g
Saturated			19g
Cholesterol			150mg
Sodium			260mg
Total Carbohydrate			27g
Dietary Fiber			0g
Sugars			23g
Protein			8g

1) Heat oven to 350°F. Line bottom only of 13x9-inch pan with foil; spray foil with cooking spray. In large bowl, beat cream cheese with electric mixer on medium speed until light and fluffy.

2) In medium bowl, mix sugar, malted milk powder and cocoa. Add to cream cheese; beat on low speed until combined. Beat on medium speed until smooth. Beat in sour cream, vanilla and salt. Add eggs 1 at a time, beating just until combined after each addition. Pour batter into pan.

3) Place pan in larger shallow pan in oven. Add hot water to shallow pan until half full. Bake 50 to 55 minutes or until set.

4) Remove cheesecake from water bath; place on wire rack. Cool until lukewarm, about 1 hour. Invert cheesecake onto cookie sheet; remove foil. Refrigerate at least 3 hours or overnight.

5) In small bowl, beat whipping cream until stiff peaks form. Cut cheesecake into squares; place on individual dessert plates. Top each with whipped cream and chopped malted milk balls.

HIGH ALTITUDE (3500-6500 FT.): No change.

Pistachio-Coconut Pie

PREP TIME: 20 MINUTES (READY IN 2 HOURS 20 MINUTES)
SERVINGS: 8

 EASY

1 package (8 oz.) cream cheese, softened

1 cup milk

1 teaspoon vanilla

1 box (4-serving size) pistachio instant pudding and pie filling mix

1 container (8 oz.) frozen whipped topping, thawed

½ cup flaked coconut, toasted

1 shortbread crumb crust (6 oz.)

Nutrition Information Per Serving:

Calories:	370	From Fat:	200
Total Fat			22g
Saturated			13g
Cholesterol			35mg
Sodium			410mg
Total Carbohydrate			37g
Dietary Fiber			0g
Sugars			24g
Protein			5g

1) In large bowl with electric mixer, beat cream cheese on medium speed until fluffy. Gradually beat in milk and vanilla until mixture is smooth and well blended. Add pudding mix; beat on low speed 2 minutes.

2) With rubber spatula, fold in whipped topping and ¼ cup of the coconut. Spoon into crumb crust. Sprinkle with remaining ¼ cup coconut. Refrigerate until set, at least 2 hours.

HIGH ALTITUDE (3500-6500 FT.): No change.

Merry Cherry-Chip Pie

PREP TIME: 15 MINUTES (READY IN 3 HOURS 55 MINUTES)
SERVINGS: 8

 EASY

1 box (15 oz.) Pillsbury® refrigerated pie crusts, softened as directed on box

½ cup sliced almonds

2 cans (21 oz. each) cherry pie filling

½ cup semisweet chocolate chips

1 teaspoon water

2 teaspoons sugar

Nutrition Information Per Serving:		
Calories: 500	From Fat: 190	
Total Fat		22g
Saturated		7g
Cholesterol		5mg
Sodium		220mg
Total Carbohydrate		71g
Dietary Fiber		4g
Sugars		42g
Protein		5g

1) Heat oven to 425°F. Make pie crusts as directed on box for Two-Crust Pie using 9-inch glass pie pan. Reserve 1 tablespoon almonds; sprinkle remaining almonds in bottom of crust-lined pan.

2) In medium bowl, mix pie filling and chocolate chips. Spoon over almonds in pan. Top with second crust; seal edge and flute. Cut slits in several places in top crust. Brush water over top; sprinkle with reserved almonds and sugar.

3) Cover edge of crust with strips of foil; bake 30 to 40 minutes or until crust is golden brown. Cool at least 3 hours before serving.

HIGH ALTITUDE (3500-6500 FT.): Use 9-inch deep-dish glass pie pan. Bake 35 to 45 minutes.

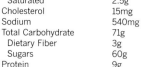

Raspberry pie filling makes an equally delicious and festive looking pie. Or, use one can of cherry pie filling and one of raspberry!

Fruit-Topped Angel Food Cake Squares

PREP TIME: 30 MINUTES (READY IN 4 HOURS 30 MINUTES)
SERVINGS: 12

1 loaf (1 lb.) angel food cake (12x5 inch)

1½ cups milk

3 containers (6 oz. each) Yoplait® Original 99% Fat Free French vanilla yogurt

1 can (14 oz.) sweetened condensed milk (not evaporated)

1 box (6-serving size) vanilla instant pudding and pie filling mix

2 cups quartered fresh strawberries

2 cups fresh blueberries

2 cups fresh raspberries

Nutrition Information Per Serving:		
Calories: 360	From Fat: 40	
Total Fat		4.5g
Saturated		2.5g
Cholesterol		15mg
Sodium		540mg
Total Carbohydrate		71g
Dietary Fiber		3g
Sugars		60g
Protein		9g

1) Spray 13x9-inch (3-quart) glass baking dish with cooking spray. Cut cake into 1-inch cubes; place in single layer in dish.

2) In medium bowl, mix milk, yogurt, condensed milk and pudding mix with wire whisk until well blended.

3) Pour pudding mixture over cake pieces; spread until cake pieces are completely covered. Gently tap dish on work surface to remove air bubbles. Cover; refrigerate at least 4 hours or overnight.

4) Just before serving, in another medium bowl, gently mix all berries. Cut dessert into squares; top with fruit.

HIGH ALTITUDE (3500-6500 FT.): No change.

German Chocolate Cream Pie

ANNETTE MEASE | BOISE, IDAHO

PREP TIME: 1 HOUR (READY IN 2 HOURS 30 MINUTES)
SERVINGS: 8

CRUST

12 pecan shortbread cookies, broken into pieces

4 Nature Valley® pecan crunch crunchy granola bars (2 pouches from 8.9-oz. box), crushed (^{3}/4 cup)*

^{1}/3 cup butter, melted

CHOCOLATE FILLING

2 oz. cream cheese (from 8-oz. package), softened

^{1}/4 cup powdered sugar

1 tablespoon milk

^{1}/4 cup Hershey®'s semi-sweet chocolate chips, melted, cooled

1 container (8 oz.) frozen (thawed) whipped topping

COCONUT-PECAN FILLING

1 container (15 oz.) Pillsbury® Creamy Supreme® coconut pecan frosting

2 oz. cream cheese (from 8-oz. package), softened

1 tablespoon milk

1 container (8 oz.) frozen (thawed) whipped topping

GARNISHES

Reserved ^{1}/2 cup whipped topping

^{1}/2 Hershey®'s milk chocolate bar (1.55-oz. size) or ^{1}/2 Hershey®'s Special Dark® chocolate bar (1.44-oz. size), chopped

1) In food processor or blender, process cookies and granola bars with on-and-off motions until fine crumbs form; pour into medium bowl. Stir in melted butter with fork until well mixed. Press mixture in bottom and up side of ungreased 9- or 8-inch glass or metal pie plate. Place in freezer just until firm, about 10 minutes.

2) Meanwhile, in medium bowl, beat 2 oz. cream cheese, the powdered sugar and 1 tablespoon milk with electric mixer on medium speed until blended. On low speed, beat in melted chocolate chips. In small bowl, reserve ^{1}/4 cup whipped topping from 8-oz. container for garnish. On medium speed, beat remaining topping from container into chocolate mixture until well blended.

3) Spread ^{1}/3 cup of the frosting evenly in bottom of crust. Spoon chocolate filling into crust; carefully spread. Place pie in freezer while making next layer.

4) In large bowl, beat 2 oz. cream cheese, 1 tablespoon milk and remaining frosting with electric mixer on medium speed until well blended. Reserve another ^{1}/4 cup whipped topping from 8-oz. container in same small bowl of topping. Beat remaining topping from container into coconut-pecan mixture until well blended. Carefully spoon over chocolate filling; spread evenly. Carefully spread reserved ^{1}/2 cup whipped topping over top; sprinkle with chopped candy bar. Refrigerate 1 hour 30 minutes before serving.

*NOTE: To easily crush granola bars, do not unwrap; use rolling pin to crush bars.

HIGH ALTITUDE (3500-6500 FT.): No change.

Nutrition Information Per Serving:		
Calories: 770	From Fat:	470
Total Fat		53g
Saturated		31g
Cholesterol		90mg
Sodium		260mg
Total Carbohydrate		67g
Dietary Fiber		4g
Sugars		47g
Protein		8g

Royal Marble Cheesecake

PREP TIME: 35 MINUTES (READY IN 12 HOURS)
SERVINGS: 16

CRUST

3/4 cup all-purpose flour

2 tablespoons sugar

Dash salt

1/4 cup butter or margarine

1 cup semisweet chocolate chips, melted

FILLING

3 packages (8 oz. each) cream cheese, softened

1 cup sugar

1/4 cup all-purpose flour

2 teaspoons vanilla

6 eggs

1 cup sour cream

Nutrition Information Per Serving:

Calories:	370	From Fat:	230
Total Fat		26g	
Saturated		14g	
Cholesterol		135mg	
Sodium		200mg	
Total Carbohydrate		29g	
Dietary Fiber		0g	
Sugars		21g	
Protein		7g	

1) Heat oven to 400°F. In small bowl, mix 3/4 cup flour, 2 tablespoons sugar and the salt. With pastry blender or fork, cut in butter until mixture resembles coarse crumbs. Stir in 2 tablespoons of the melted chocolate. Reserve remaining chocolate for filling. Press crumb mixture in bottom of ungreased 9-inch springform pan.

2) Bake 10 minutes or until very light brown. Remove pan from oven. Reduce oven temperature to 325°F.

3) Meanwhile, in large bowl, beat cream cheese and 1 cup sugar with electric mixer on medium speed until light and fluffy. Beat in 1/4 cup flour and vanilla until well blended. On low speed, add eggs 1 at a time, beating just until blended after each addition. Add sour cream; blend well. Place 1 3/4 cups filling mixture in medium bowl; stir in reserved melted chocolate.

4) Pour half of plain filling over crust. Top with spoonfuls of half of the chocolate filling. Cover with remaining plain filling, then with spoonfuls of remaining chocolate filling. With table knife, swirl chocolate filling through plain filling. Place cheesecake in center of oven. Place shallow pan half full of water on bottom oven rack under cheesecake.

5) Bake 1 hour to 1 hour 15 minutes or until set but center of cheesecake still jiggles when moved. Cool on wire rack 10 minutes. Run knife around edge of pan to loosen cheesecake. Cool at least 2 hours. Refrigerate 8 hours or overnight before serving. Carefully remove side of pan. Store in refrigerator.

HIGH ALTITUDE (3500-6500 FT.): In Step 5, bake at 325°F. for 1 hour 15 minutes to 1 hour 25 minutes. Remove from oven; immediately run knife around edge of pan to loosen cheesecake.

Berry No-Bake Cheesecake Pie

PREP TIME: 25 MINUTES (READY IN 2 HOURS 25 MINUTES)
SERVINGS: 8

PIE

- 3/4 cup milk
- 24 regular marshmallows
- 1 package (8 oz.) cream cheese, softened
- 2 tablespoons orange-flavored liqueur
- 1 chocolate flavor crumb crust (6 oz.)

TOPPING

- 2 kiwifruit, peeled, quartered and sliced
- 1 1/2 cups fresh raspberries
- 2 tablespoons powdered sugar

Nutrition Information Per Serving:

Calories: 330	From Fat: 160
Total Fat	18g
Saturated Fat	8g
Cholesterol	35mg
Sodium	200mg
Total Carbohydrate	39g
Dietary Fiber	3g
Sugars	25g
Protein	5g

1) In 2-quart saucepan, heat milk over medium heat until steaming. Add marshmallows; remove from heat. Let stand 15 minutes to soften marshmallows, stirring several times until smooth.

2) In medium bowl with electric mixer, beat cream cheese on medium speed until fluffy. Beat in marshmallow mixture and liqueur. Pour into crumb crust. Refrigerate until set, about 2 hours.

3) In another medium bowl, gently mix kiwifruit and raspberries. Refrigerate until serving time.

4) To serve, cut pie into wedges; place on individual dessert plates. Spoon fruit mixture over wedges. Sprinkle with powdered sugar. Store in refrigerator.

HIGH ALTITUDE (3500-6500 FT.): No change.

Raspberry Cookie Tart

PREP TIME: 20 MINUTES (READY IN 1 HOUR 45 MINUTES)
SERVINGS: 12

⊜ EASY

- 1 roll (18 oz.) Pillsbury® refrigerated chocolate chip cookies
- 1 package (8 oz.) cream cheese, softened
- 1/4 cup powdered sugar
- 1 tablespoon orange juice
- 1 pint (2 cups) fresh raspberries
- 1/4 cup semisweet chocolate chips
- 1/4 teaspoon vegetable oil

Nutrition Information Per Serving:

Calories: 310	From Fat: 170
Total Fat	18g
Saturated	8g
Cholesterol	25mg
Sodium	190mg
Total Carbohydrate	33g
Dietary Fiber	3g
Sugars	22g
Protein	3g

1) Heat oven to 350°F. Into ungreased 10-inch tart pan with removable bottom, break up cookie dough; press evenly in pan to form crust.

2) Bake 22 to 25 minutes or until deep golden brown. Cool completely, about 30 minutes.

3) In medium bowl with electric mixer, beat cream cheese, powdered sugar and orange juice on medium speed until well blended. Spread over cooled crust. Top with raspberries.

4) In small microwavable bowl, microwave chocolate chips and oil on High 1 to 2 minutes, stirring until smooth. Drizzle chocolate over raspberries. Let stand at least 30 minutes until chocolate is set before serving.

HIGH ALTITUDE (3500-6500 FT.): No change.

Tropical Fruit Bars

ANN HOBERT | WESTWOOD HILLS, KANSAS

PREP TIME:	15 MINUTES (READY IN 2 HOURS 25 MINUTES)
SERVINGS:	36 BARS

1 package (18 oz.) Pillsbury® Ready to Bake!™ Big Deluxe Classics® refrigerated white chunk macadamia nut cookies

1 can (14 oz.) sweetened condensed milk (not evaporated)

1 container (6 oz.) Yoplait® Original 99% Fat Free piña colada yogurt

1 bag (6 to 7 oz.) mixed tropical dried fruits

1 jar (6 oz.) dry-roasted macadamia nuts, coarsely chopped

³⁄4 cup Hershey's® premier white chips

1 cup Mounds® coconut flakes

Nutrition Information Per Bar:

Calories:	190	From Fat:	90
Total Fat			10g
Saturated			4g
Cholesterol			5mg
Sodium			80mg
Total Carbohydrate			23g
Dietary Fiber			0g
Sugars			18g
Protein			3g

1) Heat oven to 350°F. (325°F. for dark pan). Grease 13x9-inch pan with shortening or cooking spray. Place cookie dough rounds in pan. With floured fingers, press dough in pan to form crust.

2) In medium bowl, mix condensed milk and yogurt until well blended. Spread over crust to edges of pan. Sprinkle with remaining ingredients in order listed.

3) Bake 30 to 40 minutes or until edges are golden brown. Cool completely, about 1 hour 30 minutes. Cut into 6 rows by 6 rows. Store in refrigerator.

HIGH ALTITUDE (3500-6500 FT.): Bake 35 to 45 minutes.

Berry-Cherry Pie

PREP TIME:	30 MINUTES (READY IN 3 HOURS)
SERVINGS:	8

1 Pillsbury® refrigerated pie crust (from 15-oz. box), softened as directed on box

1 package (8 oz.) cream cheese, softened

¹⁄3 cup sugar

1 teaspoon vanilla

¹⁄2 teaspoon grated lemon peel

1 pint (2 cups) fresh whole strawberries

1 can (21 oz.) cherry pie filling

Nutrition Information Per Serving:

Calories:	340	From Fat:	160
Total Fat			18g
Saturated			9g
Cholesterol			35mg
Sodium			190mg
Total Carbohydrate			43g
Dietary Fiber			2g
Sugars			28g
Protein			3g

1) Heat oven to 450°F. Make pie crust as directed on box for One-Crust Baked Shell using 9-inch glass pie pan. Bake 9 to 11 minutes or until light golden brown. Cool completely, about 30 minutes.

2) In small bowl, beat cream cheese, sugar, vanilla and lemon peel with electric mixer on medium speed until smooth and well blended. Spread evenly in cooled baked shell.

3) Arrange strawberries over cream cheese mixture; press in lightly. Spoon pie filling over strawberries. Refrigerate at least 2 hours before serving. If desired, garnish with whipped cream. Store in refrigerator.

HIGH ALTITUDE (3500-6500 FT.): No change.

Sugar Cookie Shortcake

PREP TIME: 25 MINUTES (READY IN 2 HOURS 10 MINUTES)
SERVINGS: 10

1 roll (18 oz.) Pillsbury® refrigerated sugar cookies, well chilled

2 tablespoons sugar

1 lb. fresh strawberries

1 box (4-serving size) vanilla instant pudding and pie filling mix

1 cup cold milk

3/4 cup whipping cream

10 whole strawberries, if desired

1) Heat oven to 350°F. Line 2 (9-inch) round cake pans with foil so edges extend over sides of pans. Cut cookie dough in half. Press half of dough in bottom of each pan. Sprinkle each cookie layer with 1 tablespoon sugar. Bake 20 minutes or until light golden brown. Cool in pans on wire racks 10 minutes.

2) Use foil to lift cookie layers from pans; place on wire racks. Cool completely, about 20 minutes.

3) Meanwhile, slice 1 lb. strawberries; set aside. In small bowl, beat pudding mix and milk with wire whisk about 2 minutes or until thickened. In another small bowl with electric mixer, beat whipping cream until stiff peaks form. Fold whipped cream into pudding mixture. Reserve 1/2 cup mixture for garnish.

4) Remove foil from cookie layers. Place 1 layer on serving plate. Spread with half of pudding mixture; top with half of the sliced strawberries. Place second cookie layer on strawberries; top with remaining pudding mixture and sliced strawberries.

5) Spoon reserved pudding mixture onto center of shortcake. Refrigerate at least 1 hour before serving. Cut into wedges to serve. Top each with whole strawberry.

HIGH ALTITUDE (3500-6500 FT.): No change.

Nutrition Information Per Serving:

Calories:	350	From Fat:	150
Total Fat		17g	
Saturated		7g	
Cholesterol		40mg	
Sodium		300mg	
Total Carbohydrate		47g	
Dietary Fiber		1g	
Sugars		30g	
Protein		3g	

Key Lime Pecan Tart

SUE TYNER | TUSTIN, CALIFORNIA

PREP TIME: 25 MINUTES (READY IN 2 HOURS 35 MINUTES)
SERVINGS: 12

CRUST

- 2 cups Golden Grahams® cereal, finely crushed (³/4 cup)
- 6 Nature Valley® pecan crunch crunchy granola bars (3 pouches from 8.9-oz. box), finely crushed (heaping 1 cup)*
- ¹/2 cup chopped pecans, ground
- 2 tablespoons granulated sugar
- 7 tablespoons butter or margarine, melted

FILLING

- ¹/4 cup Key lime or regular lime juice
- ¹/2 package (1¹/2 teaspoons) unflavored gelatin
- 1 package (8 oz.) cream cheese, softened
- 1 box (4-serving size) lemon instant pudding and pie filling mix
- 3 containers (6 oz. each) Yoplait® Original 99% Fat Free Key lime pie yogurt
- ¹/2 cup granulated sugar
- ¹/2 cup chopped pecans

1) Heat oven to 350°F. In medium bowl, mix all crust ingredients. Press in bottom and up side of ungreased 11- or 10-inch tart pan with removable bottom. Bake 10 minutes. Cool 10 minutes. Place in freezer while making filling.

2) Meanwhile, in 1-cup microwavable measuring cup or small bowl, place lime juice. Stir in gelatin. Microwave on High about 30 seconds, stirring occasionally, until gelatin is dissolved; set aside.

3) In large bowl, beat cream cheese with electric mixer on medium speed until light and fluffy. Add gelatin mixture and pudding mix; beat until smooth, scraping bowl frequently. Add 1 container of yogurt at a time, beating well after each addition. Gradually beat in ¹/2 cup sugar until smooth.

4) Spread filling evenly in crust; sprinkle with pecans. Refrigerate at least 2 hours before serving. Cut into wedges to serve. Store in refrigerator.

*NOTE: To easily crush granola bars, do not unwrap; use rolling pin to crush bars.

HIGH ALTITUDE (3500-6500 FT.): No change.

Nutrition Information Per Serving:	
Calories: 380	From Fat: 200
Total Fat	22g
Saturated	9g
Cholesterol	40mg
Sodium	350mg
Total Carbohydrate	41g
Dietary Fiber	2g
Sugars	30g
Protein	6g

Hot Fudge Pudding Cake

PREP TIME: 15 MINUTES (READY IN 1 HOUR 5 MINUTES)
SERVINGS: 8

 EASY

CAKE

1$^1/_4$ cups all-purpose flour

$^3/_4$ cup sugar

$^1/_4$ cup unsweetened baking cocoa

1$^1/_2$ teaspoons baking powder

$^1/_2$ teaspoon salt

$^1/_2$ cup milk

2 tablespoons butter or margarine, melted

1 teaspoon vanilla

PUDDING MIXTURE

1 cup sugar

$^1/_4$ cup unsweetened baking cocoa

Dash salt

1$^1/_3$ cups boiling water

Nutrition Information Per Serving:	
Calories: 300	From Fat: 35
Total Fat	4g
Saturated	2g
Cholesterol	10mg
Sodium	290mg
Total Carbohydrate	63g
Dietary Fiber	2g
Sugars	45g
Protein	4g

1) Heat oven to 350°F. In medium bowl, mix flour, $^3/_4$ cup sugar, $^1/_4$ cup cocoa, the baking powder and $^1/_2$ teaspoon salt. Stir in milk, butter and vanilla until well blended. Spread batter in ungreased 8-inch square or 9-inch round cake pan.

2) In small bowl, mix 1 cup sugar, $^1/_4$ cup cocoa and dash salt. Sprinkle evenly over batter. Pour boiling water over sugar mixture.

3) Bake 40 to 50 minutes or until center is set and firm to the touch. Serve warm. If desired, serve with ice cream. Store in refrigerator.

HIGH ALTITUDE (3500-6500 FT.): No change.

Cherry Berry Tart

PREP TIME: 20 MINUTES (READY IN 1 HOUR 50 MINUTES)
SERVINGS: 8

 EASY

1 package (15 oz.) Pillsbury® refrigerated pie crusts, softened as directed on box

FILLING

1 can (21 oz.) cherry pie filling

1 cup halved strawberries

1 cup blueberries

Whipped cream, if desired

Nutrition Information Per Serving:	
Calories: 210	From Fat: 70
Total Fat	7g
Saturated	2.5g
Cholesterol	0mg
Sodium	110mg
Total Carbohydrate	35g
Dietary Fiber	2g
Sugars	18g
Protein	0g

1) Heat oven to 450°F. Prepare pie crust according to package directions for unfilled one-crust pie using 9-inch tart pan with removable bottom. Place crust in pan; press in bottom and up sides of pan. Trim edges if necessary. Generously prick crust with fork. Bake at 450°F. for 9 to 11 minutes or until light golden brown. Cool completely.

2) In large bowl, gently combine all filling ingredients except whipped cream. Spoon into cooled, baked crust. Refrigerate at least 1 hour. Remove sides of pan. Garnish with whipped cream.

HIGH ALTITUDE (3500-6500 FT.): No change.

Banana-Chocolate-Caramel Cake

PREP TIME: 20 MINUTES (READY IN 2 HOURS 20 MINUTES)
SERVINGS: 12

 EASY   LOW FAT

1 round angel food cake (8 to 10 inch)

2 cups (4 oz. each) refrigerated chocolate pudding snacks (from 24-oz. package)

3 medium bananas

$^1/_2$ cup caramel ice cream topping, room temperature

1 aerosol can (7 oz.) whipped cream

2 tablespoons chocolate candy sprinkles

Nutrition Information Per Serving:		
Calories: 250	From Fat:	25
Total Fat		2.5g
Saturated		1.5g
Cholesterol		0mg
Sodium		450mg
Total Carbohydrate		54g
Dietary Fiber		1g
Sugars		40g
Protein		5g

1) Cut angel food cake in half horizontally; separate layers. Spread 1 pudding snack on top of bottom cake layer.

2) Slice 2 of the bananas into $^1/_8$-inch-thick slices; arrange slices on top of pudding. Place top cake layer on bottom layer, cut side down. Top with second pudding snack. Refrigerate at least 2 hours or overnight before serving.

3) To serve, cut cake into 12 slices; place on individual dessert plates. Drizzle each with caramel topping. Slice remaining banana into 12 slices. Top each serving with whipped cream and banana slices. Sprinkle each with $^1/_2$ teaspoon candy sprinkles.

HIGH ALTITUDE (3500-6500 FT.): No change.

Brownie and Strawberry Shortcakes

PREP TIME: 20 MINUTES (READY IN 1 HOUR)
SERVINGS: 12

 EASY

1 box (1 lb. 3.8 oz.) fudge brownie mix

$^1/_2$ cup vegetable oil

$^1/_4$ cup water

3 eggs

$2^1/_2$ cups milk

2 boxes (4-serving size each) white chocolate instant pudding and pie filling mix

1 pint (2 cups) whipping (heavy) cream

3 cups sliced fresh strawberries

1) Heat oven to 350°F. Grease 15x10x1-inch pan with shortening or cooking spray. In medium bowl, stir brownie mix, oil, water and eggs with spoon until well blended. Spread batter in pan.

2) Bake 23 to 25 minutes or until brownie springs back when touched lightly in center. Cool 15 minutes.

3) Meanwhile, in medium bowl, beat milk and pudding mix with wire whisk until thickened. In small bowl, beat whipping cream with electric mixer on high speed until stiff peaks form. Gently fold whipped cream into pudding mixture until well combined. Cover; refrigerate.

4) Cut brownies into 6 rows by 4 rows, making 24 squares. Place 1 brownie square on each individual dessert plate; top each with $^1/_4$ cup pudding mixture and 2 tablespoons strawberries. Repeat layers.

HIGH ALTITUDE (3500-6500 FT.): Add 3 tablespoons flour to dry brownie mix.

Nutrition Information Per Serving:		
Calories: 530	From Fat:	260
Total Fat		29g
Saturated		12g
Cholesterol		110mg
Sodium		460mg
Total Carbohydrate		61g
Dietary Fiber		3g
Sugars		45g
Protein		6g

Key Lime Parfaits

NANCY HEIKKILA | RUSSELLVILLE, ARKANSAS

Pillsbury *Bake-Off*

PREP TIME: 15 MINUTES (READY IN 40 MINUTES)
SERVINGS: 2

- 2 cups Cheerios® cereal
- 3 tablespoons granulated sugar
- 2 tablespoons water
- 2 teaspoons butter, melted
- 1 cup frozen (thawed) fat-free whipped topping (4 oz.)
- 1 tablespoon lime juice
- 2 containers (6 oz. each) Yoplait® Light Fat Free Key lime pie yogurt

1) Heat oven to 350°F. Spray cookie sheet and 12x12-inch sheet of foil with cooking spray. In food processor, place cereal and sugar; process with on-and-off motions until fine crumbs form. Add water and melted butter; process until thoroughly mixed.

2) Spread cereal mixture evenly in center of cookie sheet. Use foil, sprayed side down, to press cereal mixture slightly; roll with rolling pin into 12x8-inch rectangle, about 1/8 inch thick. With sharp knife, score mixture into 1-inch squares.

3) Bake 12 to 15 minutes or until squares are golden brown. Cool completely, about 10 minutes. Meanwhile, in small bowl, place whipped topping; fold in lime juice until blended.

4) Break cereal mixture apart at scored lines. Reserve 4 cereal squares; crumble remaining squares into small pieces. In each dessert bowl or 12-oz. parfait glass, layer 1/4 cup crumbled cereal squares, half container of yogurt and scant 1/4 cup whipped topping mixture. Repeat layers. Top each parfait with 2 reserved cereal squares.

HIGH ALTITUDE (3500-6500 FT.): No change.

Nutrition Information Per Serving:

Calories:	450	From Fat:	60
Total Fat		7g	
Saturated		3.5g	
Cholesterol		15mg	
Sodium		360mg	
Total Carbohydrate		86g	
Dietary Fiber		3g	
Sugars		57g	
Protein		11g	

Fun With Food

Perfect for parties and special occasions,
these eye-catching treats are *almost* too fun to eat!

SEASIDE PUDDING CUPS
PG. 327

SMILEY APPLES
PG. 338

SNOW FUN SNOWMEN
PG. 343

MR. MOUSE PARTY CUPCAKES
PG. 332

Tommy Turkey Treats

PREP TIME: 25 MINUTES (READY IN 25 MINUTES)
SERVINGS: 6 TREATS

 EASY

1 tube (4.25 oz.) chocolate decorating icing

6 chocolate-covered marshmallow pinwheel cookies

6 oatmeal cookies (about 3-inch diameter)

6 small star-shaped pretzels or pretzel twists

48 corn candies (about 3 oz.)

6 miniature milk chocolate-covered peanut butter cups, unwrapped

2 red gummi worm candies

1 tube (4.25 oz.) white decorating icing

Nutrition Information Per Serving:		
Calories: 370	From Fat: 120	
Total Fat		13g
Saturated		5g
Cholesterol		0mg
Sodium		150mg
Total Carbohydrate		59g
Dietary Fiber		2g
Sugars		35g
Protein		5g

1) Squeeze chocolate icing on bottom of each oatmeal cookie. Attach 1 marshmallow cookie even with 1 edge of each oatmeal cookie to resemble body and fan of tail.

2) At area where 2 cookie edges meet, squeeze about $1/2$ teaspoon chocolate icing onto marshmallow cookie; attach pretzel to resemble feet. Squeeze chocolate icing on each oatmeal cookie about halfway around marshmallow cookie; firmly press corn candy into icing to resemble feathers.

3) With small amount of icing, attach 1 corn candy to each peanut butter cup to resemble beak. Cut each gummi worm in half lengthwise and crosswise. Squeeze chocolate icing around each corn candy beak; wrap 1 gummi piece around top of each beak to resemble wattle, pressing firmly. Pipe small dots of white and chocolate icing on each peanut butter cup for eyes.

4) Squeeze chocolate icing on largest flat side of each peanut butter cup; place over center opening of each marshmallow cookie to resemble head, pressing firmly.

HIGH ALTITUDE (3500-6500 FT.): No change.

tip

While you're getting ready to serve Thanksgiving dinner, keep the children busy making a Tommy Turkey for each person at the table. Make one model turkey ahead of time to help them understand what to do.

Honey-Nut Caramel Candy Bars

PREP TIME: 20 MINUTES (READY IN 1 HOUR 20 MINUTES)
SERVINGS: 36

 EASY   LOW FAT

¼ cup butter or margarine

1 bag (10 oz.) large marshmallows

3 cups Honey Nut Cheerios® cereal

3 cups Corn Chex® cereal

1 cup raisins

36 individually wrapped, chewy chocolate-coated caramel candies, unwrapped

Nutrition Information Per Serving:	
Calories: 100	From Fat: 25
Total Fat	2.5g
Saturated	1.5g
Cholesterol	0mg
Sodium	70mg
Total Carbohydrate	18g
Dietary Fiber	0g
Sugars	12g
Protein	0g

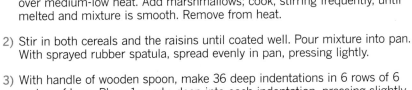

1) Spray 13x9-inch pan with cooking spray. In 3-quart saucepan, melt butter over medium-low heat. Add marshmallows; cook, stirring frequently, until melted and mixture is smooth. Remove from heat.

2) Stir in both cereals and the raisins until coated well. Pour mixture into pan. With sprayed rubber spatula, spread evenly in pan, pressing lightly.

3) With handle of wooden spoon, make 36 deep indentations in 6 rows of 6 on top of bars. Place 1 candy, deep into each indentation, pressing slightly. Cool completely, about 1 hour.

4) Cut into bars with 1 candy in center of each.

HIGH ALTITUDE (3500-6500 FT.): No change.

Seaside Pudding Cups

PREP TIME: 20 MINUTES (READY IN 20 MINUTES)
SERVINGS: 12

 EASY

6 cinnamon shortbread cookies

2 packages (24 oz. each) refrigerated strawberries and creme swirled pudding snacks (12 cups)

1 roll chewy fruit snacks in three-foot rolls (any flavor from 4.5-oz. box)

24 teddy graham snacks

12 drink umbrellas

12 ring-shaped hard candies

Nutrition Information Per Serving:	
Calories: 180	From Fat: 40
Total Fat	4.5g
Saturated	2.5g
Cholesterol	10mg
Sodium	120mg
Total Carbohydrate	33g
Dietary Fiber	0g
Sugars	25g
Protein	2g

1) Place cookies in small resealable food-storage plastic bag. With hand or rolling pin, crush cookies. Sprinkle about 1 tablespoon crushed cookies on top of each cup of pudding.

2) Cut 12 (1½-inch pieces) from chewy fruit snack. Peel each piece of fruit snack from plastic backing; place over crushed cookies on pudding for "beach towel." Top each with teddy bear and umbrella. Put ring-shaped candy around 12 teddy bears. Place on top of each pudding snack.

HIGH ALTITUDE (3500-6500 FT.): No change.

Crescent Puff S'mores

| PREP TIME: | 15 MINUTES (READY IN 35 MINUTES) | EASY |
| SERVINGS: | 16 SNACKS | |

2 cans (8 oz. each) Pillsbury® refrigerated crescent dinner rolls

16 large marshmallows

2 to 3 (1.2 oz. each) milk chocolate candy bars, broken into squares

½ cup butter or margarine, melted

1 cup graham cracker crumbs (about 14 squares)

1) Heat oven to 375°F. Spray 16 regular-size muffin cups with cooking spray. Separate dough into 16 triangles.

2) For each snack, place 1 marshmallow on shortest side of triangle. Top with 2 squares of chocolate candy. Starting with shortest side of triangle, fold corners of dough over marshmallow and chocolate, then roll to opposite point, completely covering marshmallow and chocolate; pinch dough to seal well.

3) Dip snacks in or brush with melted butter; roll in cracker crumbs to coat. Place in muffin cups.

4) Place pans on sheet of foil or cookie sheet (to catch any spills); bake 15 to 20 minutes or until golden brown. Immediately remove from muffin cups; serve warm.

HIGH ALTITUDE (3500-6500 FT.): Use 8 large marshmallows, cut in half. Heat oven to 350°F.

Nutrition Information Per Serving:		
Calories: 230	From Fat:	120
Total Fat		14g
Saturated		6g
Cholesterol		15mg
Sodium		290mg
Total Carbohydrate		23g
Dietary Fiber		0g
Sugars		11g
Protein		3g

One cup of milk chocolate chips can be used in place of the candy bars. Use 1 tablespoon of chips for each snack.

Peanut-Cereal Baseball Cake

PREP TIME: 10 MINUTES (READY IN 1 HOUR 10 MINUTES)
SERVINGS: 8

EASY

1/2 cup light corn syrup

1/2 cup sugar

1/2 cup creamy peanut butter

4 cups Cheerios® cereal

1/2 cup coarsely chopped salted peanuts

1/2 cup vanilla creamy ready-to-spread frosting (from 16-oz. can)

1 tube (0.68 oz.) red decorating gel

Nutrition Information Per Serving:	
Calories: 390	From Fat: 150
Total Fat	16g
Saturated	3g
Cholesterol	0mg
Sodium	290mg
Total Carbohydrate	52g
Dietary Fiber	3g
Sugars	30g
Protein	8g

1) Line 8- or 9-inch round cake pan with foil; spray foil with cooking spray. In 4-quart nonstick Dutch oven, mix corn syrup and sugar. Cook over medium-low heat just until mixture boils. Remove from heat.

2) Stir in peanut butter until smooth. Stir in cereal and peanuts until coated. Press mixture firmly in pan. Cool completely, about 1 hour.

3) By lifting foil, remove cereal mixture from pan; remove foil. Place upside down on serving platter. Spread frosting over top. With toothpick, draw baseball pattern as shown. Outline pattern with decorating gel to resemble baseball.

HIGH ALTITUDE (3500-6500 FT.): No change.

Peanut Butter and Cookie Ice Cream-Wiches

PREP TIME: 30 MINUTES (READY IN 2 HOURS)
SERVINGS: 12

EASY

1 roll (18 oz.) Pillsbury® refrigerated peanut butter cookies

2 tablespoons sugar

3 cups chocolate or fudge swirl ice cream

1/2 cup candy-coated chocolate-covered peanuts (from 8.5-oz. bag), crushed

Nutrition Information Per Serving:	
Calories: 310	From Fat: 130
Total Fat	15g
Saturated	5g
Cholesterol	20mg
Sodium	230mg
Total Carbohydrate	41g
Dietary Fiber	0g
Sugars	27g
Protein	5g

1) Heat oven to 350°F. Shape cookie dough into 24 balls; roll in sugar and place 3 inches apart on ungreased large cookie sheets. With fork dipped in sugar, flatten balls in crisscross pattern until about 2 inches in diameter.

2) Bake 12 to 15 minutes or until golden brown. Cool 1 minute; remove from cookie sheets. Cool completely, about 1 hour.

3) For each sandwich, spoon 1/4 cup ice cream onto bottom of 1 cookie. Top with second cookie, top side up; press together gently. Roll sides (ice cream) in crushed candy; place in shallow pan. Freeze until firm, about 30 minutes.

4) Wrap each frozen sandwich in plastic wrap. Store in freezer.

HIGH ALTITUDE (3500-6500 FT.): No change.

Giant Peanut Butter Cup Cookies

PREP TIME: 40 MINUTES (READY IN 40 MINUTES)
SERVINGS: 12 LARGE COOKIES

 EASY

1 roll (18 oz.) Pillsbury® refrigerated peanut butter cookies

1/2 cup candy-coated peanut butter pieces

1/2 cup miniature candy-coated chocolate baking bits

1/2 cup salted peanuts

12 milk chocolate peanut butter cups (from six 1.6-oz. packages), unwrapped

Nutrition Information Per Serving:	
Calories: 430	From Fat: 190
Total Fat	21g
Saturated	6g
Cholesterol	0mg
Sodium	260mg
Total Carbohydrate	53g
Dietary Fiber	3g
Sugars	38g
Protein	7g

1) Heat oven to 350°F. Into large bowl, break up cookie dough. Stir in peanut butter pieces, baking bits and peanuts.

2) Drop dough by scant 1/4 cupfuls 3 inches apart onto ungreased cookie sheets. Flatten each with fingers to 3/4-inch thickness.

3) Bake 11 to 15 minutes or until light golden brown. Immediately top each cookie with 1 peanut butter cup; press lightly into dough. Cool 5 minutes; remove from cookie sheets.

HIGH ALTITUDE (3500-6500 FT.): No change.

Sweet Fruit Baskets

PREP TIME: 25 MINUTES (READY IN 25 MINUTES)
SERVINGS: 6

 EASY

1 1/2 cups frozen (thawed) strawberry-flavored or regular whipped topping

1 package (4.5 to 5 oz.) individual sponge shortcake cups (6 cups)

1/2 cup halved seedless green grapes

1/2 cup sliced fresh strawberries

1/3 cup drained pineapple tidbits

3 orange slices, halved, sections removed

Nutrition Information Per Serving:	
Calories: 170	From Fat: 40
Total Fat	4.5g
Saturated	3g
Cholesterol	35mg
Sodium	45mg
Total Carbohydrate	30g
Dietary Fiber	1g
Sugars	20g
Protein	2g

1) Spread 1/4 cup of the whipped topping into indentation of each shortcake cup, using spoon to make indentation in topping.

2) In medium bowl, mix grapes, strawberries and pineapple. (Add orange sections if desired.) Spoon fruit evenly into indentations of whipped topping in cups.

3) Place half circle of orange rind on each sponge cup to form handle.

HIGH ALTITUDE (3500-6500 FT.): No change.

ABC Cinnamon Breadsticks

PREP TIME: 30 MINUTES (READY IN 45 MINUTES)
SERVINGS: 12 (2 BREADSTICKS EACH)

 EASY   LOW FAT

3 tablespoons sugar

1/2 teaspoon ground cinnamon

1 can (11 oz.) Pillsbury® refrigerated breadsticks

1) Heat oven to 375°F. Grease cookie sheets with shortening or spray with cooking spray. In small shallow bowl, mix sugar and cinnamon.

2) Unroll dough; separate into 12 breadsticks. Cut each breadstick in half crosswise. Shape each breadstick half into one of the following letters and place 1 inch apart on cookie sheets.

3) To form the letter A, roll breadstick half into 10-inch rope. Lightly roll dough in sugar-cinnamon mixture. Cut 1-inch piece from one end of rope. Shape main part of A with remaining 9-inch rope; use 1-inch piece to cross middle of A.

4) To form the letter B, roll breadstick half into 11-inch rope. Lightly roll dough in sugar-cinnamon mixture. Shape rope into the letter B.

5) To form the letter C, roll breadstick half into 8-inch rope. Lightly roll dough in sugar-cinnamon mixture. Shape rope into the letter C.

6) Bake 10 to 13 minutes or until light golden brown. Serve with desired dipping sauce or spread.

HIGH ALTITUDE (3500-6500 FT.): No change.

Nutrition Information Per Serving:

Calories:	80	From Fat:	10
Total Fat		1.5g	
Saturated		0g	
Cholesterol		0mg	
Sodium		190mg	
Total Carbohydrate		16g	
Dietary Fiber		0g	
Sugars		5g	
Protein		2g	

Shape these breadsticks into any fun shape you like. Make numbers or letters and spell out your child's name.

Mr. Mouse Party Cupcakes

PREP TIME: 30 MINUTES (READY IN 1 HOUR 30 MINUTES)
SERVINGS: 8

CUPCAKES

1 box (1 lb. 2.25-oz.) yellow cake mix with pudding in the mix

1¼ cups water

⅓ cup vegetable oil

3 eggs

TOPPING

8 scoops vanilla ice cream (about ¼ cup each)

16 miniature creme-filled chocolate sandwich cookies

Small candies

32 small pretzel sticks

1) Heat oven to 350°F. Line 24 muffin cups with paper baking cups. Prepare cupcakes as directed on box using water, oil and eggs. Fill muffin cups ⅔ full.

2) Bake 21 to 26 minutes or until cupcakes spring back when touched lightly in center. Remove from pans. Cool completely, about 30 minutes.

3) Reserve 8 cupcakes. (Wrap and freeze remaining cupcakes for later use.)

4) On cookie sheet, decorate each ice cream scoop to resemble a mouse, using 2 cookies for ears, and small candies and pretzels for facial features and whiskers. Cover loosely with plastic wrap and freeze. When ready to serve, place cupcakes on 8 dessert plates. Top each cupcake with decorated ice cream.

HIGH ALTITUDE (3500-6500 FT.): Make cupcakes following High Altitude Directions on box.

Nutrition Information Per Serving:

Calories:	330	From Fat:	130
Total Fat			15g
Saturated			5g
Cholesterol			45mg
Sodium			350mg
Total Carbohydrate			44g
Dietary Fiber			2g
Sugars			29g
Protein			4g

tip

Use any flavor cake that you like—just follow guidelines on the box for the amount of water, oil and eggs to use, and the baking time.

S'more Dip

PREP TIME: 10 MINUTES (READY IN 10 MINUTES)
SERVINGS: 16 (2 TABLESPOONS DIP AND 10 GRAHAM STICKS EACH)

 EASY

1½ cups semisweet chocolate chips

1 can (14 oz.) sweetened condensed milk (not evaporated)

½ cup marshmallow creme

1 box (13 oz.) graham cracker honey sticks

Nutrition Information Per Serving:	
Calories: 270	From Fat: 80
Total Fat	9g
Saturated	4.5g
Cholesterol	10mg
Sodium	160mg
Total Carbohydrate	43g
Dietary Fiber	1g
Sugars	34g
Protein	3g

1) In small microwavable bowl, microwave chocolate chips and condensed milk on High 1 to 2 minutes, stirring occasionally, until chips are melted. Stir to mix well. Pour into 9-inch glass pie pan, spreading evenly.

2) Drop marshmallow creme by tablespoonfuls randomly over chocolate mixture. Microwave on High about 30 seconds or until marshmallow creme is softened. Immediately with knife, make several small swirls through marshmallow and chocolate, creating a marbled appearance.

3) Serve immediately with graham sticks for dipping.

HIGH ALTITUDE (3500-6500 FT.): No change.

Halftime Caramel Popcorn Balls

PREP TIME: 30 MINUTES (READY IN 30 MINUTES)
SERVINGS: 10 POPCORN BALLS

 EASY

1 bag (3 oz.) Pop•Secret® Light butter microwave popcorn

2 cups Golden Grahams® cereal

1½ cups small pretzel twists

¾ cup candy-coated chocolate pieces

⅓ cup butter or margarine

¾ cup packed brown sugar

⅓ cup light corn syrup

Nutrition Information Per Serving:	
Calories: 320	From Fat: 100
Total Fat	11g
Saturated	5g
Cholesterol	20mg
Sodium	320mg
Total Carbohydrate	52g
Dietary Fiber	2g
Sugars	33g
Protein	2g

1) Cut 24x12-inch sheet of waxed paper; place on work surface. Pop popcorn as directed on bag. Pour popcorn into at least 8-quart bowl or large roasting pan; remove any unpopped kernels. Stir in cereal, pretzels and chocolate pieces.

2) In 1-quart saucepan, melt butter over medium heat. Stir in brown sugar and corn syrup. Heat to boiling, stirring constantly. Boil 1 minute. Pour brown sugar mixture evenly over popcorn mixture, stirring to coat well.

3) Spray hands with cooking spray. With sprayed hands, quickly and firmly shape generous 1 cup popcorn mixture into ball. Place on waxed paper. Repeat with remaining mixture to make about 9 more balls. Cool 10 minutes. Wrap each popcorn ball in plastic wrap.

HIGH ALTITUDE (3500-6500 FT.): No change.

Chocolate-Caramel Layer Bars

PREP TIME: 30 MINUTES (READY IN 2 HOURS 25 MINUTES)
SERVINGS: 32

🅔 EASY

1 box (18.25 oz.) chocolate fudge cake mix with pudding in the mix

$1/2$ cup butter or margarine, melted

1 cup evaporated milk

35 vanilla caramels, unwrapped

1 cup miniature candy-coated semisweet chocolate baking bits

Nutrition Information Per Serving:	
Calories: 170	From Fat: 60
Total Fat	7g
Saturated	4g
Cholesterol	10mg
Sodium	180mg
Total Carbohydrate	26g
Dietary Fiber	0g
Sugars	17g
Protein	2g

1) Heat oven to 350°F. Grease 13x9-inch pan with shortening. In large bowl, mix cake mix, butter and $2/3$ cup of the milk with spoon until well blended. Spread half of mixture (about 2 cups) in pan. Bake 15 minutes.

2) Meanwhile, in 1-quart saucepan, heat caramels with remaining $1/3$ cup milk over low heat, stirring occasionally, until melted.

3) Remove partially baked crust from oven. Sprinkle $1/2$ cup of the baking bits evenly over crust. Drizzle with caramel mixture. Drop remaining batter by heaping teaspoonfuls over caramel mixture. Sprinkle with remaining $1/2$ cup baking bits; press in lightly.

4) Return to oven; bake 20 to 24 minutes longer or until center is set. Cool completely, about $1^1/2$ hours. Cut into 8 rows by 4 rows.

HIGH ALTITUDE (3500-6500 FT.): Add 1/4 cup flour to dry cake mix. Bake as directed above.

Valentine Cookie Pops

PREP TIME: 10 MINUTES (READY IN 1 HOUR 30 MINUTES)
SERVINGS: 20 COOKIE POPS

🅔 EASY

1 package (18 oz.) Pillsbury® Ready To Bake!™ refrigerated sugar cookies

20 flat wooden sticks with round ends

$1^1/4$ cups creamy vanilla ready-to-spread frosting (from 1-lb. container)

Assorted small candies, or candy decors or nonpareils, if desired

10 yards red curling ribbon

Nutrition Information Per Serving:	
Calories: 190	From Fat: 70
Total Fat	8g
Saturated	4g
Cholesterol	10mg
Sodium	70mg
Total Carbohydrate	30g
Dietary Fiber	0g
Sugars	22g
Protein	0g

1) Heat oven to 350°F. On ungreased cookie sheets, place cookie dough pieces 2 inches apart. Insert wooden stick 1 inch into side of each piece of dough, overlapping wooden sticks as necessary.

2) Bake 12 to 16 minutes or until edges are light golden brown. Cool 2 minutes; remove from cookie sheets. Cool completely, about 10 minutes.

3) Spread frosting on one side of each cookie; decorate with candies. Tie 18 inches of red ribbon into bow around each stick next to cookie.

HIGH ALTITUDE (3500-6500 FT.): No change.

Lazy Daisies

PREP TIME: 45 MINUTES (READY IN 1 HOUR 15 MINUTES)
SERVINGS: 3-1/2 DOZEN COOKIES

 LOW FAT

1/2 cup sugar

1/2 cup butter or margarine, softened

1 tablespoon grated lemon peel

1 tablespoon lemon juice

1 egg

1 3/4 cups all-purpose flour

1 teaspoon baking powder

1/4 teaspoon salt

21 small pastel-colored gumdrops or spice drops (about 2 1/2 oz.), cut in half

1) In large bowl, beat sugar and butter with electric mixer on medium speed until well blended. Beat in lemon peel, lemon juice and egg. With spoon, stir in flour, baking powder and salt until dough forms. Remove dough from bowl; place on large sheet of plastic wrap. Flatten dough into 6-inch round; wrap in plastic wrap. Refrigerate 30 minutes for easier handling.

2) Heat oven to 350°F. Work with half of dough at a time; refrigerate remaining dough until needed. Shape dough into 1-inch balls; place 2 inches apart on ungreased cookie sheets. With floured scissors and starting at top of each ball, snip each in half, without cutting through bottom. Snip each half into thirds. Gently open cookie balls to form 6 petals. Place gumdrop half in center of each.

3) Bake 8 to 11 minutes or until edges of cookies are light golden brown. Cool 1 minute; remove from cookie sheets.

HIGH ALTITUDE (3500-6500 FT.): Bake 9 to 12 minutes.

Nutrition Information Per Serving:

Calories:	60	From Fat:	20
Total Fat		2.5g	
Saturated		1g	
Cholesterol		10mg	
Sodium		45mg	
Total Carbohydrate		8g	
Dietary Fiber		0g	
Sugars		4g	
Protein		0g	

 tip

Vary the appearance and flavor of these cookies by substituting candied cherry halves, nut pieces, chocolate chips or candy-coated chocolate pieces for the gumdrops.

No-Roll Sugar Cookies

PREP TIME: 1 HOUR 20 MINUTES (READY IN 3 HOURS 20 MINUTES)
SERVINGS: 10 DOZEN COOKIES

1 cup granulated sugar

1 cup powdered sugar

1 cup butter or margarine, softened

1 cup vegetable oil

1 teaspoon vanilla

2 eggs

4¼ cups all-purpose flour

1 teaspoon baking soda

1 teaspoon cream of tartar

1 teaspoon salt

Colored sugar

1) In large bowl with electric mixer, beat granulated sugar, powdered sugar and butter on medium speed until light and fluffy. Beat in oil, vanilla and eggs until well blended.

2) On low speed, beat in flour, baking soda, cream of tartar and salt until a dough forms. Cover with plastic wrap; refrigerate at least 2 hours or overnight for easier handling.

3) Heat oven to 375°F. Shape dough into 1-inch balls; place 2 inches apart on ungreased cookie sheets. Flatten each with bottom of glass dipped in colored sugar.

4) Bake 5 to 8 minutes or until set but not brown. Immediately remove from cookie sheets.

HIGH ALTITUDE (3500-6500 FT.): Bake 6 to 7 minutes.

Nutrition Information Per Serving:

Calories:	60	From Fat:	30
Total Fat		3.5g	
Saturated		1g	
Cholesterol		10mg	
Sodium		40mg	
Total Carbohydrate		6g	
Dietary Fiber		0g	
Sugars		3g	
Protein		0g	

For the prettiest cookies, look for a "cut-glass" tumbler with a pretty design on the bottom.

Rainbow Cookie Sandwiches

PREP TIME: 25 MINUTES (READY IN 25 MINUTES)
SERVINGS: 44

 EASY   LOW FAT

3 tablespoons butter or margarine, softened

2 cups powdered sugar

1 to 2 tablespoons milk

3 packages (0.13 to 0.19 oz. each) unsweetened soft drink mix (3 colors)

1 box (12 oz.) vanilla wafer cookies

Nutrition Information Per Serving:	
Calories: 70	From Fat: 20
Total Fat	2.5g
Saturated	1g
Cholesterol	0mg
Sodium	45mg
Total Carbohydrate	11g
Dietary Fiber	0g
Sugars	7g
Protein	0g

1) In small bowl with electric mixer, beat butter, powdered sugar and milk on medium speed until smooth.

2) Divide mixture evenly into 3 small bowls. Into each bowl of mixture, stir $1/8$ teaspoon of 1 flavor drink mix until mix is dissolved.

3) For each sandwich cookie, spread about 1 teaspoon frosting on bottom of 1 cookie. Top with second cookie, bottom side down.

HIGH ALTITUDE (3500-6500 FT.): No change.

Rudolph Brownie Cupcakes

PREP TIME: 30 MINUTES (READY IN 1 HOUR 45 MINUTES)
SERVINGS: 12 CUPCAKES

1 box (19.8 oz.) fudge brownie mix

$1/2$ cup vegetable oil

$1/4$ cup water

3 eggs

$1 1/2$ cups chocolate creamy ready-to-spread frosting (from 16-oz. container)

24 holiday-shaped pretzels or small pretzel twists

12 red spiced gumdrops

24 miniature candy-coated chocolate baking bits

Nutrition Information Per Serving:	
Calories: 480	From Fat: 190
Total Fat	21g
Saturated	9g
Cholesterol	55mg
Sodium	240mg
Total Carbohydrate	67g
Dietary Fiber	2g
Sugars	50g
Protein	4g

1) Heat oven to 350°F. Line 12 regular-size muffin cups with paper baking cups. In large bowl, stir brownie mix, oil, water and eggs with spoon until well blended. Spoon about $1/4$ cup batter into each muffin cup.

2) Bake 32 to 36 minutes or until toothpick inserted in center of muffin comes out clean. Cool in pan 10 minutes. Remove from pan; cool completely, about 30 minutes.

3) Spread cupcakes with frosting. Decorate each with 2 pretzels for antlers, 1 red candy for nose and 2 baking bits for eyes.

HIGH ALTITUDE (3500-6500 FT.): Make 18 cupcakes.

Smiley Apples

PREP TIME: 10 MINUTES (READY IN 10 MINUTES)
SERVINGS: 2

 EASY

1 red apple

8 teaspoons creamy peanut butter

16 miniature marshmallows

1) Cut apple into quarters. Remove core, cut each quarter into 4 slices. Spread $1/2$ teaspoon peanut butter on one side of each slice.

2) With kitchen scissors, cut each marshmallow in half lengthwise. Place 4 marshmallow halves over peanut butter on 8 apple slices, extending slightly over peel of slice, for teeth.

3) Top each with remaining apple slice, peanut butter side down, to make smiling mouth.

HIGH ALTITUDE (3500-6500 FT.): No change.

Nutrition Information Per Serving:		
Calories: 190	From Fat:	100
Total Fat		11g
Saturated		2.5g
Cholesterol		0mg
Sodium		105mg
Total Carbohydrate		19g
Dietary Fiber		3g
Sugars		12g
Protein		6g

Elf Hat Cookies

PREP TIME: 1 HOUR (READY IN 1 HOUR)
SERVINGS: 16 COOKIES

 EASY

1 roll (18 oz.) Pillsbury® refrigerated sugar cookies

1 can (16 oz.) creamy white ready-to-spread frosting

$1/2$ teaspoon red food color

$1/2$ teaspoon green food color

$1/3$ cup coconut, if desired

Miniature marshmallows and/or small gumdrops

Nutrition Information Per Serving:		
Calories: 260	From Fat:	90
Total Fat		10g
Saturated		5g
Cholesterol		10mg
Sodium		85mg
Total Carbohydrate		41g
Dietary Fiber		0g
Sugars		31g
Protein		1g

1) Heat oven to 350°F. Cut cookie dough in half lengthwise to make 2 long pieces; refrigerate one half until ready to use. On floured surface, roll half of dough into 8x5$1/2$-inch rectangle (use edge of ruler to make sides straight).

2) With sharp knife, cut dough rectangle crosswise into 4 (5$1/2$x2-inch) rectangles (see diagram). Cut each small rectangle diagonally into 2 triangles; place triangles 2 inches apart on ungreased large cookie sheet. Bend tops of triangles as desired to resemble stocking caps.

3) Bake 7 to 11 minutes or until edges are light golden brown. Cool 1 minute; remove from cookie sheet. Cool completely, about 15 minutes. Repeat with remaining half of dough.

4) Divide frosting into 3 small bowls. Leaving 1 portion white, stir red and green food color into remaining portions. Frost each cookie with about 1 tablespoon red or green frosting. Frost about 1 inch of short side of each triangle with about 1$1/2$ teaspoons white frosting for hat brim. Sprinkle brims with coconut. Place marshmallows on ends of hats for tassels. Let stand until set before storing.

HIGH ALTITUDE (3500-6500 FT.): In Step 3, bake 9 to 13 minutes.

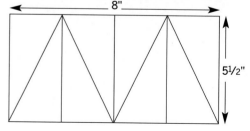

Secret Santa Trees

PREP TIME: 20 MINUTES (READY IN 25 MINUTES)
SERVINGS: 8

 EASY

1 container (12 oz.) fluffy white or vanilla whipped ready-to-spread frosting

16 small foil-wrapped milk chocolate Santa candies

8 fudge-striped cookies

8 sugar-style ice cream cones with pointed ends

2 to 3 drops green food color

Sugar sequins, sugar crystals or assorted decors

1) For each tree, place small amount of frosting between backs of 2 wrapped Santa candies; attach to bottom of cookie with small amount of frosting.

2) Spread rim of cone with small amount of vanilla frosting. Attach over Santa to 1 cookie, chocolate side to cone. Stand upright on tray. Let stand 5 minutes.

3) Stir food color into remaining frosting; frost each tree with 3 tablespoons green frosting. Decorate with sugar sequins, crystals or decors as desired. For frosting to be firm to touch, prepare the day before serving.

HIGH ALTITUDE (3500-6500 FT.): No change.

Nutrition Information Per Serving:

Calories:	400	From Fat:	170
Total Fat			19g
Saturated			8g
Cholesterol			0mg
Sodium			110mg
Total Carbohydrate			54g
Dietary Fiber			1g
Sugars			42g
Protein			3g

Attach Santas on bottom of fudge-striped cookie with a small amount of frosting. Spread rim of cone with frosting to attach to cookie.

Confetti Snowman Cake

PREP TIME: 30 MINUTES (READY IN 2 HOURS 5 MINUTES)
SERVINGS: 12

CAKE

1 box (18.25 oz.) white cake mix with pudding in the mix (not butter recipe)

1¼ cups water

⅓ cup vegetable oil

3 egg whites

2 tablespoons red and green holiday decors

FROSTING

1 container (16 oz.) creamy white ready-to-spread frosting

4 drops blue food color

DECORATIONS

1 cup coconut

Red and green candy-coated chocolate-covered peanut candies or gumdrops

2 raisins

1 candy corn

1 brown licorice twist (6 inch), cut in half crosswise, or pretzel stick

1 red or green chewy fruit snack roll (from 4.5-oz. box)

½ round oatmeal cookie

1 pretzel rod half or licorice twist half

Snowflake sprinkles, if desired

Nutrition Information Per Serving:

Calories:	450	From Fat:	160
Total Fat		18g	
Saturated		9g	
Cholesterol		0mg	
Sodium		330mg	
Total Carbohydrate		69g	
Dietary Fiber		0g	
Sugars		52g	
Protein		3g	

1) Heat oven to 350°F. Grease bottom only of 13x9-inch pan with shortening. Make cake as directed on box with water, oil and egg whites. Stir in holiday decors. Pour batter into pan.

2) Bake 28 to 33 minutes or until cake springs back when touched lightly in center. Cool completely, about 1 hour.

3) With small plate or top of jar for pattern, cut 1 (4-inch) round and 1 (5½- to 6-inch) round from waxed paper. Spread frosting over cake. Place waxed paper rounds on frosted cake to make snowman shape with larger round at bottom.

4) On each side of snowman pattern, carefully drop 2 drops of food color; swirl with knife around snowman to resemble sky. Remove and discard waxed paper.

5) Sprinkle coconut on snowman, filling in round shapes completely. Decorate with peanut candies for buttons, raisins for eyes, candy corn for nose, licorice for arms and fruit snack roll for scarf. Add cookie half for hat and pretzel rod for hat brim. Top blue area with snowflake sprinkles.

HIGH ALTITUDE (3500-6500 FT): Follow High Altitude cake mix directions for 13x9-inch pan.

Grasshopper Cupcakes

PREP TIME: 35 MINUTES (READY IN 2 HOURS)
SERVINGS: 24

1 box (18.25 oz.) devil's food cake mix with pudding in the mix

1$\frac{1}{3}$ cups water

$\frac{1}{2}$ cup vegetable oil

3 eggs

1 container (12 oz.) fluffy white whipped ready-to-eat-spread frosting

$\frac{1}{4}$ teaspoon peppermint extract

4 drops green food color

24 thin rectangular crème de menthe chocolate candies, unwrapped, each cut in half crosswise

Nutrition Information Per Serving:		
Calories: 220	From Fat: 100	
Total Fat		11g
Saturated		3g
Cholesterol		30mg
Sodium		190mg
Total Carbohydrate		29g
Dietary Fiber		0g
Sugars		21g
Protein		2g

1) Heat oven to 350°F. Make cake mix into cupcakes as directed on box using water, oil and eggs. Cool completely, about 30 minutes.

2) In small bowl, reserve $\frac{1}{2}$ cup frosting for garnish. Into remaining frosting, stir peppermint extract and food color until well blended. Frost cupcakes with green frosting.

3) Spoon 1 teaspoon reserved white frosting onto center of each frosted cupcake. Decorate each with 2 candy pieces, standing on edge.

HIGH ALTITUDE (3500-6500 FT.): Heat oven to 375°F. Make cupcakes following High Altitude Directions on box. Pour batter into 30 muffin cups.

Nutty Candy Sundaes

PREP TIME: 10 MINUTES (READY IN 10 MINUTES)
SERVINGS: 4

 EASY

4 waffle ice cream bowls

2 cups vanilla ice cream

2 peanut and chocolate candy bars (about 1.75 oz. each), chopped

$\frac{1}{3}$ cup chocolate fudge or caramel ice cream topping

Aerosol whipped cream, if desired

4 maraschino cherries, if desired

Nutrition Information Per Serving:		
Calories: 500	From Fat: 190	
Total Fat		21g
Saturated		10g
Cholesterol		35mg
Sodium		230mg
Total Carbohydrate		71g
Dietary Fiber		3g
Sugars		45g
Protein		9g

1) Place waffle bowls in serving bowls. Carefully spoon ice cream into waffle bowls.

2) Sprinkle chopped candy bars over ice cream. Drizzle with fudge topping. Top each sundae with whipped cream and a cherry.

HIGH ALTITUDE (3500-6500 FT.): No change.

Valentine's Day Meringue Dessert

PREP TIME: 30 MINUTES (READY IN 4 HOURS 20 MINUTES)
SERVINGS: 8

4 egg whites

¼ teaspoon cream of tartar

1 cup granulated sugar

1½ cups whipping cream

4 oz. cream cheese, softened

¼ cup powdered sugar

3 oz. white chocolate baking bar, melted

1 can (21 oz.) raspberry pie filling

1 pint (2 cups) fresh strawberries, halved

Fresh mint sprigs, if desired

Nutrition Information Per Serving:

Calories: 480	From Fat: 230
Total Fat	26g
Saturated	16g
Cholesterol	75mg
Sodium	95mg
Total Carbohydrate	58g
Dietary Fiber	2g
Sugars	56g
Protein	5g

1) Heat oven to 275°F. Line cookie sheet with cooking parchment paper. In large bowl, beat egg whites and cream of tartar with electric mixer on medium speed until foamy. On high speed, beat in 1 tablespoon of the granulated sugar at a time until stiff glossy peaks form and sugar is almost dissolved, about 6 minutes. Spread meringue to form 10x10-inch heart shape on cookie sheet, building up edges with back of spoon.

2) Bake 45 to 50 minutes or until firm and dry to the touch. Turn oven off; let meringue shell stand in closed oven 1 hour. Slide meringue shell and parchment paper from cookie sheet onto wire rack. Cool completely, about 10 minutes.

3) Meanwhile, in medium bowl, beat whipping cream with electric mixer on high speed until stiff peaks form. In large bowl, beat cream cheese and powdered sugar with mixer on medium speed until fluffy. Gradually beat in melted baking bar until smooth and creamy. Gently fold in whipped cream.

4) Carefully remove meringue shell from parchment paper; place shell on serving plate. Spread cream mixture evenly in shell. Cover; refrigerate at least 2 hours.

5) In medium bowl, gently mix pie filling and strawberries. Spoon 1½ cups fruit mixture over top of dessert. Garnish with mint sprigs. Serve remaining fruit mixture to be spooned over individual servings.

HIGH ALTITUDE (3500-6500 FT.): Heat oven to 250°F. For meringue, use 3 egg whites, 1/2 teaspoon cream of tartar and 3/4 cup sugar. Bake 60 to 65 minutes.

Snow Fun Snowmen

| PREP TIME: | 25 MINUTES (READY IN 55 MINUTES) |
| SERVINGS: | 6 |

1 container (16 oz.) creamy vanilla ready-to-spread frosting

6 plain mini cake doughnuts

12 plain cake doughnut holes

2 tablespoons coarse white sugar

6 thin pretzel sticks, broken in half

2 chewy fruit snacks in three-foot rolls (any flavor from 4.5-oz. box), cut into six 7- or 8-inch pieces

1 tube black decorating gel (or other colors)

6 orange candy sprinkles

12 candy-coated chocolate or fruit-flavored candies (about 1 tablespoon)

Nutrition Information Per Serving:

Calories:	540	From Fat:	190
Total Fat			21g
Saturated			12g
Cholesterol			20mg
Sodium			130mg
Total Carbohydrate			85g
Dietary Fiber			0g
Sugars			67g
Protein			3g

1) Place 12x12-inch sheet of waxed paper on work surface. In small microwavable bowl, microwave frosting on High 10 to 20 seconds or until soft.

2) For each snowman, dip 1 doughnut into frosting to cover; place on waxed paper. Dip 1 doughnut hole into frosting to cover; press on doughnut for snowman body. Dip second doughnut hole into frosting to cover; press on top of first doughnut hole for head. Sprinkle with about 1 teaspoon coarse sugar. If frosting becomes too thick for dipping, microwave on High 5 to 10 seconds to soften.

3) Gently push 2 pretzel stick pieces into opposite sides near top of each snowman body for arms.

4) Peel off paper from fruit snack roll pieces; fold each in half lengthwise to make scarf. Wrap scarf around neck of each snowman. With scissors, make several thin cuts on each end of each scarf for fringe.

5) With decorating gel, draw dots on heads for eyes; insert orange candy sprinkles for noses.

6) Gently press 1 candy-coated chocolate candy into frosting on each side of each snowman head. Draw line of decorating gel over top of each head to connect 2 candies and form earmuffs. For easier eating, let stand until frosting is set, about 30 minutes. To serve, place on serving tray or platter.

HIGH ALTITUDE (3500-6500 FT.): No change.

Alphabetical Index

General Recipe Index

This handy index lists every recipe by food category, major ingredient and/or cooking method, so you can easily locate recipes to suit your needs.

Cheese (continued)

Cheesy Tortellini Salad, 86
Chocolate Malted Milk Cheesecake, 313
Corny Sloppy Joe Pizza, 207
Cranberry-Turkey Quesadillas, 63
Doubly Cheesy Ham Divan Bake, 154
Easy Pizza Burgers, 100
Elegant Cheese and Fruit Platter, 49
Fudge-Strawberry Cream Torte, 292
Garlic, Chive and Cheese Bread, 140
Garlic-Herb Cheesy Potatoes, 158
Garlic Pepper-Blue Cheese Burgers, 123
German Chocolate Cream Pie, 315
Grilled Stuffed Pizza Burgers, 112
Grilled Tomato-Cheese Sandwiches, 121
Ham and Mozzarella Sandwich Wedges, 108
Ham and Swiss Sandwich Roll, 136
Herb-Crab Spread, 59
Herbed Cheese Spread, 38
Italian Cream Pie with Strawberry Sauce, 311
Lasagna Roll-Ups, 156
Layered Reuben Spread, 41
Make-Ahead Pizza Casserole, 161
Mexican Chili Cheese Dogs, 237
Mini Tuna-Cheese Buns, 127
Pepper Jack-Artichoke Dip, 46
Pesto-Cheese Bread, 130
Philly Cheese Steak Onion Soup, 126
Pizza Biscuit Wreath, 137
Pizza Bubbles, 223
Pizza-by-the-Yard, 217
Pizza Dunkers, 275
Pizza Lasagna, 158
Ranch Roll-Up Snacks, 61
Raspberry Cheesecake Bars, 298
Raspberry Cream Cheese Coffee Cake, 148
Rise 'n Shine Lattice Pizza, 26
Royal Marble Cheesecake, 316
Seafood Lasagna, 152
Skillet Pizza Potatoes, 172
Spicy Cheeseburger Nachos, 272
Stove-Top Chicken Enchilada Lasagna, 188
Stuffed Chicken Breasts Cordon Bleu, 208
Toasted Beef and Mozzarella Sandwiches, 127
Tomato, Basil and Cheese Sticks, 248
Topped Mini Quiches, 39
Two-Cheese and Ham French Loaf, 145
Vegetable Medley with Creamy Parmesan
    Sauce, 89
Vegetable Tree with Nacho Cheese Dip, 63
Veggie Macaroni and Cheese with
    Meatballs, 213

Cheesecakes

Berry No-Bake Cheesecake Pie, 317
Black Forest Cheesecake Dessert Cups, 307
Candy Bar Cheesecake, 294
Chocolate Malted Milk Cheesecake, 313
Raspberry Cheesecake Bars, 298
Royal Marble Cheesecake, 316

Cherries

Berry-Cherry Pie, 318
Black Forest Cheesecake Dessert Cups, 307
Cherry Berry Tart, 321
Cherry-Cranberry Sauce, 80
Cherry Fruit Punch, 45
Easy Cherry-Almond Coffee Cake, 133
Granola-Apple-Cherry Crisp, 293
Merry Cherry-Chip Pie, 314

Chicken & Cornish Hens

Alfredo Chicken Pasta Toss, 217
Bagel Shop Chicken Salad Sandwiches, 116
Baked Chicken Nugget Spaghetti, 154
Baked Taco Salad, 73
Barbecue Chicken Wraps, 111
Barbecue Cola Chicken, 252
Buffalo Chicken Layered Salad, 67
Buffalo Chicken Wraps, 272
Calabacita Chicken Stew, 222
Cheesy Chicken and Vegetables, 184
Cheesy Italian Chicken Bake, 207
Cheesy Tomato-Chicken Skillet, 174
Chicken and Vegetable Gravy over Biscuits, 187
Chicken-Bacon-Ranch Wraps, 113
Chicken Carbonara, 203
Chicken Chimichanga with Jalapeno
    Cream, 215
Chicken Dijon Shepherd's Pie, 157
Chicken Fiesta Salad, 95
Chicken Marsala Sandwiches, 102
Chicken-Ramen Soup, 106
Chicken Salad Crescent Cannoli, 224
Cinco de Mayo Glazed Chicken Wings, 60
Cornish Hens with Apple-Raisin Stuffing, 216
Crispy Oven-Fried Chicken, 195
Crunchy Asian Chicken and Vegetables, 190
Easy Chicken and Rice Casserole, 282
Easy Microwave Jammin' Jambalaya, 198
Enchilada Chicken Tart, 232
Garlic-Basil Chicken, 180
Granola-Chicken Salad Sandwiches, 119
Grilled Herbed Chicken, 226
Nutty Chicken Dinner Salad, 91
Party Chicken and Pasta Salad, 239
Pea Pod and Chicken Salad Oriental, 76
Peanut-Chicken Stir-Fry, 181
Provencal Chicken and Tomatoes, 178
Quick Italian Chicken and Rice, 170
Ranch-Style Chicken Tacos, 107
Roasted Chicken with Peach Glaze, 210
Southwestern Chicken-Biscuit Pot Pie, 230
Spanish Chicken and Rice Soup, 100
Spicy Honeyed Chicken Drummettes, 261
Stove-Top Chicken Enchilada Lasagna, 188
Stuffed Chicken Breasts Cordon Bleu, 208
Sweet-and-Sour Chicken Nuggets, 185
Warm Chicken Taco Salad, 93
Yummy Hero Sandwiches, 124

Chocolate

Banana-Chocolate-Caramel Cake, 322
Black Bottom Strawberry Cream Pie, 289
Black Forest Cheesecake Dessert Cups, 307
Brownie and Strawberry Shortcakes, 322
Candy Bar Cheesecake, 294
Choco-Peanut Butter Cups, 304
Chocolate Candy Cookie Bars, 249
Chocolate-Caramel Layer Bars, 334
Chocolate Malted Milk Cheesecake, 313
Chocolate Silk Raspberry Tart, 302
Chocolaty Caramel Layer Bars, 240
Coconut-Pecan-Fudge Bars, 312
Crescent Puff S'mores, 328
Double-Layer Mint Fudge, 306
Fudge-Strawberry Cream Torte, 292
Fudge Sundae Cake, 298
Fudgy-Peanut Butter Banana Parfaits, 295
German Chocolate Cream Pie, 315
Giant Peanut Butter Cup Cookies, 330

Grasshopper Cupcakes, 341
Heavenly Chocolate-Raspberry Torte, 299
Hot Fudge Pudding Cake, 321
Merry Cherry-Chip Pie, 314
Minty Ice Cream Squares, 297
Peanut Butter Crunch Brownies, 264
Peanut Butter-Fudge-Ice Cream Pie, 286
Praline Brookies, 258
Rudolph Brownie Cupcakes, 337
S'more Dip, 333
Sugar Cookie-Chocolate Crunch Fudge, 291
Tommy Turkey Treats, 326
White Chocolate-Iced Blueberry Loaf, 132
White Chocolate-Strawberry Yogurt
    Parfaits, 287

Coffee Cakes

Easy Cherry-Almond Coffee Cake, 133
Overnight Lemon Country Coffee Cake, 135
Raspberry Cream Cheese Coffee Cake, 148

Cookies

(also see Bars & Brownies)
Butterscotch Crackles, 263
Choco-Peanut Butter Cups, 304
Elf Hat Cookies, 338
Giant Peanut Butter Cup Cookies, 330
Jelly-Filled Thumbprints, 244
Lazy Daisies, 335
No-Roll Sugar Cookies, 336
Rainbow Cookie Sandwiches, 337
Valentine Cookie Pops, 334

Corn

Basil Scalloped Corn, 92
Beefy Bean and Corn Chili, 104
Corny Sloppy Joe Pizza, 207
Mexicorn-Topped Tomatoes, 71
Pinata Pork Roast, 206
Southwestern Layered Dip, 58

Cranberries

Cherry-Cranberry Sauce, 80
Cocktail Sausages in Crimson Sauce, 40
Cranberry-Turkey Quesadillas, 63
Granola Streusel Cranberry Muffin Mix, 142
Jingle Bell Salad, 83
Pear-Cranberry Crisp, 310
Red and Green Tossed Salad, 88
Turkey with Cranberry Stuffing, 274

Crisps

Granola-Apple-Cherry Crisp, 293
Pear-Cranberry Crisp, 310
Slow-Cooked Praline Apple Crisp, 277
Two-Berry Crisp with Pecan Streusel
    Topping, 297

Cucumbers & Pickles

Creamy Dill-Cucumber Salad, 70
Grilled Marinated Salmon with Cucumber
    Sauce, 229
Ham and Dill Pickle Deviled Eggs, 244

Desserts

(also see Bars & Brownies; Cakes, Cupcakes
& Tortes; Candies; Cheesecakes; Cookies;
Crisps; Ice Cream; Pies & Tarts; Pudding &
Parfaits)
Black Forest Cheesecake Dessert Cups, 307
Brownie and Strawberry Shortcakes, 322